PLAYING IT FORWARD

POUR CELLES QUI SUIVRONT

PLAYING IT FORWARD

50 Years of Women and Sport in Canada

POUR CELLES QUI SUIVRONT

50 ans d'histoire de femmes en sport au Canada

Edited by / Sous la direction de
GUYLAINE DEMERS, LORRAINE GREAVES,
SANDRA KIRBY, MARION LAY

Feminist History Society / Société d'histoire féministe
Ottawa

ISBN
978-0-9866478-3-3

EDITED BY
Guylaine Demers
Lorraine Greaves
Sandra Kirby
Marion Lay

COPY EDITED BY
Sandra Bialystok

DESIGN
Zab Design & Typography Inc.

Feminist History Society is a project of
the Women's Education and Research
Foundation of Ontario Inc.

BECOME A MEMBER
www.FeministHistories.ca

La Société d'histoire féministe est un
projet de la Women's Education and
Research Foundation of Ontario Inc.

DEVENEZ MEMBRE
www.FeminHistoires.ca

CONTENTS

PART TWO | UP AGAINST THE ODDS
Athletes, feminism and experiences

PART FIVE | FINDING LEADERS
Developing coaches, role models and icons

FEMINIST HISTORY SOCIETY

The Feminist History Society is committed to creating a lasting record of the women's movement in Canada and Québec for the period between 1960 and the year of the Society's founding, 2010. Our objective is to celebrate 50 years of activity and accomplishment by creating a written legacy, for ourselves, our families and friends, our communities, students and scholars. The beautiful books we publish, with membership support, will be as spirited and diverse as the movement itself, meant to stand together and to encourage and challenge those who follow.

Some writers reject the concept of "waves" with respect to the history of the women's movement, but many have described the feminist campaigns for suffrage and temperance during the nineteenth and early twentieth century as the "first wave of feminism." The upsurge of feminist activism that began in the 1960s has often been characterized as the "second wave."

Feminism has a history that predates the 1960s and will continue long after 2010, but our series is intended to encompass events during the "second wave." In 1960, the Voice of Women was founded in Canada and Québec. The decade of the 1960s also saw the appointment of the Royal Commission on the Status of Women and the creation of "women's liberation" groups across the country. By 2010, as some of the founding mothers of our generation of feminism have begun to die, it serves as a wake-up call regarding the pressing need to chronicle our history. Our movement is not at an end. But the third and fourth waves are upon us, and now is the time to take stock of what we did and how we did it. To preserve our memoirs for posterity before we lose many other key players or our memories begin to fail.

Over the next decade, our goal is to publish one or two books a year chronicling different aspects of the movement from sea to sea to sea. Members of the non-profit Feminist History Society receive an annual book at no extra charge and may also purchase other books published by the Society. The topics will be as diverse as our wide-ranging campaigns for equality through transformative social, economic, civil, political and cultural change. We will make every effort to be inclusive of gender, race, class, geography, culture, dis/ability, language, sexual identity and age. We maintain an open call for submissions.

Our first volume, edited by Marguerite Andersen, was *Feminist Journeys/Voies féministes* (2010). Michele Landsberg's *Writing the Revolution* (2011) was the second, and *Feminism à la Québécoise* (2012) by Micheline Dumont, was the third.

M. Elizabeth Atcheson, Constance Backhouse, Lorraine Greaves, Diana Majury and Beth Symes form the working collective for the Society. Shari Graydon has shared her expertise and time to help move the Society forward. Mary Breen helps with the Society's administration. Sandra Bialystok served as this volume's very skilled editor. Dawn Buie has created the Society's website, making it simple to join and contact us. Zab of Zab Design & Typography has created the visual identity for the Society as well as the book design for the series. We offer our heartfelt thanks to all of the talented and committed women who are providing encouragement, advice and support.

M. ELIZABETH ATCHESON, CONSTANCE BACKHOUSE, LORRAINE GREAVES, DIANA MAJURY & BETH SYMES

www.FeministHistories.ca | info@FeministHistories.ca

A project of Women's Education and Research Foundation of Ontario Inc. Charitable Registration No. 889933669RR0001

LA SOCIÉTÉ D'HISTOIRE FÉMINISTE

La Société d'histoire féministe s'est donné pour mandat de créer un portrait durable du mouvement des femmes au Canada et au Québec entre les années 1960 et 2010, l'année de fondation de la Société. Nous voulons ainsi célébrer cinquante ans d'activité et de réussites en créant un legs imprimé pour nous-mêmes, nos familles et nos proches, nos communautés et nos élèves, et en facilitant la recherche féministe. Les superbes livres que nous publions, grâce au soutien de nos membres, sont aussi vivants et diversifiés que le mouvement lui-même, et nous espérons que leur combinaison encouragera et stimulera celles qui nous suivront dans cette voie.

Certaines auteures rejettent le concept de « vagues » pour ce qui est de l'histoire du mouvement des femmes, mais beaucoup ont décrit les campagnes féministes organisées pour revendiquer le droit de vote et la tempérance, au dix-neuvième et du début du vingtième siècle, comme la « première vague du féminisme ». Ainsi, la poussée d'activisme féministe qui a débuté dans les années 1960 a souvent été caractérisée comme la « deuxième vague » de ce mouvement.

Le féminisme possède une histoire qui date d'avant les années 1960 et qui se poursuivra bien au-delà de 2010, mais notre série d'ouvrages entend couvrir des événements survenus au cours de cette « deuxième vague ». L'année 1960 a été celle de la fondation du groupe La Voix des femmes, au Canada et au Québec. Cette décennie a aussi vu la fondation de la Fédération des femmes du Québec, la mise sur pied de la Commission royale d'enquête sur la condition de la femme au Canada et l'apparition de groupes de « libération des femmes » ici et là au pays. Cinquante ans plus tard, le décès de quelques-unes des pionnières du mouvement sonne le rappel d'un besoin pressant, celui de rédiger la chronique de notre histoire. Ce n'est aucunement la fin du mouvement. Mais une troisième et une quatrième vague nous sollicitent, et il est temps de faire le point sur ce que nous avons accompli et comment nous y sommes arrivées. Il faut consigner nos souvenirs avant de perdre d'autres intervenantes importantes ou de voir s'effilocher notre mémoire collective.

Au cours des prochains dix ans, notre objectif est de publier un ou deux livres par an, qui relateront différents aspects du mouvement féministe pancanadien. Chaque membre de la Société d'histoire féministe, un organisme sans but lucratif, reçoit un livre par an sans frais supplémentaires, et peut aussi se procurer les autres exclusivités de la SHF. Nos thèmes sont aussi diversifiés que les grandes campagnes de notre mouvement pour l'égalité et pour des réformes sociales, économiques, civiles, politiques et culturelles. Nous multiplierons les efforts pour être inclusives à tous les titres : genre, origine ethnique, classe, géographie, culture, (in)capacité, langue, identité sexuelle et âge. À vous de nous soumettre vos manuscrits!

Notre premier ouvrage, assemblé par Marguerite Andersen en 2010, s'intitulait *Feminist Journeys/Voies féministes*. A suivi *Writing the Revolution* de Michele Landsberg, en 2011, et *Feminism à la Québécoise* de Micheline Dumont, en 2012.

M. Elizabeth Atcheson, Constance Backhouse, Lorraine Greaves, Diana Majury et Beth Symes forment la collective de travail de la Société d'histoire féministe. Shari Graydon nous a fait bénéficier de son expertise et de son temps pour propulser la SHF en avant et Mary Breen en administre le quotidien. Le présent ouvrage doit beaucoup aux talents de Sandra Bialystok comme directrice de publication. Dawn Buie a créé le site Web de la Société, qui aide les gens à nous contacter et à devenir membre. Zab, de Zab Design & Typography, a conçu notre identité visuelle distinctive et la superbe maquette de notre collection. Enfin, nous adressons nos remerciements les plus sincères aux nombreuses féministes talentueuses et engagées qui nous assurent sans relâche encouragements, conseils et soutien.

Nous vous incitons ardemment à vous joindre à la Société d'histoire féministe et même à y participer à titre d'auteure.

M. ELIZABETH ATCHESON, CONSTANCE BACKHOUSE, LORRAINE GREAVES, DIANA MAJURY & BETH SYMES

www.FeminHistoires.ca | info@FeministHistories.ca

Un projet de la Women's Education and Research Foundation of Ontario Inc.
Nº d'enregistrement d'organisme de bienfaisance : 889933669RR0001

FOREWORD

Lorraine Greaves and Constance Backhouse

WHY A BOOK ABOUT "women and sport" in the series by the Feminist History Society? Many readers will have lingering memories of the first time they felt the joy of running fast, or jumping high or throwing a ball as far as possible. Others will have less positive memories of physical education classes in school that were crushingly sexist or marginalizing, with vastly different standards and activities for boys and girls.

In the 1960s a second wave women's movement emerged in Canada, inspired by parallel movements for civil rights and social change, but reacting to continued oppression of women within those movements. Feminist activism embraced a range of goals, such as reproductive rights, legal rights and increased labour force participation, struggling to free women from a sexist and limited set of roles that pivoted on motherhood and marriage.

But any consciousness-raising for women in sport was strangely delayed. Despite the explicit feminist focus on the body and its experiences and limits, sport eluded full examination by academics and leaders in the women's movement of the 1960s. Only slowly did the realization emerge that women and girls did not get equal chances to participate; there were boys' rules and girls' rules, boys' teams and resources, and girls, if they got any notice at all, were always second, using second-rate spaces and uniforms. Boys' and men's sports and teams dominated school and university life, and male athletes went on to dominate media coverage and the public mind. In many ways, they still do.

Many of the women whose stories are profiled here are athletes who gloried in competition, the drive to win and becoming physically powerful. Others are leaders who often worked behind the scenes to create opportunities for women coaches, to change laws and rules to achieve access for girls and women, or to blaze trails in policy making or academia. We at the Feminist History Society felt that the girls and women who are following in their footsteps, and the wider women's movement, need to know more about the battles that have been fought along the way.

While some of the athletes and sports leaders did not identify their struggles or themselves as "feminist," it was indeed the mantle of feminism that gave support to the voices demanding access. It was the wider women's movement that helped set the context for change, provided the arguments and language, lobbied for inclusion, and worked to convince the majority of Canadians that girls and women could, and should, participate in and triumph through sport.

In 1960 there were some big gaps for women in sport. In community sport and national and international competition there was no women's soccer; there was figure skating, but no speed skating; there were some events in track and field, but no long distance running; there was long distance swimming, broomball and "gouret de salon," but no women's ice hockey. In contrast, for boys, it was a given that they could be part of any team in any sport, get a uniform and play—an experience denied to most girls at the time. Indeed, 50 years ago, girls were routinely sidelined. They watched their brothers play and were expected to be cheering from the stands. These expectations were carried into the adult world, where men's teams got media coverage, accolades and national attention and pride. The real game was the men's, with a bigger ball and real rules.

Women athletes were not represented in the media, except during the Olympics and in some national championships such as figure skating. There were few, if any, role models for young girls. Many of those who did succeed became activists who were critically important to what came next. Slowly, the notion that girls needed half of the attention, resources, time and space began to take root. In retrospect, we may say that the claims for gender equity in sport were hard to argue with, but success in achieving fairness was a very long time coming.

In the 1970s there were some pivotal events that turned the tide for women and sport in Canada. The Canada Games and the 1976 Olympics provided openings for women and girls, but at the same time highlighted the disparities between women's and men's access to sport. At the 1976 Olympics, women had less than one-third the opportunity to win a medal than men did. At the same time, physical education became a more formal discipline in schools, and women could aspire to a career in sport or physical activity. But still, femininity prevailed over feminism, and differences and diversities between women and among women were not acknowledged. The impact of language, sexual orientation, race, and disability were under-acknowledged or ignored.

Slowly, girls and women were starting to have a greater sense of their power and more awareness of discrimination. A few feminist role models became known, and a nascent women and sport movement emerged in Canada, with women in sport conferences held in 1974, 1980 and 2002. However, the women and sport movement did not enjoy widespread acceptance and support, and there was some resentment over the growing efforts to put women and sport issues on the mainstream women's movement agenda. Such issues were interesting to the movement mainly for their legal challenges that seemed to address universal feminist issues, but not for expanding options for girls and women. The world of sport was often dismissed as male, competitive and not crucial to the widespread effort to improving the status of women in Canada.

By the late 1970s and into the 1980s, research on women in sport began to appear, as feminist scholarship challenged the academy, the legal system, and social and cultural attitudes toward women's bodies, sport and physical activity. By the time Sport Canada acknowledged the importance of women in sport to Canada, there was emphasis on correcting the economic inputs to sport and rebalancing the resource allocation between women's and men's sport.

The sophistication of the goals of the women and sport movement increased in the 1980s, with a clear shift from asking for equality to demanding equity. Feminism became a more overt component of the activism and advocacy in the 1980s. The Canadian Association for the Advancement of Women and Sport was born, later to become the Canadian Association for the Advancement of Women and Sport and Physical Activity, with an enlarged mandate intended to reach greater numbers of women and girls. The importance of physical activity for a broader constituency of girls and women was mainstreamed, reducing the singular focus on sport and elite athleticism to include movement, fun, fitness and health.

CAAWS created a platform for feminist ideas in sport, where complex issues such as lesbianism in sport were addressed. This was not easy to broach, however, as lesbians were often told "not to rock the boat," to minimize talk about sexual orientation, and keep the public focus on "women in sport," not lesbianism in sport. But by 1982, when the Gay Games took place in San Francisco, a new route was forged for discussing the complexity of diversities and sport, setting the stage for an ongoing conversation about homophobia in sport.

The challenges and successes of the 1980s were memorable. Slowly, the opportunities for participation for girls and women expanded, and the images of active women increased. Even so, there were long, relentless fights to acquire equal access to practice time, travel funds and uniforms in school leagues across the country and in public facilities supported by tax dollars. Landmark legal cases made history in this decade as more parents began fighting for equity for their daughters.

On the public policy front, the first Sport Canada policy on women and sport was launched in 1986, building on the *Canadian Charter of Rights and Freedoms* and setting the stage for legal challenges on behalf of women. CAAWS contributed to all of these advocacy efforts and played a key role in raising awareness about media portrayals of women and sport in Canada.

By the 1990s, the first woman Director General of Sport Canada, Abby Hoffman, had been appointed. More women leaders were in positions of power, and there were more women coaches in a range of sports. The Gay Games were held in Vancouver in 1990, contributing to even greater diversity in the Canadian sport scene. The women and sport movement became globalized, with the first international conference on women in sport taking place in Brighton, UK in 1994. Following from that conference, the Brighton Declaration brought together governments around the world to take action for equity in sport. These were exhilarating times for women and sport.

These developments led to ever more attention to ethics, equity and issues such as doping, gender testing, sexual harassment and abuse in sport, and other concerns that were gendered in their effects. Researchers and activists alike identified the unhealthy relationship between femininity, diet and girls' performances in some sports. It was no surprise that there was persistent concern over the representation of femininity, not only in terms of gender testing at the Olympics but also with regard to the wider fitness industry and the emergence of sexualized sporting fashions for women. The link between fitness and fashion had a special emphasis on women and girls, exploiting body image insecurities and reinforcing widely established and unrealistic aspirations for body shape and size.

By 2000, the momentum to improve women and sport was in full swing. On the bright side, there were numerous role models among Canadian women athletes such as Chantal Petitclerc, Silken Laumann, Cindy Klassen, Sylvie Bernier, Clara Hughes, Melanie Turgeon, Hayley Wickenheiser, and many more. These successes showed that women had made it to elite sport and achieved success—perhaps suggesting to the general public that the battles had been won.

And some had been. Indeed, recent Olympics Games have had more focus on women's sports and more events for women. The Own the Podium program leading up to the 2012 Olympics in Vancouver awarded more funding for women in Olympic sports than ever before. And the number of sports open to women at the international level has improved dramatically.

But these changes have been very hard won and not without controversy. The legacy of the efforts of activists in the decades prior to the turn of the century was paying big dividends for sport. The commitment to sport equity was being made at the highest levels and Canada was at the forefront through the activities of CAAWS, the leadership provided by key women in the national sport system, and strong performances of the female athletes on the international stage.

And yet, on the other side of the scene, were the "non-sporty" women. Indeed, some of the women involved in compiling and editing the stories in this book would describe themselves in this way. These were women who dreaded physical education classes and were mortified when forced to participate in mandatory sporting events; they were women whose embarrassment at wearing exposing sportswear was acute and whose physicality was comparatively undeveloped. Yet they proudly defined themselves as feminist and saw the connections between sport, physical activity and women's power. It was their feminism that brought them to recognize that equity in sport was a key indicator of gender equality.

The linkage between women's physicality and gender equality was not initially self-evident to either group—the athletes or the "non-sporty" feminists. Sport was an issue that arrived on the feminist agenda belatedly, and not without challenge. Yet the issue of women and sport invades some key feminist terrain: the interpretation of women's bodies in the public domain, the experiences of the female body and the exhilaration of movement, and the questioning of the notions of competition and winning as feminist ideals.

Even for the distant feminist observer, the widespread and masculinist resistance to the claims of women seeking access to sports was shocking. We were left gasping at arguments we thought were long discredited: that biology was destiny, that men were entitled to privilege and power, that women should be feminine not athletic. We came to realize that the primacy of male sport was one of the strongest bulwarks of sexism in Canadian society and the world. It showed itself as a key element of the public image of male superiority and it permeated our world view through the media, education, government and beyond. It affected our most basic experiences—how we as women and girls live in our own bodies, how we challenge ourselves physically and how we might gain personal and political power. This book describes a slice of the journeys that sought to overcome and dissolve that sexist, masculinist reality that bubbled in Canadian consciousness between 1960 and 2010.

INTRODUCTION

*Guylaine Demers, Lorraine Greaves, Sandra Kirby
and Marion Lay*

THE 1960S USHERED IN the best and the worst of times for women in sport in Canada. Earlier in the century, women athletes had achieved remarkable success even in the face of extraordinary gender barriers, but these gains were always in constant danger of being eroded. Canadian women had gone to the Summer Olympics in Amsterdam and won gold for Canada in track and field in 1928. Despite this victory, pressure mounted to ban women from the 800-metre event because some women had fainted after the race. In the 1930s the Edmonton Commercial Grads, a women's basketball team, won 502 out of 521 games, traveled internationally and brought considerable fame to Canada. And in 1948 Barbara Ann Scott won gold and lasting recognition in figure skating at the St. Moritz Olympics. But by 1950 sporting women in Canada were caught up in the post-war domestication that affected women in so many walks of Canadian life. The early wins had not translated into high status or widespread opportunity for women in sport in Canada. The 1960s, with the winds of change sweeping across society at large, set a promising stage for new initiatives.

This book reveals the voices of many athletes, coaches, leaders and activists who contributed to this systemic change using legal, social and activist methods. The women and sport movement included privileged women using their influence as well as schoolgirls complaining about no space or opportunity and making their views known. What they have in common is the courage to stick their necks out, take chances, make claims and be role models.

This is also the story of the women's movement in Canada, 1960-2010. Sport is an important part of women's lives and clearly reflects the impact of feminism and the seeking of women's liberation. Sport for women calls up the experience of the body, control over image and energy, engagement with competition and the confronting of stereotypes about women's strength, idealism and perseverance.

Many of the athletes in this volume reflect on their beginnings. Often alone and unconnected, they started small, competing in makeshift venues, training alone in imperfect locations or with substandard equipment. They talk of the joy of movement, playing, teamwork and competition. Eventually, sisterhood developed among women in and around sport, as leaders emerged and the need for programs was identified. Organizations with overt feminist goals were formed.

There are many details that will resonate with the non-elite woman athlete as well. The pressures for change in the status of women athletes in Canada between 1960 and 2010 were hard won and raised numerous issues from the wider women's movement in the context of sport. The legacy of the women and sport movement in this era is felt today in the abundance of female role models, acceptance of women's participation in iconic Canadian sports such as hockey, and increased opportunities for physical activity for women and girls. But despite these many changes, it is clear that there is still much to do to advance women and girls in sport in Canada and around the world.

GUYLAINE DEMERS

Lorsqu'on m'a invitée à joindre l'équipe de rédaction d'un livre sur l'histoire des femmes et du sport au Canada, j'ai regardé derrière moi pour être certaine que cette invitation s'adressait bien à moi. Comme bien des femmes, ma première réaction fut de mettre mes compétences en doute pour la réalisation de ce projet. Puis, j'ai commencé à réfléchir sur ma propre histoire et à l'impact du sport dans ma vie de femme. Une seule conclusion s'est alors imposée : sans le sport, je ne serais pas qui je suis, ni où je suis.

Je crois que je suis féministe (sans le savoir !) depuis que j'ai 7 ans. C'est à ce moment que j'ai commencé à vivre les iniquités entre les gars et les filles dans le monde du sport, c'était en 1971.

Mes frères jouaient au hockey, pas moi… parce que j'étais une fille. J'étais passionnée et j'excellais dans ce sport, mais la place des filles était dans les estrades. Aujourd'hui, je suis en mesure d'apprécier le chemin parcouru et les nouvelles possibilités qui s'offrent aux filles en sport. Si jamais une de mes nièces souhaitait jouer au hockey, la question qu'elle se poserait serait « où vais-je jouer? » et non pas « pourquoi est-ce qu'il n'y a pas d'équipes de filles? » Et ça, c'est merveilleux.

L'aventure de ce livre a été pour moi une occasion unique de me rappeler tout le travail qui a été accompli depuis 1960. Je suis redevable à toutes ces femmes qui se sont battues, qui ont ouvert des portes et surtout qui n'ont pas accepté le statu quo comme réponse aux injustices. C'est la raison principale pour laquelle j'ai accepté de faire partie de l'équipe de rédaction : je veux qu'on se souvienne de ces femmes d'exception. L'histoire de la 2ᵉ vague féministe en sport est peu connue et ce livre pallie cette lacune.

Aujourd'hui, je travaille quotidiennement pour rendre notre système sportif plus inclusif et équitable. Et cela, je le dois en partie à des femmes exceptionnelles qui ont cru en moi, qui sont des modèles incroyables et qui font de moi une meilleure personne. Deux de ces femmes sont éditrices de ce livre: Sandra Kirby et Marion Lay. La fierté que je ressens d'avoir mon nom apposé à côté du leur est indescriptible. Ces femmes continuent sans cesse leur travail pour aider les filles et les femmes en sport. Elles ne travaillent pas pour la gloire ni pour l'argent ; elles sont généreuses de leur temps, de leurs connaissances. Bref, elles placent la cause bien au-dessus d'elles-mêmes et c'est le plus grand message que je retiens d'elles.

Mon parcours m'a rendu très sensible aux injustices que vivent les filles et les femmes dans le monde du sport. Mais je sais que le sport peut aussi être un moyen incroyable de réalisation de soi. J'espère que vous sentirez toute l'énergie qui se dégage de ce livre. Car, malgré toutes les embûches, ces femmes racontent des histoires de passion, de dépassement et d'amitié. Bonne lecture.

LORRAINE GREAVES

I am not an athlete and only a sporadic participant in physical activity. Unlike my co-editors, I am not interested in competition, team sports or sweating much. My "personal bests" include a 14 km fun run and a first place in school badminton topped off by a few years of swimming every day. Cross-country skiing, a little bit of downhill and a passing acquaintance with curling complete the picture. Nothing exceptional and, like most women, nothing near the league of elite sport, the domain of my co-editors.

However, I have been an observer and supporter of the women and sport movement in Canada for decades. I suggested this book on women and sport to my sisters in the Feminist History Society as a critical one for our project recording the second wave women's movement in Canada. Luckily, they agreed.

Why do I think this book is important? I have been an active feminist for decades, completely committed to improving the lives of girls and women. My emphasis on women's health has included an assessment of how the world, and Canada, has barred women and girls from safety and freedom of movement and full participation in life. In sport and physical activity, like many other areas of life in Canada, there has been discrimination, sexist attitudes and outright legal, economic, and social barriers. From this perspective, I have been intensely involved in the women and sport movement, applying feminist analyses to issues such as physical activity, fitness, health promotion and sexual abuse and violence in sport.

I see the women and sport movement as a site of critical struggle for women and girls in Canada in the past 50 years. The struggle to get resources, attention, space and respect is a decidedly feminist struggle for rights and acknowledgement and one that transcends women and sport. The struggle to express ourselves and to use our bodies in a free and active way remains a universal issue for women and girls. The struggle to do sport and physical activity free from sexual harassment and abuse, free from sexist glare and a sexualized gaze is intrinsically linked to women's liberation and to the broader women's and human rights struggle.

Defining a field of academic interest pertaining to women and sport is linked to other critical developments in thinking, writing and research in Canada in the past 50 years. And the intense legal and activist fights to acquire rights, space and equal resources for women and girls in sport from government and the courts are tightly laced into the women's movement's history of the second wave. The efforts to change policies and develop programmes for women and girls and to build coaching capacity and women leaders are reminiscent of the wider struggle to highlight women's abilities and skills in a range of areas of life in the past 50 years.

All of these issues emerge in this book. Stories of success, change and exhilaration stand alongside stories of struggle, pain, loss and discrimination. The energy and commitment of women in Canada to changing the playing fields in the past 50 years shine through. These stories are resonant of, and intrinsically linked to, the wider effort of making political and social change in Canada brought on by the second wave women's movement. They are exemplars and indicators of things done, and in some cases, not yet done. They are inspirational to all of us—whether we are elite-level athletes or occasional participants in sport.

SANDRA KIRBY

I loved sport from the moment I got to represent my school and wear a uniform—though the uniform was a hand-me-down from the boys' team the year before. I think I was in Grade 7. I still love being an athlete. I love competing—lining up with other equally trained people to get the very best performance from each other. My athleticism is ongoing. I am a Canadian Olympian (1976) who also has won gold medals in rowing, marathon canoe racing and cross-country skiing in competitions spanning from the local to international levels. Sport has been very good to me and for me. In return, I have coached rowing, been an event organizer and now, an international umpire.

I had to fight for a chance to go to the Olympic trials for rowing prior to the 1976 Games. I think that was my first outright feminist political action. I knew then with certainty that I, and other women, were not equal inside or outside of sport. Also, while it is not fair, the fact that I am an Olympian has opened doors for my social activism. People who did not listen to me pre-Olympic Games did so afterwards. I realized that I had a responsibility to learn to use my voice in a way that was best for woman and sport.

In 1981 I was invited to join the Athlete Apprenticeship Program, and Marion Lay became my mentor. I learned the foundation of sport administration and was introduced to women who loved sport, worked for the betterment of sport and took care of each other along the way. I became a founding mother of the Canadian Association for the Advancement of Women and Sport and Physical Activity (CAAWS) and have been so fortunate to work with those wonderful women (and equality-seeking men) who love sport. Lorraine Greaves and I were Vice-Presidents of the National Action Committee on the Status of Women (NAC) at the same time as I was on the CAAWS Board. In those roles I was able to bring sport to the women's movement and vice versa, particularly on the issues of equality, violence and abuse.

Through the creation of WomenSport International in 1993, immediately followed by the International Task Force on Harassment and Abuse in Sport, I met Celia Brackenridge of England with whom I worked on harassment and abuse, eventually co-authoring a book on sexual harrassment and abuse in sport. Our work with the International Olympic Commission and UNICEF enabled some of the child protection messages to reach a global audience. My contribution to that work was largely in the area of vulnerabilities for those with disabilities and for gays and lesbians in sport. In the past decade, I have been able to work with Guylaine Demers on these issues.

So, the invitation to participate in this book from the wonderful visionaries of the Feminist History Society represented a logical continuation not just of my career in activism but also of the work that I had already engaged in with my friends and co-editors, Guylaine Demers, Lorraine Greaves and Marion Lay. I am thrilled to be part of this group that has helped the stories in this book come forward. And I am impressed by the myriad of ways that Canadian girls and women have found their path in sport, despite some of the obstacles and negative consequences along the road.

MARION LAY
I have learned through my women and sport work in Canada just how difficult it is to bring about change. Indeed, when I first became involved in women in sport in the early 1970s, I never dreamed that to increase opportunities for girls and women in physical activity and sport would become my life's work. It has definitely been an amazing personal journey, full of accomplishment, setbacks, learning, struggle and friendship.

Despite this rich experience that became central to my life, it was only recently that I became aware of the importance of recording some of our history. In November 2011, the Canadian Association for the Advancement of Women and Sport (CAAWS) organized a small thirty-year celebration dinner. CAAWS is the main association in Canada aimed at advancing sport and physical activity among Canadian women and girls from a decidedly feminist perspective.

At the dinner, past CAAWS Chairs and executive members told stories about the women in sport highlights that occurred during their tenure on the CAAWS Board of Directors. It was an amazing evening. We all laughed and cried together as we talked for hours and shared our common and collective memories. After, I felt so proud of our work together and such tremendous respect for all of the women who have had the courage to lead the women in sport movement in Canada.

However, as I listened to the stories and remembered many of the successes and failures over the years, I felt not only a sense of pride but also a sense of urgency. I had become acutely aware of how much of our history was being lost because we had so few records of our work.

So it was with those intertwined feelings that I responded to the invitation to become involved with the Feminist History Society to help produce a book on women and sport in Canada. The aim of the book—to record the contribution to the second wave women's movement in Canada and to ruminate on the influence of feminism on the women and sport movement—is close to my heart. I have been proud and honoured to be an editor on this book and to be one of the athletes profiled.

This effort to produce a book of feminist stories about the women and sport movement in Canada has been a rewarding and inspiring experience for me. I hope that you will find many of the stories in this book amazing. Taken as a whole, they create a book that silences my worry about not having a record of our 50 years of activism, achievement, effort and struggle. This book fulfills the goal of recording that history.

PLAYING IT FORWARD

POUR CELLES QUI SUIVRONT

1 | THE PLAYING FIELDS
The importance of sport and feminism in the
second wave women's movement in Canada

THE DECADES BETWEEN 1960 AND 2010 saw the slow emergence of a feminist view of women and sport in Canada. There were many players in this effort, including women and men who tried, and in some cases succeeded, in opening doors. These five stories illustrate different realms, but overlap considerably in their themes.

All of the individuals in this section stood up and spoke out against the injustices they perceived. Sometimes, they were very much alone while making inroads in politics, academia, journalism or government. This meant taking risks and bearing the consequences of challenging the status quo. They endured sexism and personal confrontation, and yet still created new ways of thinking.

They succeeded in path finding, fighting for women and shining a light on women's stories. Simultaneously, personal and political transitions were made. Profound, life long transitions were made. Feminist identities were formed, lives of social activism emerged and new opportunities for women in sport imagined.

SAYING YES TO TRUDEAU

Iona Campagnolo

It's been nearly 40 years, but I still remember the morning that my phone woke me up in Washington, DC. I was at the State Department of the US capital researching proposals for crude oil tankers to traverse the Inside Passage of British Columbia (that this issue is still current tells you how little some things "political" really change over time) and the blinking red light on the phone came from the Prime Minister's Office. The order was brusque: "Be back in Ottawa by tomorrow morning for 08:00 hours."

The next day my appointment ended up being delayed, but eventually I was ushered into Pierre Trudeau's "Spartan" office, where he asked me to become Canada's first Minister of Fitness and Amateur Sport. "But Sir," I blurted out, "I am such a hothouse flower!" I had been a broadcaster and worked in amateur theatre for years, and the closest I had come to sports was as a children's figure skating trainer. "Why me?" I asked. To which Mr. Trudeau gave me that famous clear-blue stare and said: "You are forever haranguing me about equality for women in Canadian society. Sport is entirely dominated by men, so take the job and see what you can do with it."

I knew that having a place at the Cabinet table would give me the opportunity to weigh in on some of the national issues touching my northern BC constituency of Skeena, such as oil tankers, First Nations land claims and wild salmon sustainability. I also knew that this might give me the chance to advance feminist causes. So with the old theatre maxim in mind, "There are no small parts, only small actors," I said "yes" to Mr. Trudeau! I was determined to learn the Sport and Fitness portfolio fast and to do my best.

In retrospect, if there was any cynicism in the offer, I didn't see it; in fact, it might have been calculated to make a woman the "front-man" of Canadian sport, but it was a still a bold stroke. And ultimately, the appointment just might have boosted the self-esteem of other women who were also seeking achievement across the country. All in all, I think it worked out pretty well.

On September 16, 1976, following the success of the Montreal Olympics, my friend Monique Bégin and I were appointed to Her Majesty's Privy Council. We were the fourth and fifth women in the history of the country to enter the inner sanctum of Canadian governance. While driving to Rideau Hall that morning for the installation ceremony, I listened to the radio sport jocks joking about my appointment. "Is she fit for Sport?" they laughed, or "Is she coachable?" – on and on they went. Was I going to be a joke? Amongst the congratulations I received that day were those of a high-ranking Party man who snarled: "It's up to you to get rid of those lesbians in national sport." My reply was less than lady-like! The whirlwind had begun.

Back on the Hill, my first duty assignment was one I dreaded: HOCKEY. I was to go to the fabled Montreal Forum to appear on the "Hot Stove League" of CBC's Hockey Night in Canada. Two super hockey men were dispatched to me almost immediately. They had been assigned to fill my ears with hockey talk. But in spite of their best efforts, I was a disaster. I was so dreadful in fact, that after hearing the exchange broadcast in Vancouver, Ian Howard, a previous staffer to PM Lester Pearson and Minister of Health and Sport John Munro, phoned to urgently offer me his services as Chief of Staff (and resident "Coach").

Ian Howard was originally from Hamilton and had a long association with John Munro and all aspects of national sport development. He arrived quickly to assemble my Sport and Fitness ministerial staff and office. My only instructions were that other than competence, I wanted as many women on the staff as possible. Ian Howard proved to be an amazingly informed, fair, well-connected and effective Chief of Staff, and ultimately became a life-long friend. In those early days he often saved me when I interacted with the hundred-plus sport and fitness associations and related Crown corporations.

Although there were only nine women in the House of Commons at the time, I was confident that our time had finally come. With the close of the 1960s, we were seeing a great ferment of activism that had advanced the nascent women's movement.

We honestly thought things had changed and that women's place in Canadian society was permanently assured. (This was before the inevitable backlash). In Canadian sport, hockey always dominates the agenda. But a team of memorable men and women helped me set an energetic pace as we worked for enhanced development of both elite and mass sport and a Fitness National Policy Agenda that included equality for both sexes. The 1977 paper *Toward a National Policy on Amateur Sport*, for example, advocated increased emphasis on junior development and recommended a comprehensive athlete profile information system. Both of these initiatives were to be gender balanced.

Women who were vital to this effort were Carol Pugliese in Sport, April Holland Wright in Communications and Lucy Lambert, whose contacts and Quebec background helped me enormously. Other high-performance women like Gail Gibson, Marion Lay, Debbie Brill, Diane Jones Konihowski and many others also joined the effort. On the organizational side of the Ministry, I consulted with memorable women such as the late Carol Anne Letheren, who eventually became the first woman Chief Executive Officer of the Canadian Olympic Association. She was a trusted advisor, in marked contrast to the International Olympic Committee itself. This organization was still profoundly influenced by the blatant 19th-century sexism of modern Olympic founder the Baron de Coubertin and the arrant bigotry of Avery Brundage who had recently vacated the office of IOC President, leaving a legacy of open misogyny in 1972.

The advice and support of good men were also critical to the successes we enjoyed. I remember journalist Charles Lynch referring to the exceptional women on my team as "Madame Minister's Praetorian Guard." Yet even with my high profile ubiquitously mentioned in nearly every media report and newspaper sport section, women remained a rare sight on Parliament Hill.

Just as on the current television series "Mad Men," many managers at that time referred to their women staff assistants as "my girl" (nudge, nudge, wink, wink), as in, "my girl will get your coffee," and other equally demeaning comments. In my office at the Hill, two wonderful women, Jane Cane and Alice

Massad, held the fort, and Tom McIllfaterick kept me on course with my competing duties at the Ministry, constituency, the House of Commons and the Party—in that order. In all these responsibilities much of the old 1960's "My Girl" ethos remained, but as one of Trudeau's Ministers I was simply not prepared to either acknowledge or accept it.

The first "scandal" I faced occurred soon after I became Minister. An alert print journalist breathlessly exposed that a Ministerial plane full of women had landed for a Prairie-based re-fueling en route to Vancouver. The implication was that something salacious was afoot since there were no properly certified males on board to legitimize the government flight— only me! Of course as a Minister, I had the same right as other Ministers to use a government airplane for governmental business. There was no scandal—only old attitudes.

It was hockey that often nearly overwhelmed the Ministry. By delving into this male-oriented sport I came to know some of Canada's great sportsmen (and some who were not). I warmly remember protracted discussions and remarkable mentoring on hockey and sport from former Dean of the Parliamentary Press Gallery Douglas Fisher, former *Toronto Sun* Sport Editor George Gross, Torrance Wylie and others. At my first International Ice Hockey Federation Championship in Vienna in 1977, Doug Fisher and George Gross directed my replies to European media regarding Canada's presumed "rough play" and supposed misdemeanors. I was repeatedly advised, especially by prized staffer and friend Dan Pugliese, that when "those NHLers put on their Canada jerseys for international ice hockey" they become "your boys" and are your number one priority. They were, and they still are. I also built a fairly good working relationship with then-National Hockey League (NHL) Commissioner John Zeigler. The result was some surprisingly positive and productive negotiations concerning the role and place of Hockey Canada in regard to international competition.

But there were others. Once named the NHL's miscreant owner, the Toronto Maple Leafs' Harold Ballard was a sexist bully who famously dismissed Canadian Broadcasting Corporation's iconic Barbara Frum on *As It Happens*—the radio show she co-hosted—

by saying "the only place for a woman is flat on her back." In response to Ballard's outburst and in Ms. Frum's defence, I rose in the House of Commons on a Point of Privilege as "a woman standing on her own two feet in Canada's Parliament."

I was also subjected to a particularly sexist, hockey-related bullying incident in New York. During an NHL League dinner, I was seated beside another belligerent, now-deceased American team owner, who shall be nameless (but whose sister was the first woman to have her name engraved on the Stanley Cup). Throughout the meal, he needled me with various obscenities about being a woman in a "man's job" and then proceeded to derogate Canada, my gender and me. I retaliated and left. Later that evening our little team stopped at a bar for a nightcap. The offending owner reappeared and began with more sexist jabs. This time, though, not satisfied with verbal assaults, he grabbed my tuxedo lapels and blouse collar in frustration, slightly tearing both. Suddenly, NHL Players' boss Alan Eagleson and George Gross flew into the fray in a chivalrous determination to "protect our Minister." They prevailed, and the man was dispatched and I remained with my honour—if not my dignity—intact. A *Windsor Star* reporter who witnessed the scene kindly kept the exchange secret. He advised me that regardless of the circumstances, if the story were to be revealed, I would be blamed (unfairly in his opinion), because ("anti-woman") hockey culture would always prevail. I later donated the tuxedo and blouse, along with a Commonwealth Games sport-engraved Solingen steel sword, to the British Columbia Sports Hall of Fame. As far I am aware, the garments and the weapon remain somewhere in the bowels of the BC sport museum, without recognition of their collective symbolic value as feminist sport artifacts. Should there ever be a feminist museum, perhaps these articles might find their place illustrating another phase of human evolution.

Despite these shocking incidents, I recall that time as one of progress. There were many supportive and encouraging women and men who assisted us, and there truly was a generally positive outlook. This positivity was for good reason: this was the era when Canada began to find its way out of its colonial straightjacket. Montreal's successful 1967 Expo and the celebration of the national Centennial showed us and the world that Canada had begun to grow up at last. Other revolutionary advances also came about during this time, thanks to the strong foundations that had been laid during the late 1960s. The women's movement was strengthened and pushed ahead on a wave of support that had begun with the fight for women's suffrage. The environmental movement emerged, sailing aboard the vessel *Greenpeace* out of Vancouver and into history, a precursor to today's multitudes of global environmental organizations. Women across the country stood up and demanded choice for our persons, our bodies, our fertility. This was a time of enormous hopefulness and legally-binding achievement. There was a sense that women could face any challenge: we were free to choose our destinies and demand society's respect in the process.

Discrimination, racism and sexism wear many faces. I recall an African sport boss being especially negative as we prepared for the Edmonton Commonwealth Games in 1978. Apartheid in South Africa had reared its ugly head and might have scuttled participation from all other African Commonwealth nations in the Games. I took the gentleman aside and let him know that while he was black and suffered from rank discrimination from some of the participants, as a woman I was also subject to a similar sort of arrogance. The message was clear: we were here, we had the power to act, and act we must! He backed down, and African Commonwealth Nations (without South Africa) were prominent in the winning Edmonton Games.

I have long lived by an 1895 definition of feminism: "a feminist is a woman or girl who has within herself the will to fight her way to independence." We are mothers, homemakers, professionals and achievers—many times all at once. As Canada's first Sport and Fitness Minister I was always aware that in spite of everything, my gender was an advantage, not a hindrance. I look back now on many pivotal sport meetings, negotiations and interchanges at national and international levels, where having been a different kind of "front-man" for Sport and Fitness made progress and agreements possible that might not have been had I not been a woman. Nevertheless, after a lifetime of work, I have seen that regardless of our advances and the passage of time, society continues to remain uneasy with women of achievement in any field of endeavor, including sport—the fight for independence continues.

Canadian women's successes in sport can be measured in many ways, but perhaps the most salient is in the Olympics. All you need to do is count how many Olympic medals have been won by Canadian women in recent years and then note women's successes across the board—from hockey to soccer to individual achievements—and you can see that the future for women in sport is virtually unlimited.

HOMAGE TO THE SISTERHOOD
Bruce Kidd

"Only she who attempts the absurd can achieve the impossible!"
— NELLIE McCLUNG

Few changes during the last 50 years have been as profound as the transformation of sports brought about by the exuberant, persistent and insistent participation of girls and women. Today, there's not a sport that women do not play, excel at or attend. After many years of activism, the last barriers to female Olympic participation fell in 2012 when women competed in boxing, and the last national Olympic Committee that had refused to enter female competitors, the fiercely patriarchal Saudis, sent female athletes to the Games. Despite fewer events to choose from, Canadian women have earned places on Olympic teams in roughly the same numbers as men and have brought home a larger share of the medals. Women can now find suitable gear for all sports, and they constitute the majority of participants in many of them. And with such high numbers of female participation, the cultures of these sports have changed. In many Canadian cities, for example, most runners pounding out the kilometres in training and races are female; they've made the sport more welcoming, social and health-conscious. More women watching sports has transformed the design, comfort and fan behaviour in arenas and stadia.

Across Canada, the place of girls and women in sport is now affirmed by policy, protected by human rights legislation and upheld by the courts. The prohibition of gender discrimination, including on the basis of sexual orientation, is widely accepted as necessary to realize the "level playing field" and "fair play" values of sports. Even the way we think about sports has been altered dramatically. Feminist scholarship has effectively demolished the view that sports are trans-historically essential. Sport can no longer be regarded as an apolitical form of culture; mainstream social science has demonstrated how sports are gendered (and racialized and classed)—and has highlighted the attendant problems that go with this gendering. Organizations such as the Canadian Centre for Ethics in Sport (CCES) and the Canadian Association of Women in Sport and Physical Activity (CAAWS) disseminate these critical perspectives in their advocacy. Although important battles remain—women are woefully under-represented in leadership, especially coaching, and by the mass media—the legal, theoretical and organizational basis for waging these battles is strong.

In this current landscape, it's difficult to adequately describe the breadth and depth of the chill against female participation that followed World War II and the tremendous obstacles second wave feminism has overcome in the years covered by this volume. When I recount the horror stories of the 1950s and 1960s to young women today, they are incredulous. Yet girls' and women's access to sport, now taken for granted, simply did not exist a generation ago. On the contrary, as I can attest, having been a boy growing up in the sports-loving east end of Toronto in the 1940s and 1950s, the norm at that time was that sports were an exclusive masculine domain. For us, there were school and community programs and teams galore, all organized, funded and celebrated by supportive parents, neighbours, teachers, local businesses, politicians and the media. But there was nothing comparable for girls and young women. If any girl my age had tried to take up a spot on a community team, even if she had found the right equipment (CCM stopped making hockey skates for women in 1954), she would have faced patronizing or hostile refusal of her participation. Had she persisted, there would have been ridicule and warnings that she was endangering her health and contributing to race suicide (some authority could always be found to say that vigorous sport damaged the reproductive organs).

I'm not making this up. In 1955, the then 9-year-old Ab Hoffman was outed from western Toronto peewee hockey when she was selected for the all-star team after an official, who checked her birth certificate, discovered that she was actually Abigail and female. Her presence on the team quickly became front page moral panic. I can no longer remember my reaction at the time—it has been distilled through my subsequent friendship and collaborations with Abby and my gradual embrace of gender equity—but I can imagine my teammates and I were relieved that she was not playing in our midst. I could never have articulated it at the time, but I'm sure we all understood unconsciously that our identities as males were bound up with sports, and sports brought males privileged benefits; having a young woman on the team would undermine both our masculinity and our claim to privilege. As a historian, I've come to understand that these male-empowering aspects of sport were always intended— that modern sport as we know it was fashioned, enjoyed and celebrated for shoring up masculinity at a time when many traditional roles were being undermined by the devastating changes of the industrial revolution.

To be sure, some Canadian women excelled in sports in the 1940s and 1950s. We all knew about Olympic figure skating champion Barbara Ann Scott—some of the younger women of my generation were named after her. I distinctly remember the city-wide alert when 16-year-old Marilyn Bell completed her epic marathon swim across Lake Ontario to the Toronto shoreline. And a teammate's aunt played in the highly competitive women's softball league at Coxwell Stadium. (I had heard stories about the heyday of women's softball in the 1930s.) In high school, a few women played intramural and interscholastic sports. Despite these achievements, male hegemony in sports continued, as teams, clubs and games were organized primarily for the benefit of boys and men. Furthermore, the women who were able to excel were always categorized and marginalized as "unusual," i.e. not to be followed. In the case of Barbara Ann Scott, in spite of her exceptional athleticism, steel nerves and competitive resilience, she was presented—and presented herself—as the "girl next door," always beautifully available to support men in charge; figure skating was presented as a decorative art. Marilyn Bell was considered an athletic aberration, even though she joined the ranks of a long list of outstanding female distance swimmers in Lake Ontario swims. The women's softball league folded by the early 1960s, and Coxwell Stadium was renovated for men's high school football. For high school women athletes in my school, the separate physical education and intramural programs were decidedly unequal, with poorer facilities and shorter and less interesting schedules. We scorned their inadequacies, attributing them to lack of character and serious interest.

It was only years later that I realized that the very few programs that did exist for girls and women in the 1950s were the vestiges of the remarkable achievements of first wave feminism. In the 1920s and 1930s, Canadian women competed in and excelled at every sport there was. They generated headlines wherever they went, eventually pushing the mass media to give prominent coverage to female athletes and events and to hire female reporters and daily columnists. Women's teams and leagues attracted sizable crowds. The Edmonton Grads in basketball and the Preston Rivulettes in hockey set attendance records in many of the arenas they played. Women's softball teams in Toronto also generated sizable crowds. I have analyzed the attendance records carefully compiled by the Toronto Harbour Commission, which owned and operated both Sunnyside and Maple Leaf Stadia, and discovered that in the interwar years, more people paid to watch women play softball at Sunnyside than men play professional baseball at Maple Leaf Stadium. Many of these athletic activities for women were coordinated by the Women's Amateur Athletic Federation, a pan-Canadian governing body that promoted "girls'" sports run by girls from 1926 into the early years of WWII. WAAF won the right for Canadian women to compete in the International Olympic Committee's Olympic Games, and they also entered Canadian teams in the Fédération Sportive Féminine Internationale's Women's Olympics and Women's World Games, to give Canadian women the best of both international experiences. Some historians have called this era "The Golden Age of Women's Sports."

Yet the "separate sphere" strategy, influenced by first wave feminism and executed during the interwar years, left little room to contest the power dynamic that kept women's sports underfunded and marginal. Women were the first to be fired during the Depression, leading to decreased independent means and opportunities to pursue sports, and as resources dried up, female-led female sport was harder and harder to sustain. Another huge contributing factor to the underfunding of women's sports was when men's sports and advertising became linked. By the mid-1930s, advertisers became aware that the most effective way to attract male consumers to products was through sports. Following this realization, men's sports dominated mass media broadcasting schedules, bringing to a close the era of women's sports coverage. In theoretical terms, the "masculinizing synergies" and "symbolic annihilation of women" that sociologists have attributed to the "sport media complex" were the result of pure economics. While I was growing up, I read the sports pages voraciously, but neither my female sport-loving classmates nor I knew of the history of "The Golden Age of Women's Sport." It was as if it never happened. Moreover, it was not until much later that I realized how high the obstacles were for the women who did provide sporting opportunities for girls and women in the 1950s and 1960s, as they fought open opposition, lesbophobia and fear-mongering. If they appeared timid and conservative, it was only because they found that it was better to proceed quietly lest too much visibility provoke an outright attack.

My education in feminism began in track and field. I had a strong mother who valued sports and physical activity, and sisters and aunts who were always adventurous. One of my aunts had cycled from Toronto to Vancouver in 1926, long before the construction of the Trans-Canada highway, and I knew some of her stories. (Lots of "gumbo," i.e. mud, but "no big deal" is what she usually said.) But even with these influences, I did not question my view that sports were a male preserve until I became a teenager and gave up playing organized baseball and hockey to concentrate on track. (My immersion in track changed my views on hockey violence as well.) While there were no track and field teams for women at the schools I attended, there were outstanding female athletes at the club I joined, the East York Track Club, and women competed in all the meets. Although they had far fewer events, they trained and raced as hard or harder than we did, and their performances were as exciting to watch. It was clear that they belonged in sports.

It was also clear that they encountered all sorts of obstacles we didn't—from the number of opportunities they had to compete (school and university competition was still in the distant future) and the events available to them (800 metres/880 yards was the longest distance, and that was re-introduced in 1960; triple jump, pole vault and hammer were prohibited), to everyday training conditions. While men usually enjoyed dressing rooms and showers, women rarely did, and were forced to change in a public washroom, someone's car or even behind a bush and then go home from workouts and races sweaty and cold. I think that witnessing this two-tiered system was my first realization that the treatment of women in sports was unfair and could not be justified as the natural order of things. I have always depended upon a hot shower for recovery after a workout or race, especially after a run in the cold and wet, and it was a shock to see our female teammates forced to go without.

Most of the female athletes I knew bent my ear about the double standard in sport, but Abby Hoffman was public about it. Barred from hockey, Abby became a successful swimmer and then took up track. By 1962, at the age of 15, she had become the dominant Canadian middle distance runner and was named to the Canadian team competing at the British Empire and Commonwealth Games in Perth, Australia. The following year, she won the 800 metres in the Pan American Games in Sao Paulo, Brazil. During an exemplary career, she represented Canada on four

Olympic teams, and was chosen to carry the flag into Olympic Stadium in Montreal in 1976. She twice reached the Olympic final of the 800 metres, and won championships and medals at the Commonwealth, Pan American, World Student and Maccabiah Games, as well as Canadian, US and British championships. Her thrilling races earned her headlines and fans wherever she went, and she took advantage of her celebrity to argue for more accessible, democratic and professionally organized Canadian sport. She was articulate, eloquent and passionate and linked what was happening in sports to social theory. She had an acerbic wit and brilliant repartee. Once I was congratulating her after she won a race in Toronto's High Park when a well-dressed woman came up to her and crossly told her that if she kept up running she would "destroy her uterus and not be able to have babies." "Can I patent that?" Abby replied, without missing a beat. She became as frequently quoted for her critical views and proposals for reform as she was for her post-race feelings. It was hard not to admire her and think about what she said.

Abby was also a brilliant public educator. She deconstructed and made fun of the myths about women in sport, presented policy proposals and offered encouragement and practical tips to help women become active. One of the very few who knew about the accomplishments of first wave feminism, gleaned through her remarkable mother Dorothy Medhurst, Abby taught this history and gave women a confident sense of the possibilities, while forging a distinctly different direction. She also had trenchant views on contemporary male leadership in Canadian politics and Canadian sport. She spoke at schools, colleges and universities. She made regular appearances on Peter Gzowski's widely-heard CBC Radio program *This Country in the Morning* and other radio and television outlets, and frequently wrote opinion pieces for newspapers and magazines. For several years, she had a monthly column for *Chatelaine* magazine. During the heady days when feminism was known as women's liberation, she was one of the best known and most influential women in Canada in any field.

In arguing for a better deal for Canadian women, Abby drew upon her own bitter experiences: changing outside or in cold washrooms, while her male teammates enjoyed heated locker rooms and showers; getting less expense money from amateur officials simply because she was female; being told that what she was doing was inappropriate and dangerous for her health; and training outside during the long winter because the only indoor track in the city was closed to female athletes. Abby fought against these injustices, even at the institutions to which she belonged. At that time, the only indoor track available in Toronto for daily training was at Hart House at the University of Toronto, where she was first an undergraduate and then a graduate student, as well as a distinguished, well known Olympian who brought significant prestige to the University. But Hart House was a male-only facility. When it was opened in 1919, the University promised women a similar building, but it took it 40 years to realize and only after a tremendous lobbying effort by the women's athletic association in the 1950s; in the end, that building did not have a track. On occasion, men let female teammates in the back door at Hart House, where they had to run in hoodies and pass as men. By the winter of 1965-1966, Abby would have none of that, and on three separate occasions she openly tried to run on the track, only to be physically thrown out into the snow.

The previous summer, Abby had been a member of the first Canadian team to compete in the World Student Games (also known as the FISU games after the Fédération Internationale du Sport Universitaire), winning a bronze medal in the 800 metre race. The team had been organized by the national students' federation, the Canadian Union of Students (CUS), because the football-preoccupied Canadian Intercollegiate Athletic Union (CIAU) was uninterested. I was the manager of that first team, and since we had to send it on a shoestring, we got contributions from the men's athletic departments of the universities represented. When the U of T men's athletic director discovered that Abby was one of the athletes subsidized, he went ballistic, and immediately demanded the money be returned. Abby's presence on the team was always a sore point for the men's athletic director, and when we subsequently became colleagues, he never forgot to remind me that "Abby Hoffman was never a representative of the University of Toronto Athletic Association" and he always asked for the money back. That summer's events coloured and gave context to the decision to toss Abby in the snow the following winter. But rather than walk quietly away, Abby turned the episodes into a *cause célèbre* to fuel the growing pressure to open Hart House (a cultural centre with a theatre, art gallery, library, music hall, and eating and common rooms as well as an athletic centre) to women. Women were finally admitted in 1972, and the first women's dressing room opened in 1980. Abby was invited to cut the ribbon at the opening and unveil a plaque commemorating the history behind the dressing room that bears the same Nellie McClung quote found at the beginning of this chapter. But 14 years earlier in 1966, what she attempted really did seem absurd.

Abby, also a brilliant policy maker, had her hand in most of the significant advances for Canadian women in sport over three decades. In 1967, as chef de mission of the Canadian team to the World Student Games in Tokyo, she gave such prominence to women's participation that when CUS folded and the male-only CIAU finally assumed the FISU franchise in 1973, it had no recourse but to send female athletes to the World Student Games. In 1974 she worked with Marion Lay and Petra Burka (two other remarkable athlete activists) to organize the first national conference on women in sport since before World War II, setting the agenda for legislation, policy and programs that continue to this day. In 1975, when she created the financial aid program for Olympic athletes that became the basis for today's Athlete Assistance Program, she made sure that female athletes received exactly the same benefits as men. She was just as prominent at the local and provincial levels. In Toronto, she contributed to a landmark study that slammed municipal recreation for gender stereotyping, where boys played sports and girls did arts and crafts. As the Executive Director of the Ontario Human Rights Commission, she prepared the ground for the subsequent challenges that brought sports under human rights legislation. Not surprisingly, she quickly became one of the most influential sports leaders in Canada. She was the first woman elected to the Executive of the Canadian Olympic Association and the first female Director General of Sport Canada. In that latter position, she led the creation of the 1986

Sport Canada Policy on Women in Sport. When I asked a group of distinguished female Canadian coaches and sports leaders whom we should invite to give a keynote at a conference about sport and social change—specifically about the changes brought about by feminism between 1968 and 2008—their response was unanimous: Abby Hoffman.

Of course, there were other remarkable athlete activists during these decades, Marion Lay most notable among them. Marion was a world record holder, Olympic medalist and Commonwealth champion, and she became an eloquent public educator and a determined, strategically astute policy maker. No one in my experience can thread her way through a complicated, often hostile bureaucracy as well as Marion. In 1972 she established Canada's first government-led Women in Sport Program and developed the high performance funding plan for women training for the 1976 Olympic Games in Montreal. Marion also helped establish the leading non-governmental organizations that advocate for girls and women in sport, including the Canadian Association for the Advancement of Women and Sport and Physical Activity (CAAWS), WomenSport International and PROMOTION Plus in British Columbia. Marion, too, made a huge contribution to mainstream sport, ensuring the full integration of women in the process. She was the founder and first chair of the Canadian Sport Centre Vancouver, now PacificSport. A leading member of the Vancouver bid for the 2010 Winter Olympic and Paralympic Games, she spearheaded the province-wide campaign during the plebiscite to win public support for the bid. Once the Games were awarded, she created and led Legacies Now, the innovative NGO that enhanced opportunities for British Columbians in the build-up to those Games. I have learned tremendously from her over the years.

Many other women were involved in the struggle, pushing for better opportunities in clubs, municipalities and schools, colleges and universities, and striving for a more representative, less sexist portrayal of female athletes and coaches in the mass media. The photograph of the women who constituted the "Founding Mothers" of CAAWS on that organization's website shows the breadth of their activism. Their goals resonated with the rise of second wave feminism across the world, as women entered higher education and employment in record numbers—only to find a host of overt, structural and ideological barriers—and struggled to overturn them. In turn, second wave feminism drew upon and contributed to the widespread mobilization of young people in civil rights, anti-war, anti-apartheid and environmental movements. As women (and their partners) fought for reproductive rights, including accessible childcare, they also turned their attention to health and education issues, and in the process more and more women discovered sport and physical activity. The desire for self-defence in the face of sexual assaults also provided impetus for physical training. Although much of girls' and women's sporting activity was isolated from the broad currents and debates within feminism, some leaders were making the connection: Florence Bird's Royal Commission Report on the Status of Women in 1970 paved the way for the first national women's conference in 1974, Abby and Marion were closely linked to the women's movements in Toronto and Vancouver, and Muriel Duckworth of the Voice of Women was among the women from across Canada who founded CAAWS.

A comprehensive history of the contributions of second wave feminism in sport must consider the larger transformations in Canadian and global societies during recent decades, especially now when some of the social forces that empowered sportswomen in the 1970s, 1980s and 1990s undermine and threaten certain gains. The triumph of neo-liberal ideas and their preoccupation with unmediated market solutions to social challenges have contributed to a frontal assault on the public institutions that provide the most accessible opportunities for girls and women to engage in healthy sports and physical activity; they have also had an effect on the social policies (affordable childcare, accessible housing, income equality) that enable women and their families to live dignified and rewarding lives. Many athletes and sports organizations depend on capitalist sponsorship, but this reliance on private funding is inherently problematic in a world where the beauty industry promotes a confining, heterosexist view of femininity, and has complicated the appeal of vigorous sport and physical activity. In some parts of Canada, it seems like the battles for equitable policies have to be re-fought.

Yet at the same time, girls and women are engaging in sports in record numbers, confident that they belong in sports and have every right to mould sports to their particular needs. For that freedom they owe several earlier generations of sportswomen a tremendous debt. They should know that the opportunities that they currently enjoy were not created naturally or inevitably, but came about because a brave group of sportswomen and feminist activists fought for them—strategizing, persuading, organizing, and in some cases, committing civil disobedience and going to court. Many of these leaders were athletes like Abby Hoffman and Marion Lay. They should be remembered with admiration and gratitude. This book is a contribution to that end.

OPENING DOORS FOR WOMEN
In Conversation with Marion Lay
Sheila Robertson

" ... ask for what you deserve."
— MARION LAY

My family was living in Covina, California when I was a youngster because of my father's business as a motel owner. He died when I was 11, and the swim club became my family. I was a welfare child, and my club helped me to swim and raise money so I could go to competitions. Although I knew there was an Olympics, I had no idea that people like me, poor kids, could ever go there. Also, sport wasn't part of my family culture.

My recognition of the issues regarding women in sport began when I was 14. I was told that, although I was a Canadian citizen, I was not eligible to compete for Canada at the 1964 Olympics even if I made the team. I was also told by the United States that, because I was a Canadian citizen, I was not eligible to compete for that country. Nevertheless, I swam at the American trials and would have qualified for their relays. I then went to Canada's Olympic trials at the University of British Columbia. My coach, Vince Van Detta, said, "just swim your best, and if you aren't selected for the team, at least you will show what a good swimmer you are."

This became my first battle. I swam well enough to make the team, but many people questioned my even being at the trials and why I should be allowed to swim for Canada when I was a non-resident. During the meet, Vince spoke on my behalf to officials of the Canadian Olympic Association (COA) and others who were supportive of a non-resident being named to the Olympic team. I also wrote a letter to the COA, appealing to them for support because I really believed I was a Canadian despite where my family was living. I asked for the opportunity to do the best I could and help Canada.

When I was announced to the team at the end of the four day meet, I celebrated, but I was then faced with the situation of the head coach Howard Firby not agreeing with my selection and banning me from team workouts. I was billeted with the James family, and Mrs. James took me to the workouts, watched and made notes, and during open swim, took me through the same workout. She was wonderful!

After two stressful days, Howard allowed me to train with the team, asking only that I be the hardest worker and cause no problems. It is my nature to work hard and that has stayed with me throughout my life; only later have I caused what some might call "problems." Through his actions, Vince taught me a lesson that has been with me ever since: if you're going to bring about change, you have to be present. I won the battle because somebody looked at the rules on my behalf and because my coach supported me.

All my life I have tried to belong to Canada, and I think I overcompensated from that moment on to show that I was of value. Even though everyone was so kind, I always felt like an outsider. When I did make that Olympic team, I told Howard that if he let me swim, he would never regret it, and I would give 100 percent in everything, and I did that. I made the commitment that I would come back to Canada and try to give back to sport.

Aside from winning the bronze medal in the 4x100-metre relay, the 1968 Olympics were also important for human rights. In Mexico City, the African American athletes Tommie Smith and John Carlos raised their fists in what became known as the "human rights salute." It was the time of the civil rights movement in the United States and the beginning of the women's movement. Bruce Kidd, who was also on Canada's Olympic team, created a network called Athletes' Concern to advocate for athletes' rights. I joined because I believed athletes must have a voice and be acknowledged as people and not just as products. That network became very important for me. It was also the time when I met Roger Jackson, who later invited me to join his group at the Fitness and Amateur Sport Branch (FAS) to set up the first high-performance sport programs funded by the federal government. While in Mexico, he heard me talking about issues athletes faced, and I think he found that intriguing given my age. He also noticed that on the flight home I was playing chess so he assumed I must be a thoughtful young athlete with ideas. I didn't know chess was going to be my calling card into Sport Canada.

In the four years between 1968 and 1972, when I joined the FAS, I learned about women and sport through Marie Hart, my undergraduate advisor who wrote the first major article about discrimination and women and sport and was one of the best thinkers on the subject in the States. In 1968, because of her influence, I chose women in sport as a statistical analysis project, which gave me the opportunity to examine the issues facing women in sport, not just as athletes but as coaches, officials and administrators. I later followed Marie to Cal State Hayward because I wanted to do my master's degree with her.

The late 1960s and early 1970s saw protests against the Vietnam war and for human rights and race relations, the beginnings of the feminist movement and the Haight-Ashbury hippie movement. Rights for people with a disability were starting to be talked about and the Special Olympics began for people with developmental issues. It was really a time for people committed to bringing about change.

Before joining Sport Canada in 1972, I had come to realize that society did not believe there was an issue around girls and women in sport and also didn't think it was very important. The thought was, the opportunities are there, all you have to do is choose. There was no understanding that all the opportunities were for boys and men. In fact, when I had my interview at Sport Canada, I mentioned to the director, Lou Lefaivre, that women in sport was one of my areas of interest and, in case he hadn't noticed, there was a problem. Just like that, he said: "Let's fix it. Get out there and talk about it." He was so positive! I think he thought women and sport was an issue that could be changed quite easily. We both learned that women weren't present because of the male culture of sport; sport was seen as a male birthright and only those defined as tomboys would choose to go into sport. Those of us who did sport didn't fit the typical "girl" role but it was understood that at a certain age we would have to start doing appropriate "girl" things and stop this childhood, tomboy behaviour. We competed as an extension of the male and never as a dimension of the female. For years, psychological tests defined sport as a male characteristic and nursing as a female characteristic; in other words, defining by our gender what we were supposed to like or dislike. There was a lot more tradition to hold us into roles, and when you have tradition, roles and rules are very important.

Two pivotal events happened to help bring legitimacy to the issues facing women in sport. The first was the 1970 Royal Commission on the Status of Women Report, which included two recommendations on women in sport (#77 and #78). The second was in 1973 when the Canadian Advisory Council on the Status of Women was created to monitor and report back to the federal government on the implementation of the Royal Commission's recommendations. The Royal Commission and the Advisory Council were so important for our legitimacy in women in sport.

As a result of the Royal Commission Report, Sport Canada decided to be more proactive in the area of women in sport. We gathered statistics on the state of sport for girls and women at all levels and presented the results at national workshops and conferences. In all areas the results showed clearly that women should be doing better in terms of numbers and opportunities. They revealed an absolutely unacceptable situation that society and the sport community thought was okay. But girls and women who were athletes and/or who wanted to become coaches said, "Hey, this is not okay." It was a lonely, isolating world at that point for those of us who wanted to bring about change. The group of women who were talking about the issues was not considered legitimate. We were second class.

I was absolutely naïve in thinking that after a few presentations things would change, that the situation existed only because people hadn't noticed. I was so shocked at the reaction I stirred up. There was a huge backlash after we produced the paper with all its damning facts and statistics. And that backlash was: "How dare you use the word 'discrimination' in sport? How dare you give us these numbers? You're attacking the men who are in power but in actual fact, according to the numbers, girls and women don't want to be here." Others said: "Marion, sport has been so good to you. How dare you criticize? I thought you were one of us." Those reactions depressed me. I thought, I'm fighting an issue that hardly anyone cares about. And I've hurt a lot of people's feelings, some of whom theoretically supported me. The reaction was really intense, and I was attacked on a personal level. I started to get angry about the situation around women and sport and stayed that way for several years, approaching the issue from a very angry place because I was hurt. Because of the backlash I thought: "Oh, I didn't present it well. It's my fault. I was too hard. I should have done something different," although I wasn't sure what that was. I felt like I had failed everybody, that it was my fault.

Given the backlash, Lou said: "This probably means you are right, but now we have to do it differently." He suggested a national conference, and Canada's first women and sport conference was held in 1974. It was there that I finally realized it wasn't my fault! When you fight discrimination, you end up feeling like you've done something wrong, rather than understanding that you have a legitimate right to ask for what you deserve. The conference solidified that it wasn't my personal failure that we were unable to start to bring about change; it was the fact that we were in a system based on values that only honoured and allowed opportunities for men. Agreed, I definitely could do better presentations and I definitely had to get rid of my negative attitude, but I now knew our issue was absolutely legitimate and my work changed from "How dare you!" to "How can we?" The conference validated that the problem was not just an oversight that women were second class citizens in sport, and being in a position of power and status in effecting change is important.

Out of the conference we created a network of women and men, but a careful look at the conference recommendations clearly showed the need for women in sport organizations. At the time, there were many women's organizations in other sectors, but it took sport several years to form one for women in sport and part of the reason was that we had very little money. The common thinking was: "Do you want to spend money on an organization or on trying to do something?" Eventually we decided we needed a national organization to help us figure out what we wanted, and in 1980 the Canadian Association for the Advancement of Women and Sport (CAAWS) (later renamed Canadian Association for the Advacement of Women and Sport and Physical Activity) was formed, and I became its first chair. Our initial approach was to "ask" the system to do more for girls and women, making small incremental changes in areas such as coaching and officiating.

CAAWS gave me a safe place to talk about issues and also to make mistakes. I learned how to chair a board of directors in an all female environment, how to lead, how to bring motions forward, and how to use the system to bring about change. It also gave me a platform to talk about the issues. I could call myself a feminist in a safe environment where nobody ever said, "Oh, the 'f' word!" as often happened in the external sport community. Here, being a feminist was celebrated. Of course we had to understand the power dynamics of leadership and of course we had to talk about systemic change.

After educating ourselves, we started to build actions to develop national and provincial programs and policies in order to get funding. It is important to know that initially, CAAWS funding came from the federal government's Women's Bureau and not Sport Canada. That happened a few years later.

Once we had our key messages, we had to get on the sport agenda. And then we started working with the national sport organizations (NSOs) to get women on committees. As we learned and talked about our issues, we realized we had to create tools, which became a very important element of CAAWS work. We had to learn how to make decisions, how to transfer money from men's programs to women's programs, and to get new money for women's programs.

In the early days, CAAWS worked with women and men who were really committed and involved in sport and physical activity. Later, we started to work with women and men who were "on the edge" and not sure they wanted to be involved in our areas. This priority changed as people became more aware of health issues and of the importance of a healthy lifetstyle. CAAWS work in helping people to make the decision to become involved came to define its mission. Many of the CAAWS tools, such as those on Leadership and the Audits and Snapshots, describe how to bring about change and remain really important.

On a personal level, my work concentrated on getting women and sport on the sport agenda and providing the feminist analysis and evidence that this was a systemic problem, not just the opinions of a few whining women. When we got on agendas, people started to ask what to do and we were able to provide the CAAWS tools.

My work changed to that of oversight once there were many people talking about the issues. As the watchdog I would ask: "You're saying the correct things, but are you doing anything, and if so, what?" People may say the right things, but often because of priorities that are driven by tradition (the male agenda), women in sport do not get the same opportunities and funding. It was said: "We'd like to do more for you, but we don't have the money this year." We had to push hard and say: "That's not okay."

A "wow" moment was the Justine Blainey case in 1981. When her claim became a court case, all of a sudden women in sport and our choice to play became legitimate. Win or lose, the case was important enough to go to the Supreme Court of Canada.

In 1986 Sport Canada's Women in Sport policy came into effect and did several things. First, it gave us a backdrop. I always thought policy was something abstract, and I was a doer, a champion of creating programs. But I realized that this policy meant the sport system had to start doing something. It enabled us to tell NSOs that Sport Canada has a policy that says you must start to do something. It put us in a very different position and also provided protection. It was no longer just me, Marion, calling for change.

Now that there was some incentive, change began. However, there have never been ramifications for inaction and consequently, change has been very slow. We don't have a government that applies the necessary big stick, such as denying funding to non-compliant NSOs. We've set targets, but never quotas. I personally feel that the only successful model is one in which there are very clear targets for change, along with consequences if change is not made. I refer to the Canada Games, which has a successful policy that specifies coaching positions for women. The provinces know they have to bring women coaches to the Games too. If not, there are stated ramifications. Canada Games also supports a Canada Games Apprenticeship Program for women coaches.

When women believe they can't become coaches because they also want to have a family, we shouldn't say: "Worry about that later. Just become a coach." If we wanted to have women coaches, we would have policies that allow women to bring their children to practice, offer baby-sitting and nanny services, permit women to bring their newborn babies with them when their teams are overseas, and give women flexibility. We have to realize that women have to take some time out to have children. Overtly or not, our system absolutely says to women: "Don't plan a coaching career if you plan to have a family. You have to choose." People might deny it, but everything in our system screams that. Either we fix it or stop pretending we want to have women coaches.

We have people who measure slow- and fast-twitch fibres, biomechanics, the science of sport, sport psychology to ensure we're mentally prepared, nutritional expertise, but when it comes to coaching, we exclude 51 percent of our population and yet we say we're giving the athletes excellence in coaching. It's said that there's no skill set that women could bring to coaching. Yet, we also say the number one thing in coaching is communicating with your athletes, and that's the best skill set women have.

So we have to debunk myths, name things, talk about them, and then say, this is what we need for excellence and we're going to go there. And we need excellence from the very beginning of the sport experience.

I'm very proud of the fact that I'm a feminist. This means I have an analysis of power and organizational dynamics in society that either enable people to have opportunities or prevent them from having opportunities. This is fundamental. The new generation of young women talks a lot about "girl power," about getting women into coaching and officiating—we're way behind in those areas—but at the same time we're losing that academic look at what the power dynamic is and how we make change. People individually feel they've failed, they've tried and got burned out because we don't say it's the system that has to change. We have women who have been the pioneers, but many others don't have the perseverance, the stamina, the resources, the network, the mentors—it is so hard. It's hard, hard work.

In describing my leadership style, I first look at the dynamics of change and who owns most of the world. I look at the issues and ask how to bring about change. It's very important to name the issue and to say, even though it's hard, that it's discrimination or exclusion or wrong, or in some cases evil, such as coach abuse of an athlete.

We do not yet have a system for everybody; we have a system that limits the opportunity for women, multi-cultural groups, disadvantaged people, and people with disabilities to have a positive and enjoyable experience. Many, many people are excluded from the system. We have to say that it's not because these people don't want to be involved as is often claimed.

My strength is having a vision and making it come to life. I am also blessed with the ability to sell a dream. Some call my gift being a dream weaver, others a team builder; the result is the same—being able to translate dreams into reality. When people ask for help, I can usually set them on a course. I believe that asking for help is the greatest compliment you can pay another person. I am good at creating something and empowering others to take over because I don't need ownership. I've always had the ability to let go of transitional power. A lot of people think you need positional power to get things done; I think personal power is as important. I have allowed myself the freedom to not get involved in hierarchies so I can position myself wherever I want.

The progress made on the high performance side is visible. In organizations such as the International Olympic Committee (IOC), change has been slow, but it has added women's events, which then opened up funding of these events from government, sponsors and private donors. And the corporate world, because of the demands on them by society and the women's movement, has basically said that if you're going to sponsor men's events, you have to do the same for women's events. Those changes have been positive.

The sport system gets a huge benefit from high performance women athletes and media attention. The 1988 Calgary Olympics and the Own the Podium program have made a huge difference. At Calgary, women athletes obtained funding and corporations started to support them. Many of today's advocates for women and sport came from those Games. But even today, many people in sport say women win more Olympic medals because there is little depth of competition. The men, now that's "real" sport. It doesn't matter what we do; we're still second class.

So name it! Very clearly "name" an organization when it says it's going to do something and doesn't. When people say all the right things, you believe things are going to happen—and too often they don't. Such people have to be held to account and I do believe the next step is quotas with appropriate penalties, and yes, I know that's controversial, but how many years have we been waiting for people to do the right thing? I thought this work would be over in my lifetime, but we have such a long way to go. I'd like faster change so that I am around to see it. Canada has so many top women athletes who are going to want to coach, officiate, talk to corporations about sport, be paid for what they do and be part of our system, so our tipping point could almost be there because we have the numbers of women to really start to change the system.

And you have to be present. When I wanted to make the 1964 Olympic team, I had to go to the trials and show what I had to offer Canada. So we have to talk about the issues, see people, listen to their fear of change, debunk the myths with positive examples. People have actually asked me if you have to be a lesbian to be involved in women and sport! We have to name this (and other) issues and talk about them. We need to talk about the realities in very plain language.

Self-reflection is really important, asking yourself: "What am I good at and what am I not good at?" I'm very good at getting issues on agendas. And I'm pretty good at keeping an issue on the agenda. I'm not as good at what exactly we should do to increase our numbers in women and sport so I have networks of friends and colleagues and I empower them to do that work and I support and celebrate that. Through self-reflection, I know my weakness is having my feelings hurt. I walk around with insecurity and always ask friends if what I am about to say is okay. I constantly do that, but then I step forward and I'm willing to lead. Because of the insecurity, I try different ways of presenting so my weakness becomes a strength. When I get really nervous, I tell myself, okay, I'm going to do a good job—and I do. Self-reflection has taught me how to use my nervousness positively.

In the end, I've learned I just need to be myself. I can bring certain things to women and sport or to the sport system, but it's just being me, and I constantly lose me. I have to always go back and think about what I want, about my beliefs. Early on, that angry, hard person wasn't me. That was my reaction to being hurt and experiencing that backlash. So I try to stay really true to what I believe is my core centre and so when I present, I often say to myself, just be Marion. I've created a network around Team Marion, and my network has three parts: dear friends, people who love me and who I love; men and women within the sport system working together on change to the system; and those who lead the current system and really don't want change. I make sure I have those leaders in my network because if there is going to be a backlash, at least these people will let me know and, unlike when it happened earlier in my career, I will be prepared. Take the case of the 15 women ski jumpers who, in April 2009, argued in court that under Canada's *Charter of Rights and Freedoms*, they had a constitutional right to compete at the 2010 Games. There was a huge sport backlash around the issue; they agreed with the IOC decision and its discriminatory practices that did not allow the women to compete. Interestingly, we had huge support from the population at large. I'm uncomfortable with that kind of backlash, but going to court was the right thing to do.

In building my networks, if I hear something good about someone, I check it out. I try to find solutions to criticism about why we can't move forward because, that way, real changes can happen. I try to park issues that are going to hurt us and find areas where we can build consensus. To me, the strategy is always the struggle to move forward. There is no right or wrong; rather, you need a network of people who support you, including some who are critics who tell you that you're going too hard or too fast.

I'm not a complicated thinker, nor am I an academic, but I can move agendas and I can recognize opportunities. For example, when the Liberal government was elected in British Columbia in 2001, I looked at their strategic plan to figure out how we in sport could help them to reach their goals through sport and deliver some of their messages. I have done most of my work with governments and very little with the business world because I feel that government is committed to the social responsibility and health agendas.

In the end, I would like to have a sport system that is different than the system I grew up with, a system with a real ethic of care. I get ideas from books that talk about how to create your own realities. I listen to great speakers. I also learn by talking about ideas. I put ideas out and I like to get reactions. I enjoy the debate. I learn a lot from colleagues and friends who dream about how to make a different world. A small group of people really can make change; all you have to do is inspire them to get together to do it.

Making tough decisions doesn't come naturally to me. I prefer the carrot to the stick. With CAAWS, I always said: "Do the least amount of harm." I am into change through transition, not sweeping change. Chaos can bring about positive change, but it is very hard on people.

Every step along the way, small or large, must be celebrated and thanks given. Mentorship is really important and so I am doing that with our history because I am one of the people who has that history, and I think it important that I am a feminist. As such, I do believe in system sector analysis of the issues, of power, and of who benefits from the power.

Because I don't have so much to risk now, advocacy, like getting involved with the 2010 ski jumpers, is also very important to me, as is being willing to use the court system to learn what is legitimate change and what isn't. We did not get the women ski jumpers into those Games because the court said the IOC was an independent body. We had made assumptions that its processes would be fair and they were not. It is the same with the 2015 Pan/Parapan American Games. Women's events are not there and we are told that's because the Pan/Parapan American Sports Organization runs the show and if we took them to court in Canada, we probably would lose again. We've learned that some international sport bodies are discriminatory according to the Canadian way of doing things. We've learned that you need to entrench the concepts of fairness and equality into the original agreements around hosting an international Games.

The Vancouver 2010 Games taught me how important such events can be to profile athletes. Imagine if coaches were also profiled. Doing that would be a huge step forward, especially for the women. Games can be levers for huge sport development. We just have to learn from the transfer of knowledge, learn ahead of time so that we're directing the impact they are going to have on Canada rather than being directed by an international body that has different values.

> "Never doubt that a small group of thoughtful, committed citizens can change the world. Indeed, it's the only thing that ever has."
>
> – MARGARET MEAD

"Yes is just one word away from no."

– MARION LAY

These are quotes I live by. You go in and get a "no." Celebrate that you got a "no" because you got in and had a chance to hear what they had to say and why they said "no." And you had a chance to say things that are important to you. I honestly believe that "no" is just one word away from "yes."

*This article contains material from Sheila Robertson, "Meet Marion Lay: Sport Leader Extraordinaire," *Canadian Journal for Women in Coaching*, Vol. 4 No. 3.

BECOMING A FEMINIST ACADEMIC
M. Ann Hall

The word "feminist" was not part of my vocabulary until I read Betty Friedan's *The Feminine Mystique* in the mid-60s while completing my after-degree teacher training. I grew up in Canada in the 1940s and 1950s, when career women, and certainly feminists, were unusual if not controversial. Earlier feminists had fought for and eventually won the right to vote, and according to Friedan, they had destroyed the old image of women, but they could not erase the hostility, the prejudice and the discrimination that still remained. Her book interested me, though I found it difficult to identify with her central thesis that white, middle-class American housewives were lost, incomplete, disappointed and almost despairing because of "the problem that had no name." At the time, I was in my early 20s, freshly trained, wildly enthusiastic and about to embark on a career as a high school physical education teacher. It was full speed ahead into the world of work—not marriage and a family—and I was smugly confident that I would escape the boredom and despair Friedan described.

After less than a year in my first teaching job, I was shocked at the blatant discrimination and impossible conditions in which I was expected to teach and encourage young girls to acquire an interest in physical activity. The only female physical education teacher at my school, I was working around the clock: preparing lessons (in three subject areas), administering an intramural program, coaching all the girls' teams, and teaching my lessons in a small, dingy gym while my three male counterparts took the best facilities and equipment, and lounged about just waiting for me to crack. My solution at the end of the school year was to leave and return to university. No one ever asked why I was leaving, and I carried those awful memories with me for a long time. In fact, they fueled much of what I did and thought from then on. It has now been more than 45 years since I landed at the University of Alberta to begin graduate work.

At an international conference held a few years after I returned to graduate school, I was giving one of my first academic papers entitled "The Role of the Safety Bicycle in the Emancipation of Women" (the safety bicycle was the first bicycle with pneumatic tires rather than bone-jarring solid ones). I concluded, rather grandly, that not only did women use the bicycle as a means of defying tradition, but it was plausible that many reforms in women's rights would not have come about so quickly without the safety bicycle. The paper was a product of my Master's thesis, a history of women's sport in Canada prior to World War I. After my presentation, an American fellow approached me and stated accusingly: "You must be a women's libber." My quizzical expression prompted him to tell me about the women's liberation movement in the United States, and I listened in amazement. It was the late 1960s, and I knew of no such movement in Canada; even if there was one, I was too busy with my new career as a university physical education instructor to take notice. I was teaching a variety of sport activities, coaching the women's swim team, administering women's athletics, establishing a new subfield called the "sociology of sport," and trying to work out how, and in what specific area, I would conduct research.

In 1971 I went to the University of Birmingham in England to do doctoral work, which allowed me space and time to think about feminism again. I read a number of influential books, all published in the early 1970s—specifically Kate Millett's *Sexual Politics*, Germaine Greer's *The Female Eunuch*, Shulamith Firestone's *The Dialectic of Sex*, Eva Figes' *Patriarchal Attitudes*, Robin Morgan's anthology *Sisterhood is Powerful*, Juliet Mitchell's *Woman's Estate*, and Sheila Rowbotham's *Women, Resistance and Revolution* and *Women's Consciousness, Men's World*. These books are now considered among the classics of second wave feminism in the English-speaking western world. I also read Simone de Beauvoir's *The Second Sex*, which had been published in French in 1949 and in English in 1953. I simply could not get enough of these books, but paradoxically, although I knew beyond question I was a feminist, I could not relate this extracurricular reading to my doctoral research. How would the researcher and the feminist become one?

To my knowledge, I was the first Canadian to undertake a doctorate in physical education in England. I was also an oddity because the area was not fully recognized in Britain as a legitimate university subject. My degree was earned entirely through research, and I had taken to England a straightforward question: why do some women make sport and physical activity an important part of their lives and others do not? When I began my doctorate, I had no formal background in either sociology or sport sociology. Along with physical education, my undergraduate training had been in mathematics and statistics; consequently, the natural science model seemed the most appropriate to answer my question. I was interested in the "whys" of women's involvement in sport, or lack of it, and building a causal mathematical model to explain these whys seemed eminently worthwhile and challenging. Moreover, our exemplars in the sociology of sport at this time were proponents of empirically verifiable, formal theory. In the end, I produced a substantial multivariate statistical analysis, which "proved" among other things that the more you liked physical activity and sport when you were younger, the more likely you were to keep doing it when you were older. My dissertation, which was titled "Women and Physical Recreation: A Causal Analysis," certainly lived up to a quote I had placed at the beginning:

"Don't be afraid to oversimplify reality. It will always be possible to introduce complexities a few at a time."

I had become, to put it simply, a positivist, or someone who believes in the following: reality consists of what is available to the senses; the natural and social sciences share a common logical and methodological foundation; the goal of social research is to create universal laws of human behavior; and there is a fundamental distinction between fact and value creating the grounds for an "objective" social science. Unfortunately, I had then no clear understanding of the epistemological and methodological foundations of social research and little knowledge of the variety of research methods, including qualitative ones, available to us now. I learned all this on my own, an experience that later prompted me to introduce a course for incoming physical education graduate students on social research applications to leisure and sport, which I taught for over 20 years.

My supervisor at the University of Birmingham was Charles Jenkins, a wonderfully sensitive man. His intellectual interests were amazingly eclectic, and although he supported the positivist turn in my work, he did try to interest me in the work of those at the Centre for Contemporary Cultural Studies, and especially, men like Stuart Hall, Paul Willis and Charles Critcher. The Birmingham school, as it became known, was at the forefront of cultural studies, a form of critical cultural analysis initially developed among left-leaning, post-war British intellectuals. However, there was little work being conducted on leisure or sport at the Birmingham Centre in the early 1970s. There were also no women in the centre and certainly no feminists, although by the end of the decade, feminism had forced a major rethink of every substantive area of work within cultural studies.

In 1973 Charles Jenkins and I organized a conference at the University of Birmingham on Women and Sport. Our purpose was to explore the relationship between biological and cultural influences on women's sport participation through a series of invited papers. Among others, we invited Paul Willis from the Birmingham Center to give a paper. At the time he was working on his dissertation, the often-cited "Learning to Labour: How Working Class Kids Get Working Class Jobs." He and I presented papers during the same session. His was a brilliant and insightful discussion of the role of sport in the reinforcement of common-sense ideologies that assert the superiority of men and of how women collude in these ideological definitions. Mine was a complex multiple regression analysis in which I tried to explain the relationships among all the variables in my dissertation. At one point, I remember displaying a slide with the title: How to Regress in One Easy Lesson. The irony of all this escaped me at the time.

I returned to the University of Alberta with my newly-earned doctorate. I wanted to continue doing research in the area of "women in sport" but the disciplinary perspective was unclear. Having narrowed down the options to the social sciences, I was uncertain whether it would be history, sociology, psychology or social psychology, not that I had much training in any of these disciplines. American sport sociologist Susan Birrell was absolutely correct when she observed that the 1970s marked an unevenness in focus and quality as the field struggled first for identity and then for legitimacy. "Women in sport" as an area of study, she argued, must be seen against a backdrop of other social forces. Certainly significant were changes in physical education, which at the time was transforming itself from a profession into an academic discipline, or more accurately a series of sub-disciplines now readily identified as the history of sport, sociology of sport, psychology of sport and so forth. It was, therefore, logical to develop a multidisciplinary area called women in sport. Of equal importance was second wave feminism, which produced the women's movement and a steady growth in women's sport.

The context of Susan Birrell's observations was the United States, and although Canada has followed the American experience in some areas, it has not in others. Legislative and institutional changes in women's sport in the United States, such as the passage of *Title IX* in 1972, the formation of the Women's Sports Foundation in 1974 and the expansion of opportunities in sport for girls and women, were only marginally felt in Canada during the 1970s. From the Canadian perspective, 1974 marks the beginning of federal government involvement with the organization of the first National Conference on Women and Sport. On the academic front, since most Canadian physical educators teaching in universities went to the United States for doctoral level training (I was an exception), they brought back the need to compartmentalize the field into its various sub-disciplines, and we all felt the same pressure to create our own research specialties. Mine was to be the vaguely defined area of women in sport.

By the mid-1970s I had become immersed in the Canadian women's movement. My tales from that period are too long to narrate here, but through helping to found, or volunteer in, several feminist organizations like the Alberta Status of Women Action Committee, the Canadian Research Institute for the Advancement of Women and the Canadian Association for the Advancement of Women and Sport and Physical Activity, I gained an invaluable network of feminist colleagues across the country. I interacted with them through committee meetings, board meetings, funding crises, hiring committees, marches, lobbying and by celebrating women's culture with feminist sisters both within and outside academe. My involvement taught me an extremely valuable lesson: as feminists, our theory, politics and practices are inextricably linked. Those working in the academy, whose focus is research and scholarship, must work with those on the front line — be they activists, "femocrats," shelter workers, or volunteers — so that together we are doing critical political work. Through the years, I have continued to help document our progress in challenging gender inequality within sport and physical education in Canada and to speak out when necessary.

Feminist theory, a more sophisticated understanding of sociology, and feminist political work were the major influences on my academic research and scholarship as I undertook the task of helping to shape the sociological study of women in sport. As I mentioned earlier, our work in that area during the early 1970s was dominated by psychological rather than sociological analyses of women's place in sport. In fact, my first research article, published in England in 1972, was entitled, "A 'Feminine Woman' and an 'Athletic Woman' as Viewed by Female Participants and Non-Participants in Sport." Using an attitude measurement tool, I found a statistically significant difference between participants and nonparticipants, who showed considerably more "dissonance" between the two concepts. What was I trying to do? Mindful of the popular and often pejorative image of the female athlete as "unfeminine," I wanted to see if this stereotype prevented some women from taking an active interest in sport and show that for women who did participate, there was a greater congruence between the two images. I concluded that participation in sport among women could be increased if the image associated with athletic women was changed so that it became more congruent with the stereotype associated with feminine women. This would also involve changing the feminine image to be more like the athletic image. In retrospect, my research was naïve and demonstrated a minimal understanding of the cultural forces and ideological practices at work.

Susan Birrell hit the proverbial nail on the head with her critique that this early research, mine included, not only relied on methodologically primitive attempts to measure complex psychosocial constructs, but it also conceived of women as not fitting into sport. Therefore the problem behind women's low involvement lay within, and women themselves were to blame for their lack of participation. The topics in Psychosocial Aspects of Women in Sport, a course I introduced to my department in the early 1970s, reflected this psychological and individualistic bias. These included sex differences, sexual role behavior, tomboyism, attitudes toward women athletes, the personality traits of women athletes, fear of success, role conflict, psychological androgyny, the feminine apologetic and socialization. An understanding that sporting practices are historically produced, socially constructed and culturally defined to serve the interests and needs of powerful groups in society was clearly missing.

Despite the growth of the sociology of sport in the 1970s, it was clear that girls and women were not represented in the studies and literature. By 1976 there were 13 texts and anthologies (all from the United States) that had the sociology of sport as their focus. Only three of these had a separate chapter or section devoted to females. Less than one-tenth of some 200 separate articles in the anthologies were written or co-written by women. In sum, the material on females in these texts and anthologies represented less than three percent of the total content. This made me angry. I knew there was more research and scholarship about women than was being acknowledged, and I was becoming acutely aware of the male bias in sociology. Feminist sociologists were addressing this androcentric perspective, as were feminist scholars in the humanities and other social sciences.

Though there was little feminist scholarship to read in the late 1970s, I searched out and consumed everything I could find with one objective—to apply it to the study of girls and women in sport. My published writing from this period, aside from attempting to expand the sociological knowledge base about females in sport, represents a plea to my colleagues in physical education and the sociology of sport to recognize the relevance of feminism.

Early in my academic career, wanting to learn more about sociology, I embarked on a self-directed reading course in the history of social thought, contemporary social theory and the epistemological debates within social research methodology. Several colleagues helped me, most of them males who were engaged in producing radical critiques of sport in Western societies. They were reading social theorists like Anthony Giddens, Pierre Bourdieu, Paul Willis, Antonio Gramsci and Raymond Williams and were attempting to apply theories of power, social reproduction and practice, and cultural struggle and production to an analysis of the historical and cultural construction of modern sport. I read their work as well as the theorists from whom they drew their inspiration. I also read with great fervor emerging feminist theory, which, for the most part, my colleagues and the social theorists ignored.

Slowly I came to two major insights. The first was that social psychological research, with its emphasis on sex roles and sex identity, not only demanded a substantive critique but was potentially harmful because it continued to perpetuate the very stereotypes that researchers in the field wished to eradicate. Within the context of women and sport research, social psychological research needed to be replaced by a gender and sport discourse that treated gender as a relational category just like class or race. This led me to my second insight: for most radical theorists, class was the primary form of domination, and it was going to be a long, hard battle to get them to recognize the gender blindness of their critiques.

By the mid-1980s I was no longer alone in recognizing the potential of feminist theory and analysis for gender relations and sport. Susan Birrell, herself one of those who has contributed significantly to the women in sport discourse, has documented this work, although primarily in a North American context. Certainly we all owe a debt to the earlier efforts of scholars like Eleanor Metheny, Marie Hart, Ellen Gerber, Jan Felshin, Pearl Berlin, Dorothy Harris and Carole Oglesby. The work of Hart and Felshin in particular should be singled out because, as Birrell rightly argues, it was grounded in a feminist sensibility even though there was little theoretical work available to help them frame their arguments. Years ago I was unduly critical of this work because in my view it lacked the necessary theoretical sophistication. In hindsight, now that I am in my 70s, with several generations of feminist scholars coming up behind, my own work also lacked the sophistication they now bring. We are products of our times in ways we do not realize until we look back.

Feminism and Sporting Bodies: Essays on Theory and Practice, published in 1996 by Human Kinetics, traces my 30-year journey across the feminist terrain from the mid-1960s to the mid-1990s. It tells of my struggle to understand what various feminisms could contribute to our understanding of women in sport and to our efforts to make the sports world a better place for women. The book was one of the most difficult writing projects I have ever attempted. Limited by the publisher to a small paperback, it was agony deciding what to include and what to leave out, and then condensing it all into something clear and accessible. The book is now out-of-print, but it sold over 2,000 copies and is listed in the catalogue of nearly 500 libraries worldwide. It has also been translated into Japanese.

My nonsporting feminist colleagues were mostly bemused by my continuing fascination with sport. For them, the highly competitive, sometimes violent, overly commercialized sports world represented distinctly non-feminist values and was a place they generally ignored. Few were active in sports, although some certainly exercised for health and well-being; for many, negative childhood experiences in school physical education had turned them off long ago. In my Women's Studies classes, I sometimes had to overcome the initial negative reaction of a student who found it difficult not to associate me with a much disliked PE teacher.

I saw my task as advocating for the inclusion of sport on the feminist agenda and ensuring that feminism was very much a part of the sport agenda. One way I tried to do this was through my university's Women's Studies program that I helped establish. Over the years, I taught and held a variety of administrative positions in the program. However, I found it a continual struggle to get discussions about women's sport included in the Women's Studies curricula.

After more than 30 years at the University of Alberta, I retired in 1997. Retirement, however, has not meant the end of my research and writing. Some 25 years after completing my Master's thesis, and before I retired, I had decided to continue researching the history of women's sport in Canada. Why? First, there was still no comprehensive history of the area, which in some ways I found disappointing, but given the enormity of the task, I now understand. Second, I wanted to write a much different history than I could have 30 years ago. Along with many exemplary studies in women's sport history, there were now several decades of feminist historiography, none of which was available to me in the 1960s. Finally, I was fortunate to receive a substantial research grant that provided the necessary funds to hire research assistants, travel to archives, conduct interviews and much else. The project was nowhere near completion when I retired, and it kept me occupied for several more years. *The Girl and the Game: A History of Women's Sport in Canada* was published in the spring of 2002 by Broadview Press (and is now distributed through the University of Toronto Press).

Immodest and Sensational: 150 Years of Canadian Women in Sport, an illustrated history written for the general market, was published in 2008 by James Lorimer. Most recently, *The Grads Are Playing Tonight!: The Story of the Edmonton Commercial*

Basketball Club was published by the University of Alberta Press in 2011. The reception of this book, which is the story of a group of ordinary women who accomplished the extraordinary, has been most rewarding, especially in Edmonton. I have also published several articles and book chapters, all concerned with women's sport history, and have kept up a steady practice of encouraging and reviewing the work of others. Historical research, especially cultural history, continues to attract my attention, and I have several writing projects on the go.

The field of feminist sport studies today is exciting, diverse and theoretically sophisticated. The work is being continued by bright scholars usually with academic backgrounds in feminist and cultural theory. Some would argue their scholarship represents a "third wave" and signals a new generation of feminism representing women who came of age in the late 1970s through to the late 1980s. They were born into a world changed by feminism. Third wave feminists clearly wish to distinguish themselves from "postfeminists"—best described as young, conservative anti-feminists who explicitly define themselves against and criticize feminists of the second wave.

Third wave feminists prioritize not just gender but all of the intertwining axes of identity and experience including race, class, ability and sexuality. The third wave movement and aesthetic, argues one commentator in the book *Turbo Chicks: Talking Young Feminisms*, is associated with cultural activism (like zines, riot grrrl bands and guerilla advertising) and the challenging of identity boundaries. It revels in female power whether it is through our bodies, sexuality, work, art or activism. Third wave feminists are at ease with contradiction and accept pluralism as a given. According to others, such as Leslie Heywood and Shari L. Dworkin in *Built to Win: The Female Athlete as Cultural Icon*, strong female athlete images perform negative and affirmative cultural work simultaneously: competitive and participatory models of sport both offer a range of possibilities for women (and men), where market conditions can be oppressive to some and offer the potential to do progressive and regressive cultural work, sometimes at the same time.

Third wave feminism should not be seen as a major break

from second wave feminism because it continues the work of second wave feminists, and it is also a useful antidote to the increasing number of anti-feminist tracts appearing in press. However, there is still a noticeable absence of sport studies within feminist academic literature and scholarship. Feminist sport studies, whether second or third wave, is making little impact on feminist scholarship and women's studies programs, at least in North America.

Finally, there is an ever-widening gap between those who "do" theory and research and those who are the practitioners and activists in women's sport. To put it simply, the critical academic work of feminist sport studies is often ignored by the new policy makers and "femocrats" of women's sport, who are sometimes reluctant to engage with those criticizing the status quo. National and international women's sport movements have become overly governmental, while grassroots organizers (and critics) are increasingly ignored, sidelined or displaced by glossy new committees. I suggest that unless feminist sport scholars (of both the second and third waves) find better ways to contribute to feminist scholarship in general and women's studies in particular, and at the same time influence the practitioners and policy makers of women's sport, we and our work are in danger of becoming irrelevant.

* Previous versions of this chapter have appeared in M.A. Hall, 1996, *Feminism and Sporting Bodies*, Champaign, IL: Human Kinetics, 1-9; and, in M.A. Hall, 2005, "From Pre-to Postfeminism: A Four-decade Journey," in *Feminist Sport Studies: Sharing Experiences of Joy and Pain*, Ed., Pirkko Markula, Albany, NY: State University of New York Press, 45-61.

MY BRILLIANT BEAUTIFUL BICYCLE
Laura Robinson

I kept the cover shot of the *Toronto Star TV Guide* for years. The issue was from 1970, the same year I decided I wanted to be a runner. Abby Hoffman stared out from the picture, a calculating woman in the starting blocks with her steely eyes and wild hair, mesmerizing me. I was in Grade 7 and had joined the track and cross-country running teams, never to finish any better than at the back of the first third of the pack. But I had ambitions, and Abby Hoffman inspired me.

The shot was part of a feature on the Toronto Star Maple Leaf Indoor Games held at the Gardens. Ah, how amazing to be in Maple Leaf Gardens when a woman who wasn't an Ice Capades princess stole the show! My brother and I saved up our money and bought seats way up in the grey section for those Games. Coming in from Mississauga on the subway was exciting enough, but watching all the busyness from the Gardens' rafters like two country church mice put us in track and field heaven, especially because it meant I could be in the same place as the great Canadian women track and field athletes.

My track idols were Abby Hoffman, Debbie Brill and Glenda Reiser. Hoffman and Brill didn't walk—they strode—into the Gardens or wherever else they were working their magic, the first as an 800 metre runner, the other as a high jumper. Here's how *Sports Illustrated* describes the women at a California track meet and how Hoffman's, or should I say "Abby's," chutzpah throws off this sexist reporting from 1967:

> The withdrawals dimmed but did not destroy the race, which still included Canada's curly-haired Abby Hoffman, a British Commonwealth Games champion; Charlette Cooke, the strawberry blonde with a dancer's body who holds a wide assortment of US distance records outdoors, and, of course, Marie, a heroine of US track …
>
> … Marie, who feels she must set a brisk pace because she lacks the natural speed to really zing out on the last lap or so,

survived some unladylike bumping around at the start, before getting the lead on the first lap. Her quarter-mile time, as a result, was a slow 67.5, but she and Miss Hoffman really stepped through the last quarter mile. With two and a half laps remaining, Abby bounded into a lead and held off Marie to win by 20 feet in the good time of 2:11.4. ...

Miss Hoffman was ecstatic. "That's a Canadian record, you know," she chirped to a meet official after the race. "I'm planning to run faster later on this winter, but maybe we'd better fill out an application just in case."

Abby is a 20-year-old junior at the University of Toronto who gave up swimming at the age of 14 because she had not set a world record yet and was discouraged. If she can continue to compete south of her border she may yet attain her goal, but on the running track.

"The best competition in my event is right here in the US," she said last week. "Your runners are getting right up there. But it's the same old story. Whenever you people put your mind to something you can do it. You've ignored the middle distances up till now."

I wanted to be just like Hoffman; but I wanted to look like the long, lithe Brill, who often jumped with her hair loose, which always seemed to represent for me the spirit inside that wants to fly. But just like Hoffman, I had a head of insolent curls. I did, however, even out somewhere in the middle of Hoffman's and Brill's height. And both these women were part of a larger group of role models who profoundly influenced who I became as an athlete, a writer and a woman.

My plans for my future were inspired not just by Hoffman and Brill, but also by Joni Mitchell, Michele Landsberg, Doris Anderson, Margaret Laurence, Margaret Atwood, Alice Munro, my Grade 8 English teacher Pamela Higgins, Marilyn Freeman, the feminist bike racer I met in 1973, and my mother June and older sister Leslie (though at one time, I would never have admitted to these last two as I thought this would have decreased my chances of being cool).

In fact, as I write this I am listening to Joni Mitchell's *Blue*. She and Debbie Brill remind me of one another—they had the hair, body and talent I longed for, but I would have passed on these qualities if I could have been as cool as them. You could tell they liked men, had sex with men, and both even had a child without being married. These were the days of revolution for women: we were not apologizing for loving sex.

What times they were, the sixties and seventies. What promises, what threats. Almost everything and everyone in those days was either cool, or terrible and horrible. Joni Mitchell, Woodstock, protests that took up blocks and blocks—now that was cool. In 1996 Buffy Sainte-Marie spoke at the Women in the Media conference in Ottawa about that window of opportunity we had at that time for democracy, justice and freedom called the sixties. She was another woman who put power to words. Ostracized because of her tribute to the universal soldier, she sang about the violent disposal of young men through wars planned by old generals. There was Vietnam, but there were also the disappearances and murders of civil rights workers in the Southern United States and Latin America, strangling freedom, justice and democracy. These were the unimaginable nightmares revealed in those days. The media broke through and started to tell real stories from the frontlines as the critical written word gained traction and we wondered how on earth we could challenge it all.

There was good reason for Mitchell's album being called *Blue*. She had a blue hotel room, but she sang, as did so many others, of another blueness. The feeling that we could not win over the force used by The Man (probably the most accurate description of the oppressive violence of the military industrial complex and all it entails). I just wanted to let freedom reign, as Martin Luther King, Jr. said until he was gunned down.

It was the summer of 1972 when I was 14 and decided I would let freedom reign in my own corner of the planet. I knew then I would be a cyclist, a journalist and a writer. I loved the thought of going beyond borders. That spring, some of the boys in my Grade 8 class rode over to my place on their new ten-speeds. It was the first warm night of the year—a time that calls to children to stay out and let the warm wind wash over them. I looked outside and saw a long line of ten-speeds, shining under our sunroom lights. A switch turned on. From that second I knew my calling.

It took me only a few months of saving my babysitting money and I had a clunker of a ten-speed. They didn't make them for women then so I straddled a bike meant for someone closer to six feet tall. I had just turned 14; my brother David, who was 12, also wanted to ride. By then I had injured myself trying to run in Adidas Mexicana—the beautiful black and gold track shoe that, like all real running shoes then, only came in men's sizes. Running in a too-spacious shoe on hard surfaces had given me shin splints, but I left that pain behind as I hopped on my bike. That was it ... my life was never the same again. I began to use my bicycle as the measuring stick for almost everything. Wind in my hair, fresh air on my face, muscles strengthening with each revolution of the pedals: could anything be better?

In that magical summer of '72, on the advice of my mother, my brother and I joined the Mississauga Cycling Club. Although she denied it, I think sending us to this lovely group of people was her way of taking good care of the two middle kids of five as she prepared to leave an emotionally abusive marriage. It was one of her best decisions ever. We traded a stressful place for the freedom of the white lines of the highway, as Joni would say, though we generally chose country roads.

Around the same time that I began to experience the pure freedom of a strong body and a beautiful, brilliant bicycle, my Grade 8 teacher Pamela Higgins opened the door to the freedom of the intellect, the excitement of a curious mind and the seductiveness of the written word. She included me in a special reading group for her students. That exposure to literature and discussion swept me away—like with my bike, I flew off planet earth and into a world where anything was possible. It was then I knew I would be a writer and journalist.

My curiosity continued to grow throughout my teenage years, which I spent reading, in my eyes, the best columnist. Training for cycling after school meant I missed most dinners with my family; as a teenager that suited me just fine. After I got home, I'd shower, grab the food my mother had kept hot and settle in to read the *Toronto Star*, turning first to Michele

Landsberg's column. I read and listened to others too: Atwood, Munro, Laurence, Gallant, Engel, Steinem, Friedan, and Walker. My sister and I bought the records of Joni Mitchell, Joan (Baez and Collins), Carole King, Connie Kaldor, Buffy Sainte-Marie, Aretha Franklin and a few years later, Kate and Anna McGarrigle and k.d. lang (to give you the short list). My list of places to ride and books to read became infinite.

While figuring out who I was as an athlete and a thinker, I was also discovering sex. It was at the World Cycling Championships in 1974 where I lost my virginity. This sexual foray proved to be very pleasurable. Susan Swan's book *Stupid Boys Are Good To Relax With* made me realize I was not the only woman who wanted men in my life only some of the time. Yes, they could be very good to relax with, but were they as much fun, and profound as riding my bike or diving into a story by Marian Engel or Margaret Atwood?

I realized sex was going to be lots of fun and went straight to the local birth control clinic. I had participated in all the pro-choice marches in Toronto and I knew from a primal and powerful part of my body that no one had the right to tell me whether or not my body was going to be pregnant. I knew what I wanted: sex, but not single-motherhood; to fly forever on my bicycle; and, to write in ways that would steal people from their lives for a while and let imaginations soar.

I knew what I wanted to do, but I didn't know how to go about getting it. I also couldn't understand why there was so little help for girls and women to realize our dreams. I expressed my exasperation to my mother often. Why did we have to wait until men decided women cyclists could be in the Olympics, that women writers really did have something to say and that women athletes deserved the same space in the sports section that men automatically were afforded? My list of discontent was long. "Patience dear, patience," she would reply. "Things will change." I had to be ready for that change.

After several years I thought I had figured it all out—first, I would become the World Cycling Champion, and then Canadian newspapers would clamour for my column. Of course I would write about the unendingly exciting world of women's sport: a world that a quick glance at any sports section or sport broadcast showed to be virtually invisible to all except me. But I had that cover of the *Toronto Star TV Guide*—Hoffman's steely eyes looking ahead, telling me what was possible.

Ultimately, my ideal plan wasn't realized. I could ride a bike better than I could run, but I was still not World Champion material. I floated between being the fourth to sixth fastest Canadian female. In those days you had to be a guy before those results would send you to the World Championships. Other competitions were out too: women cyclists were still not allowed to compete at the Olympics, Pan Am Games or Commonwealth Games. So without a World Championship or Olympic win behind me, what was to become of my column? A series of twists and turns in my life meant that I never did get a column in the *Globe and Mail* or the *Toronto Star*. But the opportunity to be a freelance writer came about when I was 30-years-old, mainly because five years previously, a 12-year-old girl named Justine Blainey would not take "no" as an answer for why she could not play hockey.

Blainey had made the same team as her brother: the Toronto Olympics A peewees. When she went to register, the Metro Toronto Hockey League (MTHL) (now the Greater Toronto Hockey League) barred her from playing because she was a girl. When Blainey decided to take the hockey brass to the Ontario Human Rights Commission, I knew I'd be working on her team. A small group of us supported Blainey and we could not understand why everyone in the world of sport wasn't on hockey's case, letting them know it was unacceptable to discriminate against someone because she has no penis. The MTHL and the Ontario Hockey Association argued they weren't being sexist at all, they just wanted to protect girls from being harmed from the physical roughness of boys' hockey and to protect girls' hockey from being depleted of its best players.

The Blainey case was one of the few times women's sports did make the front page and the sports page on a regular basis. Contrary to the conservative sports circles, the public, generally speaking, was on her side. The *Toronto Star* published multiple articles on the case and was flooded with letters to the editor.

The powerful sports lobby predicted dire consequences if boys and girls and men and women actually played side-by-side: the sky over the patriarchal sporting "family" (as they love to call themselves) would surely fall; and coaches, who in their eyes came in only one sex, would leave en masse rather than put up with girls.

The media, however, had a lot of fun with these dinosaurs and it gave the Blainey team an opportunity to raise equality issues. Our small group, that included some of the other contributors in this collection, met frequently. We committed in a huge way to this case, juggling extraordinarily busy lives to meet in person. Fast friendships formed and great food was prepared as we plotted our freedom march through documents, legal procedures and well-crafted dispatches to the media. If fax machines existed then we certainly didn't have access to them, so we generally hand delivered our press releases, which I did courier-style by hopping on my bike.

Before my foray into the average newsroom, I hadn't realized what journalists looked like in the 1980s. Let's just say you wouldn't have looked to them as healthy living specimens. One day I was delivering a press release to a newsroom, just off my bike with the adrenaline necessary for two-wheeling through Toronto traffic. People took one look at me and said, "Well you're a female athlete. Can we interview you? We go to air in five minutes." And with that, I became familiar with Toronto newsrooms and TV and radio studios—still the hub of media power in this country.

Soon, if I wasn't in the physical confines of Toronto media, I was on the phone with them. Once, when being interviewed by Ann Rauhala from the *Globe and Mail*, I tried to sound as professional as possible. By then I had met women from Ottawa who spoke as if they were reciting a textbook on bureaucracy. They had an "I'm in charge" air about them and I wanted to sound as authoritative as them, with their use of phrases such as "will endeavour to ameliorate" or "will facilitate the actualizing of..." Soon into the interview, Rauhala interrupted me. "Don't you know how to speak English?" she said.

Ann Rauhala taught me one of the most important lessons I received during that formative time: to speak and write like a human being. I am so glad she is now a journalism professor at Toronto's Ryerson University, no doubt churning out gutsy journalists. I know now that it goes a long way to speak clearly with as much intelligence as you can muster and without the fogginess of the meaningless doublespeak that reigns today and only confuses and misleads. Unfortunately, this strategy of clarity isn't followed in the current, official world of sport, where the Canadian Olympic Committee, Own the Podium, and all the minions (also called consultants) who endeavour to ameliorate and facilitate whatever their "cause" have demonstrated their inability to speak clearly in English. It's doublespeak or nothing for them. This is because often their job is to prop up a system that does not allow for change.

One great example of meaningless sentences and space fillers, or "weasel words" as we would say in journalism, can be found in the 2009 Canadian Policy on Women and Girls in Sport, "Actively Engaged." It states:

> The "Logic Model" for the policy ... has three main parts: policy interventions, outputs and outcomes. The logic of the model is depicted by arrows flowing between activities and from policy interventions to outputs and outputs to outcomes. There are three levels of outcomes: immediate, intermediate and ultimate. The policy interventions are operationalized as outputs; these outputs are expected to contribute in the short term to the immediate outcomes. In turn, the immediate outcomes are expected to contribute to the intermediate outcomes, which create conditions favourable to the achievement of the ultimate outcome in the long-term. Measurable indicators associated with each of the outputs and outcomes will be used in evaluating progress associated with the policy.

Three years later, an online search of the *Globe and Mail*, the *Toronto Star* and the *Ottawa Citizen* does not show any mention of that 2009 policy. If those papers didn't carry the announcement of the new women's sport policy, it is doubtful any paper did. Either it had the softest of media launches, and/or the media could care less about what the feds say they are going to do about women's equality, knowing that it won't matter anyway.

The media's indifference is not surprising: who on earth dreamed up that framework? The inputs, outputs, interventions, immediate, intermediate and ultimate outcomes in it go on for pages. Nowhere does it state the obvious fact that the patriarchs of sport are not prepared to share power and give women an equal portion of the pie. In actuality there is only one policy intervention that will work: if an organization cannot show that all its funds and resources are divided equitably and programs and staff are in place to increase opportunities for women's equality, then the organization risks losing its funding and status. Even today, Canadian male athletes still receive the lion's share of Sport Canada funding and most of the highly placed sport bureaucrats and directors are male. After suffering through years of listening to extraordinarily boring people drone on at workshops and conferences using flow chart rationalizations and dreadful PowerPoints, only to see a sports system work in favour of men, I cannot stomach these utterly meaningless but expensive policy platitudes.

Eventually, despite being blacklisted for daring to speak out about sexism, racism and classism in sport, my dream of becoming a journalist and author did materialize. I used the self-discipline I learned on my bike and skis and applied it to writing. With one credit left to go in an Honours degree in history, I abandoned my classes when a great story came along and never looked back. But my history professors taught me well. I could write and think critically partly because of them. In my Modern European Intellectual History class with Dr. Bernie Lightman at York University, I was encouraged to follow my dream to be a writer after he gave me Simone de Beauvoir's *The Second Sex*. When I thought about the relationship between the past, the present and what the future might hold, and how I might write about it all, I was just as excited as I would have been about a great bike ride.

Although I never had a column in a daily, I am happy to be on op-ed pages and writing features and books—a task far more grueling than the most difficult of bike races. But every one of the six books and many chapters I have written have been worth the effort, and even now I feel there are at least two books stirring about inside me.

Back in the 1980s when I rode my bicycle to the CBC, the *Globe and Mail* and the *Toronto Star* during the Blainey case, I honestly believed that real and lasting change was going to occur. I was even willing to be blacklisted in my future career in sports if the equality we had worked so hard for could be realized by the next generation.

Although the blacklist materialized, the equality did not. Even as recently as 2010, women ski jumpers had to fight for inclusion at the Vancouver Olympics. Amazingly, they lost their case. It was decided that because the Olympic organizers signed a contract with the IOC in Switzerland, the contract was not subject to Canadian human rights law. (Can't a contract reside in more than one country?) To add injury to insult, if it wasn't enough that the Canadian government spent billions of dollars on an Olympics where women could be legally discriminated against, the Vancouver Police Department indicated a 233.3 percent increase in reported sexual offenses in District One (Vancouver's entertainment area) during the Olympics. This violence was understood first-hand by the Vancouver organization Women Against Violence Against Women, which received requests from four women to be accompanied to the hospital for a rape kit in the 24 hours following the Canadian men's hockey team gold-medal victory (WAVAW usually receives four such calls over two weeks). All four women had been at hockey parties. I was one of only three journalists to report on this violence—why was it not a front-page story?

With the exception of special events, such as the Olympics, Pan/Parapan American or Commonwealth Games, women's sport has been covered even less in the first years of the millennium than it had been during the 1990s. As I write this piece in late 2012, all I hear about is the NHL lock-out. But I long for the CBC to tell me how the Canadian Women's Hockey League teams fared the night before, or how the women are training for the April 2013 World Championships to be held in Ottawa.

In writing this chapter, I love remembering the passion, energy and changes that I and many other women were able to effect. It is a travesty that after all this time patriarchy still reigns. Still, dwelling on what still needs to change could lead to depression and then where would the energy for our fight come from? So I continue to take long rides on my beautiful bike, ski on fresh snow and go on hikes with the amazing kids I coach. This is how I practice patience. But I can never forget the days when there was revolution in the streets and how watching Abby Hoffman and Debbie Brill take flight made me think anything was possible.

< Earliest known
photograph of women
playing hockey, Rideau
Hall, Ottawa, circa 1890.

> Eva Ault, January 1917.
One of the game's first
female stars, Eva Ault
helped put women's
hockey on the map
in the early 1900s as
women began to form
their own leagues and
championships. Ault
played for the Ottawa
Alerts, earning the
nickname "Queen of the
Ice."

∨ Girls' Hockey Team, 1931

Tour à tour nageuse, plongeuse, sauveteure, enseignante, entraîneure, organisatrice, animatrice, juge, gestionnaire, Fernande Dionne aura consacré sa vie aux activités aquatiques et contribué directement à la formation d'un grand nombre de jeunes filles et de femmes dans chacune de ces catégories.

< Abby Hoffman, 1955.
At the age of 8, Abby
Hoffman cut her hair
short and joined a
boys' hockey team as
a defenseman. She
passed as a boy until just
before an all-star game
that required players
to submit their birth
certificates. When her
secret was revealed, Abby
became an overnight
sensation. Hoffman
went on to an illustrious
career as an athlete and in
human rights and policy
development.

∧ Rita C. Proulx (1919-)
est un pilier du curling
au Québec et au Canada.
Présidente du Québec
Winter Club de 1950 à
1954, elle fonde en 1956
l'Association féminine
de curling du Québec.
Sous sa gouverne, l'AFCQ
deviendra l'organisme
responsable de tous les
championnats féminins.
À compter de 1976,
elle siège à titre de
directrice de l'Association

canadienne de curling
féminin et en atteint
la présidence en 1978.
Elle siège au comité
féminin de la Fédération
internationale du curling
en 1980-1981.
Rita C. Proulx est
admise au Temple de la
renommée du curling
canadien à titre de
bâtisseuse en 1987 et au
Temple de la renommée
du curling québécois
en 2012.

< Marion Lay, 1964.
Marion Lay was a
member of the Canadian
Olympic Swimming
Team and helped win the
bronze for the Canadian
relay team in the 1968
Olympics.

v Iona Campagnolo MP,
1974. Iona Camapagnolo
was appointed by Prime
Minister Pierre Trudeau
to be the first Minister
of State for Fitness
and Amateur Sport
(1976-1979) and later
became the first woman
Lieutenant-Governor of
British Columbia.

< Gabrille Pleau (1920-
2000). À une époque où
le rôle de la femme se
résume à s'occuper du
foyer, Gabrielle Pleau
devient la première
Québécoise francophone
à faire partie de l'équipe
canadienne de ski alpin.
Sa carrière compétitive
s'échelonna de 1938 à
1946, se classant toujours
parmi les trois premières
dans les rencontres tant
provinciales, canadiennes
que nord-américaines. En
1950, elle fonda le club-
école *L'univers du ski* au
mont Saint-Castin, alors le
plus grand centre de ski
de la région de Québec et elle
oeuvra particulièrement « à
la séparation des hommes
des femmes » lors des
compétitions. Elle fut
intronisée au Temple de la
Renommée du ski canadien
au titre de « bâtisseur »
en 1984 et à l'Ordre de
la Renommée du ski de
Québec en 1999.

< Ann Hall is Professor
Emeritus at the
University of Alberta
and an expert on the
history of women's
sport in Canada. She has
published several books
and articles and was a key
activist in the women's
movement in the 1970s.

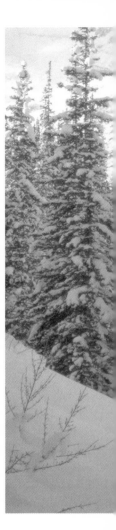

∧ Bruce Kidd, a Professor at
the University of Toronto
and a long-time supporter
of women and sport in
Canada, was a founding
"mother" of the Canadian
Association for the
Advancement of Women
and Sport and involved
with the Canadian
Sports Hall of Fame, the
Commonwealth Games
and the Olympics.

^ Laura Robinson at Lake
Louise, 2009. Laura
Robinson is a journalist,
a long-time activist
advancing women and
sport, and an avid cyclist
and runner.

2 | UP AGAINST THE ODDS
Athletes, feminism and experiences

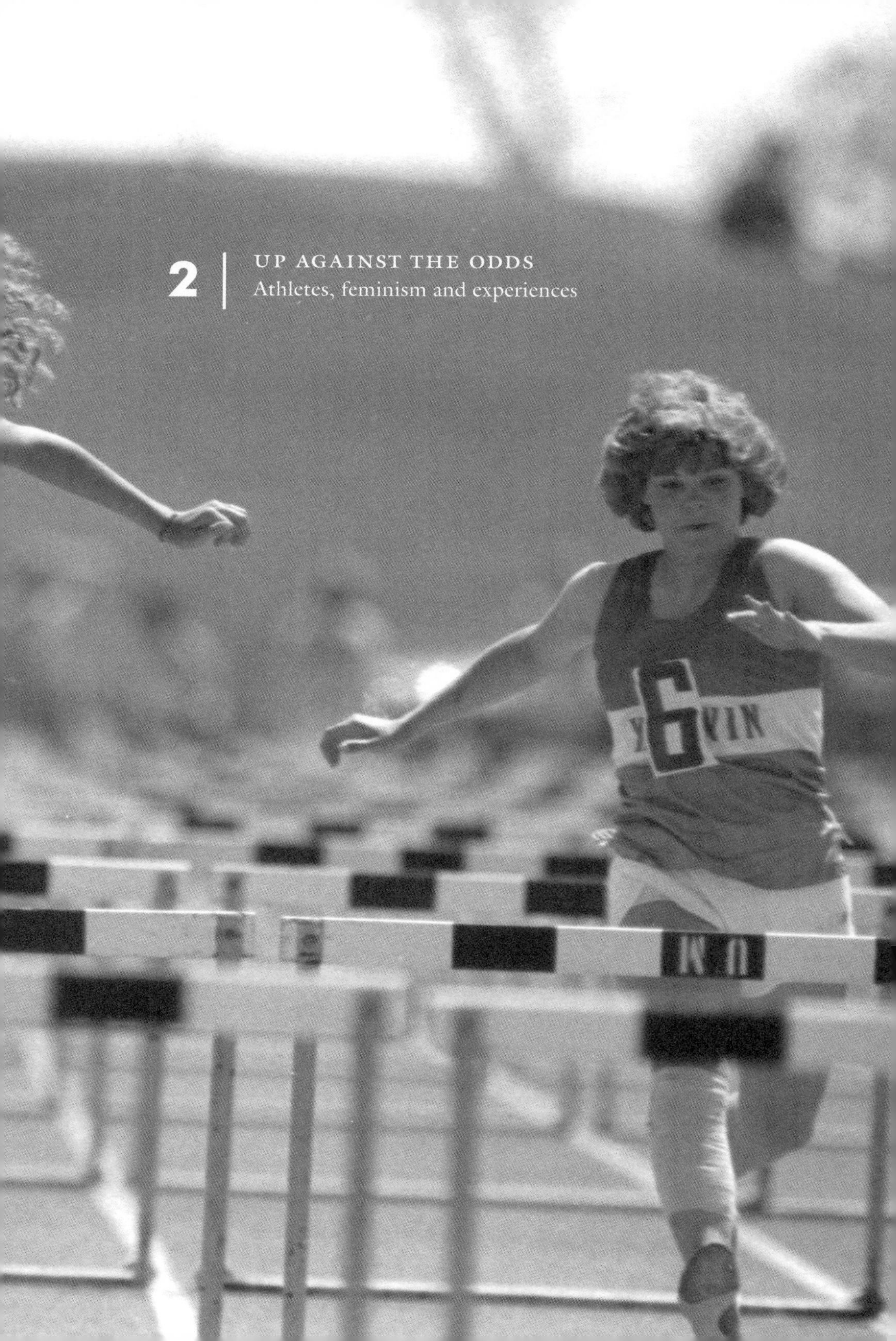

IN THIS SECTION, 14 athletes describe and reflect upon their sport experiences. While there is joy in sport for many of these women, there are also ongoing challenges. There is a certain similarity to many of these stories. Barriers and experiences of sexism and discrimination had, in some cases, profound and lasting effects. There are stories of inadequate resources and equipment, and in some cases, no places to play or train. Overarching all of these stories is the feeling of atomization: so many women having similar experiences, but not being connected to each other.

The repeated experiences of fighting the system, not knowing how to break in or find the space to play, emerge. These women had the burden of finding the place and permission to play as well as training to compete. Nonetheless, there is a strong love of action, movement, strength and power among these women driving them forward to fight the odds. This is the foundation upon which changing sport for women is based.

‹ Grant Park High School
(Winnipeg) student Lori Cohen
winning the 100 metre Hurdle in
the Provincial High School Track
and Field Championships at the
University of Manitoba Bison
Stadium, 7 June 1986.

SKATING IN THE DRAINAGE DITCHES
Hayley Wickenheiser

I have had many defining moments in my career; certainly history would point to glory at the Olympics or some other shining moment. But I have also had equally defining experiences that have not been recorded in any books. In fact, some of them continue to be driving factors in my daily life, on and off the ice. They continue to push me to do what I can to further the female game beyond what it can do for me, to what it could do for other young girls and women who share my love of the sport.

When I began playing hockey as a little girl in Shaunavon, Saskatchewan, the sport was dominated by boys. While that is still the case today, there are so many more options for girls who want to play hockey, and they are the fastest growing demographic in the sport. But, back when I started (which wasn't all that long ago), there was no such thing as girls' skates and pink sticks, and there were very few, if any, girls' leagues. The choice came down to playing on boys' teams or not at all. I was just a kid who wanted to play hockey, so I opted to join a boys' team, but without any forethought to the discrimination I would face.

I grew up playing with my family on a rink in our backyard, and used to skate in the drainage ditches to school during the winter. So I was a strong skater and loved the game, which made me better than many of the boys my age. Great for my future career. Not so great for my daily existence at the rink.

Not just the boys I played against (and sometimes with), but also their parents, would chide, taunt and say horrible things to me as I entered the rink to dress in a bathroom (there was no dressing room for a girl) or hit the ice. My parents were extremely supportive and sheltered me as best they could from the politics of hockey, especially when it concerned being a female in the game, but many times it still came through.

I remember thinking that it was wrong that anyone would make a little girl feel so discouraged and frustrated just because she played a sport that closed-minded people believed belonged to boys. I became defiant and driven to deliver. Back then, I chose this behaviour so it would show on the scoreboard that I could compete. Nowadays, I'm determined to play a small role in creating an atmosphere that nurtures girls' desire to play and ensures they are provided the same opportunities as boys. One way I have done this is by developing a program for female hockey players that not only allows them to participate in high-quality tournament competition, but also gives them access to world-class experts and trainers from my own network through workshops and clinics addressing everything from nutrition to being involved in community. In addition, all the proceeds from the annual Female Hockey Festival, which is a celebration of hockey and the young women who play it, are donated to KidSport and Right To Play—two humanitarian sports organizations that promote the concept that EVERYONE has the right to access sport, no matter their gender, socio-economic class, geographic or political environment.

To this day, when I see a little girl walking up to an arena toting a hockey bag, stick in hand, smile on her face, I can't help but smile, knowing that she is entering an ever-evening playing field—or should I say rink?

REPRESENTING TEAM MI'KMAW
The Story of Sara-Lynne Knockwood
Jason Peters

Sara-Lynne Knockwood is a proud band member of Nova Scotia's Indian Brook First Nation. Sara-Lynne, the daughter of Ron and Jennifer Knockwood, was raised in the community of Enfield, Nova Scotia. Ron required his children to participate in one sport per season, and Sara-Lynne and her two sisters, Rhonda and Nicole, were given the freedom to select their sports.

One day, the Knockwoods stumbled upon McKenna's

Tae Kwon Do Club while looking for a boxing club. As their father was in the RCMP, he had witnessed the worst of it all and wanted his daughters to be safe, so he gently nudged them toward self-defense sports. Sara-Lynne took up Tae Kwon Do (TKD) and never looked back. Knockwood was instructed by David McKenna, the club's owner, and he introduced her to the thrilling style of the International Tae Kwon Do Federation. Only months after taking up the Olympic sport, she was attending her first sanctioned World Tae Kwon Do Federation tournament in Moncton, New Brunswick. The tournament used the Olympic style, known for its big kicks. Knockwood won gold.

In 2002, Sara-Lynne attended the first North American Indigenous Games (NAIG) in Winnipeg, Manitoba. This was her first multi-sport games, and she represented Team Mi'kmaw Nova Scotia. At NAIG, Knockwood, competing as a junior, received a double gold in sparring and "poomse," the Korean term for "form" or "pattern." Four years later, she returned to NAIG (Denver) and won the silver medal in the sparring competition (Senior Black Welter Weight division) and the gold (Senior Black Poomse division).

Later that same year in November, Sara-Lynne attended the 6th World Open Championships Tae Kwon Do International in Miami Beach, Florida, hosted by the TKD Association of Great Britain and with teams representing Canada, United States, South America and Europe. McKenna wanted Sara-Lynne to try different events offered by TKD because competitors were allowed to compete in team and/or individual sparring and patterns. So McKenna walked over to introduce himself to Team Canada and to see if they had enough individuals to compete in the team events. He was told that that they didn't want anyone else—they had their team. Knockwood understood. Soon after Knockwood's first fight, the Team Canada coach sent her cards asking her to compete with his team. The strong-willed Knockwood simply responded, "You didn't want me before and I'm doing fine on my own; it was nice to meet you and thank you for the opportunity."

In the Tae Kwon Do final, after the first round, Knockwood's British opponent had a slight advantage. McKenna advised his prodigy to "let her be first." Knockwood mentally disagreed. "If I let her be first, she is going to beat me," thought the girl from small-town Nova Scotia. "I have to be first, I have to be quicker and overpower her." During the second round, Knockwood's newfound aggression kept the British fighter on the edge of the rings as she continued to step out. Knockwood's determination led her to an Under-16 World Championship. Reflecting on that tournament, Knockwood said "McKenna was a great coach, but as an athlete I had to be able to listen to my coach's advice, but also listen to my own body and understand what I'm capable of. That was the one time that I didn't listen to him."

Immediately after the fight, her father passed her a cell phone to make the call home. Sara-Lynne shed tears. This was not her normal calm composure. When Knockwood fights, it is to compete, but it always has meant more to her to be able to phone home and tell her family how she performed. The larger Knockwood family has always supported Sara-Lynne in her efforts, pitching in for fundraisers and other events. "I felt like I was competing for all of my family and everyone at home as they worked so hard to fundraise for me to attend these tournaments," acknowledges Knockwood.

Upon Knockwood's return home, a celebration was held in her honour at the local community centre. She explains, "I think that winning this world championship was a bigger thing for the community of Indian Brook First Nation."

Knockwood continued to compete in World tournaments as she travelled to the TAGB European Championships, which took place in Bristol, England. She came back with her second international championship gold medal.

After her competition days were done, she obtained a human kinetics degree from St. Francis Xavier University. Currently, Knockwood is putting her degree to good use working with the Mi'kmaq Sport Council of Nova Scotia sport, recreation and health in Mi'kmaw communities. She has been involved with many sport and recreation committees, like the 2014 Halifax North American Indigenous Games Bid Committee and has sat as a member of the Board of Directors with AthletesCAN, the Association of Canada's National Team Athletes.

32 ANS DANS LE SYSTÈME, ET PUIS QUOI?
Sylvie Béliveau

Au début des années 80, j'ai reçu ce cadeau d'être appelée à la barre d'une équipe de soccer. Cette opportunité m'a été offerte malgré l'absence de femmes à des postes de leadership et les mentalités sexistes qui ne favorisaient pas le recrutement de femmes en sport. Tout au long de mon parcours, j'ai eu le privilège d'être soutenue, du bas de l'échelle jusqu'à l'équipe nationale. Les obstacles sur la route ont été nombreux, mais je les ai surmontés grâce aux appuis autour de moi. Cependant, après toutes ces années, ma déception est de constater que si mes réalisations avaient pour but de tracer la route pour d'autres femmes, il est évident qu'il y a échecc... Être pionnière dans un domaine ne devrait-il pas signifier que les portes s'ouvrent pour celles après nous? Suis-je donc une exception ou un accident de parcours du système?

En quelques décennies, le jeu du soccer a évolué de façon remarquable pour les femmes. À preuve, plusieurs Coupes du monde ont été obtenues ainsi que plusieurs participations aux Jeux olympiques. J'ai eu cette chance de côtoyer de nombreuses personnes compétentes. J'ai évolué avec ma discipline et j'ai été appelée à œuvrer à titre d'analyste pour toutes les Coupes du monde grâce à mon expérience à titre d'entraîneure de l'équipe du Canada en 1995.

Je revendique aujourd'hui que l'inclusion des femmes et leur chance d'obtenir des postes de haut niveau passent par leur présence dans les hautes sphères de la performance. J'ai ressenti cette magie associée à la haute performance et je désire que d'autres femmes puissent aussi l'expérimenter et s'y épanouir. Malheureusement, les « hauteurs » du système sportif sont de plus en plus prisées par les hommes et le système semble les favoriser.

Voilà ce qui est contradictoire à mon histoire : « dans mon temps », les opportunités de performer au plus haut niveau pour une femme n'existaient pas et cela nuisait à leur avancement professionnel à titre d'entraîneur. Pourtant, j'ai obtenu la direction de l'équipe nationale. Aujourd'hui, bien des femmes sont en mesure de dire qu'elles ont évolué au plus haut niveau. Elles ont donc une excellente connaissance des exigences de la haute performance. Leurs expériences de joueuses lors des Coupes du monde et des Jeux olympiques resteront toutefois emprisonnées dans leurs souvenirs. En effet, toute cette expertise ne sera pas mise à contribution pour l'évolution du jeu au féminin ni même pour le bénéfice de vivre l'expérience du haut niveau dans un poste de leader afin de redonner à leur sport ce qu'elles ont reçu.

Bien entendu, si peu de femmes œuvrent à titre d'entraîneure dans les hautes sphères du sport, il en sera de même pour les formatrices. Déjà à un jeune âge et très tôt dans ma carrière, on m'a permis de partager mes connaissances avec toute la clientèle des entraîneurs en tant qu'instructrice, sans qu'à mes débuts, je sois appelée à vivre des expériences internationales. Tant que les participants n'avaient aucun préjugé par rapport à la présence des femmes dans le soccer, il n'y avait pas de problème. Pour ceux qui étaient plus hésitants à la venue d'une femme pour leur enseigner, je savais que j'avais à faire mes preuves avant d'être appréciée. Je sais aussi que mon expérience au plus haut niveau m'a permis de faire la différence auprès de ces gens. Comme on le voit souvent, lorsqu'une femme fait sa place, elle jouera plusieurs rôles à la fois. Au cours de ma carrière, j'ai eu l'occasion de combiner administration et technique, en plus de siéger au sein de plusieurs conseils d'administration et pourtant, mon bagage et mes connaissances acquises relevaient principalement du terrain. Quel est donc le parcours à suivre pour les femmes expertes dans ces domaines sportifs et qui voudraient bien avoir une place dans le système à tous les échelons de la pyramide? La question doit être posée, ne croyez-vous pas?

Ma présence au sein des groupes de travail ou conseils d'administration m'a permis de constater non seulement que les femmes sont en nombre insuffisant, mais qu'elles y jouent un rôle essentiel. La présence d'une seule femme dans une salle amène un langage différent, ce qui est un début. C'est ce que j'ai vécu. Soudainement, les intervenants faisaient plus attention à employer un vocabulaire incluant les deux sexes. Ma présence a également permis aux partisans du volet féminin de s'exprimer, confidentiellement ou publiquement; avoir des appuis silencieux contribue au changement.

Une question me revient toujours en tête : doit-on bénéficier d'une structure propre aux femmes afin de faciliter leur intégration et ainsi être considérées équitablement ou est-ce que l'intégration doit continuer à être privilégiée? Mon parcours m'a permis de côtoyer les deux types d'organisation (système séparé et système intégré) et la réponse n'est pas toute simple. L'intégration est essentielle quand on parle de services qui ne font aucune distinction entre les hommes et les femmes. Mais comment assurer aux femmes la disponibilité de programmes conçus pour elles, et ce, à tous les échelons de l'initiation à la haute performance? Les expériences de ségrégation ont un coût que peu sont en mesure de financer puisque les femmes sont encore bien moins soutenues par notre système sportif. Cependant, toutes les instances sportives doivent offrir aux athlètes, entraîneures, officielles et dirigeantes les mêmes opportunités qu'aux hommes. Mon expérience m'amène à croire que la seule façon d'y arriver est de désigner une personne avec un mandat très clair et spécifique en ce sens.

En 1999, je prenais part à la Coupe du monde de soccer féminin tenue aux États-Unis et leur slogan m'a marquée profondément: « This is my game » « This is my future » « Watch me play ». À ceci s'ajoute: « No decision about me without me ». Si chacun et chacune de nous travaillent dans le système sportif canadien en ayant en tête cette vision, je serai rassurée sur l'avenir : un avenir où toutes les filles et les femmes seront bien servies. « Alors, ne prenez pas de décision à propos de moi sans moi! ».

MARGINAL BELONGING
Danielle Peers

It took two seconds for everyone around me to decide that my thirteen-year-old body didn't belong there. This drop-in basketball court (like most) was only for boys.

It took two minutes of my shooting before one of the weaker teams made an exception, ambition trumping sexism. After an afternoon of winning games, I was officially welcomed with a "you're pretty good, for a girl." This compliment was always paired with chastisement by the boys that I beat—"pussies" and "fags" as they were called—my young queer self wishing that I was literally playing with "a bunch of pussies and fags."

By the time I was 18, I was habituated to gender binaries. My college basketball team was called the "Lady Griffins," the (under) qualified Other to the "Griffins" men's team. Our mandatory game-day skirts demarcated us from the tie-wearing males, and from those manly lesbians that we feared were among (and inside of?) us. We were also distinguished by the size of our balls. Smaller, lighter basketballs ensured that we could not train with, compete against or be considered on par with men. In the words of a young boy, while he batted away one of our balls with disgust at a camp where I was coaching, "I'm not a girl, I shoot with a real ball!"

It took me two seconds to decide that my "able" body didn't fit in. It took them two minutes to ratchet me into the titanium wheelchair, lead me onto the basketball court and convince me otherwise. When I spoke of my new sporting passion to others, it took mere moments for most to decide that I didn't belong: wheelchair basketball was only for "cripples."

It took two years of playing recreational ball to finally lose my able-bodied status. One day I walked into a doctor's office able-bodied, and walked out an hour later officially diseased. Show three pieces of disabled ID, pee in a cup, prove you are a woman (enough), train 40 hours per week, and you, too, can try out for the National Women's Wheelchair Basketball Team. Of course, when I spoke of my new elite sporting career to others, it took mere moments for most to decide that I didn't belong: "elite" sport (like most sport) is only for the able-bodied.

By the time I came back from my first Paralympic Games, those in charge of our sport (not a female wheelchair basketball athlete among them) had decided to mandate the smaller ball into the women's wheelchair game. It was sold to us as a favour, a service, a physiological inevitability. After all, women are just weaker than men. Eight-year-old boys and the men's wheelchair team had a larger ball than we did. Apparently, shooting without a penis was a serious detriment to strength. A group of athletes tried contesting the decision, but we were told there was no recourse. This disability sport decision (like most) was only for "objective" experts.

It took two seconds for everyone around me to decide that my body didn't belong. This professional French league (like most) was only for guys.

It took two minutes of watching me shoot before they realized I wasn't a player's girlfriend: I was their new teammate. When they reproached the club for the decision to hire me, the team captain replied, "She's not really a girl, she's a dyke. You'll see: she totally plays like a guy." Stereotyping, it seems, trumped sexism. While playing pro, I became a poster-child of sorts: amazingly skilled for a girl, amazingly athletic for a "crippled." Amazingly able, compared to rampant stereotypes of inability: stereotypes that such "amazing" stories recreate.

By the time I came back home from France, I had earned a men's French Championship, a women's World Championship, and a health-induced retirement. And now? I work in academic fields, activist circles and sporting communities where my embodiment, still, is rarely imagined to belong. I often play in the margins of these same communities. I play along with the "pussies and fags," the "cripples," the "dykes," the racialized, the colonized and the gender-queer. Together, we wait out the two-second reactions, re-imagine the two-minute responses and deconstruct the two-category systems. From the margins, we start to build communities we can imagine ourselves, and each other, within: communities of staggering complexity and possibility.

MAINTAINING CONTROL OF THE BALL
WHILE RUNNING
Heather Thompson

"Ab" Hoffman was my favourite athlete, role model and sports story. An eight-year-old girl from Toronto, Abby pretended to be a boy so she could play hockey for the local boys' team. She was my inspiration and helped me believe that girls could participate and achieve on an equal playing field and be proud doing so. In grade school, I remember choosing to do biographies and research projects that related to Abby's life. At the same time, my dad, with three daughters, was teaching us early on that we could do whatever boys could do: car repairs, heavy chores, sciences, math, physics, aviation, self-defense, finances or sport. With an older brother who rode BMX on the weekends, we three sisters found ourselves at the track a lot in the summers. We'd race against the boys on the Newmarket, Kingston and Orillia tracks on a regular basis, and sometimes we'd win. Although I did not pursue "boys'" sport, I did learn that in physical activity, anything is possible for girls. That is how I learned to navigate the world: playing grassroots sports and challenging whomever said I could not do something.

My role models began to change as my aspirations in sport and recreation developed. I worked in summer camps, sports camps, leadership camps, and moved my way up the employment ladder within several recreational organizations. I discovered it was not as much the competition between individual athletes that interested me, but rather how sport was organized. More importantly, I asked myself, "Where are the opportunities for young women to participate and to enjoy a variety of sports?"

In the early 1990s at Brock University in the Movement Education program, I looked for answers to that question. The program focus was elementary school children but I also worked with one of the teaching assistants in the Physical Education Department and organized a women's field hockey club for the university. This was a very humbling experience. Forming a team was not as simple as posting a homemade sign asking for players while grabbing a few lawn mowers and using our teammates and boyfriends to cut the grass on a forgotten field that Brock owned at the bottom of the Niagara Escarpment. We roughly and awkwardly began promoting the club. My naïve vision that we could immediately join in with the prestigious, university-sanctioned league OUA (Ontario University Athletics) and gain varsity status for Brock Field Hockey left me embarrassed and deflated. Yet the officially recognized university teams were still willing to play exhibition games with us. All this was part of my education as a leader. Good athletes are modest and help each other for the better of the sport. I learned from the experience that creating a new team in a new league takes a lot of work, organizational skill, lots of communication, skill in politics, and knowledge of protocol and the Ontario University League criteria for men's and women's teams. I did not have many of these qualities during that year. With my tail between my legs, I left with a feeling of a failed mission: no varsity status approval for field hockey in my "lifetime" at Brock University.

Coming from a family of teachers, it was inevitable that I went on to teachers' college the next year at Queen's University in 1994. By hanging around the lacrosse fields, watching men's competitions, playing impromptu games and selling my boyfriend's line of clothing at tournaments, I learned a lot about men's lacrosse—especially box lacrosse—and ball handling skills. At the same time, I was introduced to and became fascinated with the women's game of field lacrosse. I liked the finesse of the game: playing without padded equipment, no pocket in the stick, and still the expectation of maintaining control of the ball while running. To be honest, I loved how many of my big, burly male friends could not manage to cradle with the women's stick. After I acquired some basic skills for "Canada's national summer sport," I began to learn the women's field rules, such as having to stop on the whistle with no movement before the play resumed. Officiating also became important to me; I realized that without officials and coaches, we really wouldn't have these local games. At this time, I met Dr. Lori Livingston, a women's field official who was representing Canada at the National and

World meetings. She was instrumental in getting Canada on the map for women's field lacrosse. In addition, she was a coach at Wilfrid Laurier University, and, I would later learn, a key figure in the success of women's field lacrosse teams at both Laurier and the national level.

While completing my teacher certification, I tried again to start an "official" team for women's lacrosse at Queen's University. I thought this time that the process would be quite easy since I had learned from my mistakes during my undergrad years. I was in love with this newfound sport. At the same time, many women at other universities had the same idea and were gathering players and lobbying for recognition, field space, uniforms, equipment and varsity team status. Many of the emerging teams started as clubs. It was through networking with wonderful and driven athletes, coaches and grassroots leaders such as Cheryl MacNeill (Carleton University) and Todd Pepper (University of Toronto) that a league quickly developed.

Reflecting back, Lori has commented on how some schools benefited from more experienced leadership than others, resulting in their introducing new teams faster than others. When the sport started gaining traction in the first few years, universities were skeptical about the sport and the organization, and preferred to wait and see what came of the league. Lori also notes that the quality and experience of coaches for each university varied. Some schools dominated while others really struggled to keep players and coaches and even their clubs. During those preliminary years, Lori volunteered her time, patience and detailed sport-related resources; these were invaluable contributions for maintaining a professional process and helping us to pursue the official application to the OUA and fight for varsity status. With determination, Lori persevered as a coach, official, representative and ultimately a voice for women's lacrosse. Eventually, the sport gained varsity status with the OUA governing body. From Lori's leadership came my knowledge of and confidence in coordinating groups of people, running league meetings, negotiating issues and problem solving. Although the women's university lacrosse league faced many challenges, its growth was significant and contributed to the overall quality of women's lacrosse. Increased opportunities to play often created higher quality lacrosse and helped the sport as a whole in Canada.

Some historical context to my story is that Canada's participation at the first World Cup for women's lacrosse in 1982 marked the starting line for the sport's development. The Canadian team consisted of transformed box lacrosse players who demonstrated a national passion and competitive spirit for the sport. This team came home with a bronze. Following this victory, growth was slow, and only a few people took leadership of the sport, but by 1995 momentum was building. Canada was ready to compete at the first World Under 19 (U19) Championship and leagues were developing at the U19 level to meet the growing demand from high school players. There were still few leaders, and many players also volunteered as coaches and umpires. As the number of communities offering programs started to expand and interest from younger girls increased, by the turn of the millennium, youth teams Under 15 began to appear.

Today, some clubs are equipped to offer programs for girls and women ages 4 to 40 and beyond. Players who started as pioneers in the early- to mid-90s are following their own career paths, but are returning to the sport in leadership roles. It has taken time, but we can see that the system is now complete and feeding itself.

In many ways, the women's game in Canada is still in its infancy as compared to the US, England and Australia, but just as growth has taken place here at home, the game has expanded worldwide. When Canada played in 1982, there were six countries competing. In 2013 the World Cup will be hosted in Canada for the first time and 20 countries will participate.

Having leadership in sport helps program excellence develop. Sport cannot evolve with just athletes and coaches—someone needs to pull all the elements together in a professional, collaborative and communicative way. I have always looked up to Joanne Stanga, who held the role of Ontario Women's Lacrosse Commissioner from 1988-2005. The stability and consistency that she offered the sport reflects her commitment and passion. Joanne received a Queen's Jubilee Medal in 2012 for her contribution to the game on the provincial and national levels for more than 25 years. Lori Livingston was awarded the Governor General's Commemorative Medal for the 125th Anniversary of the Confederation of Canada for her devotion to the development of this wonderful sport. These women were my role models as a young adult. I still get chills when I look at the OUA website and see the official stats on the fall season Patterson Cup that I started with these leaders more than 15 years ago.

The efforts of Joanne, Lori and a handful of women and men who worked tirelessly to provide opportunities at the community, high school, university and national levels have given young girls today so many options. Twenty years ago, girls were only being introduced to the sport in high school with no possibility of playing beyond that level unless they were able to break into the NCAA. Today, girls can play from youth to university and beyond. Imagine … getting a quality education, playing a game that you love in your home country, and then having the ability to share it as a mentor for younger players in your own community. Priceless!

BREAKING NEWS: WOMEN LOVE FOOTBALL
Michelle Lee

I love sports. I love football. It had never occurred to me that these are radical sentiments or something I should not say as a woman. Although female involvement in football has increased, it might still be labeled a non-traditional sport for girls and women. I have been involved in football for many years, and I am driven to promote it so others can develop a love for the game.

I come from an athletic family and sports have always been a natural part of my life. My brother teaching me how to play sports is one of my fondest childhood memories, and I still tell the story of how he taught me to catch a football. I was a shy and quiet child and sports were a great way for me to make friends. I think I also gained satisfaction knowing I was doing something that not all the other girls were doing. I played the "traditional" sports, like basketball, soccer and volleyball, and I was a fan of others, like track and field, hockey and especially football. Football always seemed to be the realm of boys and men, but I grew up watching and learning to appreciate the skills and beauty of the game. There were no opportunities for girls to play football when I was younger, but as soon as I could, I started playing organized football in grade nine on the girls' varsity touch football team. I have not looked back since.

It has been well over 20 years since I first started in organized football and I still love to play. Throughout these years, I have been fortunate to meet many knowledgeable and experienced people who have taught me about the game, and my passion for it has only grown. Of course, it helps that I have some skill and ability that have led to success at provincial and national levels. Still, there is always more to learn, and I have recently become involved in the game in different ways. Although I cannot point to a single moment that drove me to become more involved, with my knowledge, experience and love of the game, it seemed only logical. I am now training to be a certified official, pursuing my coaching certification and volunteering with local football organizations to support and build their programs for girls and women. These new experiences are both rewarding and frustrating at the same time.

I have never considered myself a natural teacher, but I love to learn and passing on my knowledge is an opportunity not just for others, but also for me. At first, I started helping a women's team that was formed for pure recreation reasons, with no purpose other than to have fun. When we started, there were several novice players and I was happy to teach them. That team has now existed for over 10 years and I take much pleasure in knowing that I taught the players a few things. More recently, I have been a mentor and coach in a local girls' touch football program. I remember the reaction from the girls when I first introduced myself. They were visibly happy to meet a female football player and seemed more at ease asking questions and taking instruction than they would have been with a male coach. I have had similar positive feedback from parents who are happy to have a female coach for their daughters. As I continue to develop my coaching and teaching techniques, it gives me no greater thrill than to see the girls achieve personal or team success based on something they have learned from me. Equally rewarding is the reaction I have received as a female official. While officiating is a means for me to expand my knowledge of the game, players, parents and coaches are glad to have female referees, and I believe my position garners some respect for football as a female sport.

While I see some progress in making football a common sport for girls and women, there are still many obstacles to overcome. It is a game that remains dominated by men in all aspects—as players, coaches, officials and organizers. Women are making progress in breaking down these roles, but there is more to be done. I continue to observe a lack of respect for girls and women playing football, which may come from less engaged referees or coaches who lack passion. There are men who think because they are men, they know more about the game than I do. Of course I do not purport to know everything, but there should not be an assumption, either due to ignorance or arrogance, that because I am a woman I do not know about football. While I have been welcomed as a participant and volunteer, there is still little support for female football. Many girls want to play more, but organizers do not seem to have the will, drive or resources to expand the current programs—this is a missed opportunity for the growth of the sport.

It is only since I started reflecting on what I would like to do next in football that I have come to realize how important it has been for me to play sports all these years. Sports have shaped me and will continue to influence me. I want to give back to the community through the sport I love, but I believe there needs to be a new way of thinking about how to grow football, especially for girls and women. Girls and women are capable; they just need respect and support to be successful and to enjoy the game. I hope I can contribute to developing the same passion for football in others that I myself have for the sport.

OLD BASKETBALL PLAYERS RUMBLE ON
Heather Waddell

"Your feets are too big," announced Madame Lavoie, my formidable ballet mistress. "No man could lift such a grosse ballerina!" I was just twelve, but in a flash all my dreams were destroyed. I would not be dancing with the New York City Ballet.

But within two months, another developer of talent, teacher Les Martin, discovered me playing in the mash of intramural basketball games at little Semiahmoo High in White Rock, BC. He and his senior girls' team soon knocked me into shape. He was delighted with my big feet and was betting I would grow into them (I did!). He was more delighted as he watched me bounce into grand jetés as I snagged rebounds at both ends of the court.

Soon our once-a-week practices were not enough for me—I wanted to learn the moves I saw the male centre-forwards use on our 10-inch TV. My father, a customs officer, buried his disappointment in my being born female, and rallying his colleagues, converted the chicken coop on our acreage into an open-air court. I developed a jump, hook shot and some other strange manoeuvres that mystified the referees of the day—most females didn't play like that—so they nailed me for travelling.

In 1953 our team went to the provincial finals held in Kamloops and met South Burnaby High School at the championship. In that final game we rarely missed a shot and we controlled the backboards. Anne Fennell, our gutsy forward, fast-broke down the lanes to the hoop to sink key baskets. I remember a feeling of invincibility as I soared over taller girls to take a shot or gather a rebound. We played deep in this zone of enchantment until the final buzzer woke us from this sweaty dream. We were hoisted high on the shoulders of our male fans to parade around the arena. One man kept repeating, "You girls won me 200 dollars!"

Within weeks, Gordie MacDonald, the coach of the Vancouver Eilers—the top women's commercial team in BC—was on my parents' doorstep, promising me a trip to Mexico for the 1955 Pan

American Games if I joined his team. It was my Grade 13 year at Semiahmoo but my father drove me the 40 miles to Vancouver to practice with the Eilers. (That summer I also competed as a high jumper in the 1954 British Empire Games.)

The next year I attended Normal School in Vancouver, supporting myself by working as a nanny, but in March I went with the Eilers to the Pan American Games in Mexico City. Our transportation costs were paid by our team's sponsor, Mr. Eiler; unable to find a sponsor to pay their way, the men's basketball team was left behind.

Teams from other countries had arrived earlier to acclimatize themselves, but Canadian wisdom of the day declared that to play well at an altitude of 2,240 metres we should rest to conserve our strength, and that is perhaps why we lost every game: too rested, too much altitude for sea level dwellers. We were also unconditioned (I passed out and needed oxygen many times, for I had contracted mononucleosis the year before at the British Empire Games). And we were vertically challenged by the powerful, but unpopular, American women. When we returned to Vancouver after the games, I was approached by a sports reporter who asked me why we had lost all nine games. "Because we didn't play ten," I told him. Our coach, Gordie MacDonald, was not pleased with my smart-aleck answer and threatened me with expulsion.

At the beginning of my last year at UBC, the Physical Education Department found a fine basketball coach in Marnie Summers, and I was asked to play for my university. Thrilled to have my first woman coach, I regained a joy for the game. Our UBC team was a match for the Eilers, but they won the final game of the BC series that year, making them eligible for the Dominion Championships in Calgary. The Eilers chose two UBC players, Marilyn Peterson and me, to round out their team, but we lost the finals in Calgary to the Aidleman Aces. Now the Aces were eligible to represent Canada at the Pan American Games in Chicago in 1959, but to bolster their team they added two Eiler guards and me at centre.

Cleveland had been first choice for the Pan Am Games, but when they opted out Chicago was persuaded to fill in. The city was blanketed by an intolerable heat wave and it was all snafus and confusion. We won our first game, but in the second contest we played a heftier American team. I tangled with a large player who fell to the floor on top of my ankle, and as I struggled to get to my feet, my new husband impulsively ran onto the floor and lifted me into his arms to carry me to our bench. The crowd went wild. They thought it was so romantic. I just kept saying, "Stop! Put me down! We'll get a technical foul!" After the game, all the Canadian players accompanied me to a nearby emergency room where I sat for hours in a wheelchair while the ice pack melted and my leg ballooned. Meanwhile, the police herded in their inebriated victims and the staff calmly dealt with a collection of stab and gunshot wounds.

This accident sounded the whistle on my active playing career, so before the final parade of the Games was over, my husband and I packed my crutches into our car and left for Winnipeg where my career as a coach would begin.

BORN WITH A JIB SHEET IN MY HANDS
Erika Vines

My first job as a sailing coach was in the summer of 1994. My list of ten young athletes included only two females, and I had to check the list twice, as I hoped there would be more girls. Was this a fluke? Nope! The more I looked around, the more it became evident to me that significantly fewer females than males were involved in the wonderful sport of sailing that I'd grown to love. I then began to think …

The doctor said I was born with a jib sheet in my hands. My first regatta was when I was still in my mother's womb when she competed in the Soling class at the 1974 CORK Regatta. Typical for this time period at CORK (and many club races), she was one of two women racing amongst 60 competitors.

I grew up in Ottawa and was a part of the Britannia Yacht Club (BYC) culture from day one. By the time I showed up on planet earth, many inroads had been made for women in sailing. Women could join as associate members of BYC starting in 1919. A BYC regatta for women started in 1954, girls were allowed in the Club's Learn to Sail (LTS) program by the mid-60s, and the BYC women's committee was disbanded in the mid-1980s when folks thought there was no longer a need for it because women's participation in the Club was so strong.

So from a young age I was given the impression that girls could do anything in life. In 1985 I started in the LTS program at BYC. I didn't move through the levels quickly, but did have great fun with friends out on the water. I wanted to be just like the cool, older coaches and racers at the Club. When I was 12, I entered my first Optimist sailboat regatta, got hooked, and haven't turned back since.

Despite my positive experiences, in 1998, while studying Physical Education at Queen's University, I noticed that girls seemed to be dropping out of the Canadian LTS program at a higher and faster rate than boys. I started a study to see if my observations were correct. In the clubs I polled I found that on average, 36 percent of the participants in the LTS programs were female, although there was a 45 percent female participation rate at a club that only offered the beginner level. At the senior racing level, the average rate of female participation was 22 percent. And 30 percent of participants were women in the National 18 and Under championships between 1988 and 1996.

Statistics from 2012 also show a similar trend with female coaches and officials. At the first certification level, 26 percent of race officers, 40 percent of coaches and 18 percent of judges are women. At the highest Canadian certification level, only 10 percent of race officers, 28 percent of coaches and 19 percent of judges are female.

Since my eye-opening experience as a first-time coach in 1994, I have continually asked myself that if equal opportunity truly exists for females in sailing, then why is there a discrepancy in the numbers? When I spoke with one woman about this, she looked at me in horror and said, "How could girls keep on sailing ... as soon as they get their periods they can't be expected to be out in a dinghy!" Others have questioned how girls could survive without going to the washroom during long regatta days. These beliefs may have caused high attrition in the past, but now we've got to dig deeper to find answers.

Girls want to have fun with friends. Sailing is not a high-profile media sport, so if at a local level it is not presented as a "cool" way to spend time with friends, girls may look elsewhere for fun. Using role models to pique people's interest and to keep them involved is another key component to the equation. Also, after they are hooked, I've found you have to tell many girls that they are good (if indeed they are) and teach them not to take criticism personally (as you want to improve skills, not lower their self-confidence). I'll always remember a few horrible experiences of coaches yelling and screaming at athletes. You can't make a blanket statement saying girls should be taught one way and boys the other ... each individual has different needs, and some coaches have not taken the time to realize this.

But there is more ...

When I was a team leader at an international event in 2000, I ended up in the protest room for failing to sign the team out for the day's racing. I messed up, and the hearing was to determine the team's penalty. The majority of the judges were male and there was another Canadian coach with me. When presenting the judges' decision, one of the male judges joked, "Well, we won't make you sleep with the principal race officer." I and the other Canadian coach (and the other judges) were so shocked that no one responded to the remark. Many months later, the judge officially apologized and insisted he was only trying to be funny. I believe he was telling the truth, yet this incident made me realize how a supposedly "innocent joke" can reinforce people's perceptions of women's role in sport and society. On the bright side, I now know exactly what I would say to the judge if I were put in the same situation again today!

There is no doubt women's sailing has come a long way. Women have had an official event at the Olympics since 1988, and sailing heroes like ocean racer Ellen McArthur are recognized throughout the world. On the Canadian front, we have many role models to be proud of, such as Fiona Kidd (International Sailing Committee), Marianne Davis (CORK Executive Director), Nikola Girke (Olympian), Lynne Beal (International Judge), Jennifer Spalding (Youth World Champion), Joanne Abbott (Olympian) and Sheila Murphy and Beverley Brown (Club builders).

We are certainly on the "up and up" in terms of female participation in sailing—the sport has definitely become more inclusive since that day in 1994 when I first realized that not all women had had the same positive experiences as me. While there is still room for improvement, I am excited for my two young daughters: if they so choose, the opportunities available to them in sailing are plentiful. If we continue to tweak our club LTS and race official programs, promote opportunities for participation, facilitate mentorship and encourage fun out on the water ... the sky is the limit!

BEING A POWERFUL GIRL
Fiona Joy Green

Having my photo taken by a local Winnipeg newspaper for placing well in a provincial swim meet was one of the most poignant moments of my life. At age eight and the youngest in the group, I remember thinking at that time, and then again when I first saw the picture, that I was strong and powerful. I liked what I had accomplished by practicing hard and swimming well at the meet. I also liked that others recognized my determination, commitment, and achievement. For the first time, I believed that I had worth as a girl and that others took me seriously. Little did I know that this insight of being a powerful girl would assist in my fitness, feminism, and career over the next four decades.

At age 15, I left age-group swimming and played water polo for the Manitoba Junior Women's team into my early 20s. I set the Manitoba Masters women's 25-29 year-old long course records for the 200, 800 and 1500 metre freestyle events—which each stood for 19 years, until 2006.

Swimming ensured that I developed the skills to survive in water, the confidence to become a swim instructor, and moreover, the ability to save lives. As a junior lifeguard (at age 15), I successfully and safely pulled both an adult and a child from the bottom of a pool, while the on-duty male senior guard stood paralyzed, white-faced and open-mouthed. I again felt confidence as a female, this time for rising to the challenge when an older male could not. Swimming also contributed to my valued lung capacity and the tenacity I needed to train and successfully complete 10 marathons, including three Boston Marathons, between the ages of 18 and 50.

Observing various body types during the many hours I've spent in pools, coupled with my experience in teaching swimming to folks with diverse physical, emotional and mental abilities, has taught me how to see everyone as valued and unique regardless of body type, capacity and personality. While my teammates were certainly members of the middle class, they did not all identify as Euro-Canadian or heterosexual. Learning that folks are different due to their cultural, ethnic and sexual identities influenced my lifeguarding and provided the groundwork for my university education. Swimming not only directly financed my studies, it also laid the foundation for my understanding and accepting of diversity.

As a student, I learned how to name and articulate my observation that males tended to be valued and rewarded more than females. I also recognized my own internalized male-identified success. Until then, I had only considered boys and men worthy of competition. My delight in easily beating boys in arm wrestling (as an 11-year-old in Grade 5) is an example of my own internalized sexism. In university, I developed a more sophisticated understanding of the sexism, misogyny and gender power dynamics that I had witnessed and experienced in aquatics as a team member and employee.

My studies introduced me to feminist frameworks that valued girls and women. They nurtured the development of my own feminist theorizing and practice as I earned a BA (Sociology), an MA (Women's Studies) and an Interdisciplinary PhD (Education, Sociology and Women's Studies). The skills I established as a swim instructor have easily transferred to teaching university students. They have also helped me secure a job that I still enjoy, more than two decades later, and permit me to share my feminist knowledge with students and colleagues alike.

Swimming continues to nourish others and me. I voluntarily teach adults how to swim—as I've done throughout my life—and I've returned to Master's swimming after a 20-year hiatus to help me work through a nagging running injury. These days, I'm witnessing many more positive interactions between coaches and swimmers of various ages and genders at the pool. I believe this affirming environment offers girls and women (as well as boys and men) many more opportunities for empowerment than I had when I was an eight-year-old girl. Oh, how I love swimming and the encouraging influence it can have on fitness and feminism!

YOU'RE GOING TO HAVE TO CHANGE
WITH THE BOYS
Keri Cress

Shocked. Bewildered. Angry. This was the succession of emotions I felt after being informed that I was not permitted to try out as a goalie for my high school hockey team. It was boys only. Not permitted? Boys only?! Welcome to men's hockey in Winnipeg, Manitoba circa 1993.

It began with a sign-up sheet posted to the gymnasium doors for tryouts for a newly-formed high school hockey team. I had been playing goal in ringette since the age of five and pickup hockey with the boys at the local community centre for as long as I could remember. I instinctively added my name to that list, only to be pulled aside the next day by one of my gym teachers (and would-be hockey coach) who informed me that I was not allowed to try out.

One of my courses at the time happened to be intro to psychology, where we were required to submit a weekly journal. I adored my teacher who was a very strong woman and outspoken feminist. Every significant occurrence in my life at the time—from my boyfriend unsuccessfully pressuring me to relinquish my virginity, to not being permitted to try out for the "boys'" hockey team—made its way into that journal. After reading my journal entry about hockey, my teacher approached me to gauge my level of commitment to the tryouts. She subsequently helped me approach the school board. Since there were no plans for a girls' hockey team, the school had no choice but to allow me to try out.

There were three goalies at the beginning of tryouts and the team was formed with two, me included. Truth be told, I did not see much ice time as I was the second goalie and was not nearly as skilled as the first string. However, when I did play, I tucked my waist-length hair inside the back of my jersey, as I found that once the opposing team discovered I was a girl they either lightened their shots or attempted to take my head off.

The changeroom experiences were nothing that I could have possibly anticipated. My friends on the team were very respectful. Some of my teammates were a grade behind me, and we were less close. At times they would parade around the locker room naked, bragging about the scratches on their backs and varied sexual exploits. The open shower was altogether another can of worms. When I confronted the coach with these issues, I was told, "You want to play with the boys, you're going to have to change with the boys." At times my dad or boyfriend would accompany me in the locker room and, strangely enough, the antics would stop.

Halfway through the season I broke my tailbone during practice. That was it for me; my season was finished. After the injury, my coach was kind enough to give a statement to the local newspaper, stating I was "just not cut out for boys' hockey." Added to that was the extra humiliation of walking from class to class carting an inflatable rubber doughnut on which to rest my broken bottom—not exactly a cool fashion accessory in Grade 12. Years later, I popped into my high school and ducked my head into my former coach/gym teacher's office. Pinned to his billboard I happened to see a picture of my hockey team (which I had never received a copy of). I mentioned this oversight to him. He then turned around, unpinned the photo from the board, handed it to me with a handshake and apologized for my experience. You could have knocked me over with a feather (or a hockey puck, as the case may be).

It thrills me to see how far women's hockey has come; my former high school now has its own girls' team. Despite the progress, I still encounter people who appear to be shocked when I tell them I play hockey. Would they have the same reaction if I told them I figure skated or played soccer? Not likely. There are still an unfortunate number of gender stereotypes to overcome, but we have made some serious strides in the past few decades, which warms my heart and makes me proud to have contributed in my own small way.

Sport has been the cornerstone of my life: from being an athlete, to obtaining a degree in kinesiology, I cannot imagine the person I would be today without it. My experience in boys' hockey taught me a few valuable life lessons. First, never accept "no," "you can't," or "you're a girl." You truly CAN do anything you set your heart and mind to. In fact, 18 years later, I am still playing hockey and have now ventured into the world of roller derby at the ripe-old age of 36 as "Violent Femme." Second, I have learned that your true friends will stand by you (those who supported me in that hockey change room are still my friends to this day). Third, I have seen that people change; they can and will surprise you, long after you have given up on them. And, finally, it is important to fight for what you want, for what you believe in. Do not give up, not ever. That is my life's mantra.

L'ATTEINTE DU RÊVE OLYMPIQUE :
À QUEL PRIX?
Guylaine Dumont

Depuis aussi longtemps que je me souvienne, le sport m'a procuré une joie, une liberté et un bien-être indescriptible. Sans le sport, je n'aurais pas pu être qui je suis aujourd'hui. À travers celui-ci, j'ai appris à me définir, à mettre mes limites, à me respecter, à m'adoucir, à trouver cette paix intérieure qui est si précieuse pour moi et pour les autres que je côtoie.

Je suis originaire d'un petit village de la Rive-Sud de Québec. Je suis la plus jeune d'une famille modeste de quatre enfants : trois filles et un garçon. Mon père, un homme attachant, mais autoritaire et violent, nous a poussés vers le sport. Sans être conscient des effets nocifs, il nous mettait constamment en compétition les uns contre les autres, peu importait notre sexe ou notre âge. Étant la plus jeune, mon talent athlétique m'a servi à obtenir la reconnaissance et l'amour de mon père. Du moins, c'est devenu ma croyance : pour être reconnue, je devais gagner, je devais être la meilleure. Une croyance qui m'a poussée à aller au-delà de mes limites sportives, mais aussi à bafouer mon corps. Pendant cette période, j'ai intégré le dialogue intérieur de mon père, éternellement insatisfait si je n'étais pas parfaite et constamment en compétition avec tout un chacun. J'ai mis des années à en prendre conscience et à le transformer.

Les abus physiques et verbaux de mon père ont fait fuguer mes deux sœurs aînées qui avaient un tempérament rebelle. La fuite semblait la seule option pour elles. L'une d'entre elles a sombré dans l'alcool et la drogue et l'autre n'en est jamais revenue. Son corps fut retrouvé 9 ans plus tard. Mon verdict : victime d'un mal de vivre dû à une faible estime d'elle-même, elle s'est retrouvée dans un environnement malsain mené par la drogue et la boisson.

De mon côté, pour me sortir de ce tourbillon familial malsain, à 16 ans je suis partie jouer au volley-ball (VB) pour le club de Sherbrooke. Mon frère a fait le même choix pour aller jouer au hockey.

Le sport est donc devenu mon sauveur. Je me sentais vivante sur un terrain de VB. Mon talent m'a permis d'être sélectionnée sur l'équipe nationale dès l'âge de 15 ans, de voyager (de fuir)... de m'épanouir et d'ouvrir ma conscience.

Un moment décisif dans ma vie sportive et personnelle fut lorsque j'ai quitté l'équipe nationale de VB en juin 1995 en raison d'un entraîneur, un mois et demi après avoir été sélectionnée pour aller aux Jeux olympiques (JO) de Barcelone en 1996. C'était la fin de mon beau rêve olympique.

Ayant quitté une première fois l'équipe nationale en 1991 pour fuir l'abus de pouvoir et le harcèlement psychologique de la part de ce même entraîneur, je suis allée jouer dans une ligue professionnelle en Italie pendant cinq saisons où j'étais régulièrement sur les équipes étoiles et parmi les meilleures joueuses de la ligue.

Mon talent et mon audace m'ont servie, car j'aurais pu quitter le sport comme plusieurs de mes collègues, mais je refusais qu'un homme manipulateur éteigne mon feu intérieur. Durant ces années en Italie, j'ai commencé un suivi psychologique et petit à petit, j'ai appris à reprendre mon pouvoir et à sortir de la victimisation.

Ayant été élevé par un père violent et une mère incapable de mettre ses limites, il m'était difficile de déceler des comportements d'abus et de harcèlement psychologique. J'avais tendance à mettre ça sur le dos de mon mauvais caractère en me remettant en question et en me diminuant.

Comme je le disais précédemment, en 1995, à 15 mois des Jeux olympiques, j'ai dû mettre mes limites ; mon corps me trahissait par les blessures. Ma confiance de joueuse était à son plus bas, pourtant, j'étais arrivée en pleine forme au camp de sélection et avec une confiance et une motivation débordante. Mes tentatives pour recevoir de l'aide auprès de mes collègues de l'équipe, de la Fédération canadienne, du psychologue sportif et d'autres instances furent sans succès et je dû me résoudre.

Ayant encore une fois l'impression que c'était moi qui avait le problème et non l'entraîneur, j'ai donc abandonné toutes tentatives de dénonciation … et je suis partie sans trop faire de vagues. Un classique des victimes d'abus.

Ce fut déchirant de devoir renoncer à mon rêve olympique, mais je refusais que mon parcours pour y arriver soit un cauchemar dicté par un homme charmeur, manipulateur et sans scrupule pour les femmes qu'il entraînait. En prenant cette décision, je me suis respectée comme femme et non comme sportive. Je me suis choisie et non mon rêve. Lorsque j'ai fait les JO à Athènes, en pensant à mon aventure pour les JO de Barcelone, tout un chacun a partagé avec moi qu'il se sentait malheureux de s'être laissé prendre et d'avoir choisi l'agresseur plutôt que les victimes.

Ma croyance est que les décisions basées sur le respect et l'amour de soi nous reviennent d'une manière ou d'une autre (la loi du retour). Cela s'est concrétisé huit ans plus tard lorsque j'ai réalisé mon rêve olympique dans la joie et la légèreté.

Lorsque j'ai entrepris une formation en relation d'aide pour devenir thérapeute, un de mes buts était de m'outiller pour aider les femmes et les athlètes à mieux s'affirmer dans le sport. Suite à la découverte du corps de ma sœur en 1993, j'ai toujours porté cette motivation à l'intérieur. Cela dit, j'ai commencé par m'aider moi-même en me dédiant à un travail intense de découverte de moi-même. C'est durant cet arrêt de presque trois ans que je me suis mariée avec un entraîneur merveilleux, ouvert et sensible aux athlètes. Je suis aussi devenue maman de ma première fille.

Et après un coup de téléphone d'Annie Martin en 2002, j'ai pu vivre avec elle un rêve inespéré ; celui de faire les Jeux olympiques à Athènes en VB de plage à l'âge de 36 ans ! Je l'ai fait à partir de toutes les leçons apprises et en partant des outils et des stratégies nouvelles que j'avais acquis pour atteindre mon objectif de manière plus saine et équilibrée.

Avant d'accepter, j'ai cherché la motivation et la raison profonde qui m'animait pour faire ce retour: « Aller au bout de moi-même peu importe le résultat, et être un modèle pour les jeunes filles et pour toutes les femmes qui veulent se dépasser et s'affirmer. » Cela a été mon carburant dans les moments plus difficiles pour me recentrer et me ramener à l'essentiel et à poursuivre mon objectif.

Bien que j'aie cessé la compétition, je continue à œuvrer dans le monde du sport à titre de conférencière dans les écoles, les clubs ou les organismes sportifs. Mon message est axé sur la persévérance et sur le respect de soi et des autres. Je dévoile les côtés moins glorieux derrière mon succès olympique et je donne espoir aux jeunes qui vivent des situations d'abus ou de violence dans leur famille ou à l'école.

Je travaille comme thérapeute en relation d'aide spécialisée dans le sport. À travers mes conférences/ateliers, j'aide les parents et les entraîneurs à mieux comprendre et guider leurs jeunes athlètes à optimiser leur performance de façon globale. Puisque la vie m'a amenée à vivre ces genres de difficulté et d'expériences et à réaliser mon rêve à l'âge de 36 ans d'une manière aussi légère et magique, je souhaite maintenant partager mon message et aider les femmes et les jeunes.

A JOYOUS, NEVER-ENDING FLOW OF WOMEN
Phyllis Berck

In 1992 I participated in a most remarkable event, one I never thought possible. Nearly 10,000 women bicycled through the streets of Stockholm in a mass ride. As I walked up a slight rise to get to the start line, I could see an endless flow of women ahead of me and behind me. Women in Lycra shorts with high-end racers, women in long skirts with flowers in their baskets, the very young, the middle-aged, the elderly. It was a joyous, never-ending flow of women, only women, on bicycles; all the volunteers and most of the spectators were men. I had never imagined that women could so enjoyably be the centre of sporting attention.

Until that ride, it had never occurred to me that a well-funded event focusing solely on female recreational participants was possible. Yet today, less than two decades later, the world of road running has become very much like that bike ride in Stockholm. The transformation of road running from sexist and exclusionary to gender equitable, and, in some cases, female dominated is one of the most extraordinary achievements of the Canadian sport and recreational environment.

In 1984 the Olympic Games included the women's marathon for the first time: Joan Benoit of the United States won and Canadian Sylvia Ruegger came 8th, Canada's best performance in the women's Olympic marathon to date. The reason it took so long for the event to be included was that some decision makers, all men, felt this distance could be injurious to women's health, and if that was not enough, destroy their reproductive organs.

The inclusion of the marathon in Los Angeles was the culmination of incremental opportunities. The first was at the 1928 Olympics in Amsterdam. The Fédération Sportive Féminine Internationale (FSFI) persuaded the International Olympic Committee (IOC) to put three running events on the program, the longest being 800 m, in exchange for dropping the word "Olympics" from its quadrennial event. Canadian women did very well in Amsterdam, but the IOC said that the "exhausted condition of the women" at the end of 800 m was reason enough to drop the event from the program. The event was not reinstated until 1960. Under pressure from the FSFI to include women, the IOC did so reluctantly. It would appear that if participation by women was necessary, the IOC did not want to see effort. That was too real, too athletic and too inconsistent with their notion of femininity.

For distance runners, there were other "events of struggle." The most important was the Boston Marathon. Kathrine Switzer officially entered in 1967, registered as K.V. Switzer, but an official tried to stop her—unsuccessfully—from finishing. It was once again a battle between entrenched notions of femaleness by men and the desire by women to be athletic—to sweat, to get red in the face, to tire from exertion and know that they are no less female because of that. Boston did not officially invite women to run until 1972. While some women runners waited for Boston, Canadian Maureen Wilton – for a time, the fastest woman marathoner – created her own events. In 1967, when she was 13-years-old, she ran 3:15:23.

While the International Association of Athletic Federations (IAAF) and the IOC dragged their feet to include women's events, the commercial sector was quicker off the mark. Bonne Bell (a cosmetics company in Canada and the US), owned by Jesse Bell, who believed in the value of running and physical activity, began a series of seven 10 km events across Canada in 1979. The winner from each of the races went to Boston to run a women's 10 km. Jacqueline Garneau of Canada won the inaugural event in Boston.

What was so smart about the Bonne Bell series (and later Avon, when they bought out Bonne Bell) was that the event focused on participation rather than high performance. There was room for both, but the majority of participants were there for fun, fitness and a safe entry into a sisterhood of runners where you only had to show up. You did not need to wait to be selected for a team; a school experience many women will recount as turning them off Phys. Ed. and physical activity permanently.

Calgary was one of the seven cities to host the first Bonne Bell race in 1975, and it has continued to hold the event since then. Now the race is known as the Calgary Women's Run, and it is one of the oldest women's-only running events in Canada. It has since been joined by others, such as the Emilie Mondor Memorial 5 km Race for Women in Ottawa and the Toronto Women's Run Series founded by Cory Freedman.

Entrepreneurs like Toronto's Elaine McCrea, a marathoner since 1979 and owner of The Runners Shop, have brought many new women into the sport by featuring women-friendly running apparel and "learn to" clinics. While there was little women-only clothing 30-40 years ago—no running bras, shorts, shoes or shirts for women—there is a wealth of choice now.

Where once it was only competitive running clubs that provided training and support for athletes, there are now running clinics and training programs available in person or on-line. Stores like Elaine's and the Running Rooms across the country regard women runners seriously, regardless of their aspirations. They train them to be ready for the start line and to reach the finish.

One organization working to create a fairer, more equitable high performance sport system, and accessible, supportive opportunities for recreational participants is the Canadian

Association for the Advancement of Women and Sport and Physical Activity (CAAWS). One early CAAWS program was "On the Move," focusing on adolescent females. The program articulated the values of inclusion, participation, social networking, and avoided talk about skill or body image. All of these components characterize the world of women recreational runners today. While many women start running because of fitness, to fundraise or to celebrate a milestone birthday, they stay because they make friends, are welcome regardless of body type, and become fitter. While they may not consider themselves athletes, they do see themselves as serious runners. Beginning with the CIBC Run for the Cure—the first event of its kind that raises money for a cause—which attracts over 50,000 runners, women are participating in running events not just for personal benefits but also to raise money for organizations that improve the quality of life around them. While CAAWS did not create "On the Move" for this age demographic, it is so interesting to see the way in which women runners have taken these values and "run with them."

Because of CAAWS, after I returned from the cycling event in Stockholm I became involved in many sports. I came into running with Elaine McCrea as my coach in 2008. My goal was to get fit so that I could be a better cross-country skier, but thanks to opportunity, I discovered I had capacity I never knew I had. Since then, I have run in three major marathons (New York, Berlin and Boston) and have won my age category in many shorter races. In these races, women comprise 45-60 percent of participants. My niece runs with me, and her daughter (age 8) has run her first 5 km. That makes three generations of female runners. Running has become what women and girls do. The sexism of a sport world that once excluded us has largely disappeared from road running. That Stockholm bike ride is coming to Canada.

REFLECTIONS OF A CENTENNIAL BABY
How Sport Has Shaped My Life
Lori Johnstone

I was a Centennial baby. Growing up in the 1970s with very young parents, my brother and I were raised to believe that we could do anything. We were taught that differences were attributable to nurture, including societal expectations, education, our experiences and exposure to role models. Our mother embraced many aspects of feminism (although I do not recall her labelling herself as such) and our father was supportive and encouraging, although he had a traditional provider role (as a soldier).

When I was a young child we lived in a very rural area. What we did not have in material possessions was more than made up by our close-knit family, a healthy and active lifestyle and an idyllic setting. I spent a lot of time outdoors with my brother and male cousins, and to me, it made perfect sense to try to outrun, outclimb and outfight them. More importantly, I was not labelled for my physicality or the way I dressed or acted. I was not subjected to negative gender-based comments about my behaviour or pressured to "act like a girl." As a preadolescent, school-based sports, family activities and Brownies provided opportunities to be active with few barriers. My mother's non-traditional job as a cable installer also reinforced my idea that women and men were equal. I was too young to grasp the confidence my mother needed to do her job, the skepticism she faced from customers, the respect she earned from coworkers—I didn't know that her small body size and her "can do" attitude were ideally suited to sites where climbing through, under and over obstacles was necessary. All I knew was that anything a man could do a woman could do too ... because my mom was doing it.

It was the mid-1970s when I found female sport role models. Nadia Comaneci emerged as an international star at the Montreal 1976 Olympic Games. She wasn't much older than I was, and my friends and I wanted to be just like her. We spent hours practicing somersaults, cartwheels, round offs, backbends and splits on lawns, in living rooms and at school gymnasiums. We celebrated when someone learned to do a back handspring or a front walkover. Looking back, I recognize the safety hazards of our unsupervised play, but these experiences and skills undoubtedly contributed to our physical literacy, fitness levels and dreams. Two years later, my family and I attended the 1978 Commonwealth Games in Edmonton, Alberta. There were not a lot of sports for women, but Canadian divers Linda Cuthbert (10 m) and Janet Nutter (3 m), gymnast Elfi Schlegel and other members of the women's gymnastics team contributed to Canada's domination in the medal count and our pride as fans. These women gave this young girl a taste for high-performance sport and the belief that being the best in the world was attainable.

As a child and young teenager participating in many individual and team sports, I was fortunate to have parents who ensured I had the right equipment, could go to practices and events, and was able to participate in fundraising activities. They actively supported me in all my pursuits. At the same time, we continued to do outdoor family activities, such as canoeing, skiing and horseback riding. It was my father who introduced our family to racquetball, and we were part of a club that became my home away from home. A young woman from my club, Glenda Schenk, who was three years older than I, became my training and doubles partner and my closest friend. I see now how I thrived through our friendship. I also realize that during those years I was very fortunate to have good facilities, quality coaching, family and peer support as well as opportunities to train and compete. There were even exceptional female athletes in the region (such as Carol Ross and Carol Dupuis) who served as role models. These women competed and won against men, and I wanted to be as good as them.

In my teen years, sport was my salvation. My involvement in individual and team sports and the network of support and friends they provided inoculated me to some extent against the risks of troubled family times and frequent moves. Sport also kept me engaged in school and at home when I might otherwise have drifted into some difficult situations out of frustration, resentment or teenage angst. During that time, I became increasingly aware of the "body on display" factor. It was daunting, even as physically conditioned young female athletes, to know we were being checked out or watched by someone, whether we were working out, competing or minding our own business walking down the street. In all settings we were learning how to deal with being teased for our various body shapes, getting wanted and unwanted attention, hearing sexual innuendos and experimenting with relationships.

Fast forward a few years, and I was a young adult regularly training and competing against men (because there was a limited number of women playing racquetball at the open level). While I recognized that there were strength and speed differences, my goal was to play the men's style of game with its power and aggressive shots. Ironically, while I was gaining confidence and competence as an athlete, the whole "being a woman" thing had become rather complicated: body image issues, relationships, attention, sex—these experiences were both distracting and confusing.

Even though I was a young, female athlete, I wasn't particularly aware of all the issues I was navigating. For the most part, I took the assets for granted and shrugged off the challenges. Increasing awareness of the various and competing factors in my life (and more globally for girls and women) arose during my university studies and my involvement with AthletesCAN (originally known as the Canadian Athletes Association) and the Canadian Association for the Advancement of Women and Sport and Physical Activity (CAAWS). My exposure to these organizations and my studies in applied social sciences allowed me to name and explain many of my experiences through terms such as objectification, hyper-sexualization, homophobia and harassment. I began to see how my efforts to affirm my heterosexuality and femininity came from the pressure to "prove I wasn't gay" and show that female athletes could be attractive and strong and straight. At the same time, I was also dealing with women who assumed I was after their boyfriends and husbands — the men who served as my training partners and opponents. Lesbian or femme fatale, I must be one or the other. Before long, I ignored the noise and began working to create welcoming and supportive environments for all.

I also struggled emotionally over training with and competing against women I considered close friends. I was concerned that they would be hurt, either physically or emotionally, or that I would be rejected on a personal level if I beat them. Much later, I learned this is called the "challenge of competition," and a more common concern for female athletes than male. My paternal grandfather, a former high-performance boxer, cured me of that mental obstacle when I was preparing to compete against a close friend and training partner. He explained that I simply had to move faster and hit the ball better than my opponent, that it was part of the game and not personal. I took his advice and learned I was capable of distancing myself emotionally when necessary.

Racquetball provided many such personal lessons, opportunities and challenges. It also served as a source of income for over 20 years. When my national team career ended due to a permanent injury to my right elbow, I continued to play with my left hand, teaching lessons and competing for fun. My commitment to the sport led me to roles as an athlete representative, national program coordinator and volunteer on the high-performance committee. The on and off ramps for my continued involvement ensured that I was able to stay connected and contribute for many years.

As my understanding of and commitment to issues affecting girls and women increased, so did my appreciation for what my parents had done for me. I was indignant that so many girls and women have not benefited from sport and physical activity. However, I was now sensitized to the larger issues and the comprehensive approaches required to address them. I became actively involved in advocacy, influencing policy, developing and contributing to programs, networking, mentoring and being mentored, among other actions. Through diverse roles, including Chair of AthletesCAN (1997-99), Special Advisor to the Secretary of State for Amateur Sport (1999-2001), GO NB Provincial Coordinator for the NB-Canada Bilateral on Sport Development (2003-2008) and as a Sport NB board member (2002-2009), I have supported and championed gender equity in sport, physical activity and society.

One experience in particular has stayed with me. In 2002

I participated in the International Women in Sport conference while eight-and-a-half-months pregnant. That conference was intellectually engaging, but it also generated a strong emotional connection among delegates. I remember all the topics we covered at that meeting, but I also recall thinking that if I had a girl she would be very fortunate that we live in Canada. From my travels, and the literature, conversations and presentations at this conference, I was acutely aware that our rights as girls and women in Canada exceeded those of so many others, whether in safety and security, education, the pursuit of sport and physical activity, reproductive control, autonomy and freedom to make decisions, the ability to own land, marry by choice, etc.

As a mother and someone who works in sport, wellness and health promotion, I believe it is urgent to create optimal conditions and systems that support women and girls (as well as boys and men) to be active at all stages of participation and in all roles. As a policy analyst, I try to figure out what researchers say, what policies mean and what actions are likely to be effective. I do the same thing at home, observing my children, reflecting on what researchers recommend and what my experiences have taught me. In some ways, it is not as simple as I believed growing up. The complex interactions among the determinants of health (of which gender is one) influence who we are and the quality of our lives. I still believe that women and men are equally capable of doing mundane and extraordinary things in sport and in life. I follow in my parents' footsteps, actively supporting my children and trying not to burden them with negative stereotypes and labels. I know firsthand how positive attitudes, expectations and experiences can have the power to shape our journeys and our dreams.

I embrace Bruce Kidd's idea that equity means providing everyone with a full range of opportunities and benefits, the same finish line. We have to continue to champion gender equity because girls and women are still less likely to participate, coach or lead sport than their male counterparts. But I know we can do these things. My daughter and my son know we can too. They know it with all the confidence and enthusiasm of healthy, active children ... in part, because I do it and my mother did it before me.

IN THIS SECTION, 14 women reflect on how a movement for women and sport gained momentum and structure in Canada. Women began to organize nationally, provincially and municipally. There emerged a common recognition of the need to break or bend institutional rules to create a legitimate space for girls and women in the world of sport. In part, this effort was represented by a crystallization of demands: for more space, resources, programs and initiatives for women and girls. But the effort also lay on an ideological level: these women do not just describe being second class in sport but also feeling second class in the growing women's movement. As a result, it became essential to define a strategy for identifying the resisters to change and figuring out how to unearth them. Furthermore, as public money began to reach these fledgling organizations, usually for short-term projects, responsibility for long-term change began to weigh heavily. Eventually however, a collective ideology emerged.

As the women in the section recount, sometimes it was feminism that led them to activism in their sport; sometimes it was the sport experiences that brought them to feminism. Whichever way it happened, they worked hard, celebrated, recorded the history and reveled in joining a larger movement of change for women and girls in Canada.

< A group shot of the women (and two men) who were most of the "founding mothers" of the Canadian Association for the Advancement of Women and Sport (CAAWS) in 1981. The organization has provided the leadership for most of the key activities changing women and sport in Canada in the decades since.

WHERE ARE THE WOMEN IN SPORT LEADERSHIP?
Debunking the Myth that it was Federal Government Policy Priority
Pamela Lewis

As a very athletic girl growing up in small town Ontario in the 60s, I played most sports with both boys and girls of all skill levels. There was always a game of pick-up scrub happening on the schoolyard. If there wasn't a game going on, I would round up enough kids to get one started. In high school, I played competitive basketball and volleyball and firmly believed that a life lived well was anchored in a gymnasium. The large high school I attended in London had a major problem with drugs, even in the early 70s. To help get girls out of the smoking pits, I was keen to organize girls' intramural tournaments in basketball, volleyball and tennis. My first job was as a Municipal Park Supervisor, where I coached teams and organized tournaments for local youth during the summer. Sport was a way of life for me.

I was selected to represent my high school at the Ontario Athletic Leadership Camp, where I realized that I wanted to pursue a career in sport. I set my sights on being a high school physical education teacher and coach who would inspire and train female athletes to be provincial, possibly national, or even world champions. However naïve I might have been, this was my heartfelt dream and aspiration.

Fast forward to 1979. After completing my undergraduate degree with a major in physical education, the teaching market was flooded. Teacher's college seemed like a waste of time and money, with no jobs anywhere in the province. What else could I do to have a viable career in sport if I couldn't be a physical educator? As I scanned the horizon of potential job opportunities in sport, there were no local coaches being paid a salary. I was among the first women to be an internationally certified basketball official, and was officiating men's and women's college and university games, as well as high school and city league games. But this was not exactly a career.

It also seemed, from casual observation of major Games, that there was a shortage of women on the national team staff for the Pan Am, Commonwealth and Olympic Games. As I looked a little further into the administrative ranks of the National Sport and Recreation Centre in Ottawa, it seemed like there also weren't many women Executive Directors or technical staff in the burgeoning National Sport Organizations (NSOs). What was wrong with this picture?

Intent on finding out what career opportunities there were for women in the national sport system, I undertook a Master's degree with a focus on the Canadian sport system from a public policy perspective. Specifically, I looked at the Fitness and Amateur Sport Branch (FAS) policies as they pertained to women in sport in Canada. I wanted to know why there were so few women national coaches and administrators. I received funding for this research in 1980 to survey 68 national sport governing bodies, thanks to the commitment of a few women advocates within Sport Canada. The data I collected confirmed my observation that there was a blatant under-representation of women in leadership positions at the national level in Canada. But was anything being done to change that?

The Fitness and Amateur Sport Branch, under the umbrella of the Department of National Health and Welfare, was the Government of Canada's policy making unit responsible for the disbursement of public funding for sport and recreation in Canada. Significant policies were established within the FAS pertaining to women in sport in Canada between 1974 and 1979; however, my research found that the policy makers within FAS did not regard the lack of gender equity in sport leadership positions as a problem. Therefore, no specific policies or programs for women in sport were implemented. Furthermore, no systemic targets for improving the representation of women in leadership positions were established. Despite this neglect on the policy level, there was a great deal going on during these years as the Canadian sport system was taking shape.

In 1961 the Government of Canada assumed an active role in promoting sport in Canada and passed Bill C-131, *An Act to Encourage Fitness and Amateur Sport*, which signified a commitment to supporting fitness and amateur sport in Canada. Eight years later, the combined effect of a rise in prestige of nations' international successes in sport, specifically at Olympic Games and World Championships, and Canada's inconsistent presence on the podium at major international competitions, prompted the Minister of National Health and Welfare, the Honourable John Munro, to commission the 1969 Task Force on Fitness and Amateur Sport. The ensuing Report of the Task Force on Sport for Canadians, led the Minister to present a proposed sports policy for Canadians in March 1970. This policy was significant because it initiated the formation of a centralized national support structure for sport in Canada.

This policy was also instrumental in getting government to earmark a substantial increase of public funds for amateur sport. To oversee the programming and disbursement of these funds, in 1971, Sport Canada and Recreation Canada were formed within the Directorate of Fitness and Amateur Sport. The Coaching Association of Canada (CAC) was established to develop coaching education programs across different sports as well as a Coaching Certification Program.

Concurrently, there were significant legislative changes to promote women's equality. The 1970 Report of the Royal Commission on the Status of Women in Canada precipitated the formation of the Office of Equal Opportunities for Women within the Public Service Commission in 1972 and the Canadian Advisory Council on the Status of Women in 1973. This Report issued the following specific directive to the Fitness and Amateur Sport Directorate: "Pursuant to Section 3(d) of the Federal Fitness and Amateur Sport Act, a research project be undertaken to a) determine why fewer girls than boys participate in sports programs at the school level, and b) recommend remedial action." No such project was undertaken, although a "Women in Sport Program" was referred to in three FAS Annual Reports. In an interview, Dr. Tom Bedecki, Director of Sport Canada 1970-1974, stated that the concept of a Women in Sport Program was rejected by Sport Canada on the grounds that it would be viewed as a "token initiative of minimal effectiveness."

Amateur sport and women's issues gained further political

visibility by 1974. For one, the Fitness and Amateur Sport Directorate attained Branch status. In addition, the advent of International Women's Year in 1975 prompted the federal government to allocate funds for projects to improve the status of women in Canada (or at least appear that way). In response to this new funding initiative, the FAS supported the National Conference on Women in Sport to discuss women's place in Canada's sporting culture. The underlying assumption by the participants in this "think tank" was that their numerous recommendations would serve as directives for policies and programs within the Fitness and Amateur Sport Branch.

The National Conference on Women in Sport was held in Toronto in May 1974. This meeting of prominent women athletes, administrators, coaches, and some of the men involved in sport at that time, articulated the issue of gender inequality in sport, particularly in coaching and leadership positions. Their recommendations were listed in the Report of the National Conference on Women in Sport, 1974. Action Proposals for Government were developed for three categories—Participation, Coaching and Administration. Although the recommendations were published by FAS in 1974 and ostensibly gave birth to a Women in Sport Program, when the political visibility of women's issues faded after International Women's Year in 1975, the program was no longer acknowledged in FAS publications. Given this context, it is pertinent to examine whether and how these directives determined policy throughout the rest of the decade.

If there were in fact equal opportunities for women, it would be logical to see women occupying roles at all levels of the sport system, including in the top leadership positions. Such equality existed at the elite athlete level, where women made up 52 percent of the Game Plan Carded Athletes (athletes who were competing at the highest level nationally, with proven international success or potential to make a top 10 ranking in world competition). The same ratio was also present in team manager and chaperone appointments, where women comprised 51 percent of Games team staff. However, such equality did not exist for women in administrative and governance positions, where only 31 percent of paid administrative positions in National Sport Governing

Box 1
THE ACTION PROPOSALS
FOR GOVERNMENT

Participation
Overall, more Canadians should be encouraged to engage in physical activity. Specifically, there should be equal opportunity for participation in all physical activity programs, and women and girls should be encouraged to participate. Lower-income women should benefit from subsidized programs, and physical activity programs should be integrated into the corporate structure; at the same time, childcare services should be available to allow women to participate.

Coaching
Women's leadership programs should be supported. Government funding should be earmarked for a coaching development plan for girls and women. A joint survey between the FAS and the CAC should produce a directory of women coaches throughout Canada, and list coaching course and certification programs that are open and available to women. Federal and Provincial governments should give consideration to positions that could be filled by women with appropriate experience.

Administration
The NSOs should seek out and hire competent female sport administrators while also issuing a monthly publication for women working in the field. Audio-visual presentations should depict women in sport administration. Sports governing organizations should be encouraged to give more recognition to volunteer sports administrators.

Box 2
INEQUALITY IN THE NATIONAL
COACHING RANKS

Between 1972 and 1979, the Coaching Association of Canada (CAC) reported that only 25 percent of nationally ranked coaches were women. Furthermore, 55 percent of "predominantly female sports" were coached by women, but only 6 percent of "integrated sports" had female coaches. This inequality is especially startling since half of elite athletes were women.

The already paltry number of female coaches was further reduced through the selection process for national coaches for international Games and championships, when the representation of women coaches dropped from 24 to 15 percent in predominantly female sports and less than 2 percent for integrated sports. The peak level of female national coaches was reached in 1976 during the Montreal Olympic Games; that level dropped off to 13 percent and then 11 percent.

Bodies Organizations (NSGB, later changed to National Sport Organizations (NSOs)) were women; in volunteer governance positions, women accounted for 27 percent of all positions. The situation was also dire for nationally ranked coaches, especially in Games team staff, as highlighted in Box 2.

The very low number of women in high level coaching positions indicated a lack of equal opportunity in the selection process for coaching staff of international Games. In fact, the data collected for this survey indicated that the "glass ceiling" that excluded half the population from the higher echelons of leadership was well entrenched in the Canadian sport system.

The combined data on the percentage of women holding either coaching or administrative positions did not support the common assumption within the national sport system that equal opportunity existed for women. Indeed, most leaders interviewed for the survey did not think there was an under-representation of women in leadership positions or a need for a specific policy pertaining to women. At the same time, between 1972 and 1979, female Carded Athletes rose from just under 50 percent to over 50 percent, while the baseline level of female participation in sports across the provinces increased by as much as 300 percent, particularly in sports such as soccer. Despite this significant increase in female involvement in sport at the grassroots and elite levels, women were still not occupying more leadership positions. And the few advances that were made in this area during that time were essentially due to constant advocacy by a few women.

In short, the recommendations from the 1974 National Conference on Women in Sport had been completely disregarded by FAS and the National Sport Governing Bodies. Sport Canada and the Coaching Association of Canada had representatives on the hiring boards for coaches and administrators, but these appointments did not result in improved results. In fact, with no set standards or goals to increase the number of women in leadership positions, there was no incentive to increase these numbers or any commitment to recruit or hire women during the growth spurt in the Canadian sport system.

In 1977 the Working Paper Toward a National Policy on Fitness and Amateur Sport was tabled in the House of Commons. It was intended to generate feedback from the sport community across Canada to shape the eventual white paper: A National Policy on Amateur Sport, Partners in Pursuit of Excellence. However, the working paper contained only marginal mention of women in sport, thereby limiting the discussion on this issue. It was clear with the publication of this Fitness and Amateur Sport Branch policy paper that women in sport was not a priority and certainly not a policy determinant.

Two years later, in 1979, Status of Women Canada published its own document Towards Equality for Women, which specifically outlined "A Plan of Action," directing Fitness and Amateur Sport to address future policy and programming for women. The directives for the FAS Plan were to "encourage greater participation by women on all hiring boards with the Branch and the National Sport and Recreation Centre." This Status of Women initiative essentially forced FAS to make women in sport a priority. The political impetus for change, sadly, had to come from outside the Fitness and Amateur Sport Branch.

The results of my survey and research were published by Fitness and Amateur Sport in 1980 in the document Women in Sport in Canada: Leaders and Participants from a National Perspective. Armed with these data, a group of us gathered at McMaster University for a meeting of like-minded advocates for women in sport. This meeting gave birth to the Canadian Association for the Advancement of Women and Sport (CAAWS) in 1980.

The Women in Leadership Program was established within the Fitness and Amateur Sport Branch in 1981 as a result of the advocacy of CAAWS members and the ongoing commitment of the few women within the national sport system and Status of Women Canada. The resulting program for women in apprentice coaching and administrative positions gave aspiring young women greater opportunity to access careers in the national sport system. A directory of women in leadership positions was published in an effort to mobilize women within the system and develop a network for recruitment and hiring procedures. The lifespan of the program was somewhat vague, but CAAWS took on a more prominent role in advocating for women in sport leadership. As a founding member of CAAWS, I was so grateful and delighted to see that this organization sustained the programs and advocacy role necessary to carry the torch for women in sport in all capacities. It would be interesting to see how many of the women who participated in that program are now employed within the national sport system.

After completing this research project in 1981, I was hired as the Technical Coordinator for Judo Canada. I advocated for the Women's National Team, which received less than 10 percent of National Team funding from Sport Canada. This team was not considered a priority at the time, as women's judo was not an Olympic sport. I was viewed as a radical feminist on a mission for funding. At that time, I had the great honour of being a mentor to a highly talented national team athlete on the Women's Judo Team. She had aspirations of being a coach or technical administrator within the sport. The internship ended quietly, and I was "let go" in 1984 to be replaced by a male with more technical qualifications than I had (i.e., a black belt in judo). I had been tipped off by a Sport Canada consultant for the organization that the Executive was seeking a way to remove me from my position and by changing the job description and qualifications they were able to achieve that end. However, the female apprentice who did have a black belt was also not selected for the position, despite her extensive technical expertise and international experience. They succeeded in getting rid of us both. Discriminatory? It sure felt like it! I moved on to work at Sport Canada as a High Performance Quadrennial Planner, a position I loved and later regretted leaving in 1987 for an international sport management project, the 1989 Golden Oldies Rugby Festival. Thus morphed my short career in sport into event management!

RUNNING TO CATCH UP
Women in Sport Canada
Diane Palmason

I have two well-worn black cotton T-shirts from the 1980s that still hold a place of pride in my closet. The white print on one reads "Canadian Association for the Advancement of Women and Sport." The other reads "Women and Sport et les femmes / Ottawa." These shirts hark back to a time of my growing awareness of the inequities for women in my sport, athletics and road running, and in so many other sports as well. These inequities affected not just the participants but also the coaches, officials and administrators. What synchronicities led to an inactive mother of four becoming, eventually, the manager of the Women's Program in Sport Canada? As is often the case, the personal led to the political.

As a teenager in the 1950s, I was not allowed to compete in the middle and long distance for which I knew I was best suited. So I retired from running at the age of 17. Twenty-seven years later, inspired by a news report on the woman who won the first National Capital Marathon (NCM) in Ottawa, I started running again. One year later, May 1976, I ran the second NCM, along with several other women. That summer there was widespread coverage of the Olympic Games in Montreal. I watched and realized that not only was there no Olympic marathon for women, but there were not even any races longer than 1500 metres. Not much had changed since 1955. I resolved to mobilize the women runners I was meeting to begin lobbying the IOC to add the women's marathon to their program.

At about the same time, Kathrine Switzer, one of the first women to run the revered Boston Marathon, was gathering forces for a similar campaign from her US base. Her strategy included recruiting the Avon Corporation to sponsor women-only races all over the world, the goal being to convince the IOC that it wasn't just in America that women were excelling in distance running. In 1978 I ran the Avon Race that Kathrine brought to Ottawa. We met and agreed to join forces. In August 1980, I and 350 other women ran in the Avon Women's World Championships marathon in London, England on the same day that the men-only race was held in the Moscow Olympics. IOC dignitaries who witnessed this event were positively influenced, and by the next year the women's marathon had been added to the Summer Olympics program. On August 5, 1984, millions of TV viewers watched as 50 women, including three Canadians, demonstrated their strength, endurance and guts in the heat and humidity of Los Angeles. That first Olympic marathon was a "best moment for women and sport" for me.

Other events in the early 80s led to my steadily growing awareness of inequities for women in all sport. While participating in the Female Athlete Conference at Simon Fraser University in 1980, I met women academics, researchers and athletes who presented reports, statistics and stories on the lack of opportunity for girls and women at all levels of sport, from community playing fields to international competition. From this conference grew the initiative to form a national organization to address these problems. Meeting at McMaster University in 1981, a representative group of women from across Canada, plus two men, debated and finally settled on a name: the Canadian Association for the Advancement of Women and Sport (CAAWS). This was the source of the words on one of my prized T-shirts. The founders also agreed on a mission "to promote, develop and advocate a feminist perspective on women and sport." For the next five years, I collaborated with this pioneering group of women, serving as a member of the Board of Directors until 1986.

A key focus for the Association in those early years was the collection of data on the utilization of publicly funded sports programs and facilities. Studies in various communities confirmed the casual observation that girls and women were underserved, with girls in the 13 to 17 age bracket having particularly low rates of participation. Among the communities not just taking count, but actually initiating plans to reverse these figures, was the City of Ottawa. With support from City Council as well as staff members of the city's Department of Parks and Recreation, the Women and Sport et les femmes program was introduced, specifically targeting these inactive teenagers. As one of the CAAWS members living in Ottawa, I was involved with this program, acquiring my second prized T-shirt. The initiative proved so successful that it was decided to draft a "how-to" resource to assist other communities in reaching out to so many girls who were previously inactive. Thus the "On the Move" kit was created, receiving design and editing support from Canada's Fitness and Amateur Sport (FAS) Women's Program, a program I came to manage in 1986.

My steps to that position were set in motion with the establishment in the early 80s of the FAS Women's Program, another initiative resulting, indirectly, from the Female Athlete conference. Research at the federal level had indicated that women were seriously underrepresented in the decision-making process of National Sport Organizations (NSOs). These and other findings about women's lack of opportunities in all aspects of NSO activities led to the development of two major components of the Women's Program: the National Association Contributions Program (NACP) and the Internship Program for Women Athletes. This latter opportunity had a direct appeal for me. By 1983, I had grown disillusioned with my role at the Canadian Medical Association and enrolled in a Health Administration program at the University of Ottawa. The internship that the program offered me, a position in a long-term care facility, had no appeal. So I applied to the 1983-84 Internship Program, was accepted, and found myself working for the Canadian Track and Field Association (CTFA—now Athletics Canada). When the year of support from the Women's Program ended, I stayed on in a research and writing role. Now inside the NSO environment, I next connected with the Canadian Amateur Rowing Association (CARA—now Rowing Canada). In that office, I took over as the Acting Executive Director, another opportunity to observe the interaction between paid and volunteer officials and the exercise of power and decision-making within an NSO. All of this was practical experience I called upon, particularly with regard to the NACP, when I agreed to accept the role of Manager of the Women's Program in 1986.

The position had become vacant after the resignation of

Kathy McDonald. During Kathy's tenure, she had advanced the implementation of the recommendations for the formation of the Program in a number of ways, not the least of which was the drafting of what became the Sport Canada Policy on Women in Sport. With the collaboration of Abby Hoffman, Director General of Sport Canada at the time, Assistant Director Sue Neill, and others, Kathy oversaw the development of the policy statements and implementation plans in 12 areas: Policy and Program Development, Sport Stratification, Sport Infrastructure, Leadership Development, High Performance Competition, Participation Development, Resource Allocation, Liaison, Research, Education, Promotion and Advocacy. As her successor, my role was to prepare the final document for publication and then to integrate its recommendations into the planning process for the Women's Program. The Policy provided a framework for assessing the applications that came from NSOs to the NACP, for example, helping determine how a specific proposal met the needs for leadership or participation development in a sport. It gave the Women's Program additional legitimacy in dealings with the leadership of NSOs; and it also set standards against which the Program Manager could ask an NSO to measure its progress toward the Policy's stated goal of attaining equality for women in sport.

The existence of the Women's Program contributed to an increased awareness of the need for more opportunities for women throughout the sport system, but it was not the only source of pressure for change. Besides the activities of CAAWS, there was the Canadian Advisory Council on the Status of Women, which provided support for the publication of *Fair Ball: Towards Sex Equality in Canadian Sport*, written by M. Ann Hall and Dorothy Richardson in 1982. Some provincial and municipal governments conducted their own assessments, and women leaders in sport organizations at the provincial as well as national levels pushed for changes in funding and other resource allocations. A prime example was the efforts of women in provincial hockey associations to lobby for international competition opportunities. The eventual outcome was another "best moment for women in sport": the hosting of the First

Women's World Ice Hockey Championships in Ottawa in January 1990. When the word got out about the quality of hockey being played at this tournament, the lineup for tickets for the championship game stretched for two city blocks.

Other successes in those years included initiatives to support women as coaches, with Rowing Canada leading the way. In soccer, progress was made in providing training for former athletes to obtain officiating certification. Women's committees were formed, not only in specific sport organizations but also in related associations such as the Sport Medicine Council of Canada. By the time I left Sport Canada to take up a coaching career in Colorado, the momentum for increased participation by girls and women in all areas of sport had become unstoppable. It continues to this day, and is still needed, as the issues and problems confronted by women shift and change both in sport and in all areas of human endeavour.

GAINING MOMENTUM:
The Formation of the Canadian Association for the Advancement of Women and Sport and Physical Activity (CAAWS) 1981
Karin Lofstrom

The decades between 1960 and 2010 saw many firsts for girls and women in sport and physical activity. The Canadian Association for the Advancement of Women and Sport and Physical Activity, CAAWS as it is commonly known, was the catalyst for much of this progress. CAAWS has always been a feminist organization, born from the same period that the *Canadian Charter of Rights and Freedoms* became a reality in 1982. Indeed, the Charter's equality section, s.15, has had implications for all of Canada and CAAWS specifically. The Association's objective has always been clear: the equitable participation of girls and women at all levels and in all areas of the Canadian sport and physical activity system as athletes, participants, leaders, officials, coaches and trainers.

In the two decades before CAAWS was founded, the climate in the sport world was not accepting of difference. Girls and women who insisted on an equitable sport system were outsiders. They were considered odd, tomboys, even marginal. There was no room for women in professional sport. Women did not run marathons. Women were meant to study home economics, and be teachers, nurses or secretaries. Women did not sweat. In fact, by its very nature, physical activity was "unfeminine." Sport for girls and women was not on the national agenda. It was not an issue and the majority considered the status quo acceptable. Even the women's movement did not see sport as important.

In the decades since CAAWS was founded, gender equity in sport has been tackled head on. Many challenges continue to exist, but at the same time, girls and women have celebrated incredible victories. Canadian women participate in sport in unprecedented numbers. At the last Winter Olympic Games hosted in Canada, women enjoyed incredible successes on the podium. However, women coaches are barely visible. CAAWS has helped achieve progress, but this advancement is part of a continuum.

Before CAAWS was formed, many battles and victories were fought on an individual and small-group level. At a certain point, women leaders decided that a national body was needed to effect change at a national level. The idea was that this body would encourage a gradual societal shift benefiting girls and women, and in the long run society as a whole, because more Canadians would be active as leaders and participants.

Women, and some men, who were agents of progressive change throughout Canadian society, started asking questions. Why should the status quo be acceptable? Why did girls and women have less opportunity than boys and men? They knew equity would have to be achieved strategically, suffering setbacks and challenges, and requiring a great deal of effort, exchange of ideas and even some conflict. These leaders would become the founding mothers of CAAWS in 1981, along with a few male allies.

Many people in the sport community thought women's sport was not important. CAAWS worked with those who wanted to see progress. The Association grew slowly and advocated strategically. It entrenched values and developed tools and resources, and promoted a more equitable system. It pointed out the systemic barriers while being part of the system, which was no easy task. The Association worked with a small staff and budget and a core group of sport leaders across Canada who volunteered their time to support progressive change. They achieved results but also faced animosity from those who supported the status quo.

Early on, CAAWS inspired many women who realized they were not alone in their frustration over what was accepted as the natural order or in their personal goals for improving society. The leaders of the Association knew they could make a difference to individual and large groups of women, and this motivated them. The challenges were monumental because they had to poke holes in the common (mis)conception that sport was already equitable.

One reason CAAWS was instrumental in spearheading positive change was because it created a pocket of valuable programs and resources that it perfected over the years and shared with the Canadian sport community and partners. CAAWS led a nationally coordinated effort to develop policies, strategic communications vehicles and promotion around gender equity. It then invited all Canadians to participate in a discussion on sport and excellence—which by definition had to include girls and women. It also moved the issue of women in sport out of the personal and asked for better practices in general. The ripple effect from the development tools CAAWS created, such as workshops, was significant.

Once "women and sport" was on the national sport agenda, CAAWS worked hard to chart its course and define objectives that would have the greatest impact. Key concerns were how to identify the underlying issues and determine the Association's strategy around them. At the same time, over the decades CAAWS developed an open resource library that includes a focus on increasing girls' participation with programs like On the Move. Furthermore, CAAWS created women and leadership workshops and publications, such as *Towards Gender Equity For*

Women In Sport: A Handbook for Sport Organizations. CAAWS has also tackled issues that had previously been largely ignored, including sexual harassment and homophobia in sport. By broaching these topics, dialogue has opened up, contributing to Canada's reputation as a world leader in human rights in sport.

It is one thing to point out the inequities in a society and quite another to develop a roadmap to positive change. Over the decades, CAAWS has helped realize concrete change—but this has been a slow and gradual process that has included many challenges along the way. CAAWS leaders have focused on making women and sport a national issue. They sent the message that if girls and women could succeed in sport, they could succeed everywhere.

CAAWS has welcomed many allies over the years. Together, CAAWS and its partners have increased understanding that access to sport and physical activity is a human rights issue. In fact, since its inception in 1981, CAAWS has made a concerted effort to work with Sport Canada, national sport and multi-sport federations, provinces, associations and groups. It has also collaborated with the broader women's movement, as well as various governments and organizations. The Association has participated in key events and conferences, such as the historic International Association of Physical Education & Sport for Girls and Women (IAPESGW) conference that resulted in a breakaway group, which founded Women Sport International. As a result of this work, the contributions that girls and women made to sport from 1960 to 2010 have created a stronger national sport system.

Over the years, CAAWS has also partnered and developed resources critical to gender equity with key players, such as the Coaching Association of Canada, the Canadian Interuniversity Athletic Union (now Canadian Interuniversity Sport), the Canadian Colleges Athletic Association, the Canadian Association for Health, Physical Education, Recreation and Dance (now PHE Canada), the Harassment and Abuse in Sport Collective, as well as Health Canada and the Public Health Agency of Canada.

CAAWS has benefited from cross-fertilization with organizations like the Women's Legal Education and Action Fund (LEAF), the National Action Committee on the Status of Women (NAC), as well as with movements such as the gay rights movement and aspects of the women's health movement such as the Healthsharing Regina Women's Health Collective. All of these partnerships have been essential in influencing societal change.

The strong leadership and vision of some of the best sport leaders in Canada have shaped CAAWS over the decades. There are so many brilliant women who invested their time and energy because they wanted to achieve a high standard of excellence for their shared vision of fundamental equality for all. They knew CAAWS would champion this vision with intelligence and skill and improve the lives of girls and women. When it comes to CAAWS leadership, it would be unfair to mention one name without mentioning them all. However, a visit to the CAAWS website is worth the time as it tracks the history, names and stories of the founding members.

A major strength of CAAWS is its willingness to accept challenges head on and to work with integrity. For example, over the years CAAWS has developed solid relationships with Aboriginal communities, partnering with them to improve opportunities for girls and women to participate in sport and physical activity. As our population has aged, the Association has also begun to create resources for women 55 to 70+, a group that was largely invisible to the sport system. Since the turn of the century, CAAWS has continued to embrace topics that others may not want to face because they are seen as marginal, such as gender testing, homophobia and the lack of women coaches. The Association continues to work on building excellence within our sport system and with other partners in sport and physical activity.

As CAAWS explores how to best contribute to excellence, it has been part of a greater discussion and respectful debate with the sport community on defining excellence. From its early days, CAAWS has been ahead of the curve by normalizing diversity. It said it is OK to be a girl and play hockey. We can laugh at this idea now, but in 1960 this was a battle. More recently, in 2010, women and Olympic ski jumping was the battle. CAAWS has always supported these girls and women, as well as providing them with insight and leadership.

Although CAAWS was created to effect change for Canadians, its reach and reputation have gone beyond our borders to make sport and physical activity more accessible and safe to girls and women in many nations. The Association has become respected internationally and its members are often asked to speak at conferences, to share policies and resources. CAAWS has been involved in creating international legacies. It has shared best practices for gender equity and inclusion at the 1994 Commonwealth Games in Victoria and the CAAWS Skills Day at the 2002 IWG World Women and Sport conference in Montreal.

Good intentions, hard work and a commitment to change took CAAWS from where it was (a small group of women who knew they could improve the system by making it more equitable) — to where it is now, as a respected leader in sport and physical activity. The decades between 1960 and 2010 have been a journey of advocacy, advances and accomplishment. Participation in sport and physical activity for girls and women is on the rise. However, women are still highly underrepresented in leadership roles. The world has become even more complex. Some young girls are denied opportunity to play sports because they wear a headscarf; gender testing can be a humiliating, internationally-communicated experience; obesity is on the rise in Canada. From 1960 to 2010, we were on a continuum of progressive change. We are still on that continuum … and unfortunately there is still a lot of work to do.

With contributions from Marion Lay and Phyllis Berck, both previous Chairs of CAAWS.

FOR SHE WHO IS NOT THERE: ON THE MOVE
Sydney Millar

On the Move is a national initiative founded on the fact that a sector of the population is missing out on the benefits that come from sport and physical activity. Studies have shown that girls and young women understand the importance of physical activity to their health and want to increase their participation in it. However, their low participation rates in such activity suggest that social and systemic barriers are preventing them from engaging to the fullest extent.

The underlying premise of On the Move is to work towards attaining gender equity in sport and physical activity. This means providing girls and young women with access to a full range of opportunities and choices that meet their needs and enable them to achieve the social, psychological and physical benefits of sport and physical activity. To do so, On the Move works at the organizational level to address barriers and create positive environments where girls and young women can make positive choices and build a foundation for active living.

Specifically, this initiative is designed to increase the opportunities for inactive girls and young women ages 9-18, to participate and lead in sport and physical activity. It does this in two ways. First, it helps practitioners increase girls' and women's physical activity through the creation of fun-filled, supportive, female-only, recreational sport and physical activity programs. Based on the experiences of On the Move programs across Canada, the user-friendly *On the Move Handbook*, the initiative's foundation document, discusses the issues and barriers that girls and women face in their participation and provides information about program design and implementation, leadership, promotion and building community support. Second, On the Move has created a national network of practitioners involved in female-only programming, as well as individuals and organizations concerned with the health and well-being of girls and women. The network is a resource for information on the importance of increasing girls' and women's participation, and shares research, events and program successes and challenges.

The On the Move concept is guided by four principles. First, the program is conceptual, not prescriptive. Structured time-lines and rigid program design have been purposefully avoided to allow each community to respond to the unique needs and interests of girls and young women. This has allowed On the Move programs to reach a wide demographic of participants—pre-teens, teenagers, recent immigrants, Aboriginal peoples, those living in poverty and inactive females. Second, On the Move is participant-driven. The initiative depends on collaboration between service providers and participants. Girls and young women have a wide variety of skills, needs and interests. Involving them in program planning and implementation will directly contribute to success and provide participants with positive experiences upon which to develop a foundation for active living. Third, On the Move is programming for she who is not there.

While the existing sport and physical activity system offers many girls and women positive recreation experiences, the majority are considered inactive. Therefore, On the Move programs are designed to attract inactive girls and young women and provide them with positive experience. Finally, On the Move is not based on supply and demand. Since many girls and young women have had few or negative experiences with sport and physical activity, they are not likely to demand more of the same programs, nor are they in a position to demand programs that do meet their needs. The result is a lack of recreation programs for this group. Service providers need to find other success indicators to support special efforts like On the Move.

On the Move was launched nationally in 1994, based on the learnings from girls-only programs in Ottawa and Port Coquitlam. After their overwhelming success, and based on the abundance of research about the lack of programming for girls and young women, Sport Canada agreed to support CAAWS in its involvement in this positive and progressive initiative. On the Move programs have since been organized in almost every province and territory in Canada.

On the Move has grown over the years to include other demographics and focuses. For instance, the initiative Team Spirit: Aboriginal Girls in Sport and Aboriginal On the Move, were national, multi-year projects to increase community sport opportunities for Aboriginal girls and young women (ages 9-18). Communities received funding to develop and implement community sport and healthy living programs for Aboriginal girls and young women, increase their capacity to address the needs and interests of this target group, and raise the profile of female Aboriginal leaders and role models.

Similarly, the CAAWS Newcomer On the Move Project was designed to address disparities in the availability and utilization of physical activity and sport opportunities for newcomer girls and young women. This was started to address the underrepresentation of immigrant and minority girls and women in the Canadian sport and recreation system. Most recently, a research project led by CAAWS examined the sport and physical activity experiences of racialized girls and young women.

CAAWS involvement in the Canadian Active After School Partnership (CAASP), designed to increase healthy living opportunities during the after-school time period, will ensure the needs of girls and young women are integrated into the creation of quality active after-school programs. The after-school time period, between 3pm and 6pm, is an important opportunity for children and youth to be physically active—approximately 50 percent of total daily steps taken by children and youth occur during this time. By increasing quality opportunities for children and youth to be physically active during this period, CAASP activities will contribute to addressing rising rates of physical inactivity and obesity amongst children and youth.

On the Move has been influential in increasing awareness and understanding of the needs, interests and experiences of diverse girls and young women. However, continued low levels of physical activity amongst this target group indicate the need for further work. In the 2000s, "girls' programs" was a trendy topic in recreation programming, but other target groups have recently pushed girls and young women down the priority list. CAAWS works with a variety of sport and physical activity service providers and healthy living advocates to ensure that girls and young women stay relevant in the minds of policymakers and programmers.

WOMEN, LET THE GAMES BEGIN!
In Conversation with Sue Hylland
Jennifer Hughes

The year was 1967 and all across the country organizations were putting on special celebrations to mark Canada's Centennial. After 100 years, our young nation was having a big birthday party and the whole country was invited. One exciting part of this celebration was the very first Canada Games, held in Quebec City in February 1967. At these Games, 1,800 young athletes from 10 provinces and two territories came together to compete in 15 different sports. Since that first year, the Canada Games have become the country's largest multi-sport competition for young, amateur-only athletes. Held every two years and alternating between summer and winter games, athletes representing each province and territory compete against each other under the motto "Unity through Sport."

The Games have a history of being a springboard for some of Canada's most illustrious champions, and have seen numerous alumni, both male and female, go on to win Olympic medals and other national and international competitions. The role of the Games as a groomer of future champions, and as a celebration of young Canadian athletes, is undeniable. The Games have also produced some of the country's most prominent female champions. Colleen Jones (Team Nova Scotia, 1979), Hayley Wickenheiser (Team Alberta, 1991), Catriona Le May Doan (Team Saskatchewan, 1983, 1987, 1993), Jennifer Botterill (Team Manitoba, 1995) and Jenn Heil (Team Alberta, 1999) are just a few of their strongest success stories.

"I have been blessed with a great deal of success as an athlete, from the Olympic Games, to World Championships, to World Records, but I can say, with all sincerity, that one of my most cherished memories is participating at the Canada Games."

– CATRIONA LE MAY DOAN, *Canada Games alumnus (Team Saskatchewan, 1983, 1987, 1993) and two-time Olympic Gold Medalist*

"Playing in the Canada Games gave me some extremely valuable experience in a multi-sport event. It gave me a taste of the environment, and motivated me to strive to the next level. I remember loving the energy and the atmosphere!"

– JENNIFER BOTTERILL, *Canada Games alumnus (Team Manitoba, 1995) and three-time Olympic Gold Medalist (Women's Hockey)*

Perhaps the strongest success story to come from the Canada Games over the years is the advancement of girls and women in sports in general. In the late 1980s and early 1990s, gender equity policies for both sports selection (athletes) and coaching helped drive change towards a more balanced playing field — both literally and figuratively — at the Canada Games. Prior to these new policies, from the years 1967 to 1989, male sports, and therefore athletes, dominated the Games. The gender imbalance was even more remarkable at the coaching level.

"There was a marked imbalance in the number of participant opportunities (around 60 percent male, 40 percent female), and coaches were probably closer to 80 percent male and 20 percent female in the 70s and early 80s. The only sports that had a clear majority of women coaches were generally those practiced exclusively by women: synchronized swimming, rhythmic gymnastics, field hockey. Even women's artistic gymnastics had many male coaches. Ringette was a surprise in how many male coaches there were."

– ANDRÉ GALLANT, *Director of Sport, Canada Games, 1991-2008*

To bring about more equal opportunity for Canada's young athletes, sport selection quotas were implemented for the 1989 (summer, Saskatoon) and 1991 (winter, Prince Edward Island) Canada Games. Equity was achieved when sport selection was combined across the winter and summer Games, due to some sports favouring one gender over the other. For example, there were more male athletes in the summer Games (due to baseball and rugby being male-only) and more female athletes in the winter games (with female-only synchronized swimming and ringette on the roster). Today, the balance of gender stands at approximately 51 percent male and 49 percent female athletes. Actual numbers for the 2011 winter Canada Games in Halifax showed 1,212 male and 1,115 female athletes—proof of a strong and lasting shift in balance as a result of the policies that were put in place 20 years before.

In 1987 the Canada Games developed a new coaching policy implemented at both the 1989 and 1991 Games, which introduced quotas for gender balance at the coaching level as well. The policy stated that teams with female athletes must have at least one female coach (and likewise, teams with male athletes must have at least one male coach). Such a seemingly simple policy initially met with resistance. Some protest was philosophical, but mostly overwhelmingly practical, with the provinces and national sports organizations being concerned that there simply were not enough qualified female coaches. In the first few years of the new policy being in place, some allowances were made and the challenges of training were overcome in cooperation with the National Coaching Certification Program, the National Sports Organizations and the Provincial Sports Organizations.

The entire system adapted quickly and, eventually, enthusiastically. Coaching ratios are now at 70 percent male, 30 percent female for summer Games (a ratio that reflects the fact that baseball has all male coaches), and 60 percent male, 40 percent female for winter Games (again, thanks to sports like synchronized swimming and ringette). At the 2011 Canada Winter Games in Halifax, there were 276 male and 182 female coaches. This shows a huge positive change over time. Even so, there is still room for improvement.

"From the late 90s to the 2005 and 2007 Games, the percentage of female coaches held steady, and the percentage of fully certified at Level 3 held steady. There was perhaps incremental progress, but nothing as dramatic as the first few years. The reality is that women are still the primary care givers to their children, and thus their coaching careers are interrupted, or ended early. Sexism may still play a role, but less so, or maybe just less overtly now. The policy and program supports are in place to help women succeed."

– ANDRÉ GALLANT, *Director of Sport, Canada Games, 1991-2008*

Following the new coaching policy, the Canada Games sought to provide a program to support the development of women as coaches, which would not only help their policies on a practical level, but also drive a long-term system change toward greater equity in the future for Canadian women in sports. The Women in Coaching Program launched with the 2005 summer Canada Games in Regina, Saskatchewan, as a joint initiative of the Coaching Association of Canada, the Provincial/Territorial Coaching Representatives and the Canada Games Council. This national campaign seeks to increase the number of coaching opportunities for women at all levels of sport. The program matches apprentice coaches with mentor coaches throughout the Games.

To date, 61 coaches from 24 sports have participated in the program. The hugely positive impact that the Women in Coaching Program has had on its participants is undeniable. Many have launched successful coaching careers, and gone on to coach at the national and international level.

"Today, the Canada Games Women in Coaching Program is an integral part of the Games experience."
– SUE HYLLAND, *President and CEO, Canada Games*

"The Canada Games Women in Coaching Program helped me define a clear vision of my objectives, values and philosophy as a coach. The program gave me confidence in my coaching abilities and effective networking tools. It also gave me the opportunity to build relationships with several coaches from different sports and levels. Finally, it was a pleasure to fully participate as a coach in a major competition like the Games and to see one of our athletes win two medals. I hope that all women coaches can benefit from the support and experience of this program."

– MANON LOSIER, *2011 Apprentice Coach, Cross Country Skiing*

"Being able to participate in the 2011 Canada Winter Games as an Apprentice Coach was an amazing experience. It was my first time at the Games and I wouldn't have been able to go that year, if not for the program. Since February 2011, I have coached at two national championships (for the BC Provincial Team), and I started working for the BC Speed Skating Association as the Technical Director. The program gave me the opportunity to 'get my foot in the door' at a higher level."

– CHRISTINA ACTON, *2011 Apprentice Coach, Speed Skating*

In 2002 the Canada Games Council took another leap into the future when Sue Hylland became the first female President and CEO. An alumnus of the Canada Games (Team Quebec, 1979), she had been the Executive Director for the Canadian Association for the Advancement of Women and Sport and Physical Activity and spent 18 years with the Canadian Olympic Committee. And while many of the gender equity policies for athletes and coaches were developed prior to her arrival, Hylland has continued this progression in other areas of Canada Games operations.

"My experience at CAAWS definitely helped me to better examine and address gender issues in many other areas, such as setting hosting standards for communities winning the right to host the Games that would reflect gender equality and address gender sensitivities. We have advanced in areas such as: developing a mascot that is gender neutral; using appropriate quantities and visibly acceptable photos in all communications; having appropriate gender representation and diversity on Canada Games and Host Society Boards; developing new policies such as our Support for Nursing Coaches to assist new mothers; and ensuring a connection between CAAWS and the Canada Games through establishment

of an MOU and delivery of CAAWS Women in Leadership sessions to the many women engaged in volunteering with a host society. There is a new mindset within the Games family that has been set on all gender issues which is very positive. We have progressed."
– SUE HYLLAND, *President and CEO, Canada Games*

As a strong champion of women in sports, Hylland has witnessed the monumental change of the last 35 years as an athlete, coach and leader.

"Over the last 25 to 30 years, there has been much greater awareness and more opportunities for young girls in sport. When my daughter was 9, she was playing competitive hockey, basketball and soccer. When I was 9, I was waking up at 6 a.m. to go watch my brother at his hockey practice! What a difference. We have a lot to celebrate."
– SUE HYLLAND, *President and CEO, Canada Games*

WAIT A MINUTE, THIS ISN'T EQUAL
In Conversation with Pat Hunt
Sheila Robertson

These days, girls and women fill Canada's playing fields, enjoying and competing in virtually every sport. But even as recently as the 1980s, active girls and women were a rare sight, with organized sport, physical activity and recreation almost exclusively the domain of boys and men. This status quo was for many years largely accepted. However, as second wave feminism swept across Canada, there was inevitably an impact in these areas, with lasting and important consequences.

The flourishing scene we know today has its roots in Girls n' Women and Sport (GWS), a City of Ottawa initiative endorsed by City Council and initiated in 1985 after two years of research and planning. The initiative can be traced back to a City-School Boards Liaison Committee sub-committee composed of representatives of the various school boards, the regional office of the Ministry of Education and community and City of Ottawa representatives. Out of this came the Women and Sport Committee, an advisory group that surprisingly reported in 1983, "teachers, coaches and principals ... [perceived] that there was no discrepancy in participation levels between girls and boys." However, the data collected proved that this perception was incorrect.

Those working in the field, particularly the City of Ottawa's Parks and Recreation Branch, also knew this summary to be untrue. Consequently, in 1984, Jeanette St. Amour, a director of the Branch, undertook a study for the city and found that, contrary to the advisory group's report, "girls' participation rates were nowhere near that of their male counterparts." In fact referring to Sara Dorken's 2011 dissertation, Pat Hunt recalled that "for every five males participating in sport in the city, there were correspondingly only two females" in group-oriented activities, competitive and inexpensive programs. "Jeanette's meticulous research showed clearly that girls were under-served," says Pat Hunt, who led GWS until she retired in 1995. "Girls were mostly participating in high-priced individual activities like figure skating and gymnastics rather than the lower-priced team sports such as basketball and softball and recreational activities."

The result of St. Amour's research was a pilot program backed by leaders who were "skilled, articulate, committed women in significant political positions who helped us take Jeanette's research, vision, political wisdom and leadership and build a program," says Hunt.

Hurdles were inevitable. Not surprisingly there were those who questioned a program for girls, including community centre staff, politicians, recreation staff at all levels and volunteers who were finding their gym time squeezed because of the new program. "Why not for boys?" was a frequent query. Having the research showing the need was invaluable in responding to the criticism.

Other questions focused on the funding level. "Certain

people feared losing some of their resources to the GWS, and so there was a little jealousy, a lack of understanding and a lack of awareness," says Hunt. Others were angered by the additional financial support for promotion, a rarity in the recreation field where publicizing programs is under-funded. "We did a lot of work in planning and delivering programs, but never had the funding to really promote them the way they should be. In this instance, we did! We had really strong promotion with signs on buses, newspaper coverage and ads on radio and television."

Hunt and her staff were learning important lessons as they went along, not least of all, the importance of building understanding, "a huge first step." She adds: "I wonder, when I look back, if we should have spent more time doing that. But we didn't have time. We had the green light and we had to go ahead. Our feeling was that those who were resistant would come along if they saw success, but we constantly had to make our case."

Despite the opposition, community centres seemed to be natural partners as GWS took shape with Hunt's two-woman staff preparing to offer programs and providing liaison and support. "Yes, there was lots of resistance to coming on board and a resistance to understanding this opportunity and the responsibility that came with it," says Hunt. Undaunted, they began by developing a "Basketball Hoops Day." Success came quickly and before long, it was mandated that every community centre in the city have a girls and women in sport program. Hunt says that while it might have been easier to concentrate on a handful of sure-bet community centres, this approach was overruled by the belief that in order to change the mindset each and every girl in the city had to be given an opportunity to participate, in particular those who would never make a school or community team.

Along with the challenge of encouraging community centre staff's cooperation came a number of other issues. These included the girls' unfamiliarity with sports' rules and a lack of skills, access to playing facilities and maintaining stable schedules. Pat quotes Sara Dorken again: "An unanticipated barrier ... in its initial stages was the attitudes of those for whom the programs were created." Hunt recalls getting [them] to understand that there was a place for them in sport and that they were welcomed and encouraged in this program was a huge barrier that needed jumping. On the plus side, the city's generous subsidy program was a significant factor in enabling many girls and women to participate.

It was a learning process for everyone concerned. "We had to do a lot of skill building so the girls would have the confidence to play," says Hunt, adding that ongoing encouragement was essential. "Also, the sport language – 'you throw like a girl' – was so loaded that it created an inhospitable environment for girls to participate, so we used the language of the Canadian Association for the Advancement of Women and Sport and Physical Activity (CAAWS) that urged girls to 'Get onto the playing field.'" The GWS personnel were a determined lot and met each issue headlong, reassured by the overwhelming response to the program in terms of registration but also, importantly, of participation.

An unexpected outcome of all the promotion was the demand from women to be included. Hunt reports telephone calls from women saying, "I'd like to play volleyball. I haven't played for 20 years. I loved it and there's never been any volleyball for me." And: "Can I play basketball? I haven't played in 15 years. Ever since I left high school, I've wanted to play and there's been nothing for me." The result was a very strong women's component to GWS. It was, says Hunt, an untapped market. "The need was out there and we told that to the decision makers. We believed including the women would be a return on investment—and it certainly was!"

Another catalyst was the 1990 women's ice hockey world championship. Canada played the United States for gold at Ottawa's Civic Centre, winning 5-2. "Our registration for hockey went through the roof and so, of course, did the demand for ice time, the purview of the Minor Hockey Associations," says Hunt. "We got involved in re-writing the ice allocation policy, another important step in creating change."

Beginning in the early 1970s, Hunt found herself evolving from her roles as a middle-class wife and at-home mother of three children into an ardent feminist. Consciousness-raising had become prevalent and feminists such as Betty Friedan were constantly in the news. "I began to think more and more about how all of this had an impact on me and where my place was, as well as the place of my daughter, my sons, and my husband." She was the first mother on her street to have a job outside the home (a part-time position with the Nepean Parks and Recreation Department where she first met St. Amour, who would become her director at the City of Ottawa) and encountered subtle impressions from neighbouring mothers that she was abandoning her children. "That's how new it was in the suburbs where we lived," she says.

By 1979, her metamorphosis was completed after encountering situations as a community centre director in a low-income neighbourhood. "Every day I was part of a system of inequity for women," she says. "It was a daily challenge to sort through what these mostly single mother-led families were facing systemically. So, as I was unfolding as a feminist, so were many women I got to know. Those of us who were involved in sport and recreation were shaking our heads and saying, 'Wait a minute! This isn't equal by any stretch of the imagination.'"

Hunt's responsibility as director of GWS paralleled her involvement with CAAWS, first as a member of the board of directors and later as a contractor. Ottawa-based CAAWS, a "national non-profit organization dedicated to creating an equitable sport and physical activity system in which girls and women are actively engaged as participants and leaders," was a natural partner for GWS. It was engaged in identifying low participation rates nationally and was also the prime advocate for accessible sport and physical activity.

Shortly after GWS was up and running, a similar program began in Port Coquitlam, with much the same results as the Ottawa program. The overwhelming success of both convinced Sport Canada, through its Women's Program, to provide support. Its policy on women in sport "recognized that increased participation of girls and women in 'grassroots,' community-level sport programs is the best base on which to build improved participation and involvement at all levels of the sport system."

With financial support from Sport Canada, CAAWS collaborated with PROMOTION Plus, the BC organization for Girls and Women in Physical Activity and Sport, to pilot programs modelled on GWS and Port Coquitlam in 10 communities throughout the province. Learnings from the pilots were compiled into a practical handbook, launched in 1994, that provided the foundation for a national On the Move initiative, established to increase the participation of inactive girls and young women, ages 9 to 18, in sport and physical activity. Nowadays, successful On the Move programs are running in almost every province and territory.

Today, GWS is mainstreamed and integrated into the regular flow of programs. With the slogan, "Everyone Gets to Play," it continues to offer over 6,000 Ottawa area girls and women "quality, fun, and safe opportunities for the girls and women of Ottawa to participate in all sorts of sports and physical activity."

Hunt says with pride that Ottawa was the first community that recognized inequity in programs, facilities and staffing and the first to take action on the inequities through GWS, the first program of its kind at the municipal level. She and her staff were very proud to be the first community in Canada to speak about the inequality of girls and women in sport and physical activity, to develop an initiative, to find the resources and to model strong advocacy of communities taking responsibility. "If your mandate as a recreation branch is to serve all members of your community, then girls and women must be included," she says.

> "Never doubt that a small group of thoughtful, committed citizens can change the world. Indeed, it's the only thing that ever has."
> – MARGARET MEAD

Citing Margaret Mead in describing the importance of GWS, Hunt says that change "usually takes a small group of visionaries, people who care passionately about an issue, who are committed to whatever that change may be, are prepared to go out on a limb and stay the course, and who don't back down. It's that initial sparkplug, and it's having the tools to do the job, and it's understanding the steps needed to work towards achieving the vision. 'Who do they need to partner with? Who needs to be on board? What kind of language do they use to excite people about the vision?' GWS, like CAAWS, had a small group of committed people who didn't take no for an answer, who stayed the course, brought like-minded people together, developed the skills and the tools, found the role models, and celebrated successes."

D'INCONNUE À ALLIÉE
Égale Action, sport et équité
Élaine Lauzon et Guylaine Demers

C'est en janvier de l'année 2000 que la fondatrice d'Égale Action, Sylvie Béliveau, approcha quelques collègues en sport et en activité physique afin d'échanger sur la problématique qu'elle percevait et vivait en tant que femme dans son milieu sportif. Cette démarche allait devenir la première étape de la petite histoire d'un grand projet. Un long périple que celui de ces quelques femmes convaincues qui décidèrent alors de poursuivre leurs rencontres. Au départ, elles se sont réunies afin d'établir les points communs qui ressortaient de leurs expériences respectives. Chacune de leur côté, elles avaient rencontré, vécu et traversé des obstacles dans leur milieu. Elles ont pensé que sans doute d'autres femmes vivaient la même situation et apprécieraient sûrement recevoir l'aide et le support qui leur permettraient de mieux se réaliser en sport et en activité physique. C'est ainsi que ce groupe de femmes a établi une stratégie de démarrage et approché l'instance politique de l'époque responsable du loisir et du sport au Québec dans l'espoir qu'il reconnaîtrait la légitimité de la démarche. De cette initiative est née une large consultation en région auprès des femmes ainsi que de la direction générale de fédérations sportives et d'organismes du milieu du sport, de l'activité physique et du loisir. Cette démarche, échelonnée sur une période d'un an, a permis de déterminer les besoins concrets des femmes et de confirmer le bien-fondé d'une association qui ouvrit officiellement ses portes en juin 2001.

La mise en place d'un organisme quel qu'il soit demande

à coup sûr le soutien de partenaires et l'appui de personnes engagées. Égale Action ne fait pas exception à cette règle. Sur sa route vers l'obtention d'une reconnaissance officielle, Égale Action a pu compter en première ligne sur l'engagement du groupe de femmes de départ, le soutien financier du ministère de l'Éducation, du Loisir et du Sport (MELS) et de Sports-Québec pour l'utilisation de ses ressources matérielles, certains services administratifs ainsi qu'un espace de travail. La consultation aura également mis sur la route d'Égale Action plusieurs personnes intéressées (hommes et femmes) qui ont appuyé la démarche par leur participation active aux diverses consultations et comités. Quelques organismes se sont également joints au mouvement et ont fait sentir leur présence au moment du lancement officiel de l'organisme en appui à Égale Action et à sa mission; notamment le Centre National Multisport-Montréal (CNMM), le Conseil du statut de la femme et quelques fédérations sportives, partenaires des premières heures.

Ayant pour mission de promouvoir la participation des femmes de tous âges en sport et en activité physique et de veiller à l'équité de cette participation en sol québécois, il est clair que la démarche et la mise en place de l'offre de services ne se sont pas faites sans causer quelques perturbations dans le système en place, dont la majorité semblait s'accommoder sans trop se poser de questions. Pour parvenir à faire passer son message et à la limite faire comprendre et accepter sa mission, Égale Action a dû surmonter quelques obstacles.

Étrangement, les réticences se sont fait sentir davantage après le lancement officiel de l'organisme et non pendant les étapes de sa création, où nous ressentions alors davantage le désir des gens d'avancer avec nous. Même nos partenaires de premières lignes démontraient d'une part le désir de s'impliquer, mais se gardaient une porte de sortie. Quoique nous ayons dès le départ utilisé une approche très ouverte et axée sur le respect à la fois de nos partenaires et de notre mission, nous sentions que la plupart craignaient non pas Égale Action mais le message que l'organisme véhiculait, à savoir qu'il existait un problème avec nos filles et nos femmes en sport et activité physique et qu'il était grand temps qu'on s'en occupe. Nous bousculions leur compréhension du système, leurs façons de faire et leurs certitudes. Cette incertitude et cette réticence à notre égard ont fait en sorte que les milieux d'intervention n'ont pas embarqué dans l'aventure pendant les cinq premières années d'existence d'Égale Action, limitant par le fait même l'utilisation de l'offre de services rendus disponibles. Qu'à cela ne tienne, cela n'a pas empêché Égale Action de mettre en branle ses premières initiatives concrètes, « amenant » le milieu à agir concrètement un pas à la fois.

Égale Action est le seul organisme québécois reconnu par le MELS dédié exclusivement à la cause de toutes les femmes dans le sport et l'activité physique. L'organisme s'adresse bien entendu aux filles et aux femmes sportives et actives physiquement ou qui désirent l'être. Mais les services d'Égale Action s'adressent aussi aux femmes et aux hommes qui interviennent auprès de celles-ci dans les contextes du sport et de l'activité physique, peu importe leur milieu d'intervention.

Depuis l'adoption de son premier plan stratégique en 2002, Égale Action a laissé sa trace. La première réalisation essentielle à la venue au monde de l'organisme fut la définition de son fonctionnement administratif et politique. Ils s'en est suivi une première série d'activités publiques comme le Gala Femmes d'influence en sport et activité physique, les conférences annuelles « Les succès au féminin » et l'offre des formations « Leadership au féminin » de l'Association Canadienne pour l'Avancement des Femmes, du Sport et l'activité physique (ACAFS).

La création d'Égale Action a contribué à mettre en place une multitude de programmes, d'activités et d'ateliers de formation. Parmi les plus marquants, notons la réalisation du projet de leadership MentoreActive destiné aux jeunes filles de 15 à 17 ans, le programme de soutien aux fédérations sportives pour améliorer le développement du sport féminin au Québec et la création d'ateliers de formation pour toute la communauté sportive dans le but d'influencer le système sportif. Égale Action est non seulement devenue une structure de soutien pour la participation des femmes mais elle est également une organisation ayant un impact politique qui donne ses recommandations et agit comme organisme de référence. Nul doute qu'elle a permis aux acteurs sportifs du Québec de prendre conscience de la problématique de l'équité en sport et en activité physique et des changements à adopter. Désormais, Égale Action est considérée comme une source d'information crédible sur tout ce qui touche les filles et les femmes en sport et activité physique.

Malgré la création d'Égale Action en 2001 et les avancées réalisées dans plusieurs secteurs, le contexte a malheureusement peu changé en termes de statistiques concernant la participation des femmes, particulièrement au chapitre du leadership. Selon l'étude de 2008 réalisée par Égale Action sur la place des femmes dans le sport au Québec, la plupart des fédérations sportives sont dorénavant conscientes de la réalité des femmes dans le milieu sportif, sans compter que la majorité des fédérations aspirent à une représentation masculine et féminine équilibrée. En contrepartie, des conceptions et des préjugés relatifs à la sous-représentation féminine sont encore bien présents: certains ne voient pas la pertinence de la parité entre les hommes et les femmes et expliquent la sous-représentation des femmes par des raisons qui leur sont propres, c'est-à-dire que cette situation est de leur faute! Quoique la place des femmes représente une préoccupation grandissante des divers organismes en lien avec le sport et l'activité physique, on constate dans la réalité un manque d'équité dans les efforts de développement des filles et des femmes par le milieu. La préoccupation des instances pour le « fait » filles et femmes dans le sport et l'activité physique n'est toujours pas une priorité. La peur de la réaction des instances et des individus ainsi que la création de précédents lorsque l'on parle de mettre à l'avant-scène les réalisations des femmes ou l'instauration de programmes spécifiques pour les filles et les femmes sont encore présents. Il reste encore beaucoup de chemin à parcourir pour la prise de conscience de la situation réelle

Une autre des préoccupations importantes de l'organisme touche le désengagement des jeunes filles à la pratique de l'activité physique et du sport, souvent accompagné de problèmes d'excès de poids ou encore du poids insuffisant chez certaines jeunes femmes. La perception négative de la population face à l'image de la jeune fille sportive (homophobie) en décourage plus d'une à persister dans le monde du sport de compétition. Ces jeunes sportives font face à une grande pression sociale concernant leur image.

Depuis 10 ans, nous sommes passés d'un organisme inconnu ayant une mission et des objectifs dérangeants à un organisme reconnu pouvant contribuer à mieux outiller les intervenants et à améliorer « la statistique » de participation des filles et des femmes en sport et activité physique au Québec. Ce rôle conféré à Égale Action est lourd de responsabilités. Ce nouveau statut ne constitue en fait qu'une étape dans un processus qui doit être envisagé à long terme, et ce, par l'ensemble des partenaires, gestionnaires et intervenants. La sensibilisation n'a pour limite que l'action volontaire et autonome qui en découle. C'est cette action concrète du milieu qui sera un gage du succès pour les filles et les femmes. Dépasser cette perception du « programme » à livrer pour s'approprier la cause et la faire sienne, non pas parce que la statistique le dit, mais parce que plus de 50 % de la population est concernée et parce que la santé d'une société est menacée. L'avenir d'Égale Action passera par sa capacité à ouvrir les œillères et les barrières politiques et à ancrer de nouvelles attitudes et habitudes auprès des décideurs, des bailleurs de fonds, des gestionnaires de programmes, des intervenants et finalement, auprès de la femme elle-même, et ce, tout en conservant une qualité pour l'ensemble de ses programmes et services. La partie est loin d'être gagnée.

WOMEN AND SPORT GO PROVINCIAL
The Story of PROMOTION Plus
Sue Griffin

A few months ago, I was asked by what I thought was an environmental group to speak on a panel about the role of women in creating a "sustainable" organization. I didn't understand why they had asked me—I am the CEO of the BC Sports Hall of Fame and the current Chair of ProMOTION Plus (Girls and Women in Sport and Physical Activity). I'm in sport, not the environment. I "get" sustainability and do my best to recycle—but that's it. After a few minutes of discussion with the organization's event organizer, I realized that the panel was in fact focusing on the traits and characteristics of women in executive/leadership roles. Specifically, how and why a woman at the helm creates a different culture with different outcomes than a man does.

I was honoured to be asked and to participate as a leader in sport in British Columbia. Women have a very different and unique set of leadership characteristics. Research indicates that women are more compassionate, empathetic and creative leaders. We are "doers," prepared to take risks and explore opportunities. And women leaders have a strong entrepreneurial spirit— although I wasn't entirely conscious of this before, I realize that this definition strongly applies to who I am and what I offer as a CEO. You see, I am an entrepreneur at heart and a leader by choice.

More specifically, what role does sport play in the life of a woman CEO? Stats say that among women earning over $75,000 a year, one in three was involved in varsity sport and one in six was involved in sport at some level. The opportunity to be one of the three speakers on the panel provided me with an opportunity to reflect on my journey as a woman in the male-dominated world of sport and the amazing lessons I have learned along the way; a journey that brings me now to a role that I cherish, volunteer Chair of ProMOTION Plus.

Growing up on the court, on the track and in the ring taught me the lessons and provided me with the foundation, skills and traits required to lead and, I believe, to lead well. A number of years ago, I was seeking an opportunity to share my passion and skills with a group that was committed to providing young girls with the opportunities to shape their lives through the values of sport. I came across a small organization by the name of ProMOTION Plus.

It wasn't until I joined the BC Sports Hall of Fame that I had the opportunity to actually connect with the organization. The Hall had entered into a wonderful partnership with three organizations that shared a common vision: to create a permanent tribute to extraordinary women in sport and recreation in BC. Led by ProMOTION Plus, the British Columbia Centre of Excellence for Women's Health, 2010 Legacies Now and the BC Sports Hall of Fame, a tribute to women in sport and recreation in BC was created, known as *In Her Footsteps – Honouring Women in Sport in BC*. The tribute is comprised of an annual nomination and selection process culminating in an emotional evening of celebration and recognition of the honourees.

The stories of the extraordinary accomplishments of these women are told through video in the BC Sports Hall of Fame's In Her Footsteps Gallery. I am blessed with the opportunity to see our guests visit the gallery on a daily basis. I watch grandmothers, their daughters and granddaughters stand mesmerized as they become immersed in the stories of the journeys these women took to follow their personal dreams. Storytelling has the power to inspire and motivate young women to dream and to believe that they can do anything they wish to pursue. These stories cross cultures, age and gender to move an audience to laughter and tears.

ProMOTION Plus captured these stories, and I knew then that I had to take on a greater role with this organization. I wanted to have an opportunity to work with them, to assist in expanding the reach and the impact of their programs. Basically I wanted to work with a small group of passionate, committed women who believed in providing young girls and women with access and opportunities in the field of sport—to participate, to compete, to enjoy.

ProMOTION Plus is a provincial organization that was started by a small group of extremely passionate and devoted women, most of whom are still involved with the organization today. They are committed to inspiring young women by recounting the journeys and success stories of other women in sport who have achieved their dreams, delivering leadership workshops, and setting up support networks in order to create a sustainable environment for women in sport and physical activity in BC.

The first federal Sport Canada policy for women in sport was developed in 1986. As a result of that policy, and more than three years of planning and hard work from women like May

Brown and Bobbie Steen, the BC Government decided to give annual funding to ProMOTION Plus. This funding provided the organization with the ability to hire its first Executive Director, Marion Lay.

Under the direction of the first board of directors, CAAWS and ProMOTION Plus formed an alliance. CAAWS provides national legitimacy to ProMOTION Plus and other provincial organizations with a similar mandate, and it is a key partner in assisting us to move the provincial agenda on gender equity forward in an impactful and relevant way. Indeed, as a small non-profit society, we cannot work in isolation. Collaborating with organizations such as CAAWS provides strength, creativity and an engine that will not stop. Furthermore, these partnerships give women in sport the opportunity to discuss issues and learn from each other. As the network of women in sport grew and women leaders began speaking out about the injustices they saw in the world of sport, people began naming issues and creating projects to bring about change.

One example of change was the effort led by CAAWS to promote women's ski jumping as an Olympic sport to the Vancouver Olympic Organizing Committee in 2009. ProMOTION Plus was also instrumental in this case, which eventually went to the Supreme Court of Canada, positioned as a human rights issue. The result: women's ski jumping is now a sanctioned Olympic sport and is included in the 2014 Olympic Winter Games in Sochi.

During the early days, ProMOTION Plus placed a great deal of emphasis on leadership. It developed a province-wide speaker's bureau with the BC Athlete Career Centre, and created a Women in Sport and Recreation Administration Network, providing professional development and issue awareness sessions. A major emphasis in leadership is coaching. One of the most successful women in coaching initiatives was the 1994 Commonwealth Games Coaching Apprenticeship Program, a partnership with ProMOTION Plus and the CAC (Coaching Association of Canada). It was the catalyst for a number of the bursaries and professional development programs to help women become top coaches in Canada, such as the Canada Games Women's Apprentice Coaching Program, which is still a major initiative within the

CAC. Another major initiative of Sport Canada and CAC was the National Coaching School for Women, championed by Betty Baxter, one of our coaching experts in British Columbia.

Over the years, PROMOTION Plus has changed along with its leadership. However, its work and efforts have always been with partners in four major areas. The first is in the area of recognition. Women leaders have been such an inspiration to the next generation of young women leaders and PROMOTION Plus has recognized their work through the *In Her Footsteps* Exhibit, a program that features over 40 women in sport and recreation in BC. In addition, the Bobbie Steen Award is distributed annually at Sport BC's annual Athlete of the Year Awards, recognizing a young woman who exemplifies the characteristics of our founder Bobbie Steen.

The second area is consultation: to help find solutions and promising practices to meet the current challenges. We consulted the 2010 ski jumping advocacy group, spoke out against the discrimination and helped create the Canadian advocacy network.

The last two areas are education, critical in continuing to ensure that our message is heard and reaches those who have potential to change lives, and development, to increase, broaden and strengthen the vision. We have initiated a small strategic grant fund and an awards initiative, directly increasing the opportunities for girls and women in physical activity and sport in BC. With the creation of partnerships, PROMOTION Plus has had a direct and sustainable impact on the lives of girls and women in physical activity and sport. This last year we distributed over $40,000 to various groups that provided opportunities for young girls and women to participate and be active.

A number of years ago, PROMOTION Plus introduced a community chapter in Victoria. It is a self-sustaining grassroots organization that raises funds through third party events. Funds are used to deliver Girls Only and On the Move programs for young girls and women on Vancouver Island. The women on the Victoria board are exceptional role models and mentors. They demonstrate that if we are to make change, it is incumbent upon us to join a board, learn the skills to be an effective board member and become a change agent. As women leaders, we have the natural tendency to get things done. So let's do it.

Having now been Chair of PROMOTION Plus for the last three years, I have seen how being supported and surrounded by believers makes us more confident as women. Our self-esteem grows. We question, we follow, we lead. We learn to speak our mind and we take nothing for granted. My learning curve as a volunteer on the board of PROMOTION Plus was steep. Coming to an organization that already had over 20 years of rich history, I learned about the critical issues facing young girls and women as they attempted to participate, compete and become involved in sport and recreation.

Perseverance, passion, commitment, assertiveness, embracing risk, taking a chance—these are part of my spirit and a critical part of my job as a CEO. As women, we can, do and will create a more sustainable organization and community through our leadership style. Be brave, be bold. Breathe and believe.

PLAY IT FORWARD
Sustaining PROMOTION Plus in Victoria
Patti Hunter

Here I describe and reflect on the experiences of the Victoria chapter of PROMOTION Plus, a provincial organization that advocates for equitable opportunities for girls and women in sport, physical activity and recreational opportunities. The provincial office is located in Vancouver; the Victoria office houses the regional chapter, and with its small committee of volunteers, serves the Capital Regional District on southern Vancouver Island. This piece describes this chapter's history, activities and events, and assesses our challenges, successes and key lessons.

We are a cadre of professionals with different skill sets but a shared passion and interest in physical activity, recreation and sport. I co-founded the Victoria chapter with Alison Ducharme in 1999, and over the years we have benefited from many helping hands. Most recently, Joan Wharf-Higgins and Andrea Carey have become the co-chairs of the chapter, and they have taken on the mantle of leadership by continuing to innovate and expand the organization. Altogether, the collective efforts of many women of all ages and life stages have given the organization a regular, refreshing flow of energy and enthusiasm.

I was also one of the founding board members of ProMOTION Plus for Girls and Women in Sport and Physical Activity for BC, which was advocated for by Marion Lay and Bobbie Steen through the Minister's Task Force chaired by May Brown in 1985. Our early members contributed knowledge and skills in organizational and event planning, evaluation, and marketing as well as connections to the recreation, sport, education and policy realms in the public, private and not-for-profit sectors. As career opportunities arose, we lost some of our key members in the early 2000s, but we kept going and recruited great new members. Because we were all working professionals, some with young families, we decided early on to keep the scope of our work manageable and tangible. We met once every 4-6 weeks over snacks at members' houses to discuss and stay connected with each other and the cause.

In keeping with our intent to accomplish tangible outcomes within our (entirely fundraised) modest budget and volunteer time, our efforts built on provincial and national opportunities for networking, education, advocacy and granting, delivered with a local flavour. In the beginning, our early morning networking events were well attended (30-40 people), providing a venue for women (and in some cases men) to share with each other, hear from noted speakers (Olympians, policy makers, researchers) and learn about upcoming events and activities related to advancing sport and physical activity for girls and women. Always held at a local public golf club, admission cost between $10-$20 over the years, most times securing us a small profit to help cover speakers' travel costs and other operational expenses. The somewhat awkwardly titled WISRAN (Women In Sport and Recreation Administration Network) was rebranded in 2009 as Breakfast Links to reflect the networking nature over the first meal of the day overlooking the golf links. After some time, dwindling attendance led us to hold future events at a recreation centre, bar and coffee house, all with less success than we had previously experienced.

One of our more important and sustained activities has been the creation and administration of our girls' grants: Proud to Play Like a Girl (for girls aged 10-14 and 15-18, the grant provides $250 to enable girls to attend special coaching and skills development clinics in their sport); Play it Forward Program Development ($1,000 for sport/recreation organizations or schools to serve girls); and In Training ($500 scholarships for women aged 18-25 who are in post-secondary programs related to sport, recreation, fitness). Since the inception of the grants, we have funded over 55 individuals and organizations with more than $25,000. Through the annual KidSport Victoria/ProMOTION Plus Victoria golf tournament, $6,000 is raised and re-invested through ProMOTION Plus to support girls' participation in the Capital Regional District. In addition to these annual and targeted granting opportunities, we also support female participation in leadership training and education seminars and workshops where appropriate. For example, we have sponsored delegates at the CAAWS Leadership Development Workshops and the AthletesCAN Workshop. We also strive to acknowledge and celebrate local leaders and each year nominate a recipient for our Bobbie Steen Award. Furthermore, since 2008, we have sponsored a table at the Women in Sport event, hosted annually by the Pacific Institute for Sport Excellence, which brings local, provincial and national women athletes to commemorate their accomplishments over brunch every April.

We have experienced both successes and challenges during our pursuit of these activities. One key success has been aligning ProMOTION Plus with KidSport Victoria in 2002. By providing annual funding to ProMOTION Plus for the girls' grants programs, KidSport Victoria achieved its mission to ensure that dollars were allocated equally to females and males for sport and physical activity. It can be difficult to garner support for such projects or to communicate effectively with the public, but when the advocacy work becomes tangible, such as funding girls' participation in sport and physical activity in connection with an organization such as KidSport, the "work" becomes more meaningful for all. In turn, the stories of sport success unite our work, drive policy decisions and sustain our passion and support for equity.

Strategic planning has always been part of ProMOTION Plus Victoria's organizational work. Every second year, we assess our strengths and weaknesses, opportunities and threats and are very strategic in what work we will take on and with whom. As such, we were opportunistic in offering leadership development experiences for women through the CAAWS workshops and the WISRAN or Breakfast Links networking events; our communication, education and advocacy were done through our KidSport partnership and funding of such things as the Olympic Youth Academy and the Women in Sport celebration of females in sport.

Our networking breakfast and evening meetings saw our membership grow to over 150 at one point, gathering a mix of women in education, recreation and sport to hear a featured guest speaker and then a round of introductions/announcements and networking. These events drew up to 50 people in their peak of success. We have faced challenges in attracting the same kind of interest over the last couple of years and so have anchored our events to the announcement of our grant recipients, ensuring that there is a continued public acknowledgement of our funding and advocacy efforts.

Over the years, we have learned many lessons on effective practices and strategies for furthering the mission of our organization. We have found that it is essential to share leadership roles and work through collaboration, while following proper not-for-profit procedures such as strategic and priority planning. Looking outside the organization, we have connected with other groups that share a commitment to equity and have a provincial and federal reach. As part of our advocacy work in striving for equity in the sport system, we have committed to creating programming that has tangible evidence of advocacy for girls and women in action. Finally, it is vital to continue developing and evaluating our fundraising and networking opportunities, such as the newly established Victoria Goddess Run. These best practices form the core of our work and help us continue to promote equity for both women and men in sport.

BLENDING FEMINIST PRINCIPLES AND ENTREPRENEURIAL GOALS
In Conversation with Bryna Kopelow
Sheila Robertson

In the two decades that have passed since Bryna Kopelow took the helm of JW Sporta, she and her colleague Jennifer Fenton have brought the British Columbia based consulting and marketing company to the top of its field. Specialists in physical activity and sport education, their small team consists of diverse and experienced health, physical activity and sport professionals who operate with an integrated program design, delivery and service approach. The work centres around two innovative products: Action Schools!BC™ and the Premier's Sport Awards Program (p.s.a.p.).

The first, Action Schools!BC™, is a best practices model designed to assist schools in creating individualized action plans to promote healthy living while achieving academic outcomes and supporting comprehensive school health. p.s.a.p. is a physical education resource program that helps teachers and instructors teach youth basic sport skills. Both initiatives reflect Kopelow's empathy for those who, unlike her, did not have a positive physical education and sport experience. "It is our responsibility and within our power as a sport sector to ensure that more girls and women participate and enjoy," she says.

Without hesitation, Kopelow attaches the feminist label to her company. "Absolutely it's feminist. We are totally customer service-driven, we're the 'yes' company, everything is custom designed, and we do the work for our target market, mainly the generalist elementary, usually female, 50-year-old school teacher. We want them to provide physically active opportunities for their students and so we repackage and reposition how to encourage physical activity, teach physical education and make it really simple."

The need these programs fill is traceable to the 1980s when there was a decline of physical education specialists in provincial public schools, leaving the task to a generation of generalists who, more often than not, disliked sport and were fearful of teaching physical education. Even if they enjoyed physical activity as youngsters, somewhere along the line the experience became negative. Yet, they are the ones charged with developing physically literate youngsters, creating, as Kopelow notes, a disconnect. "We hone in on the needs of these teachers by re-introducing them to something they used to love, showing them that there are many options in providing quality physical education, encouraging them and providing the necessary training, resources and support."

Kopelow's parents were of modest means, but nevertheless provided endless opportunities for self-growth, treated her and her brother equitably and set unlimited expectations about what she could accomplish. Feisty, always active in a wide range of sports and academically driven, she earned a degree in physical and health education from the University of Toronto (U of T), concentrating on sport sociology and women's studies; a master's degree in physical education from the University of British Columbia (UBC); and a teaching certificate, also from UBC. Her feminist academic work was shaped by two influences: U of T sport sociologist Rob Beamish and UBC political scientist Rick Gruneau. "Both were incredibly great professors, men who were ahead of their time in terms of their sociological, hegemonic studies," she says. "They were open to everything, they liked to dialogue, they liked to twist and turn constructed ideological frameworks, and in doing so, gave permission to challenge traditional ways of thinking. Critical reflection became my ideology; I question everything, which meshes beautifully with the feminist model of rejecting the status quo."

From her early years, Kopelow has been attracted by mass

participation, believing that physical activity and sport should be accessible to all for the social interaction, community connectedness and health benefits they provide. "Everybody should be able to benefit from being involved in the game," she says, "not just those who are skilled and talented."

Eager to put her passion into practice, Kopelow joined JW Sporta as managing director of p.s.a.p. after completing her master's degree in 1986. Before long she brought that passion to her volunteer work as well. The genesis was an invitation from the late Bobbie Steen to attend a gathering to discuss how to secure provincial government funding for an organization focusing solely on girls and women in physical activity and sport. The meeting ignited such a flame that she immediately volunteered her services to the embryonic British Columbia organization, PromOTIONPlus.

In the early 1990s, Kopelow and Fenton volunteered to develop and pilot a program and a complementary handbook to increase opportunities for inactive girls, aged 9 to 18, to participate and lead in sport and physical activity. Thus On the Move was born. "On the Move (OTM) began as a concept that initiated a project that turned into a movement, that uses a community development process, and when put all together, can be described as an approach," says Kopelow. After successful pilots in Ottawa and Port Coquitlam, OTM has grown into a thriving national initiative administered by the Canadian Association for the Advancement of Women and Sport and Physical Activity (CAAWS). "What stands out about OTM is that while it may appear to be just another program, conceptually it is much more," says Kopelow. "It is based on the premise that there is a sector of the population missing out on recreational opportunities due to various covert and overt societal barriers. We saw the need to blend the theoretical and the pragmatic by creating a professional, practical resource with a conceptual framework, encouraging people and then letting each program evolve because there is not just one way of doing this … it doesn't matter what physical activity people do; all we want is for them to enjoy being physically active and make healthy eating choices."

Meeting Bobbie Steen so early in her career would prove

to be vitally important for Kopelow. Both women led CAAWS, Steen until her untimely death in 1996 and Kopelow from 1998 to 2004. "Bobbie was my administrative inspiration," she says. "Seeing what she was doing with CAAWS showed me that I could put my feminist thinking into practice ... we realized there was a whole movement out there, girls who needed to follow the same trail, girls who owned it and felt comfortable in a physical activity setting." Another important influence was legendary women in sport leader Marion Lay, who profoundly contributed to Kopelow's understanding of the issues concerning gender equity in sport.

Asked what separates JW Sporta from similar companies, Kopelow says: "Critical analysis using a feminist lens ... we have a certain way we do our work. We call ourselves the 'translators' and by that I mean we take the technical expertise from a particular sector and translate it into something palatable and usable by a different market. In our case, that's the teacher market." With p.s.a.p., for example, the company doesn't claim to be technical experts in any of the 13 sports for which it offers manuals, coaches and skill level crests. Instead, it seeks out the technical experts to learn how each sport skill should be taught. It then develops a user-friendly manual written in clear language with skills cues, education techniques, and 30-minute lesson plans. Each manual is designed in exactly the same way and provides an overview that shows how it links to the curriculum, the resources and equipment that are required, a warm-up and cool-down chat, and a concluding activity.

Two decades of experience in developing and delivering p.s.a.p. influenced the design and implementation strategy for Action Schools!BC™. For this product, JW Sporta translates the provincial government's goals of a healthier population by assisting schools in creating individualized action plans that promote healthy living. "Our work is constantly revolving and evolving as we work with the provincial government and the education sector to make these goals achievable," explains Kopelow.

Kopelow has deliberately kept JW Sporta small—the staff numbers around ten—believing that going large results in a loss of the ability to control how the company is run and how the work is done. She hires only people who believe in the work, are team players able to multi-task, are curious, interested, passionate and loyal. There is a fine line between staying big enough that "you are able to do the work you want to do with the people you want to do it with, and being small enough to know your clients very well," she says.

The fact that the staff is all female is almost coincidental. "We're not against hiring men and we have worked with male staff and intern students. The people we are looking for are able to start anywhere and do anything, are willing to work hard, have a broad skill base, enjoy a collaborative atmosphere, will work until the job is done and thrive on multi-tasking—dominant female characteristics. It's not that we're closed to hiring men; it's just that they view the work differently."

Although JW Sporta is a hive of constant output, Kopelow places a high value on making time for reflection. She does admit that initially she tended to "copy" predecessors' leadership styles before realizing "I'm not a male leader, I don't have the size and personality. I know people don't treat male counterparts the same way, and I have quite a different approach."

As Kopelow figured out her leadership style, she realized the importance of human resources, making sure that people feel valued and are treated well. That includes enabling staff to follow their passion even if it means approving a three-month or even a year-long leave. "Why lose somebody who wants to go away and do something else great for awhile? Who made all these rules? Rules are something I question all the time."

The company strategist and office manager, she thinks big and then cuts her ideas into bite-size, manageable pieces, ready for delivery. She also willingly takes on administrative tasks, including ordering resources and supplies. "I do the big-picture thinking and some of the very detailed work and everyone else does everything else in between," she says.

In the 1980s, Kopelow suggests, her work was cut out for her. She and her colleagues knew they needed to get girls and women active. Hence On the Move, which remains relevant. The 1990s were a decade of raising physically active feminist daughters with fathers much more involved in parenting than previously. Come the 2000s and Kopelow began to have misgivings. On the surface, the tide had turned. "Kids are on the fields, girls are playing soccer, so people are thinking the job is done. But in my opinion, we are witnessing superficial success, and that is making it much more difficult to articulate the work of organizations like CAAWS and ProMOTION Plus."

So, despite the strides Canadian women have made since Kopelow was a hungry-for-knowledge student, she worries that the young women of today may not be fully aware of all the hard work that has been done and still needs to be done. "In fact, our work becomes much more difficult, not least because our feminist daughters haven't had as many negative experiences to fuel their fire and so often may not fully appreciate what the issues are."

Vitally important to Kopelow is mentorship that focuses on young women professionals as one way to raise awareness. There could be, she suggests, a cycle of re-positioning that brings with it strong feminist sport writings—a new wave of "crypto-feminist thinking—and then they will understand. Their issues will be different but as important as ours were ... I'm bracing myself for when my eldest daughter says, 'Hey, Mom! We're starting this organization for girls and women ...'"

Kopelow often speaks with students and her messages are clear. She says, "Most ideas are not original; what counts is what you do with the ideas and how you work with people." Other advice she gives includes: respect and integrity are not over-rated; don't burn your bridges; don't underestimate where someone else may end up; ask for advice and gather information; and, prioritize by giving yourself time to think clearly and to plan your legacy, whether it is career and family or work/life balance.

All Kopelow's works focuses on the long term. "We tell the teachers we're not delivering a government program that's the flavour of the day. Rather, you can count on us to be here for the long haul. We need to fundamentally change how they do their work and re-train them to enjoy being physically active. Our work is deeply rooted and definitely not quick and dirty."

She isn't dismayed when a teacher says she is no longer

using Schools!BC™-specific resources because investigation reveals that the school is in fact providing plenty of physical activity and healthy eating opportunities. What they have done is "changed the culture of their school, which is exactly what we want to happen. We don't want schools to follow a prescriptive program; we want them to create their own because that means it's theirs."

If Kopelow could wave a magic wand, school teachers would all provide quality physical activity, physical education and sport opportunities for their students during school hours. She would go even further and enact legislation to ensure access to quality physical activity and sport opportunities for all children, at no cost, in community recreation settings. "The investment made in providing such opportunities within and external to school hours would prove to be significantly less than the financial burden of coping with a physically inactive and overweight population," she insists.

BEYOND THE OPEN DOOR
Gender Equity and Municipal Recreation
Cindy Crapper

Back in 1986, I began my recreation career as a fitness centre worker at Trout Lake Community Centre in Vancouver. I was hired to work during the women-only time slots and implement strength and conditioning programs for women. I remember thinking that it was great to have a time set aside for women: for some, working out with men was intimidating and not an option. This was the beginning of my involvement in Parks and Recreation and its interest in taking gender equity seriously.

It was because of Diane Murphy, Past Chair at PROMOTION Plus and colleague, that in 1996, a Gender Equity Committee was started and developed a draft Gender Equity Policy for the

Vancouver Park Board. Diane and I co-chaired the Committee where we reviewed access and gender equity issues within the Recreation Division. The values of the committee were based on principles of co-operation and collaboration among participants, user groups, community groups, community associations, politicians, Park Board staff, families and members of communities. We believed that gender equity is not a negative process designed to disenfranchise men, but an attempt to attract and include girls, teenage girls and women, and provide equitable access and opportunities in Parks and Recreation. To this end, the Committee identified needs, addressed issues and barriers to participation, developed terms of reference, created a program plan, and worked with staff and local sport groups to develop fair and equitable opportunities to ensure girls benefited from community sport and physical activity.

The Committee devised the strategy that gender equity is the principle and practice of fair and equitable allocation of resources and opportunities to both males and females. It followed the Gender Equity Principles: (1) All participants in Parks and Recreation services have the right to a recreation environment that is gender-equitable; (2) Gender equity considers social class, culture, ethnicity, religion, race, sexual orientation, sex and age; (3) Gender equity requires sensitivity to gender, determination, commitment, political will and vigilance over time. Using these principles, we developed terms of reference that advocated for gender equity in Vancouver while supporting staff in policy implementation and development.

In partial fulfillment of these terms of reference, in 1997 and 1998, six staff training workshops were offered in partnership with CAAWS. These workshops called More than an Open Door trained 120 staff members from 22 community centres and sport groups on gender equity: what it means and how staff and community can work together to remove barriers for girls, teenage girls and women in participating in recreation and sport in Vancouver.

During these workshops, participants raised many different opinions, concerns and fears. Some wanted to make sure that subsidies were available for children and families who could not otherwise participate. Others feared that not all staff would interpret the gender equity policy the same way and that there had to be a common understanding built around it. Certain participants thought it was important to share all the information on the principles of gender equity with everyone. Another perspective was that women should be encouraged to participate both in non-traditional sports (e.g. hockey) and traditional sports and that allocation policies had to be developed for all.

Using this feedback, the Gender Equity Committee formulated an 11-point gender equity policy and program objectives that covered everything from allocating sufficient funds and resources to implementing programs and facilitating awareness on the topic. Finally, on October 18, 1999, the draft Gender Equity Policy Statement was passed unanimously at the Vancouver Park Board meeting.

Another outcome from the More than an Open Door workshops was that it became clear that some women-only programs were struggling from lack of participation. Recreation professionals were asking for help in developing their programming and marketing for these programs. So another educational opportunity was created for staff through the initiative "Girls on the Move," supported by the provincial organization PROMOTION Plus. This initiative offered a toolkit that assisted staff to develop markets, advertise programs, target populations and find creative ways to engage and keep girls and women-only programming viable.

It has always been challenging for certain sports programs to survive because traditional programming requires marketing and charging a fee for service using a break-even mentality. As a result, many programs did not succeed due to numbers and resources. However, PROMOTION Plus's support and resources gave recreation professionals an opportunity to apply for grants to develop new program initiatives to engage girls, teenage girls and women with recreation and sport. Furthermore, the British Columbia Parks and Recreation Association fully supported programs for girls and women in partnership with PROMOTION Plus and the British Columbia Centre of Excellence for Women's Health.

One of our largest girls' programs that has benefited from this funding is the girls' basketball program at the Strathcona Community Centre, which sits on the edge of the downtown East Side. Hundreds of girls have gone through this program because of the outstanding efforts of Ron Suzuki, Recreation Programmer and Leadership Award winner from PROMOTION Plus. The City has also been creating new coaching opportunities for girls and women and sporting opportunities for all through the MoreSports program. This was created in 2000 to give kids in the downtown East Side an opportunity to play sports.

The City of Vancouver embraces gender equity as well. City staff value young women as mentors and coaches, and it is possible to see many teenage girls coaching in our community centres and in local sport organizations. Furthermore, the City's staff is well represented by both women and men, and the most senior management position is held by a woman.

Still, we need to do a better job of engaging Aboriginal girls and other minorities, and inspire them to take part in programs and help them develop as mentors and coaches. As Carole Brown, supervisor of Ray Cam Cooperative Centre, says: "One of the challenges we have is women who passively work against the involvement of their peers, with attitudes and belief systems that have designated women as inferior to men in the coaching arena. They fail to realize how disempowering their approaches are to their own daughters."

There should also be a focus on building female and minority coaching and leadership. Although there is some representation of women coaches at the local level, the same is not true for coaches in the regional, provincial and national systems.

Another group that should be heard is youth. In the mid-1990s, civic youth strategies were developed as young people became interested in their health and wellbeing and the environment. We also began to expand Parks and Recreation and outreach from our youth worker team, and youth councils were formed so we could start listening to their voices. At the same time, more opportunities arose for girls and young women to get involved and be the decision makers in our community centres. More recently, the "Get Out" initiative was expanded with a grant from Legacies Now, a program designed to engage, inspire and educate people in British Columbia in sport and the Olympic Games. The "Get Out" initiative was designed for youth by youth, giving them the opportunity to work with staff and community partners to actively pursue their own programs. As part of the program, a variety of dance and outdoor sport and physical activities was made available for girls only. The impact of these programs significantly increased self-esteem, confidence and gave girls the opportunity to play.

Seniors should also not be left out of the equation. Staff at a number of community centres wanted to provide an introduction to sport and physical activity for women aged 55 and over. Targeting women who were inactive or wanting to be more active, we proposed a successful grant called "Walk your Way into Sport and Physical Activity," in partnership with community centres, viaSport, sport organizations, Sport Med BC's Walk this Way Program, and other senior-serving agencies. This program provided an introduction to walking, sport fundamentals, muscle conditioning and weight training. It gave women a second chance at sport. At the beginning of the 10-week program, the women were given a fitness test and by the end everyone had increased their strength and flexibility.

In 2008 the City of Vancouver approved the Vancouver Sport Strategy. The Park Board is the facilitator of the strategy, and in partnership with the Vancouver Sport Network, local sport organizations and the Canadian Sport Centre Pacific among others, a community plan for Sport Development in Recreation is being implemented. This plan follows the Canadian Sport for Life Long Term Athlete Development model. It gives everyone the opportunity to integrate "good sportpersonship" using ethical decision-making techniques and true sport principles. Through this strategy, we will have the opportunity to acquire good data on gender participation in order to review and determine the future scope and focus of work. Already allocation policies need to be reviewed for fields, gymnasiums and arenas to improve access to facilities. To encourage female participation in physical activities, programming for girls and women-only activities need to be encouraged and education materials developed to assist our partners with this direction.

Vancouver is in a great position to ensure its policies reflect the needs of its community partners, although more work and further consultations are still required. I don't think Vancouver knows all the answers for getting gender equity right. However, I think that we are not afraid to be inclusive, ask the tough questions and get people talking about equity. Every girl in Vancouver has the right to be included in sport and physically active programs and we are collaborating with charitable organizations and social services to reach out and include immigrants, girls from different ethnic backgrounds and those living in poverty or with low incomes. I feel that after over 25 years with the City of Vancouver, I am in a very good position to rebuild our framework to increase and improve the opportunities, programs, access and support for all girls and women in the parks and recreation delivery system in order to achieve gender equity.

EFFECTING CHANGE FROM WITHIN
My Journey from Athlete to Advocate
Charmaine Crooks

Sport is my passion and I cannot recall a time when it was not a part of my life. Whether it was running with my father after he came home from work or playing sports with my eight siblings, being active was and still is part of who I am.

As a young immigrant from Jamaica to Canada, I found that sport provided a close sense of community and a connection to my new country. Our diverse immigrant neighbourhood and free access to Toronto Parks and Recreation sport programs and facilities meant multiple opportunities to participate in sport for fun and a bit of healthy competition.

My talent as a runner grew rapidly in middle school. This was due in large part to an encouraging female gym teacher who must have known that sport would help build my confidence and self-esteem.

High school sports and another encouraging female coach helped solidify the Olympic journey I was determined to take. Ultimately, I competed in five Canadian Olympic Teams, eleven national championships, a World Cup and Commonwealth Games, winning Pan American Games gold medals and an Olympic silver medal in Athletics. These experiences and the many coaches who helped me to get to the podium shaped me as a person and gave me a vantage point outside the arena from which to view the world of sport.

While attending university in the United States on an athletic scholarship, I first experienced the stark differences between how male and female athletes were treated. As female athletes on full sport scholarships, we did not have access to the same nutritional meals, known as "the training table," that the male athletes had, nor was there any real media focus on the women's sports programs. I used every opportunity to speak with the athletic director on several occasions to voice my concerns on this and other issues while emphasizing the positive role of the female student athlete. Needless to say, not many of my recommendations were fulfilled.

My attempts at advocacy were happening at the same that the entire landscape of women's collegiate level sport in the United States was beginning to change with the introduction of *Title IX* in 1972. This important progress for the civil rights movement provided many opportunities for educational institutions to receive funding, and in the process, swung open the doors to expand scholarships for women in sport.

The female athlete role models and trailblazers who were on the "front line" of breaking down barriers for women in sport allowed me the opportunity to compete with the best athletes in the world and excel. I will always be grateful to these women.

Furthermore, these experiences fuelled my passion to advocate for the rights of athletes, in particular, women. After graduating and moving back to Canada, I continued to be driven by the deep desire to give back to sport and actively looked for sport organisations with whom to volunteer.

One of my first key advocacy roles in Canada involved working with a group of fellow athletes from Olympic, Paralympic and national team sports. Our vision was to increase the voice of athletes within the Canadian sport system. Around a kitchen table, we created the athlete advocacy group AthletesCAN that still exists 20 years later and remains a vibrant and relevant voice for all Canadian athletes.

Working with government and sport bodies, AthletesCAN represents issues such as equity, increased funding and promoting women in positions of leadership. One of our initial successes was ensuring that athletes on maternity leave would continue to get their government funding. We also encouraged government, along with other partners, to increase the monthly funding stipends for eligible athletes.

The shift of athletes into positions of leadership was not only taking place in Canada but also internationally. These new roles would greatly benefit women in sport in many ways, particularly in leadership and increased participation in sport.

In 1996 I was part of the first group of international athletes to be elected to one of the eight positions on the International Olympic Committee's (IOC) Athletes' Commission. This was the first of such elections, held by peers in the Olympic Village. Needless to say, being chosen as the Canadian representative significantly helped strengthen my role as an advocate and gave greater voice to Canadian sport and our international agenda. It would also mark a key opportunity for more women to be included on the exclusive International Olympic Committee at a time when women comprised about 10 percent of IOC membership. In the history of the Olympic movement, only the late Canadian Olympic Committee (COC) Chief Executive Officer Carol Anne Letheren, Olympic gold medalist Beckie Scott and I have been the Canadian female IOC representatives.

The most historic accomplishment of our IOC Athletes' Commission was gaining the right to be full voting members of the IOC that came as a result of the IOC 2000 Reform recommendations. This achievement led to elected IOC Athletes' Commission members serving on the majority of IOC Commissions, including the IOC Executive Board; the Women in Sport Commission—the Program Commission that makes recommendations to the IOC on inclusion of sports to the Olympic Program; and the Ethics Commission, where I was the first female member.

Full IOC membership has clearly strengthened the voice of Olympians as a whole and put more active female decision-makers at the table. IOC membership also provided me with the opportunity to continue to advocate for athletes' rights, such as greater overall inclusion in the IOC, increasing women's sports participation, concerns over gender testing and doping in sport, better engagement of alumni Olympians and increasing women's leadership within National Olympic Committees.

The 2010 Vancouver Winter Olympic and Paralympic Winter Games (VANOC) and the showcasing of Canada and our sports to the world marked a significant time in Canadian sport history. Vancouver was one of a handful of global Olympic bids to ever have a female Bid Chair. Olympian Marion Lay set the initial course during her tenure to shine the spotlight on women in sport leadership. As the first female athlete to join the initial Bid Committee in 1998, I served through to the successful completion of the Games as the longest serving board member of VANOC.

I believe that one of the many important legacies left by the 2010 Games to women in sport was leadership development, as there were many women in key executive positions. The commitment to sport expressed through the Own the Podium programme helped to raise the bar of Canadian sporting achievement. It also led to national record-breaking sport performances and helped build new role models.

Affirming women's position in sport is also a commitment of the Canadian Olympic Committee (COC), where I have been a longstanding member. There is a Women's Committee and a Gender Equity Policy in place to "encourage gender equity in its governance, administration, programs and activities." The COC also works closely with world-class women through its sport partner the Canadian Association for the Advancement of Women in Sport and Physical Activity (CAAWS) and other relevant sport organisations and multi-sport Games in Canada.

Furthering and recognising women's role in national sport governance and identifying international sport leadership opportunities for Canadian women should always be an important agenda item in order to motivate and encourage the next generation of female sport leaders. As we advance our broader sport culture across Canada, women leaders in sport are not only helping to expand the participation of girls in sport but are also actively building future leaders through mentorship and other programs. To strengthen these goals even further, we must look to best practices of leadership development in other sectors of society and business and see where we can scale the opportunities for growth and collaboration. One option is by increasing communication between female athletes and women in sport through networking, social media and forums, and providing a consistent vehicle to share and voice concerns necessary for change.

My lifelong involvement in sport has not only given me the opportunity to understand the sporting world, along with all its complexities, but also to make a long-term commitment to effect change within it. My hope is that many more athletes will take up the baton and "run a leg" in what is the rewarding marathon of sport leadership that helps contribute way beyond our days as active athletes. In my own journey from athlete to advocate, sport has been, and will continue to be, a vital part of my life.

"MISS WORLD CHAMPIONSHIPS" AND OTHER CHALLENGES
Reflections on Women at the International Level
Tricia Smith

I rowed on the National Rowing Team for 12 years, was selected for four Olympic teams, and won seven World Championships, one Olympic, and one Commonwealth Games gold medal. When

I retired, I was one of the most successful rowers from a non-Eastern bloc nation. I had also finished my studies so was ready to start a career in law. However, a few years after my retirement from rowing, I was surprised and honoured when a member of the women's commission of the international rowing federation (named Fédération Internationale des Sociétés d'Aviron or FISA) asked me if I would be interested in joining the Commission. (At that time, representatives had to be approved by their home country and be nominated by the Chair, and approved by the committee. This process is still in place although there is also an open call for applicants.) Before that, the possibility of getting involved in international sport leadership had never crossed my mind. I relate this story only to point out the obvious: often, women who have experience and possible interest in leadership positions have to be sought out, informed and encouraged in order to get involved.

Nine years after I joined FISA, in 2000, I was elected to the board of the International Council of Arbitration for Sport (ICAS), the body that oversees the International Court of Arbitration. I was nominated to this position by another well-placed, female former athlete. I am inspired by the work of ICAS. As one of three women on the 16-member board, I am able to represent athletes and women, use my background in sport and the law, and contribute to diversity in decision-making. My experience gained through my work in FISA provided me with invaluable background for the position with ICAS. I love the international work that I have been able to do with ICAS and FISA, and am always alive to promoting qualified women to international roles—I strongly believe that improving diversity in leadership is critical to strengthening international sport.

Combined with the move to promote more women to positions of leadership is the quest to encourage more women to participate in the sport. This issue was already on the table in 1992 when I became a member of the FISA Women's Commission. In one of my first meetings we were discussing ways to promote women in rowing. Our Chairman (as she was then called—how we changed the title from Chairman to Chair is another story) suggested a Miss World Championship contest where the athletes would vote on the female athlete who was "most fine." It was a concept apparently used in Europe in other sports, and there was a similar competition in tennis. I was horrified, as were most of the other members of the Commission. As is perhaps expected in an international body, societal norms vary among members of the Women's Commission as well as among the Commission and other members of the "FISA family." However, at that time, and now only slightly less so, FISA was Euro-dominant in its leadership and members. The sport and its membership can be fairly described as relatively traditional and conservative. Change takes a long time. Part of this has to do with the leadership structure.

The Chairs of each specialized Commission (Women's, Medical, Competitive, Events, Athletes' etc.) sit on Council, along with a Vice President, a Treasurer and Continental Reps. There are no limits on terms, with the exception of the Athletes' Chair, who can hold this position only for a certain time after he/she last competed internationally. Accordingly, many, if not most, of the Chairs continue until retirement age (previously 65 and now 70), and there are few challenges to incumbents.

The first members of the Women's Commission were handpicked in the late 1960s by then president of FISA Thomas Keller. This was part of a push to get the IOC to approve women's events in the Olympic Games (for more information, read "Paddling Against the Current: A History of Women's Competitive International Rowing Between 1954 and 2003" by Amanda Nicole Schweinbenz). The Commission commenced work on obtaining data on participation and writing letters of support and encouragement to nations to send female athletes to World Championships. This was important because participation in the World Championships was one of the prerequisites for entry to the Games. After a number of setbacks, it was ultimately a presentation to the IOC Executive Board that strategically included a beautiful, tall female blond rowing champion that resulted in women's events being admitted for the first time in the Olympic Games in 1976. Men had started in 1896.

When I joined the Women's Commission, two of the original members were still on the Commission, including the Chair (which might help explain some of the context behind a Miss World Championship idea). Although the primary motive behind the creation of the Commission years earlier may not have been to increase the number of women in leadership, one of its effects was to open that door slightly—five intelligent, capable, female former rowers were given an opportunity that had previously been much less likely. Three of the five ultimately sat on Council as either Chair of the Women's Commission or Chair of another Commission.

I was elected Chair of the Women's Commission, and in a governance review, we recommended changing the structure of the Commission membership. Instead of being a stand-alone Commission made up of specialist members, we proposed drawing members from the other Commissions. The idea was that the Women's Commission should be fully integrated within the work of FISA. For example, the representatives from the Umpires' Commission would raise the issues related to female umpires for that Commission to address. This would not be an issue for the Women's Commission to address outside of the work of the Umpires' Commission. The approach was to be applied across the board with the other specialist commissions. The next step was to invite males from other commissions to become members of the Women's Commission. We meet once a year at the Joint Commissions Meeting to report on women's issues being dealt with by the relevant commissions and to share challenges and best practices.

The Women's Commission also takes on projects as appropriate. For example, the Commission sought out PhD student Amanda Schweinbenz and partially sponsored her doctoral research into the history of women in rowing (mentioned above). It also organizes and promotes an annual Women's Development Camp for women coaches and athletes. In addition, the Commission has been instrumental in helping develop policies within FISA that guide, for example, the international development program. If FISA supports a development program, it is expected that opportunities will be offered to girls and women as well as to boys and men.

Because new Chairs of the specialist Commissions are usually selected from within the Commissions, the identification and promotion of women to each Commission has been a long term strategy for the Women's Commission. As a result, women now make up seven members of Council, six Chairs of Commissions and a vice president. In other words, the recent surge in the numbers of women in leadership position did not come about by chance.

There are still a number of challenges.

FISA overviews the historic and actual number of crews, male and female, at World Championships to determine the number of events and crews at the Olympic Games. Boxing has operated in this way, and when adding women's events to the Olympics they have not added the same number of women's events as men's. Arguably, as more women take up the sport they will gradually increase the number of events for women, but this can be a long process. Even though women's rowing has been in the Olympic Games since 1976, there has been no increase in the number of women's events. Perhaps we need to look at a different approach for women's inclusion in the sport.

In the statistics we have gathered, it is obvious that eliminating or adding events from the Olympic Games has a significant impact on the participation numbers in that event. Furthermore, eliminating an Olympic event has financial repercussions—often, it is difficult for countries with limited budgets to bring crews that have no corresponding event at the Olympics to the World Championships. This means that fewer women's events at the Olympics translates to fewer women's crews at World Championships. (The same effect was felt in the men's events that had to be excluded.)

So what are some options for FISA? Perhaps more proactive work can be done through a review and revision of the World Championship program, an option investigated by the working group set up by FISA in 2012 for that purpose. Or, FISA could change the Olympic events, which was done at the Youth Olympic Games and with new sports like rugby and old sports like cycling. There will be those who will argue there is some inequity in this approach: because there are more men rowing, it would be more difficult for men to qualify. On the other hand, it must be remembered we are trying to catch up from what has been a legacy of inequality. Men have been at the Olympic table since 1896. Women were not permitted in the Olympic regatta until 1976. If we want to reach that gender parity mark we might have to change the system entirely.

The more proactive approach is the "if you build it, they will come" argument. If we offer equal events for women and men at the Olympics, then support for women will come and they will fill those spots. There are also many other factors to be considered in this discussion, in particular, how support for women in the sport is decided. In the highest level of leadership, the decision makers are still more than 80 percent male; those who decide where to spend the money are still in large part male; and, a majority of coaching staff is male. There is nothing sinister in these statistics. It is just to point out that there may be less diversity in approach because there is less diversity in the decision-making bodies. Change is taking time.

Anecdotally, I have been informed that an argument against the "build it and they will come" strategy is that in certain sports at the Youth Olympic Games, although not in rowing, some of the places offered in the 50 percent of events open to girls go unused, whereas the 50 percent of places open to boys are full. What seems to be ignored is that it takes time to build the infrastructure and the expectation of providing women with support. The traditional offerings of sport were designed with boys in mind, not girls.

There has been some progress to increase women participating in events, but much more work remains to be done. The work continues.

WINNING AT THE COMMONWEALTH GAMES
The Achievement of Gender Equity
Judy Kent

In 1992 I was selected as the Canadian Chef de Mission to the 1994 Commonwealth Games in Victoria, BC. This meant that I was also one of three official delegates representing Canada at the 1992 Commonwealth Games Federation (CGF) General Assembly in Barcelona. At that meeting, I was the only female delegate from the 71 Commonwealth Games Associations. This was the beginning of my experiences with the Commonwealth Games Federation and the first time I personally witnessed the domination of white males in international sport leadership.

After the successful completion of the 1994 Games in Victoria, I was elected President of Commonwealth Games Canada for 1994-98. By this time, I had attended three Federation meetings as a Canadian delegate, held a high profile role as host Chef de Mission, and served on the three-member Commission for the Inclusion of Athletes with a Disability in the Commonwealth Games.

By the 1995 General Assembly, I was President of the Commonwealth Games Association of Canada (CGAC) and hence a voting delegate—in fact, the only female voting delegate at that meeting. Over the next two years, two other women became delegates from Commonwealth Games Associations (CGAs) at the General Assembly.

At that time, I was being encouraged by several individuals to use my new position to advance the gender equity agenda. In 1995 I presented a paper at the General Assembly, entitled "Women and Sport: Towards Gender Equity in the Commonwealth Games, CGF, and CGAs." This paper outlined the current state of gender equity in the Commonwealth Games movement and included a road map detailing what could be achieved and how to accomplish it. It provided specific goals and strategies related to the sports programme, participants and leadership within the movement. Finally, the paper recommended the establishment of a working group for Women and Sport and provided terms of reference.

Although there was some theoretical support for gender equity, many of the delegates were threatened by the possibility of women taking away their positions. A number of these men had occupied the same positions for decades, travelling annually to an interesting part of the world, receiving per diems and enjoying great camaraderie. In short, this was a plum position that many were afraid to lose. Hence, the position paper was tabled until the 1996 General Assembly to give all Commonwealth Games Associations time to review it before voting.

At the same General Assembly, elections were held for the CGF positions, including Officers, Regional Vice Presidents (six positions), Sports Committee (one per region) and Finance Committee (one per region). Men were elected to all 23 positions. Fortunately, having had the discussion on the position paper during the same meeting, a strong point for gender equity had been made and supporters concerned by the election results were rallied.

I worked with this group of like-minded people over the following year to build support for the motion that would be voted on at the 1996 General Assembly. By the time the 1996 General Assembly took place, there was a critical mass of support to work toward improving equity for women in the Commonwealth Games movement. The paper was accepted, and the recommendations were approved almost unanimously. Implementation was referred to the CGF Executive Board.

The Executive Board established a task force to review the recommendations and finally established a working group on Women and Sport in 1997. I was named Chair, and each of the six Commonwealth regions submitted names for the Committee. The inaugural meeting was held in conjunction with the CGF meeting in September 1997.

Since the six Regional Vice Presidents appointed their working group representative, the composition lacked some of the key supporters and included some of those opposed to gender equity. We did, however, manage to develop terms of reference and a work plan, and collaborated with the 71 CGAs/

NOCs to provide educational materials and assistance in meeting the IOC targets.

For four years the working group met annually and furthered several initiatives between meetings. The working group provided bid cities and Organising Committees with guidelines for a gender equitable sports programme. We prepared media guidelines for CGAs and CGF on the appropriate portrayal of women in sport in both words and images. In supporting the IOC targets, we strove to recruit and promote women within the CGAs, making them comfortable and knowledgeable when they arrived at the General Assembly. This was a very positive time for me, seeing the increasing number of talented women coming from the African and Caribbean associations.

At the 1998 General Assembly, office bearers were elected for the next five years. Women were nominated for several CGF positions. One Officer position was available due to the retirement of the long-standing Honorary Secretary. We lobbied actively for and successfully recruited Louise Martin, President of Commonwealth Games Council of Scotland, who was elected to the Executive Board in 1998. (Note: Louise has been an excellent Honorary Secretary and continues to hold the position in 2013.) This victory aside, men were elected to fill the other 22 positions. Although this was very frustrating initially, the attitudes of many delegates had changed, and this election result was no longer seen as acceptable.

As a result, I proposed a motion to the General Assembly: "that both genders be represented on the CGF Executive Board, all Committees and Commissions; and if this does not happen through the electoral process, the Executive Board has the power to co-opt." To further guarantee that the agreed-upon directions continued to move forward, the General Assembly also approved that the Legal Committee ensure this principle be entrenched in the revisions being made to the Constitution; and, that as a result of the 1998 electoral process, the Executive Board co-opt capable women to serve on the Sports and Finance Committee until the next election. I was co-opted to the Sports Committee, resulting in two women holding positions within the CGF. (Note: the Finance Committee was inactive at this point. During the next election in 2002, Louise was re-elected to the Honorary Secretary position and I was elected to the Sports Committee.) Overall, this was a very rewarding time and motivated me to continue the struggle.

Between 1997 and 2000 the Committee continued to work closely with bid cities and Organizing Committees on making sure the sports programmes were gender equitable, such that new events or sports included both genders. Being on the Sport Committee allowed me to undertake a review of the sports programme and provided the opportunity to include a gender equity principle in the overall regulations governing the sports programme.

As the sports programme review became more refined, equity was added to the list of criteria for assessing sports for inclusion in the Commonwealth Games. By 2002, the Manchester Commonwealth Games had a gender equitable sports programme, and the number of women participants had improved from 30 percent to just over 40 percent.

A network for women communicated regularly and took part in the international opportunities provided by the International Working Group quadrennial conference and the IOC Women and Sport Conference. I represented CGF at that International Working Group for seven years. One great achievement resulting from these regular meetings was led by Commonwealth women from several African nations, who founded the African Women in Sport Association (AWISA) at the 1998 World Conference on Women and Sport in Windhoek, Namibia. Furthermore, by the 2000 General Assembly, 11 CGAs included women in their official delegations, with four as voting delegates. Several African NOC/CGAs elected women presidents over the next decade.

The inclusion of a significant number of women delegates allowed me the opportunity to change the direction of the working group. In 2001 the Working Group on Women and Sport became a Gender Equity Forum and was opened to all interested parties. Since these meetings are held prior to the General Assembly and most delegates had nothing to do while the Sports Committee and Executive Board met, an open forum was just the thing to attract the majority of delegates. At the

2001 General Assembly, 42 delegates from 26 CGAs attended the Forum. By hosting this event annually, more women were selected by their CGAs to attend as official delegates. The number of women delegates continued to grow over the next few years. Thus the Forum became a vehicle for sharing strategies and lessons learned and to "bring and brag" ideas from the various CGAs on their advancement in gender equity.

The one downside to moving the working group to an open forum was it lost its "permanent" status and became an option in the planning of the General Assembly schedule. Although I managed to fight to have it included for several more years, its inclusion became an annual battle. However, because I was an active member of the Sports Committee and member of the CGF, I was able to influence change at another level and provide support to the upcoming women from the CGA level.

International federations often use the same rationale for reducing the emphasis on gender equity, saying they have done everything they can on the issue. The CGF itself used this excuse and claimed it could not do anything else unless the CGA/NOCs nominated women for CGF positions. To some extent, there is merit to this argument, but what is left unsaid is that once nominated, those women have to pay their dues and be at the table long enough for their turn to come around—this can be a long time to wait. Elections at the international level in sport are done primarily on longevity, not on meritocracy, with few exceptions.

After over a decade of work, we have now achieved gender equity both in the sports programme and in the numbers of women participants from the majority of Commonwealth nations in recent Games. Moreover, women are regularly selected as Chefs de Mission and flag bearers. There is still a long way to go in the decision-making structures at both national and CGF levels. However, with more women attending international meetings, and the General Assembly specifically, increasing numbers of women have become known and respected. Currently the Caribbean Regional Vice President is a woman. There is hope but it is a long, tiring process.

After working in the Commonwealth Games movement for 22 years, I resigned from the Sports Committee at the end of my term in 2007 and did not stand for re-election. It was time to pass the torch on to the next generation of women.

< Sandra Kirby, 1980. Rowing at the Royal Canadian International Henley Regatta Open. Kirby competed in the 1976 Olympic Games in the quadruple sculls event, placing 9th.

∨ Sue Prestedge (second from left) at the Royal Winter Fair, 1988. Prestedge became the first woman Olympic host for CBC in 1984 and covered 3 Olympic games, women's alpine skiing and thoroughbred racing. She received the Foster Hewitt ACTRA award for outstanding broadcasting at the Los Angeles Olympic Games and became Senior Vice President of the first-ever women's sport television network (WTSN) in 2001.

^ Jojo Carrier représente la poursuite de la tradition d'excellence en nage synchronisée, autant à titre d'athlète que d'entraîneure. À 13 ans, en 1968, elle remporte son premier championnat canadien sénior en solo. Elle conserve son titre en 1971, 1972 et 1973. Durant la même période, elle remporte les épreuves des figures et du duo avec celle qui partagera longtemps ses succès (Mado Ramsay) en 1969, 1970, 1971, 1972 et 1973. Elle devient entraîneure en 1974 et est toujours active à ce jour au club SynchroÉlite de Québec.

< Erika Vines sailing a mirror dingy at age 10, with her sister in 1985.

> Johanne Falardeau débute sa carrière en badminton à l'âge de 10 ans. Après seulement quelques mois d'entraînement, elle gagne un premier tournoi, et c'est la piqûre. Un an après elle en aura gagné 17, l'année suivante 40 et elle est encore d'âge pee wee! C'est le début d'une longue et prolifique carrière qui en fait à 15 ans la plus jeune athlète de l'équipe canadienne, dont elle fera parti jusqu'à l'âge de 30 ans. La récolte se poursuit durant ses années sénior aux niveaux canadien et international où elle remportera 31 médailles de 1982 à 1990.

< Lucille Lessard débute le tir à l'arc à l'adolescence. Elle progresse rapidement et sa médaille d'or « extérieur » au premier Championnat canadien en 1974 la conduit à 17 ans à Zagreb en Yougoslavie au Championnat du monde « extérieur » où elle remporte une autre médaille d'or malgré son manque d'expérience internationale et une autre au Championnat de la Côte Pacifique. Ses succès lui ont valu d'être intronisée au Temple de la renommée des sports du Canada en 1977 et au Temple de la renommée olympique du Canada en 1982.

> Heather Thompson, centre, with her lacrosse team, early 1990s. Heather helped develop the sport of lacrosse for girls and women at the varsity level in Canada.

∧ Keri Cress, front row left, was the female goalie in the otherwise male Shaftesbury Hockey Team, 1993-1994.

∧ Charmaine Crooks, Canadian Senior Track and Field Championships in Montreal, QC, 1995. A five-time Olympian and Olympic Silver Medalist (LA 84), she represented Canada in Athletics from 1980 to 1997, carrying the flag for Canada at the opening of the 1996 Summer Olympics. A former elected member of the International Olympic Committee, she serves on the Executive Board of the Canadian Olympic Committee.

∧ The Pasternak twins, Amy and Jesse, playing hockey. The Pasternaks launched a gender discrimination complaint to the Manitoba Human Rights Commission in 2004 for the right to play in the men's hockey league.

^ Hayley Wickenheiser won six
gold medals and a silver medal
at the Women's World Hockey
Championships, a silver at
the 1998 Winter Olympics,
and three gold medals at the
2002, 2006 and 2010 Winter
Olympics.

< Jennifer Walinga (second from left) and her teammates in Vienna at the World Rowing Championships in 1991. Walinga was a member of Canada's Commonwealth, World and Olympic gold medal rowing teams between 1983 and 1992.

> Manon Rheaume began playing hockey at age 5, and in 1992 became the first woman to play professional hockey when she joined the Tampa Bay Lightning as goalie. While with Team Canada, she won a silver in the 1998 Nagano Games and golds at the 1992 and 1994 World Hockey Championships.

4 | NAMING THE ISSUES
Challenging the status quo

THE 12 CONTRIBUTIONS in this section describe a growing activism and pressure to name the issues and imperatives that were controlling women's sport opportunities. Most of the stories reflect on the reactions to seeking changes. Some of these women fought back against inequities, but paid heavy prices for doing so. Many of these women had to persist in trying to make change just to play, get space or be recognized.

The emerging issues of abuse and homophobia were named and added to the tolls of sexism and racism. Homophobia was present both inside and outside the movement of women and sport, creating divisions and delaying progress. Demands for equity replaced demands for equality and efforts were made to sell the collective benefits of social justice for all in the movement. The resistance was broad and the status quo firm. There were ongoing pressures of stereotypes and socialization. The law and sporting bodies were resistant. Indeed, all major societal instititions were resistant—from the International Olympic Committee to municipal councils, from broadcasting networks to educational institutions—systematically denying women and girls their rightful places in sport. Traditions of sport were held up as reasons for not changing. Sometimes male athletes and coaches felt threatened.

These stories reflect on the pressures of making change in the face of systemic barriers. These contributors describe the issues, the need to be well prepared, organized and courageous and, most of all, to leave no one behind in the movement for change.

THE OLD GYM BECAME THE GIRLS' GYM
Reflections across Three Generations
Marg McGregor

I fondly remember the lively kitchen table conversations that I had with my mom when I was a child growing up in the 1960s. Mom would recount her memories of playing on the women's hockey team at the University of Saskatchewan back in the 1930s. It was inspiring to hear how, in an era when women were for the most part expected to be spectators in sport, my mom was in the thick of things refining her slap shot in Rutherford Rink. Those were the Depression years, and there was no money for shin pads for the women's hockey team, so mom and her teammates would shove newspapers and magazines into their socks to provide some cushioning. In 1939, the second year that my mother was on the hockey team, the Huskiettes won the city championships in Saskatoon, the city where the University of Saskatchewan is located.

I also recall listening to my mother's recollections of her experiences with a local golf club in my hometown. In the late 1950s, only men could join the club. My mom and her female friends set out to convince the golf club that there was an economic benefit to allowing women to play. Mom assembled a long list of women who were prepared to purchase memberships and play during off-peak times. She presented it to the board of directors for their consideration. Mom and her friends were convincing, the history of exclusion was snapped and the women took to the links! Thanks to trailblazers like my mom, my personal experiences in sport in the 1970s were more welcoming. I played on school teams, and benefited from great coaching by both men and women.

Although I was not conscious of it at the time, when I look back now on my experiences, there were subtle indications that sport for boys was more important and legitimate than sport for girls. My high school constructed a new gymnasium. We were happy because this meant we would have easier after-school access to gym time. The new gym was branded the Boys' Gym, while the old one became the Girls' Gym. The boys got new basketball uniforms, while the girls continued to play in well-worn skirts and purple bloomers.

When Canada played host to the 1976 Summer Olympics, I remember being excited because women's rowing and basketball were first admitted as Olympic events—some 40 years after men's basketball became an Olympic sport and 80 years after men's rowing made its Olympic debut. I was inspired to dream of becoming an Olympian by watching Romanian gymnast Nadia Comaneci score seven perfect 10s and win three gold medals in Montreal.

In the 1990s, I became Executive Director of CAAWS. It was a time of rapid progress for women in sport. The number of events for women in the Olympics increased significantly. Issues in sport, such as homophobia, harassment and the female athlete triad were being talked about; sport organizations were being challenged to become more inclusive. Increasing the number of women coaches became a priority.

My two daughters grew up in the new millennium. They possess a confidence and a sense of entitlement—an expectation of equality—that sport belongs to them as much as it does to their male friends. They participate as athletes, coaches, administrators and officials. They can purchase sporting gear designed for women.

There are Women's World Cups. Equal prize money for the women's tennis champion at Wimbledon (the last hold-out against equality of prize money in the Grand Slams) has been in place since 2007. There are an equal number of events for women in the Summer Olympics. Women athletes are becoming household names: Hayley Wickenheiser, Clara Hughes, Christine Sinclair and Perdita Felicien are shining role models for my daughters and their girlfriends. Countries that formerly prohibited women athletes from competing in international sporting events, such as Brunei, Qatar and Saudi Arabia, have begun to field female athletes at the Olympics. Although it might be argued that this participation was a token gesture in response to international pressure, it is a beginning. The truth remains that the opportunity to compete in sport opens doors to equity in other domains. Sport is a powerful and positive vehicle for change and empowerment in the lives of girls and women.

There has been significant progress from my mom's generation through my generation and to my daughter's generation. Many of the "old boys" have retired and a new breed of women leaders has emerged. The CEOs of many of Canada's sport organizations are women, including the Canada Games Council, ParticipAction and Own the Podium. Having said that, much remains the same and there are shocking similarities to the past.

While my mom took up the fight to open the doors of a golf club to women in the 1950s, it was not until 2012 that the famed Augusta National Golf Club admitted its first two female members. Facing intense pressure, it finally permitted two of the USA's most influential women to play on its hallowed grounds.

The Toronto-based National Golf Club of Canada continues to restrict women, allowing them to play only as guests and on a limited basis, thus illustrating that women still hit their heads on the glass ceiling not only in the corporate board rooms but also on the playing fields.

One of my daughters travelled with her provincial team to the United States for a training camp, while the equivalent boys' provincial team travelled to South America and Europe. Preferred playing times still belong to the men. Media coverage is dominated by men's professional sports.

Toronto received a franchise in the Lingerie Football League for women in 2011 and the League is looking to expand to the Prairies and West Coast. Players are obliged to sign agreements to allow "accidental nudity." The Bikini Basketball League is also making waves and garnering attention. These leagues objectify and sexualize female athletes.

As the saying goes: "We've come a long way, baby." And we still have a long way to go. We need to take heart from our successes and keep up the momentum to make the world of sport fully equitable.

If I have any granddaughters, I hope that they will: be able to take part in any sport on an equal and open basis with their male friends, spend their energies on getting prepared to play and not on trying to be allowed to play, be lauded for their performances and not for their looks, not feel afraid that they will be harassed, and not feel ashamed of who they are. Let's all hope for such times.

CRITICAL THINKING ON THE POOL DECK
Not Now, Not Ever?
Sarah Teetzel

As a young swimmer in the late 1980s, I found that when girls and boys trained together, girls consistently swam as fast as or faster than boys prior to puberty. The pool deck felt like a gender-neutral space, and I was completely sheltered from the fact that women's sport and men's sport were still far from being equal. This naïveté continued while I was a teen in the late 1990s. Most surprisingly, as an undergraduate and then graduate student and varsity athlete in the 2000s, I still remained ignorant of the challenges faced by female athletes and the gender inequity remaining in subtle ways in many levels of Canadian sport. I had what can be considered, on the surface, a perfect sport experience in the club and university systems. Competing at youth, junior and university national competitions, I thought my teammates and I were among the luckiest students in Canada, spending our time training together and competing at swim meets coast to coast.

In hindsight, the degree to which I failed to apply any type of critical thinking skills, and my lack of awareness to observe the reality of my surroundings and experiences, continue to shock me today. Some people might attribute my perception of having experienced a perfect sport experience to sheer optimism, rose-coloured glasses, or the innocence of youth. But, reflecting on my experiences as a competitive swimmer through my undergraduate degree and early stages of my graduate studies, I think it is more realistic and accurate to describe myself as wilfully blind to the challenging aspects of the sport I loved and to the inequities it perpetuated. Now, I am able to look back on and reframe some of my experiences within the Canadian amateur sport system in order to suggest areas where advocacy and awareness can strengthen athletes' leadership and development, rather than stifle young athletes' critical thinking skills.

One way to do so is to resurrect discussions of the early sport feminists, and ensure girls know the importance of their stories and accomplishments. Children grow up hearing stories of male hockey legends, such as Maurice Richard and Gordie Howe, whose names and accomplishments are likely to never be forgotten. But to poll young swimmers about past heroines of their own sport would likely result in blank looks, despite Canadian female swimmers' important roles in the history of Canadian sport. The achievements of these women and girls, some quite radical in their time, are virtually unknown to the majority of girls who spend their waking hours outside of school on the pool deck and in the water. To be sure, as a young swimmer in the 1980s and 1990s, there were many world-class Canadian swimmers to admire. Marianne Limpert, Joanne Malar and Nancy Sweetnam were consistently winning medals at the international level and served as very positive role models. But prior to their time atop the podium in Canada, my teammates and I had no idea what had occurred in previous decades.

Sadly, even the name Marilyn Bell is often met with the questioning looks and a response of "who's that?". Marilyn Bell, one of the best long distance swimmers the world has ever seen, has been a member of Canada's Sports Hall of Fame since 1958, yet young athletes are not aware of her record-breaking swims across Lake Ontario, the English Channel and the Strait of Juan de Fuca. In her swim across Lake Ontario when she was 16-years-old, she covered 52 kilometres in just under 21 hours, exiting the water as the first person to successfully complete the swim. Her accomplishments in the 1950s were recognized with every award available: the Canadian athlete of the year (Lou Marsh Trophy), the top female athlete in Canada (Bobbie Rosenfeld Award) and the Canadian Newsmaker of the Year, as well as numerous prizes, gifts, and monetary rewards. Bell was not the only long distance swimmer capturing headlines in Canada after World War II. Other great swimmers, such as Winnie Roach Leuszler, who caused waves by leaving her three children at home in Canada to swim across the English Channel in 1950, helped usher in the view that swimming grueling distances was an acceptable pursuit for women. These women swam where they wanted and covered distances previously thought impossible for any human—let alone women—to complete. It seems absurd that these women's contributions to Canadian sport history are unknown to most girls today. The accomplishments of strong, spirited, determined, talented women need to be discussed and celebrated. Young swimmers need examples like these women to show that they, too, can do extraordinary things.

I became aware of Bell and the stories of other heroines of sport as an undergraduate student athlete studying kinesiology and competing in the Canadian Interuniversity Sport system. I vividly recall my frustration that my teammates had not heard of these women either, but I did not focus on this omission in our knowledge of Canadian history. It was not until I enrolled in a master's and then doctoral program in ethics in sport that I began reading feminist theory, feminist history, and about gender inequity in sport. When I started my graduate studies, I was still competing for the university's team. Had the eligibility rules allowed me to keep competing throughout my postgraduate studies, I question whether I could have kept it up or if I would have eventually quit in protest. Would I have complacently continued participating in an environment that encouraged me to follow orders and rarely, if ever, think? Would I have pressed for more autonomy for the swimmers, a less authoritarian and conformist training program and more emphasis on developing athletes as leaders and coaches? I would like to think I would have, but I am not sure. While women take part in numerous competitive sports funded at roughly equal levels with access to top-notch training facilities, the fact remains that gender inequities and feminist concerns still permeate many sports. The most troubling part is that many young women athletes in the system do not recognize these issues are ongoing.

In graduate school, I discovered the works of the great writers of women's sport history and feminist research. Authors such as Helen Lenskyj, Jennifer Hargreaves, Bruce Kidd and M. Ann Hall opened my eyes to the magnitude of gender inequity perpetuated through sport. With my head filled with statistics and analyses of sexual harassment, discrimination, homophobia, heterosexism, power relations, powerlessness, authoritarian coaching, access and equity issues in sport, I felt fortunate that my own sport experience had been free of these all-too-common horrific examples. At the same time, my mind also buzzed with the nagging and hostile thought that perhaps I was choosing to ignore the nuanced ways in which gender inequity continues to play out in many young women's sport experiences, including my own. In re-examining my past swimming experiences through a gender lens, I was awakened to a world that was hard to continue describing as "perfect."

The reality is that, like most sports, in swimming there are very few female high-performance coaches, officials or administrators. At the grassroots levels, a gendered division of labour continues to occur at swim meets, where women tend to run the bake sales and fundraise and the men often volunteer in the more "important" roles, such as starter and referee. More shocking, though, are my reflections on my experiences as a student athlete on a university team. When I was a competitive swimmer, every member of the women's team was Caucasian from an upper- or middle-class family. Highly competitive student athletes with disabilities at the same university trained with a team across the city, not with the university. There were no Aboriginal athletes on our team. All of my teammates projected an image of heterosexuality and stereotypically feminine-appropriate behaviour. We, as athletes, had little choice in important matters that went well beyond our athletic careers. Without hesitation, we all signed on as patients for the doctor assigned to our team, we stayed in hotel rooms with roommates chosen by the coach, and we watched our calorie consumption and sat through talks about how increased body mass equalled increased drag in the pool. Some team members swam through injuries, and we knew that exhaustion and sickness were unacceptable reasons for missing a practice. Most shockingly, we did not recognize that any of this was problematic.

A significant number of swimmers on my "perfect team" of female swimmers, I now know, were suffering in silence. During our competitive days, we all acted as though we had healthy body images and eating practices, everyone was heterosexual and we were free to conduct ourselves as we pleased. Yet most of us demonstrated an extreme amount of what sociologists of sport refer to as female apologetic behaviours. Long blond hair was the norm, and it was not uncommon for girls to wear make-up and jewellery on the pool deck and even in the pool, despite understanding it was counterproductive to the desirable streamlined body position in the water. Several years into our "retirement" from high-performance sport, many of my former teammates are now living openly and proudly as lesbians, and several have dealt with, or are continuing to deal with, their disordered eating patterns that include anorexia and exercise compulsion. I cannot recall one conversation in the locker room or outside the pool environment where we discussed important topics such as homophobia, heterosexism or eating disorders in sport. Rather, we talked about more trivial things, such as strategies for making our big, strong shoulders appear smaller, instead of being proud of our strength and size. We did what we were told in and out of the pool because, as we quickly learned through the dismissal of our captain one year for her defiant behaviour, challenging our male coach meant being kicked off the team. Critical thinking was neither appreciated nor tolerated.

One might think that with hours spent swimming up and down a pool we would have had ample time for thinking and self-reflection. But at least for me, these mind-numbing hours were not put to good use, and were passed instead counting laps and singing songs to ourselves underwater. With a highly regulated practice schedule, where missing a weekday or Sunday practice was not an option, we were tied to the university campus and to our hectic schedule. Of course, the diminished free time is part of the price athletes pay to have the privilege of representing their university. However, I think there are ways of making the experience more democratic and allowing the athletes more input and decision-making powers over how they live their lives. As Lenskyj has emphasized, many female athletes spend so much time following directions and trying to please their coaches during their youth spent training that they fail to develop adequate survival strategies for coping inside and beyond the sport environment.

As a member of the so-called Generation Y, which was taught from a very young age that women and men were equal and we could excel at anything we chose to pursue, my reflections on my sporting history have been difficult. I cannot speak for my peers, but it is my perception that we, as a group, desperately want to cling to the belief that our parents were right when they told us sports were equal and equitable. It was only when I was finally equipped with an understanding of women's history and feminist theory that my blinders were removed and I began to acknowledge that feminist concerns for women's safety, participation at all levels, and freedom of choice, are still extremely relevant in sport today.

After this reflection, can I still claim that my student athlete's experiences were positive? Yes, but in a much more qualified and critical manner, which recognizes both the great times we had and the work that still needs to be done. We need to promote the drive and spirit of the athletes who made important advances during the second wave of feminism in Canada and challenged traditional gender roles about sport. We need to encourage girls and young women to ask questions and not simply accept the orders of their coaches without careful scrutiny and understanding of the rationale behind the decisions. Unless young athletes actively think for themselves and are encouraged to follow in the footsteps of our more radical and revolutionary heroines, sport will continue to promote uncritical thought and adherence to rigid, authoritarian programs. In moving forward, particularly at the university level, I believe we need more communication between feminists groups and athletes, more education for coaches on women's sport history. Organizations such as CAAWS, which routinely calls for and supports the development of more high-level female officials and women's head coaches, are on the right track in these respects. I hope that through these and other initiatives, girls and young women will be encouraged not only to take up coaching as a career but also to pursue it to the highest levels. To move forward, we need to continue to look backward by remembering the feats of the great women swimmers and reclaiming their achievements as motivation for future generations of athletes.

PRIDE AND PREJUDICE
How Aboriginal Women have Experienced Canadian Sport
Janice Forsyth, Audrey R. Giles and Vanessa Lodge-Gagné

Aboriginal women have been and continue to be critical members of the Canadian sport community. Like many women, they occupy multiple roles in the sport system, as athletes, coaches, officials, administrators and mothers and/or caregivers, and strive to find ways to balance their busy lives with their commitment to sport. This balancing act is challenging at the best of times and is made more difficult when issues of class and gender come to bear on their sporting lives. By acknowledging these different roles, it might be possible to minimize the factors that hinder their involvement in sport, while those that enhance their participation can be improved. We hope to make a small, but important, contribution to those twin objectives.

This paper draws on oral interviews we conducted with 10 Aboriginal female athletes who won a Tom Longboat Award between 1951 and 1998. The fact that they are recipients of this specific award is significant. It is the longest standing and one of the most prestigious sport awards for Aboriginal athletes in Canada. As written in Janice Forsyth's 2005 dissertation, "The Power to Define: A History of the Tom Longboat Awards, 1951-2001," while the criteria for the Award have changed since it was inaugurated in 1951, it has always been imperative that all nominees made a significant contribution to Canadian sport.

Thus, most Award winners have experience in community-level sport to elite-level competition in either all-Aboriginal sporting contexts or mainstream sport environments, as well as amateur and/or professional leagues. To put the matter another way, the women we interviewed are among a select group of athletes whose experiences offer unique insights into sport as a place where women continue to struggle for symbolic and material rewards, and take pride in their accomplishments while dealing with prejudice in active and courageous ways.

Overall, our findings show that Aboriginal women have a long and rich history of involvement in Canadian sport, whether in their home community and/or in mainstream towns or cities, and that they have had to negotiate their involvement in sport from positions of marginality, shaped along lines of class and gender. It is outside the scope of our contribution to delve into an analysis of race, class and gender; instead, we will examine how the women and their families struggled to make ends meet to enable their involvement in sport and how this shaped their sense of community and pride. We will also consider how gendered sporting patterns informed their sense of value as sportswomen in their community. While this chapter is structured around two analytical categories—class and gender—elements of each can be found in both sections, which speaks to the complexity of sport as a key social institution in modern life, especially in the lives of Aboriginal women.

Established in 1951, the Tom Longboat Award is the longest-standing and most prestigious sport award for Aboriginal people in the country. Recipients are usually provincial and territorial level athletes, but also include participants who have competed at the national and world-class levels, including the Olympic Games. Being a Tom Longboat Award recipient is thus a form of cultural capital that few possess. Among the rarified few are a small handful of Aboriginal women who excelled in their chosen activities, even though, as M. Ann Hall states in her 2012 book *Toward a History of Aboriginal Women in Canadian Sport*, ideological and structural barriers limited their ability to pursue their athletic dreams.

Consider, for instance, the structure of the Tom Longboat

Award. From 1951 to 1998, only one recipient was named for each administrative region in Canada, with the national recipient being selected from the pool of regional winners. Ann Hall writes again in her 2012 book that during that era, sport (for all Canadians) was primarily a male domain. There were more sporting opportunities at every level for men, which meant that male athletes had more and better opportunities than female athletes to reach higher levels of competitive development and to earn recognition for their accomplishments. For example, at the Arctic Winter Games, a circumpolar sporting and cultural festival that occurs every two years, men have competed in Dene games (a series of traditional Dene physical practices) since 1990, and a Junior Boys category was added in 2002. According to Audrey R. Giles in her article "Kelvar, Crisco, and Menstruation," it was not until 2004 that a category was added for Junior Girls and there remains no category for women. As such, male athletes have had an institutionalized advantage over their female counterparts when it has come to winning sport awards, since the women often toiled away in obscurity at lower-tiered events or were not able to participate at all. This gendered pattern in sport and the symbolic rewards attached to athletic achievement is obvious in the Tom Longboat Award between the years 1951 to 1998. Although there was never a formal rule that limited nominees to men only, the structure of sport itself precluded most women from being named a recipient because they did not have access to the same types of opportunities as the men (e.g., national and world championships) who were vying for the same award.

A summary of the total number of recipients versus the total number of female recipients per administrative region for the Tom Longboat Award illustrates that women were systematically disadvantaged in sport. Although some data are missing in Alberta (post 1985), Saskatchewan (post 1976) and Ontario (post 1987), the available information between the years 1951 to 1998 shows that at least 188 Tom Longboat Awards were handed out to Aboriginal athletes throughout Canada. Of that number, only 21 recipients were female (approximately 9 percent of the total). In 1999 the Tom Longboat Award was split into two categories at the regional and national levels — one for male and another for female recipients. The gender equal format continues to this day. Of the 21 women who we know won a Tom Longboat Award between the years 1951 to 1998, 10 (nearly 48 percent) were interviewed for a project funded by the Social Sciences and Humanities Research Council. The interviews took place over six years, from 2004 to 2010. All of the transcripts were read with a view to identifying two dominant themes: 1) family, class and community, and 2) gendered community patterns. Excerpts from six transcripts are used to accentuate the points made in both sections.

For the women interviewed, participation in sport was often a family affair due to the large, tightly-knit familial networks that they identified as being common in their Aboriginal communities. Vivian Underwood, from Saanich, British Columbia, underscored this point, stating, "We were a big enough family that we had our own team." Leona Sparrow, from Musqueam, British Columbia, noted, "At one point our basketball team was six sisters, and so they called me the seventh sister! It was the same playing ball over in Duncan, they were all cousins of mine." Mary Ward, from Red Bank, New Brunswick, echoed this sentiment:

> "I have 10 brothers and sisters. There's 6 girls and 4 boys in the family and I remember occasions where we'd be sitting at the supper table. There would be at least 8 of us in uniform … There was four of us [sisters] on the team. I was pitching, my sister Pam was catching, Anita was on shortstop, and Betty was on first base."

Ward further noted, "you learn about your community history when you're playing Native ball, because you're going to different villages where you have relatives, and you learn about who they are and you see the kinds of differences there are between the communities." Participation in sport thus served to strengthen family ties both within and between communities.

The participants frequently cited the key roles that their families and broader community members played in facilitating their participation in sport. Underwood recalled that there were "a lot of breastfeeding moms" at her ball games and that the players and people on the sidelines would help: "The ones that were on the bench would change the diapers." Ward's mother played a key role in encouraging her daughter's sport involvement. "I had a very athletic family and a lot of it came from my mom," she noted. She continued,

> "The enthusiasm that she had for that, we [Ward and her siblings] got it. Every day my mother had to wash a whole stack of uniforms and she didn't mind. Every day our uniforms were hanging on the line because we either played every day or we would have a practice or she just made sure once those uniforms were off at the end of the day, whatever was dirty was hung up on the line right away, it was washed."

In her 2011 article, "The geographies of Aboriginal people in Canada," Evelyn Peters explains that "the systematic underdevelopment of reserve areas and First Nations economies and populations" has contributed to First Nations' poverty in Canada. The impact of poverty on the participants in our research was particularly evident; it made family and community support all the more important due to the financial constraints that the women and their families faced. Several participants noted that because of a lack of financial resources, facilities and equipment often had to be improvised. For example, the surface upon which Leona Sparrow grew up playing soccer was "the sand on the beach. It was not a manicured field." Similar innovation was necessary for other sports. In Six Nations, Ontario, Phyllis Bomberry's brothers built a dam for a pond to ensure that there was a place to play hockey. Because it lacked lights, she told us, "we'd use a tin can instead of a puck so you could hear wherever the can went." While Bomberry explained that she did have her own hockey stick, she often did not have a puck: "If we didn't have a puck, we'd cut a tree branch into hockey pucks. That way we'd have a bunch of pucks because we couldn't afford real ones." Meanwhile, in Woodstock, New Brunswick, Carol Polchies' father cut wood intended for their wood stove into tennis racquets of sorts. Underwood poignantly recalled competing in sprints without shoes until Grade 10, at which point officials brought in a rule that athletes in the inter-city meet had to compete in shoes:

"My mom was going to get a new pair of shoes for herself. Then she bought a pair for me ... when I got the track shoes in grade ten, it made a difference. It didn't increase my speed any, but it gave me a little bit more pride, that's all."

Strong participation in sports leagues within some of the participants' communities decreased the need to travel to other communities. When travel was necessary, it could be difficult to find financial support. Several participants mentioned the need for extensive fundraising and to keep costs as low as possible. Ward explained:

"We would sleep in the van sometimes. We would bring tents with us; we had sleeping bags. It was hard but it was something at that time [that] didn't seem hard. But when I look back at it, how the hell did we do that? You know, how the hell did we do that? We were so, we were poor. Native people were very, very poor at that time."

While family, class, and community shaped the way the women experienced sport, so too did ideas about gender. Indeed, the women struggled against the constraints imposed by gendered ideas and patterns in myriad and complex ways.

Gender, similar to class, is a key organizing principle in sport, whereby contemporary elite sport is usually organized along male/female lines. There is an entire system in place that supports male sporting opportunities and, more recently, another to support female sporting opportunities. Rarely do the two overlap so that males and females compete against each other in the same category. Indeed, as Don Morrow and Kevin Wamsley write in their book *Sport in Canada: A History*, the two systems are not equal, although opportunities for females have come a long way since the emergence of organized sport in the late 19th century.

The women we interviewed all spoke eloquently about how gender shaped their sporting experiences. In some cases, the lack of opportunities for females clearly influenced the way they tried to gain access to train and compete. For instance, Beverly Beaver, from Six Nations, Ontario, explained how she pretended to be a boy in order to play hockey at a nearby pond:

"Nobody else that I knew liked to play hockey. So I just played with the boys and that was fine for everybody. There's an area around here called the Mill Pond. It's quite a big area of water and it's where the guys used to play. So I used to put my hair up under my hat and I used to go down there and they would think I was a boy. They asked me what my name was and I said "Billy"! So that's how I would get to play because they'd think I was a boy. There's another place down the other way but they knew me there. So it didn't matter. I didn't have to disguise myself. Then, when I started getting older I would tape my breasts so they couldn't tell."

While playing with the boys might have been acceptable under some circumstances to some groups, the women we interviewed almost always had to make some sort of accommodation in order to play sport. Traditionally, hockey is a sport where male Aboriginal athletes have learned and asserted their sense of masculinity, explains Michael Robidoux in his book *Stickhandling Through the Margins: First Nations Hockey in Canada*. Given this situation, Beaver had to adjust her looks so that the male players would not be offended by the inclusion of a girl, presumably because the men thought women were inferior hockey players.

The Aboriginal women we interviewed also struggled to gain access to much-needed resources for sport from their community band council. One woman, Ward, spoke eloquently and openly about the different types of support that were given to the male and female softball teams from her community. We use her words extensively here to relay the way she is able to communicate the interconnectedness of gender and community sporting patterns:

"Ohhh yes, it was a constant fighting for recognition, constant fighting for resources, constant fighting for the one ball field on the reserve. If the men had something scheduled, even if it was just a practice and you had a game, they would take the field and they wouldn't give it up. It was like a form of bullying. We encountered that a lot as women back then; we were second-class, we were not first-class. It was always that … that's one of the problems we had … was actually fighting against the men and not fighting with them. It's just that they did what they wanted and they took precedence over us even though they weren't successful and we were. But later on, as we became more and more successful, we built up the respect, respect of the men, respect of the community, respect of other communities surrounding us."

Ward's comment also speaks to a pattern in broader society, where female athletes have had to earn recognition and support, while men are habitually and automatically granted "respect" as athletes simply because they are men. This pattern reinforces the idea that sport is a male domain that women should either not intrude upon or enter into only under limited conditions. Ward explained that the men "had sort of like a superficial respect. They had respect just because they were men, that they should be number one. They didn't have the respect because they were really good, it wasn't that." The practical implications for Ward, and the other women who faced similar challenges, were that the men usually received more and better resources than the women, such as access to facilities for training and competition, uniforms, and funding for travel and competition. For Ward, the real battles for sport were fought not only on the playing fields against other teams, but also in the band council offices, which have traditionally been (and remain) dominated by men:

> "We fought initially with the chief and councils to get the same kind of help that the men were getting. The men were getting uniforms—everything was given to the men. And for us [women], we had to start fighting and getting what we got. It was really the first time, and eventually we had everything that we wanted, but it was through a lot of fighting and you had to be focused. If we weren't passionate about it, then we would have been left in the dust, we wouldn't have won nothing. We wouldn't be given nothing."

Similar to women more broadly in Canadian society, the women we interviewed responded differently to the gender inequity they experienced. The reasons for these differences varied, but had to do with a combination of the era in which they were training and competing, the history and structure of sport in Canada, access to existing sporting opportunities in their community, and ideas about appropriate sporting behavior for women, among other factors. While some athletes, like Ward, openly pushed the boundaries for women in sport in their community, other women, like Beaver, pushed the boundaries in less obvious ways. Beaver eventually played hockey on a boys' team in Six Nations, but was not allowed to compete in championship play because the rules at the time prevented mixed-gender teams. When asked if she was upset with the rules, she said, "I was disappointed, but it didn't really bother me. No." Her husband George Beaver, who was also present for the interview, further explained: "That's the way it was. Girls didn't expect to be treated the same as boys back then."

This chapter investigated the experiences of the small handful of women who won a Tom Longboat Award between the years 1951 and 1998, with the goal of gaining a clearer understanding of the challenges and opportunities they faced as sportswomen in Aboriginal communities. Our findings show that all of the women delighted in their experiences and had vivid and revealing stories to tell, stories that went to the heart of what it was like for women to struggle for access, support, opportunities, and recognition, all the while developing friendships, bringing members of their community together through play and competition, and acting as role models for other girls and women in their community. This combined behaviour shows a pattern of the pride and prejudice for Aboriginal women in sport. If there is an overarching narrative that describes their experience, it is this: in spite of the challenges they faced, Aboriginal women have developed a strong sense of pride in their Aboriginal heritage and fostered a deep sense of community attachment through their sporting experiences. These women have a great deal to offer—theoretically and practically— on how gender has shaped, and continues to shape, sport for women in Canada.

IT JUST MAKES SENSE
Media Coverage of Women's Sport
Nancy Lee

There should be more media coverage of sporting events that appeal to female audiences. And there should be more coverage of women's events period. But that does not mean these ends are easily achieved. During my time working in TV coverage of sporting events, I have had the chance to see how broadcasting decisions are made. I have also had the opportunity to reflect on current policies and think about how coverage could be changed, not just in TV but also across all sport media platforms.

There are a variety of ways to change the current status of sports coverage for women. And in fact, a lot of times change can happen when consumers point out the inequity in the coverage to the reporters, producers or media companies. Often the under-represented coverage is not necessarily intentional but based on the media's lack of results for the women's events. This is particularly true for sports events at the high school and post-secondary levels.

At the Olympics, there are several key stakeholders involved in the decision-making about the competition schedule; however, the process begins and ends with the International Sports Federations (IFs). The IFs are responsible for organizing the sports competitions at the Games. They also heavily influence which events will occur at the Olympics, the number of female and male athletes invited to compete, and the distances or weight classifications for the female and male competitors.

The other stakeholders who participate in determining the competition schedule at an Olympics are the Organizing Committee (OC), the broadcasting rights holders (RHBs), the host broadcasting company (HB), and the International Olympic Committee (IOC). By and large, the levels of influence for setting the schedule occur in that order.

The OC is naturally driven to increase revenues via ticket sales and decrease costs by avoiding overlaps at adjacent venues, thereby keeping costs down for transportation and other logistical resources. The OC also wants to maintain commuter flow and minimize chaotic spectator arrivals and departures at the venues.

The broadcasting rights holders (RHBs) are focused on maximizing television audiences. For the Olympics, this means scheduling the key competitions for their country's athletes in prime time (7-11 pm). However, a complicating factor is time zones, which creates conflict between RHBs from different continents.

The host broadcasting organization is interested in keeping its operations costs down and at the same time trying to juggle and mediate the discrepancies of the international RHBs and the time zone issue.

Finally, the IOC's responsibility is to ensure the OC, the IFs and the RHBs reach an agreement on the schedule. The IOC can be consulted regarding significant areas of conflict, but at the end of day, it comes down to a give and take amongst the stakeholders. There can easily be over 40 renditions of the schedule before it is finalized.

The day and timing of the female competitions and the impact the schedule has on media coverage of these events is a very important matter, but not one that gets enough consideration. And it is an area where those working with IFs and National Sports Organizations can influence the outcome. Consumers and interest groups can also impact the discussion by addressing the matter directly with the national broadcaster holding the rights to show the Games.

The Winter and Summer Olympic Games offer several examples of how the competition schedule could have been changed to allow greater prominence of the women's events, and consequently, an opportunity to draw in larger audiences.

To see where these opportunities lie, it is first useful to understand how television and the competition schedule intersect. TV scheduling is based on common sense: to garner the largest audiences possible. This process begins by identifying when the largest potential audience is most likely available to watch TV. In Canada, this time slot is in evening prime time (7-11 pm). A second prime time window for sports is Saturday and Sunday afternoons (generally 3-6 pm), with Sunday typically having a larger potential audience. Consequently, the Olympic events that are broadcast in prime time evenings or Saturday and Sunday afternoons will have the largest audiences.

Most networks around the world broadcast on average 20 hours of Olympic programming per day. This has been the norm since the late 1990s. This much exposure has proven a great opportunity for high performance sports to receive much needed media coverage. If greater attention were paid to making the television coverage equally allocated to women's and men's events, it could also be a great opportunity for female athletes.

As the team competitions wind down, there are fewer events to cover. This culminates at the end of the second week of the Games, particularly the last weekend. The decrease in coverage opportunities has a significant impact on the television schedule because networks worldwide need a certain volume of hours to meet their revenue targets. (In the case of public broadcasters, there is also an internal mandate to maximize coverage.) The combination of these two factors translates into the entire, three-hour men's 50 km cross-country ski competition being shown on the final Sunday of the Winter Games. At the Summer Games, the entire men's marathon is televised for two and a half hours. In both these cases, there is no need to cut away to show other events because there is nothing else on the competition schedule. Furthermore, the medals for these events are awarded during the closing ceremonies for the Games. In comparison, the coinciding women's events (the marathon and 30 km cross-country skiing) are scheduled during busier time periods. Inevitably, these scheduling choices mean that broadcasters are switching away from those women's events to provide coverage of other competitions.

There is also a fundamental inequity in the competition schedule as it relates to gold medal events on the last day of the Olympics. At the Winter Olympics, there are two gold medal events held on the last Sunday for men. There are none for women. At the Summer Olympics, there are seven gold medal events for men and two for women — modern pentathlon and rhythmic gymnastics. This imbalance begs the question that if fewer women are around to compete on the final weekend, are there also fewer women still at the Games to participate in the closing ceremonies?

Two other changes to the competition schedule would result in a significant increase in the extent of women's media coverage at the Olympics. The first change is related to women's figure skating and women's hockey. Both these events occur on the same day (the second last Thursday of the Games). A slight shift of the men's hockey schedule could result in the women's gold medal hockey match being played on Saturday, in prime time. This minor scheduling change would prevent these two key events competing for media attention.

The second change is for curling and snowboarding scheduling. The women's events are scheduled on Friday (when there is a smaller available television audience) while the men's are both held on Saturday (prime time for sports audiences.)

Another matter worth considering is the venue women's competitions are assigned. At major Games such as the Olympics or Pan/Parapan American Games, the number of teams competing in ice hockey, football and tennis require the availability of more than one venue. The IFs and the OC lead the decision-making for venue selection.

The interesting media point regarding venues is that television coverage constantly covers the size of the audience with its crowd shots. There is a massive difference in seeing a crowd in a 5,000-seat arena versus an 18,000-seat arena, which invariably leads to an assumption of second-rate competition at the smaller venue. At the Vancouver Olympics, the women played five games at Canada Hockey Place (home of the NHL Canucks). The men played 27 games there. Meanwhile, the women played the majority of their games (15) at UBC Thunderbird Arena, while the men played there twice. Do not assume that ticket sales were a major factor in this decision. Women's ice hockey sells out Canada's large arenas. And the Olympic ticket packages can be bundled in such a way to ensure sell-outs at indoor venues.

Scheduling championships at different locations and on different dates is another barrier in the coverage of women's sports. Whether it's a single print reporter or a complete television broadcast crew involving 50 staff, there are significant financial savings for coverage of women's and men's events if they are happening at the same location and within the same time period.

It is not always the event organizers who can be held responsible when women's competitions do not receive equal prominence on television. A case in point is the Canadian women's National Curling Championships. In the early 2000s, the CBC offered to schedule the women's and men's national curling finals in prime time Sunday! (Sundays generally achieve the highest TV audiences for the week.) The men took CBC up on the offer. The women did not. They preferred to continue playing in the afternoon so that the traditional end-of-competition banquet would not be displaced. That decision meant the athletes, the association and the sponsors lost out on a minimum 15 percent audience gain.

It can be disheartening to read about examples where female athletes were given less than equal opportunity for media coverage. But the positive news is that many of these situations can be changed. First, people have to appreciate that there is a problem. Then, people must take the initiative to change the status quo. And it takes perseverance to keep asking the question "why?" and not accepting the argument that changing the competition schedule would lower the television audiences or ticket sales.

Offering more hours of coverage of women's competitions is not going to cannibalize the audience—particularly when there are so many television channels simultaneously covering the Games. It makes good business sense to change the status quo. It also just makes sense.

CLASHING VALUES
Gender Equity, Canada and the International Olympic Committee
Nikki Dryden

Rather than formulating a progressive sport policy, Canada appears to be regressing in the world of sport. One reason is its continued allegiance to the Olympic Movement and other international sporting structures that discriminate against women and violate laws meant to uphold and promote gender equity. Canada is a country with strong domestic equality laws; it is a leader in international human rights regimes and boasts internationally successful women athletes. Yet women in Canada and internationally are far from equal to their male counterparts in the world of sport.

As Canadian female athletes, we have achieved successes equal to and even exceeding those of men in a myriad of Olympic sports, despite often receiving less financing and public support. However, from our participation in professional sports to our actions off the field, we are still not engaged in Canadian sport at the same level as our male counterparts. I will address the contradiction between Canada's legal obligations to promote and protect women's rights in sport domestically and internationally and its regressive sport policy and membership in the Olympic Movement, which continues to discriminate against women sportspeople. I conclude with a set of actions Canada can take to lead the Olympic Movement and the world of sport more generally toward gender equity. As host of the Pan/Parapan American Games in Toronto 2015, Canada must decide now what values it wants to promote.

A Canadian Heritage report indicates that in 2009, the general participation levels of girls and women in Canadian sport were steadily rising. At the elite level, women are achieving greater international sporting success. At the 2008 Olympics in Beijing, they comprised 47 percent of the team and won 41 percent of the medals, while at the Vancouver Winter Olympics in 2010, Canadian women made up 44 percent of the team, and won 56 percent of the medals.

Despite these positive numbers, there is a dearth of women coaches everywhere. In a 2009 article, Guylaine Demers reported that in 2007, the National Coaching Certification Program statistics showed that 30 percent of Level 1-3 coaches were women, 21 percent at Level 4 and a dismal 11 percent at Level 5. She continues that in the 2004 and 2008 summer Olympics in Athens and Beijing, women head coaches numbered just 7 percent and 9 percent respectively. Despite a Coaching Association of Canada's Women in Coaching initiative that addressed factors affecting women in coaching, including apprenticeship and mentoring programs, these low numbers persisted.

Off the field these numbers are no better. In 2005 the International Olympic Committee (IOC) called for 20 percent of National Sport Organization (NSO) leaders to be women. The IOC has not reached that mark itself, and women in Canadian sport leadership were markedly absent from decision-making positions in a variety of NSOs, AthletesCAN and the Coaching Association of Canada. In 2010, women occupied approximately one third of positions on the boards of these organizations.

Canada has two sport policies: the first from 2009 on Sport for Women and Girls called Actively Engaged and the second from Sport Canada released in 2012. The two documents contrast sharply; for instance, the Sport Canada policy fails to mention any of the following words: women, girls, gender, discrimination, sex, equity or equality. In addition, the 2012 policy states only in general terms that one policy goal of Sport Canada is for sport to be inclusive. This policy stance represents a huge step back from the 2002 Sport Policy that acknowledged the realities, trends and challenges of sport in Canada, including a section called "Barriers to Access," stating that "girls and women" among other minorities "continue to be under-represented in the Canadian sport system as athletes/participants and as leaders."

The second document, "Actively Engaged: A Policy on Sport for Women and Girls 2009," is a Canadian Heritage publication that replaced the 1986 Sport Canada Policy on Girls and Women in Sport and guides domestic priorities including funding for the Canadian sport system. The Sport Funding and Accountability Framework is used by Canadian Heritage to identify which national sports organizations are eligible to receive Sport Canada funding under the Sport Support Program. As it pertains to women generally, NSOs must affirm their commitment to funding women in order to be eligible to receive money. Additionally, they "must demonstrate their formal commitment to equity and access for all persons through their policies or equivalent instruments," with a particular focus on equity and access for women and girls. As it relates to leadership specifically, "Sport Canada encourages organizations to build in provisions for women in governance through the accountability stage."

Canada continues to be forced to discriminate against women sportspeople in order to participate in the Olympic Movement. In addition, with a weakened domestic policy there is no mandate for Canada's participation in Olympic sport to be gender equitable. The Olympic Movement encompasses all manner of sports organizations, including the IOC, International Sports Federations (IFs), National Olympic Committees (NOCs), Organizing Committees of the Olympic Games (OCOGs), national sports organizations (NSOs), and the athletes, coaches, fans, administrators and officials who participate in these organizations.

The Olympic Charter guides the Olympic Movement, and all persons in the Movement, whether they know it or not, agree to be bound by it. Thus the IOC holds tremendous power in world sport as all Olympic sports report up the ladder to the IOC. This means that the IOC touches every person associated with an Olympic sport in Canada and around the world, from the top Olympic athletes and officials down to volunteer parent coaches at the local swim club. Although the Olympic Charter, like international and Canadian law, contains anti-discrimination and gender equality clauses, the IOC continually violates its own rules; therefore, when the Olympic program, set by the IOC, discriminates against women, there is also a trickle down effect, forcing countries such as Canada to enforce those same decisions. This effect was exemplified at the 2010 Vancouver Olympics, when a court decided that only the IOC could put women's ski jumping on the list of events, and no action could be taken by VANOC, even though excluding the women's teams was in obvious contravention of both Canada's *Charter of Rights of Freedoms* and the United Nations' *International Convention on the Elimination of All Forms of Discrimination Against Women* (CEDAW). Furthermore, IOC policies also affect lower levels of sport and events held under the Olympic umbrella, such as World and National Championships and the Pan/Parapan American Games.

The Olympic Movement needs Member States. It cannot function without countries and their athletes. But at what point will international law finally outweigh the hold of the IOC? Margot Young addresses the women's ski jumping case in her 2010 article "The IOC Made Me Do It: Women's Ski Jumping, VANOC, and the 2010 Winter Olympics," writing "sanctioned sex discrimination in a publicly funded exercise on the scale of the Olympics is no small issue. It reinforces and perpetuates a troubling but traditional discriminatory message about women, athletes, and social citizenship." Public backlash against the final outcome of the women ski jump trial in Canada was huge, with polls showing 73 percent of Canadians in favor of the women ski jumpers. Despite public outpouring of support and a declaration by the judge that they were being discriminated against, very few Canadian athletes, past or present, spoke up in support of the women ski jumpers. Canada's IOC member winter athlete Beckie Scott was elected by the athletes of the Olympic Games to represent them in the Olympic Movement, yet publicly she did nothing to uphold the Olympic Charter, international or Canadian law. Canada's other IOC member, Dick Pound, called the women silly and made comments that their behavior might just keep them out of the Winter Games in 2014 too. Is it really a wonder that Canada's powerful human rights law is not being translated into the sporting arena? With no women leaders in sport, in coaching, administration or even in our own Olympic athletes, it is not surprising that Canadian sport perpetuates discrimination against women athletes.

Until now, Canada has been complicit in the Olympic Movement's systemic gender discrimination, which affects not just women in Canada but also those around the world. Will we stand up for women or continue to violate domestic and international law in order to placate the Olympic Movement?

Canada must take a two-pronged approach to effect real change in domestic and world sport. First, it should implement the mandates for women's participation in leadership and coaching positions in Canadian sport through the 2009 Women and Girls Sport Policy. It must also demand that the IOC implement similar mandates as a pre-condition of all countries' participation in the Olympic Movement. Second, Canada must require equitable access to and rights in the Olympic Movement for women athletes.

Canada has a series of options available to move ahead and mark itself as a leader in gender equity in sport. First, it could stipulate to the IOC and PASO (Pan American Sport Organization) that the number of women athletes competing at the Winter and Summer Olympics and Pan/Parapan American Games be equal to the number of men. For this to be achieved, the IOC must change the Olympic program so that all events and sports are open to both women and men. Should this move not achieve gender equity, then the IOC could affirmatively include more events or teams in sports that have large numbers of women athletes, such as netball or softball.

Second, both the Council of Europe and the Commonwealth Games Federation (CGF) have already passed recommendations and regulations addressing gender discrimination against women in sport, as have other bodies in Africa and Asia. The CGF in 2006 issued a regulation to its Constitution, which states, "future programmes in sports will have a balanced participation and profile for males and females." Should the Olympic Movement continue to institute reforms at its current glacial pace, Canada could use these and other international laws, as well as its own domestic laws and Olympic regulations, to refuse to host a Pan/Parapan American Games that discriminates against women athletes.

Furthermore, during the Pan/Parapan American Games in Toronto, Canada must argue for and implement the regulation that in order to compete, countries must send teams of both men and women, and demand the same be applied at the Olympic level. There is already a precedent for the Olympic Movement to mandate such action from Member States. The IOC has banned countries that discriminate against race and gender, the "aggressor nations" during World War I, and has issued political declarations about communism and codes about doping, all the while drawing upon international law and the international legal systems, including the UN General Assembly, to promote these international human rights.

Canada should require that all nations participating in the Pan/Parapan American Games implement a sexual abuse and harassment policy within their NOC. Canada should also end gender testing for women athletes at the Pan/Parapan American Games and stipulate that the IOC insist all international federations within the Olympic Movement end gender testing for women athletes within their sports. Canada must mandate that all NOCs, IFs and NSOs create gender equity within the administration of their organizations, should they want to participate in the Pan/Parapan American Games and demand that the IOC mandate the same at the Olympic level. With Canada's leadership, all these actions can occur prior to the 2015 Pan/Parapan American Games as well as the 2016 Olympics.

While the athletes on the podium will take the spotlight in Toronto, the Pan/Parapan American Games and the Olympics are not just about equity for Canadian women sportspeople but also about the impact these events have on the lives of women around the world as athletes, coaches, leaders and economic and social actors. Part of Toronto's bid to host the 2015 Games included the promise of grants to developing Pan/Parapan American countries to send athletes and coaches to Canada to train and learn prior to the Games; a lofty sentiment that will mean nothing if not implemented today. Will the legacy of Toronto 2015 be the same as Vancouver or will we look to Canadian, international and even Olympic law to create an equitable playing field for women in the Americas and around the world?

THE TARNISHED SIDE OF THE MEDAL
Sexual Harassment and Abuse
Sandra Kirby

The work on harassment and abuse in sport has steadily lagged behind that in the public sphere by at least a decade. In the 1960s and 1970s, women were beginning to name inequities in the workplace, support the call for childcare and, as women moved in greater numbers into the workforce, to name sexual harassment and abuse. The focus was, it is fair to say, on helping women share the home and childcare loads with their husbands as they sought employment outside the home. Violence inside the family was emerging as a public issue and lawyers were struggling with how to more justly help women whose husbands beat them, support safer child custody arrangements when exposure to violence in the home was identified and help women who chose to (or had to) work outside the home be better treated in the workplace. The first time I heard the words sexual harassment was in the early 1980s and in relation to university women faculty and their workplace.

During those decades in sport we were busy—busy getting more women athletes on Olympic teams; identifying the lack of female coaches; calling for action on gender equality, but not yet naming sexual harassment and abuse. We were trying to raise women and sport issues on the National Action Committee on the Status of Women conference agendas. What a coup it was to have our own conference—the Female Athlete Conference at Simon Fraser University in 1980. I was doing a masters degree is physical education at McGill University at that time and had been told not to focus on women and sport because it would "ghettoize me."

It is difficult to summarize in any meaningful way the enormous progress that has been made in our understanding of child protection in sport, and in particular, on the nature and scope of sexual harassment and abuse in sport.

Suffice to say that in 1960 we did not yet have words for sexual harassment, either in the sport context or in any other. We had to identify emerging issues, create the language to talk about them and then develop a knowledge about "range, type, and scale" of abuses as Brackenridge and Rhind named it in 2010. We were beginning to know a lot about sexism and racism—and the study of gender was marked in earnest by the F-word, feminism.

Research on sexual harassment and abuse in sport was in its infancy though the 1980s and 1990s. Some discussion on the topic occurred at the 1984 Olympic Congress in Oregon and again at the 1993 IAPESGW Conference in Melbourne. Some names started to emerge—Celia Brackenridge, Kari Fasting, Libby Darlison, Gertrud Pfister, Marion Lay, and Barbara Drinkwater—and these women have sustained this field since those early days. Within WomenSport International, the International Task Force on Sexual Harassment and Abuse in Sport was created. It was chaired by Celia Brackenridge, and with members such as Kari Fasting (Norway), Trisha Leahy (Hong Kong) and me (Canada), we were able to concentrate considerable attention and resources on the sexual harassment and abuse issues in sport.

The gathering of personal accounts in the sport world, mostly about young female athletes and their coaches, began by collecting reports of events that had occurred some years earlier. One of the cases that came to public attention in Canada was the 1993 case of George Smith, a track and field coach in Edmonton. Independent of each other, both Rachel Corbett and I had written and published articles on George Smith in 1993. Smith used persuasion to groom young female athletes, some as young as 12 years of age, into sexual encounters partly because he was a coach with great charisma and extraordinary control of "his" team of athletes. In fact, he acted as if he owned them.

Shortly after the Smith case, on November 2, 1993, CBC's *The Fifth Estate* "blew the lid off" harassment and abuse in sport with the program "Crossing the Line" featuring athletes from swimming, rowing and volleyball. The Paul Hickson case in the UK (Olympic Swim coach given a sentence of 17 years) added fuel to the fire. In Canada, we began the search for common characteristics of harassment and abuse between sport and other domains such as daycares, orphanages, residential schools, the military and the family. In the workplace, there was a proliferation of harassment policies and the emergence of a new professional, "the harassment officer." Sport in Canada soon followed suit.

The first reports by academics emerged at conferences and in publications—amongst those, the research by Helen Lenskyj, Lorraine Greaves, Marge Holman, Bruce Kidd, Peter Donnelly and me. In 1994, at the Commonwealth Games Conference, there were presentations on this research. The first national study of the nature and scope of abuse in sport done by two of this book's editors, Lorraine Greaves and me, was funded by Sport Canada and conducted with some 1,200 national teams and recently-retired national team athletes. It was the first wide-scale study in the world and provided important benchmarks for how athletes thought about harassment and abuse, what they had seen and heard in the sport environment, what they had experienced and how they had acted in the face of such experiences. The most stunning fact from that study was that 22.8 percent of the 266 athletes reported having had sexual intercourse with persons in positions of authority over them in sport. When these results were released at the Pre-Olympic Congress in Dallas, Texas in the summer of 1996, sport organizations and the public sat up and took notice.

Shortly after, in September 1996, Sheldon Kennedy and another unnamed NHL hockey player pressed sexual assault charges against their former coach, Graham James. In January of 1997, Graham James pled guilty and received a 2-and-a-half-year sentence. Organized sport, and in particular, hockey, sprung into action. The Canadian Hockey Association, the Red Cross and Volunteer Canada banded together to take on the issue directly. Their response was to open the issue up, to figure out where the safety issues were and to work together with researchers and advocates to bring about fundamental changes to hockey.

When the Graham James case was occupying the headlines across Canada in 1996 and early 1997, there were press queries about the sexual orientation of James and Kennedy. Caroline Fusco and I concluded that only when the reporters determined for themselves that homosexuality was not the issue in the allegations of sexual assault by a much older man of a boy 14 to

18 years of age, did the press then focus on child sexual assault and pedophilia.

On the heels of the James' case was the Maple Leaf Gardens scandal involving the facility caretakers' sexual abusing young boys. In February 1997, Martin Kruze was the first victim to make allegations of sexual abuse by three men who worked at Maple Leaf Gardens. The abuse had gone on for decades and sadly, once the men were convicted and sentenced, Martin Kruze committed suicide. As this book goes to press, more charges were laid in this case.

Lost in the shuffle of these important cases was the "normalized" sexual harassment and abuse of girls and women in sport. Many people I talked to revealed stories of coaches, always male, who had romantic relationships with individual athletes, always female, on their teams or who "slept their way through our team." Some cases involving individual girl athletes who were in romantic relationships with their older, sometimes much older, male coaches seem to be regarded by those in sport with a curious myopia. Peer abuse was certainly also known—mostly from boys and men to girls and women. My sense was always that though these events were known, people in sport tolerated them as just part of normal life creeping into sport. It was hard in those days to name the abuse through that screen of what passed as normal sexual attention. Indeed, not paying attention to girls was not a backlash, but rather a reflection of the fact that sexual harassment and abuse of girls was so normalized it was not newsworthy.

Canada has made great progress in the last decade. Sport organizations have openly sought assistance for their sexual harassment policies, coaching codes of conduct and education programs for their athletes. The associations for the training and certification of coaches stepped up their efforts to ensure that coaches were screened, trained, evaluated and educated about the harassment and abuse issues. In some jurisdictions, sport organizations received funding conditional on their progress with policies and procedures, with training and efforts to protect athletes in their sports. Screening of volunteers became required and accepted. Athletes were invited to be part of education programs and to work with coaches, administrators and researchers to create better ways of reporting suspected harassment and abuse.

A group of Canadians, Margo Mountjoy (IOC), Marge Holman, Susan Bissell (UNICEF) and Sheldon Kennedy, worked together with the IOC and UNICEF on violence against children in sport and on child protection in sport. The network of sport researchers on abuse expanded dramatically, including newer scholars such as Guylaine Demers and Sylvie Parent. Also notable was the involvement of three organizations that ensured continued and unrelenting attention to the harassment and abuse issues: Sport and the Law with Hilary Findlay and Rachel Corbett, Canadian Council for Ethics and Sport with Victor LaChance and Paul Melia, and CAAWS with Marg McGregor and Karin Lofstrom. Education programs through schools and sport teams are now widely available for athletes.

By 2010 it was generally accepted that sport coaches and athletes were well educated on the issues of harassment and abuse. They were also getting educated on the dangers in sport of sexual grooming, sexual exploitation, hazings and initiations. They found the language of discrimination a useful and familiar one when harassment and abuse education began to include issues of sexism, heterosexism, homophobia and racism. Advocacy for child protection, including a particular focus on the girl child, was reaching across the world. Attention to violence against children, including violence against children in sport and recreation, formed an umbrella framework for UNICEF and the IOC who continue to show leadership. Researchers, child protection advocates, human rights personnel, coaches, sport administrators and athletes linked together to improve sport practice around the world.

Canada is, as I like to say, ahead of the curve on the issues of sexual harassment and abuse in sport. However, there is still a long way to go to make sport safe for girls and women (and boys and men) but we have come such a long way already. We in sport have stood on the shoulders of our foremothers and some forefathers to make great progress on ending sexual violence in sport. It is through the women's movement, and the persistence of the early advocates to end violence against women within that movement, that we in sport have at least a toehold on making sport a safer place for all.

SEXUALLY SUSPECT
Single, Athletic and Female
Guylaine Demers

I am an out lesbian. It is a public fact! So writing about homophobia in sport is really a personal matter. I was born in 1964 and started to be involved in competitive sport at age 12. It was in basketball. That sport became my passion in an instant. I wanted to have fun with my friends, play with the best, and compete at the highest level possible. It became really clear to me that I would not be given the permission to be myself when I was in the sport arena. I must say that in those years, it was pretty much the same everywhere. I was able to reach the university level but I was not the best on the team. Looking back, I can now say with an absolute certainty that I could have been a better player if I had not had to carry that heavy weight on my shoulders: being a lesbian athlete. Hopefully, the situation for lesbian athletes has evolved. But in the following lines, you will be able to see that we still have a long way to go. The silence is still omnipresent and behind it are many stories of sadness, shame, secrecy and stigma. I want to break that wall of silence. My goal in writing this piece is to help create a welcoming sport environment for all homosexual athletes and coaches.

To begin, we need to have a common understanding of the word "homophobia." *The Oxford Canadian Dictionary* defines it as "a hatred or fear of homosexuals or homosexuality." Thus, the title of this chapter suggests that the sport world is not a particularly welcoming place for homosexuals. In my view, not only are they unwelcome, but also people ignore the facts, taking the easy way out by pretending that there are no homosexuals in sport. This is not the case.

Lesbian, gay, bisexual, and transsexual (LGBT) rights regularly make the news in Canada. In the world of sport, however, people seem to suffer from tunnel vision—they do not see the issue or recognize that diverse sexualities exist. The subject of homosexuality in sport is clearly taboo, and the deafening silence reflects prejudice against homosexuals, who stay "in the closet" out of fear of reprisals that can take many forms.

In women's sports, the words "female athlete" and "lesbian" are often uttered in the same breath. Researchers attribute this to the process of socialization of girls, which even today perpetuates the cult of female fragility and delicateness. It is not considered normal for a girl to exhibit athletic qualities, such as strength, at a very high level. When a girl does exhibit such qualities, she is immediately labeled as not very feminine and suspicions arise about her sexual orientation. By definition, sport and sporting attributes are a male preserve. A number of studies have shown that the source of homophobia in women's sports is the desire to discredit performances by female athletes and discourage them from participating in sports.

This perspective on athleticism is one of the major differences between homophobia as experienced by women and homophobia as experienced by men. A female athlete exhibiting several athletic qualities, such as strong physical abilities, is often automatically labeled a lesbian. It follows that female athletes may feel that they have to prove they are not lesbians. Jennifer Hargreaves in 2000 writes that as a result, many of them lend considerable importance to their physical appearance in asserting their femininity and, by extension, their heterosexuality by using make-up and wearing "feminine" clothing. Many girls and young women drop sports because they do not want to be branded as lesbians.

Another difference between male and female homophobia is the greater openness of women toward lesbian team members. Lesbians who are open about their sexual orientation to other team members are well-accepted most of the time. Some studies show that female athletes prefer everything to be out in the open and people to be clear about their sexual orientation. As a result, a new generation of heterosexual women no longer fears that they will be labelled as lesbians for practicing their sport. On that note, in 2008, Celia Brackenridge and colleagues stated that young people "often express more enlightened attitudes to diversity than older generations." There is some evidence that some changes are happening, but it is far too early to say that homophobia in women's sport is behind us. In fact, some studies reported that team members accept lesbians coming out, as long as the information stays within the four walls of the locker room. They insist on this in order to protect the team's image and reputation. Some researchers also report that teammates react in a variety of different ways when a lesbian comes out: some refuse to share a room with a lesbian on a road trip, others feel uncomfortable changing in the locker room. This so-called openness might differ depending on whether the context is team versus individual sports, or elite versus recreational sports.

The practice of labeling female athletes—especially those who demonstrate great athletic abilities—as butch, dykes, lesbians, freaks or sickos still occurs in the Canadian sport context. Female coaches are not exempt, but unlike female athletes who are labeled lesbian because of their great athletic abilities, female coaches become suspect when they do not have a male partner. There is huge pressure on female coaches to conform to heterosexual norms and pass as heterosexuals. According to Pat Griffin, much of the prejudice and discrimination against lesbians in sport arise from the fear that they are predators who will seduce and corrupt girls and young women, which, she suggests, taps into the deepest fears of parents and heterosexual athletes and coaches. So, if you are a coach, married, and, as a bonus, a mom, you are "safe": safe for yourself, but most importantly, safe for your athletes.

On that note, I had a revealing experience recently. I was giving a lecture on homophobia in sport and had invited a female coach to talk about her supporting role with her lesbian athletes. The first thing she said to the group, before even saying her name, was: "I am not a lesbian." I was speechless and at first did not understand the statement. After the class, many students told me they all had thought she was a lesbian and were surprised to hear this was not the case. I asked them why they had thought this. They replied it was because she is single and they had never seen her with a man/partner. Then I asked: "What about that male coach (I gave them his name)? Do you think he is gay?" Without hesitation, they all said: "No, he's straight." I asked: "Have you ever seen him with a woman/partner? Is he married?" At that moment, they realized that they were using different norms to judge a female coach's sexual orientation. I now knew why the speaker started her story talking about her sexual orientation. She was well aware that she was not judged by the same criteria as her male counterparts. It is very clear to me that female coaches are doubly jeopardized. As women, they are not competent in coaching unless proven competent (which is the opposite for male coaches), and if they are single, then they are lesbian without a doubt!

We have seen that as a woman and as a coach, pressure comes from everywhere, and if you happen to be a lesbian coach, it is even worse. Lesbian coaches face different impacts on their coaching career. In fact, being a lesbian dramatically limits career options and adversely affects hiring opportunities at the assistant coach and head coach levels. Hiring a coach who has been labeled as a lesbian is a major concern for an organization intent on protecting the image of its sport program. Here is a true story from the homophobia workshop developed by CAAWS: a national female coach, who is out to her employer but not to the public, is provided with a male date by her sport organization to accompany her to "formal" functions so that people won't think she is a lesbian.

Another problem female coaches face—lesbian or not—is related to athlete recruitment. Often prospective athletes, their parents and their current coaches try to find out whether there are any lesbians on the team or among the coaching staff. Insinuating that there are lesbians on opposing teams is a common recruitment tactic. This practice, called negative recruiting, involves denigrating rival coaches and programs during the recruitment process. Whether true or not, some coaches will state that rival coaches are lesbian or that there are lesbian athletes on their teams. That happened to me more than once. The other teams' coaches (all male) would approach my athletes in gymnasiums, in bars, anywhere, telling them that I was a lesbian, that they should not play for me, but should play for them. Because I was out to my athletes, they were able to defend themselves, but were traumatized by the experience. Those male coaches were using that "tactic" to undermine my credibility with my athletes. I was the only female coach in the league and I was winning. THAT was disturbing.

Homophobic discrimination can wreck sporting careers in concrete ways. Lesbian coaches can fail to secure promotions or get positions. There is ample evidence that lesbian coaches have to survive in an inhospitable climate and function in a homonegative environment.

In preparing for this piece, I had the good fortune to meet some lesbian athletes and coaches who were willing to share their stories with me. I am grateful for their openness, spirit of sharing and the trust they placed in me. I was able to draw on their experiences to illustrate the findings and conclusions of the literature on homophobia in sport with concrete examples. Note that all the women were involved in team sports and all insisted on anonymity. I tell their stories by focusing on their commonalities. Homophobia has changed over the last 30 years or so. I met women who were high performance athletes in the 1980s, others who were performing at a very high level in the 1990s, and some who are currently top-flight university athletes.

The interviewees who were competing in the 1980s and 1990s never dared to come out publicly. Just as the literature shows, they were extremely afraid of what their teammates would think of them. A number of times they referred to the fear of rejection, the fear of damaging—or being accused of damaging—team unity and spirit, and the fear of causing teammates to change their attitude toward them by becoming more distant, for example. None of the interviewees who had shared their secret with teammates whom they really trusted had suffered from this selective coming-out. This fact confirms the conclusion drawn by researchers that athletes are quite receptive to team members who come out as long as the information stays within the four walls of the locker room.

One particularly interesting fact that emerged during the interviews was that two athletes came out by confiding in their coaches, not their teammates. They told me that having a female coach was a major factor in their decision to share their secret with that person. They also referred to their coaches' values and the fact they were centred on respect for the individual. They were thus fairly confident that the coaches would react positively, and they were right in their assumption because the coaches reacted with total respect. Both athletes reiterated how significant and decisive a factor their coaches' reactions were at that moment in their lives. They were able to continue their season with one fewer weight on their shoulders.

Coming out selectively was a considerable relief for the athletes. They had at last found somebody who would lend an ear as they recounted the highs and lows of their love life. In contrast, staying in the closet is a heavy burden to bear. One of the interviewees told me that one day she came to the gymnasium sad and unmotivated—her heart had been broken for the first time. At one point during the training session, she broke down and started crying. She told the team and her coach that "Richard" had left her, when in fact it was Louise. The story speaks volumes about the heavy burden lesbian athletes have to bear when they stay silent about their sexual orientation.

Notwithstanding a few sad stories about women who never dared to come out, the situation facing lesbian athletes has changed. Some athletes who are competing today told me that all their teammates know they are lesbians, even though they have never officially announced it. This fact was left unspoken and unsaid, and all members of the team seemed at ease with the situation. None of the interviewees reported any unpleasant or disturbing events in connection with their sexual orientation. Some even told me that teammates joked with them about it and that their orientation was well accepted. For example, another player would say, "We know you're not interested in bar hopping with us and finding some good-looking guys!" The interviewees told me they did not feel the need to make an official announcement because the other players and the coach were aware of their sexual orientation. They have never broached the issue openly. They feel no pressure from their teammates and are very happy with their love life.

That being said, some lesbians do not dare come out, even though they know other lesbians on their team. I met two such athletes. They told me that they had not yet informed their parents and they preferred to keep their secret until they felt ready to disclose their sexual orientation.

Two female coaches I met have not yet come out to their athletes. One coaches a women's team sport and the other a mixed individual sport. Both are in long-term relationships. They believe that the athletes harbour suspicions about their orientation, but that they are not at all uncomfortable with it. They have never broached the issue officially with the athletes and do not feel the need to do so. However, after the interview, it became clearer to them that they might have to assume some responsibility for combating homophobia in sport. It is my understanding that they are now considering coming out in order to help lesbian athletes feel that they can openly and safely confide in their coach or tell their teammates about their sexual orientation if they so wish.

In the summer of 2006, Montreal hosted the first World Outgames, an international sporting event for lesbians and gays. I competed in golf. It is hard to describe the emotion I experienced: I felt I was part of something bigger than myself and that I belonged ... Just to be able to take my partner's hand on the golf course without fear of being judged, excluded or harassed was a totally new experience. For the first time in my life, I was in a prejudice-free space, something that mainstream sport has failed to offer me. It was quite an experience and one that I won't forget for years to come.

From that experience, I realized that I was part of the problem and part of the solution as well. I share Jennifer Hargreaves' point of view that she explains in her 2001 book, *Heroines of Sport*, about our individual role to fight homophobia in sport: "Many lesbian sportswomen live constantly with the tension created between their gayness and their desire for integration, which could be eased if they were courageous enough to come out in mainstream sport in greater numbers, and if more heterosexual sportswomen were prepared to stand up and speak out against heterosexism and homophobia."

Homophobia is not a form of discrimination that will simply go away by virtue of silence. As Helen Lenskyj observes in her 1999 book *Women, Sport and Sexualities*, "The vicious cycle of invisibility and homophobia in women's sport needs to be interrupted in a number of levels, both individual and institutional, before social change can be affected." Following Lenskyj's thought, it is imperative that sport organizations adjust to new social and legal equalities discourses. Celia Brackenridge and her colleagues wrote in their 2008 book *A Review of Sexual Orientation in Sport*, "Unless sport is able to reinvent itself and to accommodate and celebrate diversity in sexual orientation, as it has already begun to do with race, (dis)ability and gender, then it will become increasingly irrelevant to many 'outsiders' for whom a non-heterosexual sexual orientation is a significant and perhaps defining feature of their identity."

So my final word is straightforward. Everyone has to oppose homophobia and related discrimination in sport. There is no doubt that one of the most effective tools in counteracting homophobia is increased lesbian and gay visibility. Research indicates that, for most people, contact with out lesbian and gay people who embrace their sexual identities reduces prejudice. We have to give LGBT people the chance to come out safely without any fear. I hope you become advocates for gay and lesbian rights, whether you are LGBT or not, because the world of sport is still very homophobic and we need every possible ally to fight against it.

This text is an adaptation from previous publications by the author.

IN WOMEN'S SPORT, WHO ARE THE WOMEN?
Sandra Kirby

It simply never occurred to me that to participate in Olympic sport, in women's events, I would have to prove that I was a woman. It was in July of 1976 at the Montreal Olympic Games, when all 23 Canadian women rowers (my teammates and I) sat on benches looking across the room at the Russian women rowers. It was prior to competition, and we had been scheduled for anthropometric and femininity testing. I remember being puzzled at first, then simply accepted that if a sex test had to be done before I could race, then a sex test is what I would do.

So, we stripped down to our underwear, had all the measurements taken for the anthropometric study—I was a 2-5-2. Then, we each had to swab the inside of one cheek and hand over the Q-tip to the person in the white coat. Sometime later, we were each handed a "femininity card" with our registration number, height, weight, age and country of competition. This card was my passport to the starting line for the Quadruple Sculls race so that I could represent my country. I do not remember anyone giving a reason for why the test had to be done.

It took me another 23 years to figure it out and to become part of a movement against sex-testing for athletes. This is my story of our collective struggle against gender verification.

From 1976 to about 1992, I would occasionally ask about sex testing—since that is what we called it in those days. I did think it funny that I had a "femininity card" and laughed with my mother who said I had never been known for my femininity but for my sporty behavior—her kind way of saying I had always been a tomboy. Sometime during those years, around 1980 or so, Marion Lay and I had a conversation where she told me about sex testing—Mexico 1968 style. Those initial tests involved what she called the "peek and boo" test. Someone skilled at viewing anatomical sex checked out the genitalia of each athlete as she walked by in a nude parade. As Skirstad wrote in 1999, at the 1967 Pan American Games in Winnipeg, if the medical observers had any doubts, they did an on-site manual. I remember thinking, "the things some women have to do for our country, really!" The chromatin screening of 1976 certainly seemed much more civilized than a nude parade.

Between 1985 and 1991, I did a great deal of volunteer work with Marion Lay to establish CAAWS. In 1988 the Olympic Academy of Canada wanted to end the sex testing practices. And, as recounted in the briefing background on gender verification from Fitness and Amateur Sport (F&AS) Canada, a motion passed to "discontinue the use of sex chromatin tests for verification." It was race walker Ann Peel at the Olympic Academy whose words resonated most with me: sex testing was discriminatory and demeaning to women. I began to get a glimmer of the inequity of it all.

Women athletes were being tested for two reasons. The first was to confirm that no men fraudulently registered in women's events. So why were all women tested because of something a man might do? Had any man actually tried to get in to the Olympics by entering a women's event? As Judith Huebner and I wrote in 2002, the only actual record is of one Hermann Ratjen, who confessed in 1957 that in 1936 he had entered the women's high jump for Germany, finishing fourth. The other reason was to screen out the women who exhibited abnormal masculine traits. Why would that be an issue? Again, all women were tested to ensure that those with ambiguous sex (presumably chromosomally-based) would be eliminated from competition. The F&AS 1991 report included references to four athletes who participated in women's events and then subsequently had sex change operations. It also identified athletes, including the Press sisters Irina and Tamara, who many thought were abnormally strong and muscular. The International Olympic Committee Medical Commission, formed in 1964, was charged with addressing these, and many other, medical issues for the International Olympic movement. By 1966, when athletes needed a medical certificate confirming their sex from a doctor in their home country, the Press sisters had completed their competitive careers and so were never "carded." As a burgeoning sport scientist myself, I wondered whether any science had even suggested that such individuals would have performance advantages? And, even if there were sex aberrations amongst the competitors, what business was it of the sport community to know?

During that time I met Dr. Jerilynn Prior, an endocrinologist and also a member of CAAWS. It was after a discussion with her that I began to look at the questionable politics and the dubious science behind sex testing. Dr. Prior was a member of a gender verification sub-committee for the International Relations and Major Games Directorate of Fitness and Amateur Sport. In 1991 in Ottawa, they released a background briefing note on gender verification to enhance "Canadians' capability of reacting strategically to important international issues." The report concluded with the following:

> The Canadian Academy of Sport Medicine supports the recommendation that laboratory based sex testing for eligibility purposes be abandoned for all future sport competition. CASM recommends that all athletes, both women and men, undergo a thorough medical evaluation including assessment of their reproductive health. This evaluation should occur in their country of origin prior to entering the international sport arena.

From 1992 to 1999 I developed course material and co-taught "Talking about Sex" with biologist Dr. Huebner. It was wildly popular with undergraduate students and was part of the "best lecture" series for a number of years. In this course, we problematized gender in the social world of sport. We talked about the biology, gender and social pressures within specific cultural sport contexts. Because I had been sex tested and the students had not, Dr. Huebner and I asked them "Do you know what sex you are? And how do you know?" The results were interesting, and what appeared to them to be obvious answers were much more nuanced by the end of the lectures.

In the course, we looked at definitions of "masculine" and "feminine," and the generally accepted logic that gender agrees with sex. We pushed students to question heterosexual normalcy that arises from that perceived sex-gender continuum. But, we asked, what happens if someone is male, but presents socially as female? What happens to the relationship between sex, gender and sexuality? In addition to these questions, the students in that course were asked to think about the definition of "sex" itself. Indeed, there are many different kinds of "sex." There is anatomical sex—indicated by presence (male) or absence (female) of a phallus or penis, as well as by other anatomical features, body shape, fat distribution and breast enlargement. There is also chromosomal sex, defined by an individual's number and type of chromosomes. Students learned that while a normal male has a karyotype of chromosomal pattern of 46 chromosomes (including one X and one Y set of chromosomes) and a normal female has a karyotype of 46 chromosomes (with two sex chromosomes, both Xs), there are genetic anomalies that include sex chromosome anomalies where, for example, there are more than or less than two sex chromosomes. Finally, we looked at physiological sex, which is primarily dependent on the relative amounts of male and female sex hormones present in children, adolescents and adults. More estrogens (cyclical) rather than testosterone (continuous) in a body usually mean that the person is physiologically female.

The measurement of sex in the sport world has been complicated over the years. In 1966 it was anatomical sex that was being determined—hence the initial tests at international competitions that consisted of "pulling out an athlete's track pants," as Marion Lay has described to me, or in 1967 in Winnipeg at the Pan American Games, the "nude parade" of female athletes in front of medical doctors.

By 1976 when it was my turn to be tested, chromosomal sex was being measured. That quick microscopic examination of cells from a swab inside my cheek determined the presence of the Barr Body, a structure in the nucleus of the cell which contains an inactivated X chromosome. No Barr Bodies would mean that one was either an XY-normal male or an Xo-Turners female. Presence of Barr Bodies meant, for example, that you were an XX-normal female or perhaps an XXY-Klinefelters male. I was verified as a female (XX) athlete and received a femininity card with my registration number. I passed. But about 1/500-600 athletes tested do not.

What happened when an athlete went to an international

competition and after testing was declared ineligible and told to return to her (now "his") home country? What would she/he go as? An ineligible female, an eligible male … without support or any understanding of the ramifications of these tests. Skirstad wrote in 1999 about the high testing error that resulted in a number of false negatives (females designated as males) and false positives (males who pass as females). Athletes were retested at subsequent international competitions, and there have been reports of people passing, then failing, then passing the test again. Skirstad continued that by 1992 there was considerable pressure amongst those in the international sport community to use the PCR or Polymerase Chain Reaction test or a combined PCR—gynaecological examination to ensure women athletes are women.

It is not a simple matter to accurately and reliably test for sex. "Misidentification" can occur when anatomical variations, such as clitoral enlargement, unusual birth defects (e.g. "penis-at-twelve" syndrome), surgical damage, or gynecomastia (the presence of enlarged breasts in males) are present. Mistakes can also be made if anatomical appearance and actual chromosomal pattern do not agree; for example, when a "female appearing" Turners (XO) female has no penis or any Barr bodies or a "female appearing" Klinefelters (XXY) male has a penis and one Barr Body. If any such athletes tried to participate in sport in the 1990s, the Turners female would have been ineligible to compete at the Olympic Games while the Klinefelters male would have been verified female and permitted to compete.

The picture has become even more complicated with issues related to phenotypic sex: the sex one appears to be. Included in this category are those people who live and appear as girls and women but are actually male (androgen insensitive karyotype XY individuals with testicular feminization syndrome). So too, male to female transsexuals (MFTs) would appear female.

Between 1992 and 1999, the debate on gender verification mounted on both sides. On one side there was increasing pressure on the IOC to intensify gender verification with gynaecological examinations. On the other were organizations such as WomenSport International and the Canadian Association of Sports Medicine, and academics including me, Huebner, and Skirstad who were lobbying the IOC to abandon gender verification entirely.

In 1999, on the eve of the opening of the Pan American Games in Winnipeg, with IOC members present for the Opening ceremonies, Arne Ljungqvist of the IOC Medical Commission wrote in an e-mail to me that the IOC "has abolished genetic screening for gender of female entries into the Olympic Games." Although five International Federations (Basketball, Judo, Wrestling, Volleyball and Weight-lifting) continued the testing into the next decade, for me that e-mail marked the end of widespread investigation of female athletes for gender testing.

Subsequently, between 2000 and 2010, two momentous changes occurred. The first was that in 2004, the IOC at its Stockholm Convention agreed that no athletic advantage remains after gender reassignment surgery and two years of hormone therapy. This meant that from 2004 onward, transgendered athletes would be allowed to compete in the Olympic Games. The second was the creation of a growing and rather public list of athletes whose qualifications for women's events were being questioned while they were at international competitions. Caster Semenya's story is perhaps the most prominent of these. So, the gender verification issue has not gone away. Still, as Kath Woodward wrote in her book *Embodied Sporting Practice*, there remains a need for clear policy on how questions about an athlete's eligibility for entering women's events should be handled, but always conducted in safety, fairness and privacy.

So, now in 2013, I remain committed to women's sport. I still compete in rowing and in cross-country ski races, and I still have the card—I am one of the card-carrying females. Indeed!

THE HOCKEY TWINS: SKILL OR GENDER?

Amy Pasternak and Jesse Pasternak

When we were four years old, we were on bobskates with a hockey stick and puck in hand. Being on the ice was natural for us since we came from a whole family of hockey players. Both of our parents and all six of us kids grew up playing boys' hockey, our mother played women's hockey for many years, our dad coached women's hockey and our older sister also switched over to play women's AA hockey at the age of 14. Every winter, we, Amy and Jesse, tried out for and played the highest level of boys' community hockey with our friends until the age that AAA was introduced. That year, we decided not to try out for AAA because of the time and money commitment and we both enjoyed playing other sports as well. For example, we played boys' box and field lacrosse for 14 years, including playing on the Manitoba Men's U16 Provincial Field Lacrosse team in 2004 and 2005 and the West Kildonan Collegiate Institute (WKCI) men's field lacrosse team throughout high school, which won two consecutive provincial championships in 2005 and 2006. We still wanted to play competitive hockey with the friends we had grown up playing with and against, so we continued in boys' community hockey, just not at the AAA level.

Once we entered high school (Grade 9) in 2003, we were thrilled about the opportunity to play for WKCI's men's high school hockey team in the Rookie Tournament. We were even called up to spare on WKCI's men's high school hockey team that year during regular season. The following season we entered Grade 10 and were eligible to play for the high school's hockey team, so we decided it was only natural to tryout for the men's team. This was the team many of our friends were planning on playing for, and the timing of the games, which were immediately after classes, helped to balance our school, work and volunteer lives. In addition, the cost of high school hockey was significantly lower than the community league.

It just so happened that in 2004, the same year we initially tried out for the men's high school hockey team, an official women's high school hockey team was formed at WKCI. In the midst of tryouts for the men's high school hockey team, a rule was brought to our attention. We were surprised to hear that the governing body of high school hockey, the Manitoba High School Athletic Association (MHSAA), had a rule in place since 1974 banning women from trying out for any men's high school sports teams if there was a women's team available at that school. The MHSAA sets rules and regulations that are voted on by membership at the Annual General Meeting, and the Association allows for appeals relating to such rulings or bylaw interpretations. The problem we faced was not with the team, the school or the school division. The issue was in regard to MHSAA's rule. The manager of the men's team had inquired with MHSAA if it would be a problem if we tried out for and played on the men's team. MHSAA responded that if we did play on the team, WKCI's men's hockey team would be ineligible for playoffs, and if ineligible players were on the team, the team's insurance would be void. This put the coaches, as well as the two of us, in a very difficult situation. Though the coaches wanted us to play, we did not want to compromise the team's position within the league and eliminate it from playoffs.

With the help of our parents, we began trying to problem solve quickly since we were already in the middle of tryouts. Initially, an attempt to mediate the issue included sending a formal appeal of the rule to MHSAA, which included supportive letters from the Winnipeg High School Hockey League, the President of the Zone, the Principal of WKCI and the WKCI's women's hockey team coach. The women's hockey team coach's letter confirmed there were enough girls for their team to fill a roster without the two of us playing; therefore, we were not hindering their ability to field a team in the league. Despite many other attempts to mediate the issue outside of court, we were still denied the right to try out for the men's high school hockey team.

On September 22, 2004, we contacted the Manitoba Human Rights Commission and filed a formal complaint. In it we indicated that our mother, coaches, manager, administrator and the School Division Superintendent requested that MHSAA reconsider its decision to prohibit us from playing in the men's league. In response to this request, MHSAA replied that our playing on a men's team would create anarchy within the high school system.

By the time we had received a definite "no" from MHSAA, tryouts for the community league hockey teams were already over, as were high school hockey tryouts. This left us with no place to play hockey during the 2004 season. The head coach of WKCI's men's high school hockey team decided to roster only five defensemen that year as everyone was hopeful the issue would be resolved within a matter of weeks and that way at least one of us could continue to play hockey in 2004. Understandably, the coach was unable to hold a goaltender position open for one of us (Amy), because a team absolutely needs two goalies in case one gets hurt or cannot make it to a game. At that point, the only option left was to carry forward with our complaint to the Manitoba Human Rights Commission. The root of our complaint was gender discrimination, which is defined as differential treatment of an individual or group on the basis of sex. It is important to note that anyone can file a human rights complaint, and that Human Rights Commissions' services are free-of-charge.

After we filed our complaint, the Human Rights Commission sent us a Guide to the Complaint Process for Complainants, which helps plaintiffs understand the process. We were assigned a Mediation Officer, whose role was to determine if the parties were interested in resolving the complaint in a timely manner and on a without prejudice basis. Mediation is a voluntary process and was unsuccessful in this case. While the Mediation Officer attempted to resolve the matter, the file was also sent to an Investigating Human Rights Officer, whose responsibility was to conduct a neutral and objective investigation of the allegations in the complaint. The Investigating Human Rights Officer completed an Investigative Assessment Report for the Board of Commissioners, and the Board of Commissioners was responsible for any final decisions regarding recommendations made within the report.

From the investigation there are two routes that can be taken:

1) settlement of complaint, or 2) adjudication or prosecution. We were required to proceed with a settlement, but because MHSAA refused to settle, the Board of Commissioners requested that an Adjudicator be appointed to conduct a hearing on the matter. We were then assigned a lawyer from the Manitoba Human Rights Commission named Sarah Lugtig, and the adjudication process began. This whole process started in September 2004, and the hearing did not occur until May 2006. This is unusually quick for a human rights case, as many often take numerous years to be resolved.

The following year, 2005, we tried out again for WKCI's men's high school hockey team despite no success in making MHSAA budge on the rule. Once again, we could not play, as it would jeopardize the WKCI's men's high school hockey team by making it ineligible for playoffs and voiding its insurance, as per MHSAA rules. That year, the AA and A1 team in the community league had folded so we decided to work, volunteer and play many other sports instead. We participated in community men's box and field lacrosse, swimming, and we took the National Lifesaving Society's course to become certified lifeguards. We played multiple high school sports, such as indoor and outdoor track and field, cross-country, men's field lacrosse, women's soccer, women's basketball, and women's volleyball. Amy was also a goalie coach for a boys' 10 A1 community hockey team and Jesse was a team manager for WKCI's men's high school basketball team and a pre-calculus tutor. We were both the first-ever female box lacrosse referees in Manitoba in 2003, and we continued to referee that season.

In May 2006, the hearing finally began. This was our final year in high school, meaning our last chance to play on the team should a decision be reached prior to the end of tryouts in September. For those intervening two years, we completed the tryouts for WKCI's men's high school hockey team and played in the pre-season tournaments because we genuinely wanted to play on that team and the team wanted us to play with them. We were skilled enough to make their roster. However, the decision each year was never reached in time to accommodate this. By the third year, the media pressure was immense; we received constant criticism in school, in public, while playing other sports and in many other situations as well. During pre-season tournaments players from other teams would "headhunt" and we thought that parents in the stands were undeniably immature by making rude comments about us throughout the games. This made the sport quite undesirable for both of us. That was when we realized that we were no longer following through with the complaint for ourselves but for a much larger cause.

The hearing lasted for two weeks. It was eight hours each day, witness after witness. The hearing was open to the public, and in the room sat family, friends, supporters, opposers, news reporters and many others. We attended the hearing everyday and sat and listened to the defendant's witnesses describe why girls should only play on girls' teams and why boys should only play on boys' teams, without regard to personal skill and merit. We felt that these strangers were placing both of us in a category of sport where we knew we did not belong. One of the defendant's witnesses even admitted to never having met or seen us play hockey before. Having someone who does not know you or your skills sit just feet away from you, judge your abilities and argue against your purpose was frustrating. On the other hand, there were also witnesses speaking on our behalf who seemed to completely understand why it was so important for the rule to be changed.

Sandra Kirby, Associate Vice President Academic and Dean of Graduate Studies at the University of Winnipeg and former Olympic rower, holds expertise in many areas, including high performance sport. Her recent sport research includes systemic discrimination, which made her a highly credible witness for our human rights case. She explained that forcing students to play on a lower performing team, regardless of whether it is a girls-only team or any other, is not beneficial to those students, and in fact, adversely impacts the development of their skills and playing ability. Having faced such obstacles, it is highly likely that these students would leave the sport and be lost as potential leaders, including as coaches and educators.

After three long years, on September 22, 2006, the Adjudicator determined that we had indeed been discriminated against based on gender. Subsequently, MHSAA was ordered to remove its requirement that a girl must try out and play for a girls' hockey team if one was supported by the school. Kirby brought to light two highly influential statements during the process: "You may have to treat people differently in order to treat them equally;" and "Equal opportunity in a sport means everyone has an equal chance to achieve in sport—whatever that achievement may be." As with any human rights case, we were awarded damages to compensate for the two-year loss of skill, injury to our dignity, feelings and self-respect.

In retrospect, many people tend to ask us "Was it worth it"? This endeavor did not come without consequences. Dealing with the media was very difficult for us and our parents. Although we attempted to settle the issue quickly and quietly, MHSAA went to the media in hopes of making us back down due to media pressure. Various media constantly left messages on our answering machine, and cameras and news crews were often at our doorstep, at tryouts and outside the school interviewing people from the team, friends and many others. It was surprising and sometimes disappointing for us to find out on the evening news who was supporting us and who was not. Although we and our family continuously declined to comment, there would still be an article in the paper the following day that was mostly fictional and in most cases degrading and hurtful to us. There was also constant judgment from our peers while we were in school; it was not uncommon to walk through the halls or to be sitting in class and hear snickering and name-calling. Our house was vandalized on multiple occasions. It was difficult for us to participate in other sports (as a player or referee) without references to hockey. Everyday life changed, and we struggled to feel comfortable at work or out and about when strangers recognized our faces from the news and would ask if we were "the hockey twins." There was so much uncertainty about whether or not these strangers supported our initiative, sometimes it was easier for us to say "no" when asked and to simply move on.

We never asked for our picture to be taken or to be put on television; we were pushed to do it. But sometimes a push is what people need. If we had not fought for our rights then nothing would have changed. Future generations of females may have run into this problem had we not fought to have the gender discriminatory rule changed.

In the National Hockey League, an award is given out every year to the player who scores the most goals; there is no award for the player who accumulates the most assists. To some, one of the most beautiful things about the game of hockey is the assist. Not only does it require some measure of skill, but also something much more important in team sports—selflessness. While a goal comes from the hands or the head, assists come from the heart. Without the selfless act, no society could hold itself together. There is no doubt that in time more people will come to understand what we have accomplished with our "assist" in the fight for human rights.

Canadian society has benefited from our endeavor. Following the 2006 decision, legal precedent for this kind of human rights case was set, and other provinces have also been able to promote gender equity in sport. In 2009 the British Columbia Human Rights Tribunal found that Little League Canada's tournament policy adversely affected Beacon Hill Little League Major Girls' Softball Team by excluding them from the Little League Canada's travel fund; therefore, the team was deprived of benefits of subsidization and had the burden of making its own travel arrangements. The root of this case was discrimination in the provision of services on the basis of sex. Our human rights case was used in this hearing to prove that the existence of discrimination against women in sport is an historical fact.

In 2010, Courtney Greer, a 17-year-old female soccer player in Ontario, played on a women's soccer team outside of high school and desired to tryout and play for the boys' high school soccer team as well. Initially, she was denied this right, but as a result of our human rights case, and the testimony of Sandra Kirby, the Ontario Federation of School Athletic Associations changed its gender equity policy. Without Courtney's case being prolonged and having to go to a hearing, she was granted the right to play where she deserved to play. As she once said, "Equity is about choice, and as soon as we take away choice then we're already discriminating at some level."

It is worth mentioning that the worst fear of the MHSAA—anarchy—did not transpire. In fact, there are only ever a handful of girls who play within the "boys'" sport system, and most often girls will move over to women's sport when the time is right for them and they choose to. Research published by Beaubier, Gadbois and Stick in 2011 utilized our case, the Pasternak sisters' human rights case, as an argument that gender equity dilemmas could be avoided if Canadian high school athletics directed more attention to American gender equity policy and legal conclusions of gender equity issues in high school and college athletic programs. However, even after the Pasternak decision, the MHSAA's 2008 revised constitution read:

> The MHSAA endeavors to provide equal opportunities for athletes. If a school does not have a girls' team, then a girl may try out for the boys' team. If a school has both a boys' and a girls' team, then the students would play for their respective gender (except in hockey, where a girl may try out for a boys' team, even if the school has a girls' team).

This demonstrates that MHSAA failed to see the broader issue at hand, where the inequity did not lie solely in relation to the sport of hockey. More recently, in 2012, MHSAA revised its constitution again to state,

> Girls may try out for and play on a boys' team. They may not play on both the boys' and girls' team for the same sport in the same season. Once they have declared a team they cannot switch to the other gendered team during the season. If a school has both a boys' and a girls' team, they are encouraged to play for their respective gender.

This is a step in the right direction for gender equity in high school sport in Manitoba. However, further attention needs to be placed on promoting gender equity in sport within all of Canada in order to avoid forcing young women to endure legal battles in the way that we did.

SHARING TIME AND SPACE
Reallocating Public Facilities to Girls
Janna Taylor

"A gender equity policy that could have costly implications for sports and recreation programs and facilities across BC and the rest of Canada was announced Friday by the city of Coquitlam and the BC Human Rights Commission. The policy, detailed in an eight-page agreement between the city and Dave Morrison of Coquitlam, the father of two female gymnasts, commits the city to an unprecedented balancing of funding and support for male and female recreation programs." *Vancouver Sun* (March 14, 1999)

When the gender equity program for the City of Coquitlam was announced in 1999, I knew that the agreement was a wakeup call to municipal recreation departments in BC. At the time, my colleagues and I were aware that we were getting more and more requests from female teams wanting access to arenas, fields and other municipal facilities. The scene was ripe for a collision of some sort.

During my tenure in the municipal recreation field—the 1970s to the 1990s—I witnessed and was party to an evolving environment as girls and women became more involved in a wider range of sports and changing expectations. What was once an assumed domination of space and resources by boys' and men's sports teams was now being questioned, and in some cases, hotly contested. Parents were no longer willing to have their daughters take a backseat to the boys playing the same sports and getting financial subsidies in municipal facilities.

As bureaucrats, we were all faced with the same pressures— both political and resource-wise. The municipal system had been developed on a traditional model of male sports. Ice arenas, playing fields, pools, etc. were allocated following decades of male "ownership"—real or perceived. Allocation policy development was also constructed from a top-down, non-participatory approach, thereby excluding many new sports that did not have representatives or advocates at the political or quasi-political level. There were no policies as to how to handle not-for-profit recreation organizations—such as gymnastics clubs—that did not have the use of public space and had to rent space to carry out their mandate. There were also no policies to guarantee previously under-represented or non-represented sports; and, of course, no policies to grant women and girls equal access to facilities or subsidies.

Ensuring equal access and equal subsidies to municipal recreation services for girls and women could have far-reaching consequences. Politically, it was a contentious issue. Girls and women still faced barriers to accessing community recreation programs and facilities, despite the fact that many municipal parks and recreation departments had been set up to provide recreation services for the citizens of the community.

Overall, there was just a finite amount of time and space, and those who had always used both were virtually guaranteed a continuing right to do. The common allocation practice for ice, field and other public facilities was done on a seniority basis, and those teams that had come in previous years would get first choice for schedule and also would receive subsidized rental rates if they were using an arena or swimming pool or gymnasium.

For feminists working in the field, we often had to negotiate political minefields to squeeze more time for women's teams or girls' sports. Given the traditional historical model of allocations, and without policies guaranteeing equal access, we often didn't succeed in achieving progress as quickly as we would have liked. The system was dominated by a traditional male sports model, which did not allow for a whole new group of people—in this case women and girls—to share equal time or space.

I recall in Port Coquitlam in the latter part of the 1970s when a ringette team requested ice time and a subsidized ice rental. We had little ice time available other than very early in the morning, which was not a good time for an emerging female sport. The city's recreation committee had to take a resolution to the city council so that we could provide a better time in the early evening. This move required much consultation and work with other groups who used the ice, such as junior hockey, minor hockey and figure skating, to reach a compromise. The concept of equity policies was only starting to be recognized, and progress was only made after much discussion and organized political support.

And then one day in 1991, I received a phone call from a concerned father, Dave Morrison, who indicated that he was on the board of directors for the Omega Gymnastic Club. Morrison had a very personal investment in this issue—he had two daughters who were members of the gymnastic club. We had a discussion about the issue of Coquitlam recreation facilities and subsidized rental rates for minor sport groups.

Morrison had heard about some of the work of PROMOTION Plus—an organization formed in 1990 to increase opportunities for girls and women in physical activity and sport. As I was on the organization's board of directors, I was, of course, very engaged in the issue. He told me he was concerned that the Omega Gymnastic Club was not treated in a similar manner as other minor sport groups in Coquitlam were. He was gathering information and doing research to build a case for equal treatment for the gymnastic club, and was going to file a human rights complaint with the BC Human Rights Commission. I knew that if his complaint went forward, it could result in a significant ruling.

As written in a piece from the Sport Law and Strategy Group by Hilary Findlay on June 12, 2000: "Mr. Morrison's complaint alleged that the allocation of resources, either as direct financial subsidy or tax relief, by the City of Coquitlam to sport and recreation facilities and organizations, disproportionately benefited male-dominated sports over female-dominated sports." As reported in the *Vancouver Sun* article, the City of Coquitlam decided to negotiate an agreement with Mr. Morrison rather than have the BC Human Rights Tribunal hear the complaint. The essence of the agreement was that the City of Coquitlam had 10 years to develop a gender equity program that would ensure that program offerings, financial subsidies, and space allocations, such as arena time, field allocations etc. were balanced between males and females.

Leading up to the negotiated agreement, I was involved in

a number of strategic meetings with Mr. Morrison and others interested in his human rights complaint. It is not appropriate to divulge all the discussions that were held behind closed doors, but it is safe to say that the complaint was viewed as a significant change that could have serious ramifications throughout municipalities in BC.

It is difficult to gauge the impact of the City of Coquitlam's gender equity program on municipal recreation departments in BC, but there is no doubt in my mind that it was one piece in combination with the work of such organizations as ProMOTION Plus that helped to significantly move the gender equity agenda. During the decade following the agreement, there has been an increasing general awareness and involvement of girls and women in sport.

I suspect that current municipal gender policies are not what they were in 1990. Today, if a parks and recreation department told a girls' hockey team it could not get ice time because several boys' hockey teams had already booked it, such a response would almost surely be considered reckless.

Of course, now that there are minor hockey leagues for girls' teams, the fight for equal ice time is more complicated, as is any other kind of allocation of space for fields, gymnasiums, swimming pools and other municipal facilities. Indeed, the City of Coquitlam's Gender Equity Policy was a catalyst for change that would not have happened had it not been for the tenacity of Dave Morrison, who fought for his daughters and other females of the Coquitlam Omega Gymnastic Club for a fair and equitable opportunity to participate, without any financial barriers.

BLAINEY, PASTERNAK AND SAGEN
Courts and Public Opinion
Hilary A. Findlay

This chapter examines three notable Canadian legal challenges that have contributed to defining the equality landscape of sport in Canada. Those involved in some of the cases are described elsewhere in this book and bring an additional and valuable perspective beyond the legal confines of the cases. The three cases are: the 2009 case *Sagen v. VANOC*, the 1987 case *Blainey v. Ontario Hockey Association et al.* and the 2008 case *Pasternak v. Manitoba High Schools Athletic Association*.

The cases are notable from a number of perspectives. First, they provide a historical context to the legal activity that has been a part of the efforts of girls and women to gain a greater, more equitable standing within sport. Second, they represent two different approaches to the issue of discrimination. The *Blainey* and *Pasternak* cases are similar and in fact, *Pasternak* draws on the decision in *Blainey*. They reflect an "individual rights" model to claims of discrimination, an approach reinforced by the nature of human rights legislation. Both Blainey and the Pasternak twins were successful in their claims; however, the "individual rights" approach typically pits the immediate best interests of the individual claimant against longer-term systemic change. As a result, the underlying disparity, which led to the original complaint, continues. *Sagen*, on the other hand, dealt with group rights; that is, the rights of female ski jumpers to have their sport, women's ski jumping, included in the Olympic Games. It was not about one, or even several, female skiers seeking membership on the men's ski jump team. In this case, redress of historical and systemic inequities was central. The claimants were not successful through the hearing process; nonetheless, women's ski jump will finally be on the Olympic programme for the Sochi 2014 Olympic Games and a historical inequity, and the adverse effects flowing from it, will have some redress. Thirdly, the cases, and *Sagen* in particular, reflect the difficult complexity, particularly at the international level, of dealing with issues of inequality.

The Canadian case, *Sagen v. VANOC*, captured headlines leading up to the 2010 Winter Olympic and Paralympic Games, putting into question the inclusion of any ski jumping events—male or female. In this case, a group of 15 female ski jumpers challenged the IOC's decision not to include women's ski jumping in the 2010 Olympic programme. The trial judge had little difficulty finding that the IOC's decision to include only ski jumping events for men was discriminatory. Notwithstanding this finding, under Canadian law, both the trial and appellate levels of court concluded that control over the decision of what sports to include in the Olympic programme rested solely with the IOC and was beyond the jurisdictional reach of a Canadian court. The decision was perplexing to many. How could something that was discriminatory under Canadian law, and which violated Canadian values, be allowed to be part of an event taking place on Canadian soil, organised by a Canadian organisation and receive significant public funding from all three levels of government—municipal, provincial and federal?

The decision in *Sagen* was not a popular one among the public. Margot Young writes in her 2010 article "The IOC Made Me Do It," that according to one public opinion poll at the time, nearly three quarters of Canadians supported the inclusion of women's ski jumping in the Games. In the court case, it is recorded that even the trial judge found "something distasteful … about a Canadian governmental activity being delivered in a way that puts into effect a discriminatory decision made by others."

In defence of the skiers' claim of discrimination, VANOC argued that it was simply implementing a decision of the IOC and one over which it had no control, but a contractual obligation to implement. The IOC for its part always maintained that its decision not to include women's ski jumping in the 2010 Olympic programme was based on "technical merit" and had nothing to do with gender discrimination.

It became clear over the course of the trial, however, that the actual discrimination was rooted in a historical decision of the IOC passed in 1949, which introduced selection criteria for determining whether a sport, discipline and event was to be included in the Olympic programme. At the same time, an exception to the criteria was also created for sports that had traditionally been part of the Olympic Games. Men's ski jumping had been part of the Olympic programme since 1924 and was thus grandfathered into the Olympic programme. As Marcus Mazzucco and I wrote in a 2012 publication, men's ski jumping has never been subjected to selection criteria in the same way as women's; and if it had, even in 2010, it would not have satisfied those criteria.

As for the claim by the IOC that the decision not to include women's ski jumping was based on "technical merit," Patricia Vertinsky and colleagues wrote in 2009 that it was noted during the course of the trial that the IOC had made a number of exceptions to the selection criteria, including women's ski cross, in which the number of both athletes and countries involved were far fewer than women's ski jump. When asked about the admission of women's ski cross, which did not meet the selection criteria, leading members of the IOC pointed to its popularity with the public and its appeal to youth. As acknowledged in the 2009 publication, "The Future of the Olympic Movement" by Dick Pound, an IOC Executive member from Canada, "[t]here has been some pressure on the IOC to expand the program of the Games to include sports that have an appeal to today's youth, which has led to inclusion of such sports and disciplines as triathlon, snowboard, snow cross, freestyle skiing, synchronized diving and the like." Many of these were exceptions to the IOC selection criteria.

The trial court in *Sagen* recognised the significant disadvantage suffered over the years by women ski jumpers over their male teammates by virtue of the historical inclusion of the latter in the Olympic Games. The court noted that without Olympic recognition, it is difficult for women to get the training and support, both financial and competitive, necessary to reach world-class levels. At the international level for example, without recognition at the Olympic Games, there was no urgency for the Fédération Internationale de Ski (FIS) to establish a competitive circuit for women's ski jumping, and the first world championships for women were not established until the 2008-09 season. At the national level, funding from national Olympic committees, and other sources including sponsorship, is tied to the sport's Olympic status, as are competitive opportunities. Consequently, without high-level competitive and training opportunities, women ski jumpers collectively were unable to meet the IOC selection criteria. The resulting exclusion of women's ski jumping from the Olympic Games simply perpetuated the disadvantage.

Though the court concluded that there was discrimination, the ski jumpers in this case were left without remedy. The case highlights several issues. First, it demonstrates that relying on national courts to regulate international sport bodies may have little effect. National authorities can find themselves unable to intervene, even where, as was the case in *Sagen*, the decisions of the IOC violated fundamental national legal principles of equity and fairness. In this case, technical and jurisdictional constraints left the group of female skiers without a legal remedy and the IOC immune from Canadian law. Second, the case highlights the underlying pernicious and accretive effect of a historically inequitable competitive rule and shows how such a rule can create systemic inequities within a sport.

Blainey v. Ontario Hockey Association et al. and *Pasternak v. Manitoba High Schools Athletic Association* are similar cases, each making essentially the same gender equity arguments as the other, but separated by some 20 years. *Blainey* arose in 1984 and *Pasternak* in 2006. Ironically, the *Blainey* decision was heralded at the time as a watershed decision opening the doors for greater, more equitable opportunities for girls to participate in sport activity in Canada.

Justine Blainey, then 12-years-old, was selected to join a local boys' travelling hockey team. The rules of the Ontario Hockey Association did not let girls play on boys' teams, and thus Justine was denied membership on the boys' travelling team. Justine's challenge of her exclusion using the Ontario *Human Rights Code* was straightforward. As noted by Margot Young in "Sameness/Difference: A Tale of Two Girls," "the only difference between [Justine] and the other [male] members of the team as far as playing hockey was concerned was her sex which, at least in this context, was simply an 'accident of birth.'" Justine was much more the same than she was different. It was not difficult for the Human Rights Tribunal, and subsequently the Ontario Court of Appeal, to find in Justine's favour. This so-called "similarly situated" approach to equality jurisprudence ensures that people who are similarly situated are treated alike, to the extent that they are alike. Blainey was sufficiently like the boys on the team with which she wished to play to have the right to play with them.

Twenty years later, the Pasternak twins from Manitoba wanted to play on their high school boys' ice hockey team. Even though they had been playing through the ranks of boys' teams for a number of years, the local high school sport authority enforced a rule prohibiting girls from playing on boys' teams where a girls' team existed. As in the case of Justine Blainey, the Pasternaks were successful in challenging the discriminatory rule. The Human Rights Tribunal, and subsequently the Manitoba Court of Appeal, ruled the twins should be permitted to try out for the team on the merit of their own abilities, finding the girls to be more akin to the boys than to the girls in their hockey skill, i.e., more alike than different, as in the *Blainey* case.

This approach to equality decision-making has largely been the model in sport in Canada. It requires some comparator group against which difference is judged. The comparator becomes the norm against which the claim of discrimination is determined. In both *Blainey* and *Pasternak*, the comparator group was the boys' team. The more alike the girls were to that comparator group, the more straightforward the decision. On the other hand, the greater the differences the more murky the landscape.

The difficulty with this approach is twofold. First, the differences are often constructed, that is, they emerge as a result of historically and socially constructed stereotypes and environments. Second, the focus is on the difference rather than the norm itself. By simply focusing on the differences, the actual cause of the inequality is missed and an opportunity to ameliorate systemic inequities, which are at the root of the differences, is lost. Martha Minow notes in her book *Making all the Difference*, "[t]he focus of equality analysis should not be on the sameness or the difference of the equality claimant but on the practice and institutions which construct and utilize differences to justify and enforce exclusions." Those factors are some of the very ones enumerated by the trial court in the *Sagen* case discussed above — the lack of training and competitive opportunities, a lack of resources and chronic underfunding, among others.

A wider lens, one that could take in the environment that led Justine to want to play in the boys' league, would have pulled in a whole other set of equality concerns and may have been more likely to lead to greater systemic and enduring change. Instead, we saw 20 years later the Pasternak twins bringing a human rights claim eerily similar to that of Justine Blainey. And, again in 2010, the CBC news reported that Courtney Greer, a 17-year-old soccer player brought a similar complaint against the Ontario Federation of School Athletic Associations (OFSAA) regarding a rule prohibiting her from playing with the boys' soccer team.

The courts in both *Blainey* and *Pasternak* heard similar concerns against allowing girls to play on boys' teams. The wicking away of top girl athletes to the boys' teams will lead to the girls' teams remaining secondary and subordinate. And, inclusion of the top girls on boys' teams will take opportunities away from the less skilled boys. In *Blainey*, the Court said it was unlikely the floodgates would open and a rush of girls would seek participation on the boys' teams. The Court recognized that, at least in hockey, there was a difference between the girls' game and the boys' game and that most girls would rather play in a segregated environment. The Court in *Pasternak* observed that in the 20 years between the *Pasternak* case and the *Blainey* case there had been no mass exodus of girls to boys' teams (and even after the hearing, Judy Owen reported in her article "No impact seen from hockey rights' case" that there had been no exodus). In the end though, both courts rested their final decisions on the similarly situated test, necessarily ignoring the broader systemic issues underlying the case. While there may have not been an exodus of girls to boys' teams, the equality issue underlying both cases, manifest in the gender discrimination systemic to the sporting world and reflected in the discrepancy in quality and opportunity between girls' and boys' sport, remained untouched.

It may be that recourse through traditional equality-based judicial channels is too blunt an instrument to address more than the individual rights of each claimant. Although one indirect outcome of these cases is that in the context of Greer's 2010 complaint to the Ontario Human Rights Tribunal, OFSAA did revise its rule in order to allow girls to try out for and play on boys' teams. Unfortunately, as reported by Hayley Mick in the *Globe and Mail*, a number of provincial school athletic associations continue to promote gender equity policies limiting girls' involvement on boys' teams only where there is no girls' team, some maintaining they will only change their policy if challenged.

LES JEUNES ATHLÈTES FÉMININES
Les risques du métier !
Sylvie Parent

Les jeunes filles qui pratiquent un sport de compétition vivent pour la majorité de grands moments de plaisir, de complicité ainsi que des moments de dépassement de soi. Plusieurs athlètes féminines témoignent que le sport leur a permis de se développer et de vivre de belles expériences. Le sport est également connu pour ses impacts positifs sur la santé des jeunes filles qui le pratiquent. Toutefois, ces récits d'un parcours en somme positif et formateur ne sont pas le propre de toutes les jeunes athlètes. Dans le présent chapitre, je traiterai donc des côtés plus tabous et moins « populaires » de l'expérience des jeunes athlètes féminines et des impacts de la culture sportive et de certaines pratiques sur leur santé et leur sécurité !

Le monde du sport change et évolue au rythme des découvertes scientifiques et des progrès en entraînement. Les progrès sont souvent bénéfiques pour les organisations sportives et les sportifs eux-mêmes. On assiste aujourd'hui à une amélioration des techniques d'entraînement, des équipements, des résultats, etc. Ces améliorations contribuent au spectacle sportif mais ces « avancées » ont certains effets pervers. Beaucoup d'efforts, d'argent et d'espoirs sont investis dans le sport d'élite. Nous savons qu'il y a beaucoup d'appelés, mais peu d'élus. Ainsi, on demande à certaines jeunes filles des régimes d'entraînement énormes et des sacrifices substantiels dans le but d'atteindre les plus hauts sommets. En effet, on observe aujourd'hui une augmentation de la durée et de l'intensité des entraînements, une spécialisation plus précoce, des entraînements à l'année et une difficulté accrue sur le plan des différentes habiletés sportives requises. De plus, les modèles de développement des athlètes actuels sont essentiellement axés sur le développement des aspects physiques. Ces modèles ne tiennent souvent pas compte des dimensions psychosociales du développement de l'individu. Comme le mentionnent Ford et ses collègues, dans leur article de 2012 "The long-term athlete development model: physiological evidence and application", placer trop d'emphase sur le conditionnement et la préparation physique durant l'enfance peut avoir des conséquences négatives sur le plan du développement physique, social et psychologique. Les dimensions sociales et psychologiques sont pourtant d'une importance majeure lorsque l'on s'attarde aux raisons de l'abandon des jeunes en sport. En effet, plusieurs jeunes filles abandonnent le sport, entre autres en raison du manque de plaisir et du manque de temps pour socialiser et étudier, mais également pour d'autres raisons comme le harcèlement ou les abus dont elles peuvent être victimes dans le contexte sportif.

La quête des médailles et des bénéfices monétaires associés entraîne également son lot de conséquences sur le bien-être et la santé des jeunes athlètes féminines. Souvent nous regardons leurs exploits et nous sommes impressionnés par les aptitudes sportives de ces dernières. Mais est-ce que nous réalisons pleinement les heures innombrables qui sont investies pour atteindre ces sommets et les sacrifices que cela demande ? Le jeu en vaut-il la chandelle ? Bien que le sport contribue indéniablement à la santé physique et psychologique des jeunes filles, que faire lorsque ce même sport entraîne des conséquences fâcheuses sur la santé et la sécurité de celles-ci ? Si le sport était pratiqué et encadré dans une perspective de développement holistique et de respect des droits des jeunes filles et que l'on s'efforçait de faire du sport un milieu sécuritaire et sain, aurions-nous les mêmes problèmes ? C'est une question qui mérite d'être débattue en regard des informations que nous possédons sur les impacts physiques et psychosociaux des pratiques actuelles chez les jeunes filles évoluant dans le milieu sportif.

Le parcours de plusieurs jeunes filles en sport est malheureusement ponctué de difficultés diverses. Par exemple, plusieurs subissent des blessures dans leur carrière; celles-ci sont monnaie courante en sport. C'est en effet par milliers que les jeunes filles subissent des blessures traumatiques et d'usure, et ce, dans divers sports. Ces blessures peuvent être le résultat d'une spécialisation précoce dans un sport spécifique, d'entraînements excessifs et de surentraînement dans un contexte où les os sont immatures, d'un repos insuffisant après les blessures ou d'une préparation physique insuffisante ou erronée. Certaines athlètes féminines peuvent même être victimes d'épuisement et de burnout. Malgré ces risques de blessures et d'épuisement, les athlètes et quelquefois les intervenants qui les encadrent minimisent ou normalisent les blessures, priorisant la performance sportive au détriment du bien-être des jeunes filles. Les médias ne sont pas étrangers à cette culture de normalisation. En effet, les médias font fréquemment l'éloge et la promotion de comportements de prise de risque et valorisent le fait de s'entraîner dans la douleur et le sacrifice personnel pour l'intérêt de l'équipe et des résultats de compétition. Selon Peter Donnelly dans son article "Child labour, sport labour: applying child labor laws to sports" de 1997 :

> [...] dans aucune autre profession ou activité, et ce même pour les adultes, ne serait tolérés autant de burnout, de blessures d'usure, de risques de blessures traumatiques et de possibilités de conséquences sérieuses à long terme sur la santé des jeunes sans que de vives questions ne soient soulevées.

Les blessures subies par les jeunes athlètes féminines sont même considérées par certains comme une forme d'abus physique et d'exploitation du corps des jeunes filles.

Ces formes de « blessures » discutées précédemment sont très visibles. Toutefois, d'autres blessures ou traumatismes sont vécus par certaines jeunes filles et se manifestent de façon beaucoup plus subtile. Les comportements malsains d'adultes gravitant autour d'elles (ex. : abus sexuels, harcèlement, abus psychologiques, etc.) et les demandes imposées par la culture sportive sont des formes de violence envers les jeunes athlètes féminines. La question de l'importance accordée à la victoire et aux résultats est un élément maintes fois soulevé pour expliquer la violence dont peuvent être victimes ces jeunes sportives. Notamment, la philosophie sportive axée sur la victoire peut créer des situations pouvant aisément mener à l'abus de la part de personnes en position d'autorité. Cook et Cole écrivaient en 2001 :

> […] quand la victoire prend le dessus sur les autres raisons de la participation, le participant est perdu et l'enfant devient rapidement un instrument à entraîner et à discipliner pour jouer un rôle particulier. Lorsque cette situation est présente, l'athlète n'est dès lors plus vu comme un individu avec des besoins personnels et des droits, mais davantage comme un outil utilisé pour la poursuite du succès sportif, ce qui place alors l'athlète dans une position de vulnérabilité pour diverses formes d'abus.

Bringer, Brackenridge et Johnston ajoutent dans leur article de 2002 qu'à partir du moment où les athlètes décident de tout faire pour atteindre des buts de performance, leur vulnérabilité pour l'abus est augmentée par le fait qu'ils normalisent et justifient divers processus qu'ils croient être essentiels pour atteindre leurs objectifs. Les abus peuvent prendre diverses formes comme les abus physiques (ex. : exercice forcé), sexuels, économiques ou psychologiques. Selon Ashley Stirling de son article de 2009, l'abus est défini comme un mauvais traitement sur le plan physique, sexuel ou émotionnel par une personne en position d'autorité résultant en un risque de causer du tort à un athlete.

Dans le domaine du sport, on observe une certaine normalisation de comportements inappropriés qui ne le seraient pas en dehors de la sphère sportive. Par exemple, pourquoi tolère-t-on des relations intimes entre entraîneurs et athlètes ? Pourquoi tolère-t-on que des jeunes filles jouent ou pratiquent blessées ou épuisées ? Pourquoi tolère-t-on des gestes de violence ou d'intimidation sous prétexte que « ça fait partie du jeu » ? Pourquoi tolère-t-on que le corps des filles et des femmes soit exploité en sport pour projeter une image ou faire vendre ? Pourquoi tolère-t-on que l'image corporelle et la conformité soient omniprésentes dans le sport féminin et que des juges prennent en compte cette dimension dans leur évaluation des performances sportives ? Pourquoi tolère-t-on que des jeunes filles mineures investissent 36 heures par semaine dans la pratique d'un sport, même si cette situation est considérée par certains auteurs comme de l'exploitation d'enfants ? A-t-on besoin d'autant d'investissements de la part de ces jeunes filles en si bas âge et en plein développement pour « générer » des athlètes de haut niveau à l'âge adulte ? Autant de questions pour lesquelles je n'ai pas les réponses. Toutefois, les prochaines lignes fournissent quelques pistes de réponse à ces interrogations.

L'importance accordée au poids et à l'esthétisme dans plusieurs sports est un exemple parfait d'une culture sportive « violente » envers les jeunes filles. En effet, il nous vient rapidement à l'esprit le cas des jeunes filles évoluant dans des sports où la composante esthétique est importante et où les catégories de poids sont présentes, bien que ces problèmes soient présents dans plusieurs sports. Dans ce contexte, certaines jeunes filles s'astreignent ou sont astreintes par des adultes en position d'autorité à suivre des régimes, à perdre du poids ou à surveiller leur alimentation de façon importante. Pour plusieurs d'entre elles, la préoccupation à l'égard du poids et les troubles alimentaires sont des réalités avec lesquelles elles doivent composer. Nous savons à l'heure actuelle que les apports nutritionnels de plusieurs jeunes filles athlètes sont en deçà des recommandations nationales sur le plan nutritionnel en dépit du fait qu'elles ont une dépense calorique importante. De plus, plusieurs utilisent la diète pour atteindre le corps qu'elle, leur entraîneur ou les officiels conçoivent comme étant « idéal ». On pousse en quelque sorte ces jeunes filles à avoir un corps parfait par l'importance qu'on accorde à la minceur et aux standards imposés par le sport et ceux qui le dirigent. Les pressions sont particulièrement fortes sur les athlètes féminines pour rencontrer des poids et des pourcentages de gras irréalistes, et ce, de façon accrue dans les sports jugés. Ceci entrave leur développement, car elles sont dans une période où elles se forgent une image de leur corps.

La culture et les règles de certains sports soulèvent également des questionnements sur l'impact des choix institutionnels et sociaux sur la vie des jeunes athlètes féminines. Par exemple, certains entraîneurs exercent un contrôle important sur les jeunes filles, que ce soit sur leur sommeil, leur alimentation, leurs fréquentations, etc. D'autres isolent la jeune athlète de sa famille et de ses amis dans le but d'avoir une main mise sur « leur » athlète. Ces situations ont un potentiel abusif certain. Sur le plan socioculturel, certaines jeunes athlètes féminines sont, en bas âge, privées de socialisation et de liens de proximité avec leur famille en raison des exigences des compétitions, des camps d'entraînement ou des séjours intensifs avec les équipes nationales loin de chez elles. Sachant que ces liens sont primordiaux pour le développement social et psychologique des jeunes, ces situations ne favorisent certainement pas un développement sain et harmonieux.

L'âge minimum requis pour prendre part aux compétitions internationales chez les jeunes filles est également un facteur problématique. En gymnastique, l'âge minimum a été instauré pour protéger les jeunes filles des entraînements trop intensifs et des risques de blessures sérieuses. Ce n'est qu'en 1997 que l'âge minimal a été établi à 16 ans. Avant cette date, on pouvait observer des championnes olympiques aussi jeunes que 12 ans. Récemment, la Fédération internationale de gymnastique a même tenté d'augmenter cet âge limite à 18 ans, mais cette proposition n'a pas été retenue par divers membres influents du monde de la gymnastique. Toutefois, plusieurs fédérations internationales ne possèdent pas ces règles. La gymnastique mondiale a fait des pas de géant sur cette question, mais d'autres fédérations internationales n'ont pas encore emboîté le pas. En effet, selon une étude menée auprès des fédérations internationales par la commission médicale du Comité international olympique (CIO) et citée par Montjoy dans son article en 2010 "Protecting the child athlete: The IOC perspective", 45% de toutes les fédérations internationales n'avaient pas d'âge minimum requis pour participer à des événements de niveau international. De plus, 40% n'ont pas d'âge minimum pour la participation aux Jeux olympiques et 33% n'ont pas modifié leurs règles pour accommoder les besoins de développement et de croissance des jeunes athlètes d'élite.

Il est important de repenser notre façon de faire en sport et de questionner les exigences placées sur les épaules des jeunes filles dans ce contexte. L'importance accordée à la victoire ne devrait pas justifier les moyens utilisés pour y arriver lorsqu'il est question de la santé, de la sécurité et du bien-être des athlètes féminines. Comme société, nous avons le devoir de protéger nos jeunes filles, y compris dans le cadre de la pratique du sport. Rien ne devrait justifier les abus et la normalisation de la violence, pas même les discours comme « c'est comme ça dans le sport », « c'est la culture du sport » ou « ça fait partie du jeu ». Comme le dit Ryan dans son livre de 2005, *Little girls in pretty boxes, the making and breaking of elite gymnasts and figure skaters*,

> [...] il y a eu assez de tentatives de suicide, de troubles alimentaires, de corps brisés, de parents ayant des regrets et d'athlètes amères de leur expérience pour se donner comme devoir de réévaluer sérieusement ce qui est fait pour produire des championnes olympiques.

Mais l'horizon n'est pas si noir. Une attention grandissante est portée à la sécurité et au bien-être des jeunes athlètes féminines. En effet, la Commission médicale du CIO a produit des déclarations de consensus sur l'entraînement des enfants athlètes d'élite, sur la triade de la femme athlète ainsi que sur le harcèlement et les abus sexuels. Aussi, de plus en plus d'organisations sportives mettent des politiques en place afin de protéger les athlètes contre le harcèlement et les abus notamment, et quelques formations sont offertes aux entraîneurs sur divers sujets reliés à ces problématiques. Le Canada fait bonne figure sur ce plan. En effet, les dernières années ont été fertiles en actions de la part des organisations sportives et des dirigeants. Entre autres, Sport Canada a imposé aux fédérations nationales la mise en place d'une politique sur le harcèlement au sein de leur organisation. De plus, les entraîneurs canadiens doivent compléter un module sur l'éthique pour obtenir leur certification et certains entraîneurs canadiens et québécois se voient dans l'obligation de compléter la formation « Respect et sport ». Cette formation a pour but de protéger les jeunes et d'aider les organisations sportives à offrir un milieu sportif sain et sécuritaire. Des initiatives comme le *Child Protection in Sport Unit* en Angleterre ont également des échos au Québec et au Canada. En effet, cette organisation ayant pour mission de protéger les jeunes et d'offrir soutien et conseils aux organisations sportives en cette matière est citée en exemple à maintes reprises. Je viens d'ailleurs de compléter une étude ayant comme but d'analyser les possibilités d'implanter ce genre de modèle de protection ici même. Ce ne sont là que quelques initiatives canadiennes remarquables en matière de protection des athlètes.

Cependant, mon intention n'est pas de répertorier ici l'ensemble de ces initiatives, mais plutôt de soulever des interrogations sur ce que nous possédons comme outils et mesures pour protéger les athlètes féminines et sur l'efficacité de ces mesures, car malgré ces initiatives et ces progrès, il reste beaucoup de chemin à faire. En effet, nous savons que malgré la création de politiques ou de documentation (lorsqu'il y en a…), ces écrits restent souvent tablettés. De plus, les gens qui administrent ces politiques ou qui sont appelés à mettre des mesures en place manquent de compétences pour bien concevoir et appliquer ces dernières. Il existe donc un grand fossé entre la mise en place de mesures de protection et de politiques et les effets réels sur le terrain. Un défi important des prochaines années est de réussir à mettre en place des mesures de protection, mais aussi de faire en sorte qu'elles soient appliquées, connues, comprises et utilisées. Aussi, certaines problématiques sont moins connues et devraient faire l'objet d'une attention accrue. Par exemple, dans leur résolution de 2011 "Le sport en tant que moyen de promouvoir l'éducation, la santé, le développement et la paix", les Nations Unies soutiennent qu'il est

> […] primordial de se préoccuper des dangers auxquels sont exposés les sportifs et sportives, en particulier les jeunes, notamment le travail des enfants, la violence, le dopage, la spécialisation précoce, le surentraînement, l'exploitation liée à la commercialisation ainsi que les menaces et privations

moins visibles, telles que la rupture prématurée des liens familiaux et la perte des référents sportifs, culturels et sociaux.

La protection des jeunes filles dans le sport n'est donc pas encore optimale et demande plusieurs efforts supplémentaires en vue de modifier les façons de faire, les croyances, les mentalités, etc. Ne soyons pas naïfs: les prises de position en faveur d'une plus grande importance accordée au bien-être des athlètes et à leur protection rencontrent d'importantes réticences de la part des autorités politiques et sportives. En effet, plusieurs croient que de tenter de contrer ou de prévenir les effets négatifs de l'implication sportive mettra en péril le succès sportif et le sport d'élite. Là est toute la beauté de l'analyse de ce discours ! Est-ce que santé et sécurité empêchent le développement des jeunes filles à travers le sport ? Pourquoi un milieu favorisant le développement holistique et respectueux des jeunes athlètes féminines ne permettrait pas de garder nos jeunes dans le sport et de favoriser une expérience positive, indépendamment des niveaux atteints ? Doit-on prioriser le développement sain et sécuritaire aux dépens de l'élite et de la performance ? Pourquoi les deux seraient-ils absolument mutuellement exclusifs ? Il est selon moi important de faire du bien-être des jeunes filles et des femmes évoluant dans le sport un enjeu majeur. En regard de cet objectif, il est crucial de tenter de favoriser un changement dans les politiques publiques relatives au sport.

Si les jeunes filles évoluaient dans un système sportif où l'intérêt premier des dirigeants, gestionnaires et intervenants était le développement sain et sécuritaire des jeunes filles, probablement que notre système sportif et ses participantes n'en sortiraient que gagnants et les droits des jeunes athlètes seraient respectés. Selon l'article de Bissell de 2010 "Notes on international children's rights, implications for elite sport and the work of UNICEF", les jeunes athlètes devraient être considérées comme des enfants et des jeunes d'abord et des athlètes ensuite. C'est donc un sous-système (le sport) qui est appelé à se questionner sur ses valeurs, ses choix, sa vision. Pour ce faire, il faut des décideurs publics convaincus et convaincants, mais également une communauté sportive qui croit que de valoriser et de prioriser le développement sain et sécuritaire des jeunes filles en sport est garant non seulement d'une réussite sportive, mais également d'une réussite humaine et sociale. Finalement, je crois fermement qu'il est important d'offrir du soutien aux jeunes filles et aux femmes qui vivent ces problèmes, de les sensibiliser sur ces questions, mais surtout de leur redonner du pouvoir sur leur vie, sur leurs choix.

Sylvie Béliveau, 2004. Béliveau
is the former Women's National
Soccer Team head coach. She
led the Women's National Team
to its first appearance in a FIFA
Women's World Cup in 1995 and
in 2006 was inducted into the
Soccer Hall of Fame.

∧ Nancy Greene, 1968.
Greene won a gold
medal in the giant slalom
and a silver medal in
the slalom in Grenoble,
France in 1968, as well
as defending her World
Cup title, winning ten
races in a row. In 1999,
she was declared Canada's
female athlete of the 20th
century.

^ Silken Laumann rowing in Seoul in 1988. Laumann won a bronze medal at the Los Angeles Olympic Games in 1984, a gold in the single sculls at the Pan American Games and in 1991, the single sculls rowing World Championship. Ten weeks before the 1992 Barcelona Olympics, she was injured in a rowing accident and told she might never row again. Five operations later, Laumann made a great comeback, winning the bronze medal at Barcelona and in 1996 a silver at the Atlanta Olympics.

> Sandra Kirby in Quebec in 1980, just prior to the Olympic trials and the Olympic boycott of the 1980 summer Olympics in Moscow led by the United States and supported by the Canadian government.

^ Chantal Petitclerc in 2008.
Petitclerc lost the use of her
legs in an accident at age 13.
She won 21 Paralympic
medals, including 14 golds
and is the first female
Paralympian inducted in
Canada's Sports Hall of
Fame.

< Beckie Scott was awarded a 2002 Salt Lake City Olympic gold medal in the 5 km cross-country skiing event after two Russians were disqualified for using a banned substance and followed this with a silver medal in the 2006 Olympics in Turin. She became a member of the IOC Athletes' Commission.

∨ Hilary Findlay co-founded the Centre for Sport and Law in 1992 with Rachel Corbett. She is an Associate Professor at Brock University, teaching courses on intellectual property and licensing for sport managers, contract drafting and analysis, negotiating disputes and sport and law.

∧ Marion Lay in 2010 holding her bronze medal for swimming from the 1968 Olympics.

5 | FINDING LEADERS
Developing coaches, role models and icons

Leadership in the women and sport movement between 1960 and 2010 took many forms. Role models were key, some came from previous eras, others were found amongst family, friends and colleagues. Women learned how to be role models, encouraging other girls and women to embrace sport and fight for change.

Some successes were achieved in getting innovative programs in place and funding flowing to support them. Formal efforts to create leadership focused heavily on creating women coaches. This was more than simply skill building. It also included creating safe spaces, generating alliances among women, and developing a feminist approach to coaching, teaching and learning. Again, resistance from the male-dominated sport world often denied women a place among the ranks of coaches and leaders.

These contributors describe the process of building administrators for the sport system and developing skills in advocacy and action. Their efforts to create capacity were focused partly on assisting women in developing survival techniques to exist in the male-dominated sport system. The glass ceiling was also a labyrinth, and finding help to thread through the maze of barriers generally only came from other women, or a few special men.

Change for these leaders came at high prices: pain, disappointment, betrayal and rejection. High expectations abounded and little room for error or slower pace of change existed. The pressures were strong and there were unfair expectations on new leaders to show successes in very short terms. These women talk about the frustrations of gaining ground and then losing that ground afterwards. Change is uneven and it can hurt.

SENSIBILITÉ ET VICTOIRES
Linda Marquis et la dynastie du coaching!
Guylaine Demers

Linda Marquis a entrepris sa 28ᵉ année à la tête de l'équipe féminine de basket-ball de l'Université Laval en août 2012 et elle a atteint le plateau des 500 victoires le 13 février 2013. En soi, cette statistique est remarquable. J'ai eu le privilège de l'avoir comme entraîneure à ses tout débuts avec le Rouge et Or en 1985, et ce, pour trois ans. Vingt-huit ans plus tard, je me trouve encore privilégiée de pouvoir raconter son histoire, mais surtout de vous parler de l'immense impact qu'elle a eu sur plusieurs centaines de jeunes femmes et je fais partie de ce nombre. Le texte qui suit est le résumé d'une entrevue que j'ai réalisée avec elle en octobre 2012.

Linda a une formation en enseignement. Elle a obtenu son baccalauréat en enseignement du préscolaire primaire de l'Université Laval en 1980 et a par la suite amorcé une maîtrise en enseignement à l'Université McGill. Elle a mis de côté ce projet pour se lancer en coaching dès 1983. Elle a d'abord fait ses classes à titre d'adjointe à l'Université McGill pendant deux ans. Elle a ensuite accepté un poste d'adjointe au Cégep de Ste-Foy à Québec (sa ville natale). Ce séjour au niveau collégial AAA fut de courte durée : elle fut tout de suite recrutée pour prendre en charge l'équipe de l'Université Laval en 1985. Je me rappelle très bien un certain matin où notre entraîneur de l'époque a réuni toute l'équipe de basketball dans un restaurant pour le déjeuner. Il nous a alors officiellement présenté Linda, notre future entraîneure. Cette nouvelle nous a toutes réjouies. Je dois cependant avouer qu'à ce moment, notre joie n'était pas associée au fait d'avoir une femme comme entraîneur (pour la première fois de notre vie!), mais plutôt, de changer d'entraîneurs, car nous n'étions pas particulièrement heureuses avec l'équipe d'entraîneurs du moment. L'automne suivant allait nous faire vivre toute une gamme d'émotions ... J'y reviendrai plus loin.

En commençant l'entrevue, Linda a naturellement abordé

la raison de sa « longévité » dans un monde qui n'est pas particulièrement accueillant pour les femmes. Sa raison #1 : pour travailler avec des personnes. Linda adore aider les jeunes femmes sous sa charge à prendre confiance en elles par le biais du sport. Sa formation en enseignement est très représentative de qui elle est : c'est une pédagogue dans l'âme. Au fil des ans, elle a remarqué à quel point les jeunes femmes au début de la vingtaine ne se sentent « pas bonnes, pas belles et incapables ! » Il est devenu incontournable pour elle d'essayer de trouver des façons d'améliorer leur confiance. Tout au long de l'entrevue, elle reviendra régulièrement sur l'importance de semer des graines afin de voir grandir des personnes et de les amener à se dépasser. Le développement de la personne passe définitivement avant celui de l'athlète.

La deuxième raison évoquée par Linda pour expliquer sa persistance dans cette carrière : la carapace qu'elle s'est construite au fil des ans. En effet, entraîner au niveau universitaire apporte son lot de difficultés. Une de celles-ci est l'évaluation des compétences de l'entraîneur basée principalement sur la fiche victoires-défaites. Elle sait depuis longtemps qu'elle est évaluée par tout le monde incluant les parents, les spectateurs et les administrateurs. Elle qualifie cette évaluation de superficielle. En effet, le public en général ne connaît pas sa philosophie d'entraîneure et encore moins les objectifs d'équipe qu'elle fixe avec ses athlètes année après année. Pour ces raisons, elle a forgé sa carapace en s'appuyant sur des valeurs éducatives. Ceci la ramène donc toujours à l'essentiel, aux raisons profondes pour lesquelles elle entraîne encore aujourd'hui. Ceci lui permet donc de mettre en perspective cette fameuse fiche de victoires-défaites. Linda dira en cours d'entrevue qu'elle s'est anesthésiée au fil du temps, mais aussi qu'elle a appris à « fermer le contact ». Elle sait que ces attentes élevées font en sorte que beaucoup d'entraîneurs développent un gros ego. Cependant, elle souhaite que cela ne soit jamais son cas. Elle m'a d'ailleurs demandé « si jamais je rentre dans un power trip, avertis-moi! ». Linda admet volontiers qu'elle n'est pas capable de tout faire, que certains défis auxquels elle a été confrontée lui ont permis de reconnaître qu'elle n'a pas toutes les compétences et qu'elle a ses propres limites.

SES EXPÉRIENCES D'ENTRAÎNEURE

- Entraîneure-chef, Rouge et Or de l'Université Laval, 1985-...

- Programme Canada basket-ball pendant 12 ans

- Coentraîneure-chef, équipe nationale, Universiade d'été 2009 (Serbie)

- Entraîneure-chef, équipe nationale, U-20, Championnat du monde 2007 (Russie)

- Entraîneure-chef, équipe nationale, Championnat de qualification U-20 2006 (Mexique)

- Entraîneure-chef, équipe nationale, Universiade d'été 2005 (Turquie)

- Entraîneure adjointe, équipe nationale aux Universiades 2001 (Chine)

- Entraîneure adjointe, équipe nationale, Jeux olympiques 2000 (Sydney)

- Entraîneure apprentie, équipe nationale 1998

- Entraîneure adjointe, équipe nationale, Universiades 1997 (Italie)

- Entraîneure adjointe de l'équipe du Québec (1995-1996)

Il n'y a aucun doute qu'en 28 ans de carrière à l'Université Laval, Linda est devenue, bien malgré elle, une référence en coaching et en basket-ball en particulier. Avec cette reconnaissance vient une énorme pression. Bien sûr, il y a toujours la pression de bien faire, mais lorsque beaucoup de personnes nous regardent, on devient vite la cible de critiques et on se fait constamment juger. Elle a donc appris à ne pas se comparer, à bien définir ses valeurs et à les respecter. Avec les années vient aussi l'irritation : irritée de devoir encore se battre pour la place du sport féminin versus le sport masculin; irritée que l'arbitre s'adresse au physiothérapeute au début d'un match en pensant qu'il est l'entraîneur-chef, car c'est le seul homme du personnel d'encadrement; irritée de la bataille constante à mener pour trouver des commanditaires qui sont prêts à investir pour le sport masculin, mais pas pour le sport féminin; etc. Elle constate qu'encore aujourd'hui en 2012, il faut toujours se battre pour le sport féminin et la reconnaissance des athlètes féminins. Je rappelle que Linda est la seule entraîneure-chef à l'Université Laval ...

En discutant son style de leadership je vais commencer avec l'anecdote que j'ai annoncée au début de ce texte : l'arrivée de Linda à titre d'entraîneure-chef à l'Université Laval à l'automne 1985. Après deux mois sous sa gouverne, nous (les athlètes) avons commencé à questionner sa façon de nous entraîner : on la trouvait trop douce, pas assez directive, elle ne criait jamais après nous ! Bref, on ne reconnaissait pas les comportements qu'avaient adoptés nos anciens entraîneurs avec nous, tous des hommes dois-je le préciser! Étant co-capitaine de l'équipe, j'ai eu la charge avec l'autre capitaine d'aller rencontrer Linda pour lui faire part de nos doléances et surtout exiger qu'elle soit plus sévère avec nous, qu'elle démontre « plus de poigne ». Cette image restera gravée à jamais dans ma mémoire. Nous sommes en tournoi à l'extérieur et après une dernière réunion d'équipe, nous nous dirigeons dans la chambre de Linda avec notre liste bien en main. Nous entrons et nous défilons notre liste. Linda est sur son lit, les bras croisés au-dessus de sa tête et elle nous écoute sans bronchée. Une fois terminé, elle nous demande calmement : « est-ce tout ? » On lui dit « oui », elle nous remercie et on ressort aussitôt. Encore aujourd'hui, lorsque nous parlons de ce moment l'autre capitaine et moi, on se sent mal... Suite à cette rencontre, Linda n'a rien changé ! Nous avons repris les entraînements et on s'est rendu compte que c'était pareil. Ce qui c'est produit cependant est vraiment intéressant : plus les semaines passaient, plus nous avons commencé à apprécier sa différence, à apprécier être considérées d'abord comme des personnes et ensuite comme des athlètes, à apprécier (et profiter de) sa politique de la porte ouverte en tout temps. Bref, on a compris qu'un style de leadership différent ne veut pas dire pas de leadership, surtout lorsqu'on parle de coaching. Nous n'avions jamais eu de femme comme entraîneur. Le seul modèle qu'on connaissait était un modèle de coaching très masculin et très autocratique. Linda souhaite rendre les athlètes autonomes et leur donner du pouvoir. Pour elle, l'université est la dernière étape avant la « vraie vie » où ces jeunes adultes seront pleinement responsables et elle souhaite les préparer à aborder cette étape de leur vie. Elle rêve qu'un jour elle soit assise sur le banc avec les joueuses lors d'un match et qu'elle n'ait besoin de rien dire … que les joueuses soient totalement responsables de la partie.

Ce qui est troublant en 2012, c'est que Linda m'a confié qu'elle doit encore expliquer son style de leadership dès qu'elle recrute une nouvelle joueuse. Elle décrit alors à l'athlète (et à ses parents dans certains cas) comment elle fonctionne, qu'elle vise l'autonomie des joueuses, qu'elle a des valeurs centrées sur la personne et qui font en sorte qu'elle entraîne différemment. Linda m'a dit qu'elle doit faire ces précisions, sinon, au moment de commencer les entraînements, certaines athlètes se rebutent, comme nous l'avions fait en 1985. Le plus déprimant pour moi est que ces athlètes n'ont jamais eu d'entraîneurs féminins !

Il est certain qu'avec toutes les expériences que Linda a vécues en tant qu'entraîneure, elle a une préoccupation importante pour développer une relève. J'ai perdu le compte lorsque j'essaie d'estimer le nombre d'athlètes que Linda a entraînées et qui sont devenues entraîneures à leur tour. Je crois que j'ai été une des premières. Comme j'étais nouvelle dans la région de Québec, Linda m'a présenté à son frère, responsable d'un programme de basket-ball dans une école secondaire. J'y ai entraîné la première équipe féminine et j'ai développé le programme féminin. Par la suite, Linda a toujours porté une attention particulière aux athlètes qui avaient « de la graine de coach ». Elle leur a souvent offert un poste d'adjointe à la fin de leur carrière universitaire. Elle souhaite transmettre sa passion du coaching : « Je trouve que c'est tellement passionnant de coacher; c'est enrichissant de pouvoir redonner à mon tour ». En jouant un rôle de mentore, elle souhaite s'assurer que celles qu'elle a formées feront ce qu'il y a de mieux pour leurs athlètes. Pour elle, il ne fait aucun doute que le mentorat est indispensable pour recruter, soutenir et maintenir les femmes en coaching.

PRIX ET DISTINCTIONS

■ Au terme de la saison 2006-2007, première récipiendaire du prix Jean-Marie De Koninck-Entraîneur émérite remis à un individu dont la contribution au sport universitaire s'est avérée exceptionnelle à travers son dévouement et son leadership à titre d'entraîneur aux niveaux local, provincial, national et international du sport universitaire canadien.

■ Récipiendaire de la médaille du Jubilé de la Reine (2002)

■ Nommée entraîneur-chef de l'année par SIC en 200 et en 2001

■ Récipiendaire du « Prix 3M » comme entraîneure de l'année au niveau national. Sélection basée sur le succès de l'entraîneure, sur l'engagement dans le domaine de l'entraînement sur la contribution à l'avancement du sport, sur l'habileté d'organisation et de planification, sur le progrès des athlètes et de l'équipe, sur la formation des athlètes et l'image publique (1993)

■ Désignée entraîneure de l'année par la Fédération québécoise de basketball en 1988-1989

Les différentes expériences que Linda a vécues au fil des ans lui ont permis de grandir en tant que personne. Elle se rappelle avec beaucoup de passion les 12 années passées avec le programme Canada basket-ball, les participations aux Jeux de la francophonie à titre d'entraîneure et de mentore pour les entraîneures africaines, les rencontres avec des entraîneures d'autres équipes nationales dans le cadre du programme « Les entraîneures » de l'Association Canadienne des Entraîneurs (ACE). Toutes ces rencontres lui ont permis de s'ouvrir sur les autres et de devenir plus conciliante sur certains aspects de sa vie. Sans oublier que toutes ces aventures lui auront souvent permis de revenir les deux pieds sur terre et de remettre ses propres problèmes en perspective, surtout à l'égard de l'expérience des entraîneures africaines.

Malgré tout ce qu'elle a vécu, Linda considère qu'elle a été chanceuse. Elle se dit toujours que « ça aurait pu être pire ! » Elle sait que certaines personnes se sont battues pour elle, et cela lui a permis de continuer à se battre. Pour l'avenir, elle admet que ce sera toujours un défi de faire valoir le sport féminin et de continuer à se battre pour faire reconnaître les athlètes féminins. Concernant ces dernières, elle a constaté qu'au fil des ans, les générations d'athlètes changent. Son défi actuel : la communication avec les athlètes de la génération Facebook et textos. Il lui est de plus en difficile d'avoir des rencontres en personne avec ses athlètes. Ces nouvelles façons de communiquer ne cadrent pas vraiment avec son approche pour une communication efficace. Linda a appris à choisir ses batailles, mais celles concernant le sport féminin lui sont chères et elle n'a pas l'intention de laisser tomber.

Linda est une femme d'exception. Elle est généreuse, attentive aux besoins de ses athlètes et elle est centrée sur leur développement global. Elle a marqué plusieurs générations de jeunes femmes et aujourd'hui, elle peut dire sans gêne : mission accomplie. Elle a encore le feu sacré et je nous souhaite de la voir sur le banc de l'équipe féminine de basket-ball de l'Université Laval encore longtemps.

THE SNOWBALL EFFECT
Where are all the Women Coaches?
Margaret "Peggy" Gallant

In 1969 Carolyn Savoy and I were hired by John Dewar, chair of the Physical Education programme at St. Francis Xavier University / Mount Saint Bernard College in Antigonish (St. FXU), NS, to teach and coach. What a team. We became BFFs (best friends forever). We had no idea how hard we would have to fight to establish women's varsity programmes in what was, until 1969, a male-only establishment. Our job description included, but was not limited to, coaching varsity teams, running intramural programs, lecturing to undergraduate physical education students, teaching skill labs and offering classes in a variety of sport skills to all first year general students.

Our contact hours, before coaching duties performed at the

end of the day, amounted to about 30 hours a week. Fresh from our own undergraduate studies, we were keen. I was hired to coach field hockey and run the intramural programme for women along with lecturing. Carolyn was hired to coach volleyball and basketball and also teach in the physical education programme. This arrangement sounded great, until we discovered that volleyball and basketball had parallel seasons in the Atlantic Women's Intercollegiate Athletic Association (AWIAA). No problem. We just switched and became varsity coaches in two sports that we had not been hired to coach, and our athletic director, Father George Kehoe, encouraged us to do so without batting an eye. Perhaps his reaction should have been a red flag for us about the importance placed on women's varsity sport at St. FXU, but at the time it was not. It simply meant that we would have to work harder to get up to speed in these sports so that we could coach the young women who were going to show up to play. For the most part, universities had not yet started to recruit female athletes. There was no such thing as an athletic scholarship for women at St. Francis Xavier University in the early 1970s.

In contrast to the women's varsity programme, the men's had better dressing rooms and uniforms; access to the best practise times, an athletic trainer and therapy room; longer schedules; exhibition play; and more and larger trophies, spectators and booster clubs. Still, this programme was also staffed with coaches who were involved with two or more sports, and who also had to do some other job along with coaching to earn a paycheck.

As the years progressed, we fought to have the urinals removed from our women's dressing room, demanded staff dressing rooms that didn't have to be shared with officials, begged for expanded schedules for our teams that included exhibition games, argued to have some sports changed from tournament status to varsity, pursued coaching and refereeing certification, furthered our formal education and somehow found the time to get married.

In 1977, when I was pregnant with my first child and days away from delivery, Carolyn walked into my office and announced she was leaving St. FXU for a basketball-only coaching position at

Dalhousie University: She had been recruited by the athletic director Ken Bellemare. Devastated and hormonally imbalanced, I put my head down on my desk and started to sob. I congratulated her and went immediately to the athletic director to ask him to meet the Dalhousie offer and retain Carolyn. He informed me that we could not hold her back. We were unable to meet the Dalhousie offer, and in the long run Carolyn would be better off. He was right. Carolyn, now Dr. Savoy, had a stellar career as the women's head basketball coach at Dalhousie University for more than 30 years. Little did I know at the time, Carolyn's departure was the beginning of a 30-year decline in the recruitment and retention of female coaches at St. FXU and throughout other university programs in Canada.

In the early 70s all women's varsity teams at St. Francis Xavier University and most teams at sister institutions were coached by women. In the new millennium, St. Francis Xavier University has 11 women's varsity teams, including hockey and rugby, and none are coached by women despite efforts by hiring/selection committees, falling just short of affirmative action. There is a reluctance to apply affirmative action policies in case the inexperienced women are not effective in their role of coach. The argument is always to give the job to the most qualified person, who in most instances is male.

Not only are all coaches at St. Francis Xavier University now male but also we have never in the history of the university's athletics program had a female athletic director. Our university is not unique. Although many gains have been made for women in sports, the number of female coaches in collegiate athletics continues to decline. While the percentage of women in most professions approaches or exceeds 50 percent, in coaching and coach leadership, the percentages of women are very low, approximately 15 to 19 percent, according to the 2011 Centre for Sport Policy Studies' "Gender Equity Report." These statistics have prompted researchers to examine factors that might be influencing women's participation in leadership roles in sport. Numerous studies explore the decline in the number of female university-level coaches; all find that the under representation of women in university coaching positions is largely due to a variety of internal and external barriers to success that women must overcome to reach and maintain a career in high-level coaching.

Internal barriers may stem from character or personality traits that affect professional coaching opportunities, for instance, perfectionism, self-limiting behaviours and the work-family balance. As a wife of 40 years, a mother and a former varsity coach, I relate well to the research that describes how working women, especially female coaches, might feel internal conflict. The young women who entered the coaching ranks at St. Francis Xavier University and did not remain, always complained of a lack of time for friends and family, whether they were married, single, gay or straight. The coaching profession is very time consuming, and when most people are at home enjoying a meal and conversation at the end of the day, coaches are hard at work striving for excellence. Many times this work is further complicated by the fact that these coaches could be working with young people who do not share the same values, priorities or drive.

External barriers lie outside of the coaches' control and they have negative implications on female coaches' professional opportunities. These might include: gender stereotypes, unequal assumption of competence, lower salary than a male counterpart, unfair hiring practices, different leadership styles and expectations and lack of mentoring. Many times when I was sitting on selection committees for coaching positions, fear was expressed by committee members concerning a candidate's sexual preference. If a candidate's sexual preference was unknown and she had been an excellent athlete before becoming a coach, then it was assumed that she was gay and therefore not a suitable choice to coach women. My lesbian friends in the coaching ranks tell me things are better today, but I remain unconvinced that women are not still discriminated against either because they are married with children or single and gay.

Sex stereotypes play a large role in the unequal assumption of competence, further impeding women's advancement in sport leadership. Sport is seen and defined through masculinity. Women involved in sport are often judged by male standards and thus assumed to be less competent than their male counterparts.

Often these assumptions mean that women are paid less for doing the same job as men. In the early years of my career, I was always paid less than men with the same experience and the same or similar qualifications. The recognition of this discrimination impacts women's interest in coaching at all levels.

The second largest external barrier for female coaches is a perceived lack of opportunities for promotion, even though they generally have to work harder than men to prove themselves. Maybe women are more aware of the difficulties in coaching. Perhaps women are more astute than men, and even with or without the barriers, would not choose coaching as a long-term career. This may be an indication of why we have such large numbers of women who enter the coaching ranks but do not stay. They may well be smart enough to figure out that coaching is not for the faint of heart.

Another external barrier for female coaches is the absence of women in administrative positions. This has been documented as a large contributor to the lack of women in coaching positions and cited as a reason for why it is so difficult for women to even enter coaching.

Discrimination also prevents women from becoming coaches. Homologous reproduction—the tendency for people to hire someone similar to them—might not be intentional in the sport world, but it is a subtle form of employment discrimination that women in coaching experience.

Finally, the absence of female mentors and role models is a significant barrier to encouraging women into the coaching world. Indeed, the absence of women coaches is not only upsetting, it also acts as a barrier to encouraging young female athletes to become the next generation of coaches. This lack of other women in the profession makes it difficult to enter coaching and causes those who are in it to feel isolated at work. Many of the women I worked with at St. FXU cited this isolation as a significant reason for leaving coaching.

Formalized mentoring was also cited by my university colleagues and my students at the National Coaching School for Women as the most important factor in their acquisition and development of coaching knowledge and expertise. Mentoring is important at all stages of a woman's coaching career. Mentors are vital to motivating women to apply for and to secure a position, and they are equally important in facilitating networking and establishing contacts in the profession.

I feel the lack of mentors in coaching is the fuel to all other barriers women must overcome. Over the years, I have heard from my colleagues and students about the obstacles they have faced in coaching, including a lack of respect, few mentors, little support and gender socialization. Allison McGlashan, my honours student last year, spent some time interviewing previous female coaches from St. Francis Xavier University to see if we could get any further insights into why there are so few female coaches. The following are some reflections expressed by former female coaches to Allison as part of her investigation and written in her dissertation "Sociocultural Barriers to Women in Coaching: A Case Study of Female Coaches at St. Francis Xavier University."

In general, female coaches receive little respect, causing them to question their choice of career. Women entering coaching are not given the same credibility as men; they must prove themselves as competent and qualified coaches. One coach stated, "I wasn't taken seriously until there was some success, until I proved myself." This unequal assumption of competence rarely subsides and makes women feel as though they must constantly battle for respect and resources. This struggle is exemplified by one coach:

> "As long as I can remember sport has been the toughest, toughest field to work in for a woman because you were constantly trying to prove yourself. If you were the kind of woman who needed a lot of validation it was not the place to be. You had to believe in yourself and what you were doing."

The women interviewed in this study reinforced previous findings and observations that the dearth of female mentors fuels the other barriers faced by women in coaching. It diminishes athletes' desire to become a coach, contributes to coaches feeling isolated in the profession and causes people involved in sport to devalue female coaches. Many coaches referenced the profound impact the lack of mentors can have on young athletes:

"Unless you see role models in coaching that are female how can you see yourself as a potential coach down the road?"

"If it is never there it will never be an option for young women. They will never see the possibility."

Gender socialization dictates that women's traditional roles are as mothers. While such perceptions are changing somewhat, domestic duties can still be a constant source of negotiation and stress between parents. Furthermore, often in heterosexual relationships, women continue to be the ones taking time away from their career in order to raise children. One coach shared the following opinion: "Traditionally, women still have more of a responsibility with children. Their life as a coach goes down the tubes; they are the ones that go home with the baby not the dad. The majority of the childcare falls on the woman's shoulders." Because childcare is assumed to be a woman's responsibility, when a woman is required to spend great amounts of time away from home, it is highly likely she will feel conflicted about her work-life balance. Furthermore, because gender socialization has also devalued women's sport, and thereby decreased visibility of women's sport, female coaches are less likely to obtain funding and be celebrated or valued in society.

The lack of support for female coaches comes from every angle. It reduces women's desire to become coaches as well as their strength to remain in the profession. First, because there are so few women coaches, others lack sympathy for the immense amount of work required for the job. Second, women do not adequately support each other in the profession, creating additional barriers for women. The "Old Boys' Network" contributes to the lack of support for female coaches, as it inhibits women's ability to develop a support network within the profession. One previous St. Francis Xavier University coach was adamant about this, stating that "there is still a lot of chauvinism out there, and there is still what you would call 'The Old Boys' Network.'"

Those interviewed also agreed that the lack of female mentors acted as more of a barrier than all other barriers faced by women in coaching. Furthermore, the snowball effect stemming from the relative absence of female coaches is apparent. One of the former female head coaches from St. Francis Xavier University shared the following insight: "It is a snowball effect because then there aren't as many female coaches and the support network isn't there, which just makes it that much harder for female coaches."

Overall, the interviews above: (a) demonstrate that not enough effort is being put into attracting and maintaining female coaches; (b) illustrate the complex nature of the issues facing women in coaching; (c) supply a depth of understanding for new and previously indicated barriers to women in coaching; (d) indicate that initiative needs to be taken by governing bodies, such as the Coaching Assocation of Canada (CAC) and Canadian Interuniversity Sport (CIS) to train, support and retain women coaches. In order to increase the number of female coaches, organizations need to give women the opportunity to understand their role as coaches. They must also provide female coaches with opportunities to spend time with each other so that they have the chance to talk and listen to others, and to gain support from their colleagues and learn new tools and strategies. Perhaps it is time we looked at why women stay in the coaching profession rather than leave it. The insights we have for leaving seem to be many. What we really need to know is how did coaches like Coach Carolyn Savoy manage to stay and be so successful despite the odds?

FEMININE OR FEMINIST
Ruth Wilson Comes of Age with Basketball
Christiane Job

Ruth Wilson was one of the first to be inducted into *In Her Footsteps*, an exhibit at the BC Sports Hall of Fame that honours women sports heroines. She is celebrated as a woman who embodied excellence in sport and fitness through her performance and her ability to enable others to participate and excel in sport. With a stunning list of accomplishments, including four Canadian Championships as a basketball player, three trips to the softball world championships, many appearances on the women's provincial golf team at National Championships, and a bronze medal as a coach of Canada's 1967 Pan American Games basketball team, she also became the first nationally recognized woman to referee a league basketball game, earning a reputation as Canada's answer to Babe Didrikson Zaharias, as reported by Wendy Long in the *Vancouver Sun*. Incredibly focused, she worked for the professional advancement of women in sport and career. Wilson has been declared Canada's best all round athlete of the 1940s and 1950s with her commitment to sport and female achievement an evident priority throughout her lifetime.

Celebrating heroines of sport is not a straightforward matter. The concept of the heroic, as Jennifer Hargreaves points out in her book *Heroines of Sport*, must be examined through an analysis of the struggles and achievements of many women whose stories have been excluded or forgotten from previous accounts of women's sports and female heroism. Therefore, to understand and celebrate the contribution of Ruth Wilson, it is also necessary to understand the background of basketball in Canada.

According to Lynne Emery in her article on intercollegiate women's basketball, the sport played a fundamental role in both shaping and providing sporting experiences for women in North America as early as 1892. Invented for men in 1891 and taken up by women soon after, basketball took on increasing importance to girls and women in Canada as the 20th century developed. It was a sport that crossed the boundaries and limitations of socioeconomic status, required little equipment and accommo-dated the participation of at least 10 players at one time.

Despite the growing accessibility of the game, aspiring sports women were initially constrained by social mores demanding appropriate female behaviours. Basketball rules across North America in the early 20th century were initially adjusted to reflect "feminine" notions, leading to constraints that affected both physical and spatial dimensions of the women's game. In Canada these debates divided the country, where the form of the game was often determined by the region. Women in eastern Canada, for example, emulated their conservative American neighbours and adopted "girls' rules," while some in the West learned to play like the men, even if their teams were not regarded and supported in their institutions at the same level as the men's teams. Western Canadian teams benefited from this less conservative attitude, producing some of the most competitive women's basketball teams in Canada. These women were fortunate in that the period from the late 1940s through the 1950s was marked by an increased emphasis on community leagues, often called commercial or industrial leagues, where they could experience semi-professional sporting opportunities.

By the late-1950s, another shift had begun to occur in women's basketball. The generation of teams and stars, including Wilson, who had sparked the postwar renaissance, was retiring and taking on new roles as coaches and administrators in the sporting scene. Change was also influenced by the depopulation of the commercial leagues, due to an increased emphasis on inter-university sport as well as growing pressure from both the East and West to bring together the nation's top players to compete on the international stage as a nationally representative team. Additionally, as more funding became available, there were more opportunities for women from eastern and western Canada to meet and discuss the future of basketball in Canada. It was during these meetings that lobbyists (including Wilson) — influential young women coaching in the university system who had played Canadian Amateur Basketball Association (CABA) rules in community competitions and western provinces — pushed hard for the uniformity of basketball rules. As a result of their efforts within the changing social climate of the 1960s, where a competitive sports model was gaining traction, women's basketball witnessed both a surge in growth and a change in the value system underpinning the nature of play and participation in the sport. According to some scholars writing in the early 1980s, such as Mary Keyes and Barbara Schrodt, the controversy over the type of basketball women were playing in Canada thus ceased to be a constant source of contention for both female physical educators and athletes across Canada with the eventual rule unification and adoption of CABA rules in 1966.

In his book *The Struggle for Canadian Sport*, Bruce Kidd writes that with all of the changes in rules as well as the implementation of the federal *Fitness and Amateur Sports Act* (1961) and its provincial counterparts, a transformation in the Canadian sport model began to emerge. The federal government committed funding to the development and promotion of amateur sport with a two-fold mandate of encouraging mass participation as well as enhanced performance at international competitions. It was a challenging time for women's basketball because even though it was unified through its rules, few of the players participated in major organizational decisions, and those who did were discouraged from aligning themselves with radical feminists of the time. It was in this space that Ruth Wilson would make her most significant contribution to the sport of basketball in Canada.

Born in Calgary in 1919, Wilson moved to Vancouver with her family when she was an infant. At an early age Wilson excelled in tennis, golf, swimming, volleyball and basketball. Her experiences in sport were supported by her family's financial stability as well as the burgeoning sport opportunities for girls and young women in Vancouver. In Vancouver, as in many other western Canadian communities at the time, females were seeking opportunities to compete in highly competitive activities such as softball and basketball. If their labour was not crucial to family survival (as was the case for Wilson) their free hours could be easily taken up with clubs and sports—a situation discussed in detail by Veronica Strong-Boag in her book *The New Day Recalled*. Wilson's family encouraged her to play in the backyard. In fact, as reported in an interview with Barbara Schrodt in 2006, Wilson, like so many women influenced by the Edmonton Grads basketball team, spent hours playing and "dreaming that one day she would get the chance to be on the team." In fact, as Barbara Schrodt wrote earlier, in 1984, the liberal environment, in addition to the several fitness movements including the Pro-Rec movement in British Columbia, enabled Wilson to pursue her athletic endeavors.

In 1934 she experienced the loss of her father and learned to use her involvement in sport as a means to cope, as well as to please her mother (an individual well versed in the importance of physical education). With her mother's support and financial backing for her education, Wilson enrolled at the University of British Columbia (UBC) with her sights set on becoming a teacher. Already a successful athlete well before she entered UBC, she continued to be a popular and respected athlete and co-ed at university. Wilson reflected nostalgically on her many successes and joys experienced through sport at UBC in various interviews during her lifetime. Upon graduation from UBC and having completed her teacher training program, she entered the work force and remained in the educational system as a teacher and then later as a school guidance counselor.

Her involvement in basketball continued throughout her professional career. She participated in what was called the Vancouver Commercial Basketball League in both the Senior A and Senior B league divisions. This was a semi-professional basketball league where local merchants, companies and schools sponsored teams. A meat packing company and a jewelry store sponsored two of the most famous Vancouver teams, called the Hedlunds and the Eilers respectively. Wilson played on four Hedlunds Canadian Championship teams (1943-1946) and, according to Barbara Schrodt, was declared to be among the "perennial core of talent" for the team, which made her a household name in the city of Vancouver. When she retired as a player, her talents and ability to scout and nurture young players proved beneficial as she coached the first Eilers teams to two Canadian championships (1950, 1951). These were an important series of wins, for they were the first postwar competitions to involve cross-country travel. By 1958 Wilson served as the vice president of the Canadian Amateur Basketball Association (CABA), a designation she maintained for 10 years. It was in this role (1958) that she initiated and organized the first Canadian Women's Basketball Tournament held in Saskatoon. The following year she was named manager of the 1959 Canadian team participating in the Pan American Games. Her coaching accolades were also substantial: in 1966 she coached the first

Canadian national basketball team and in 1967 led the team to a bronze medal at the Pan American Games. She also coached collegiate teams at the University of British Columbia, Simon Fraser University and Western Washington University (USA).

In an interview with Fred Hume in 1993, Wilson, reflecting on her life, explained: "I have had an interesting life, it has not always been easy, I have had times, well, when it was quite [pause] sad." Only a few years after the loss of her father she also experienced the loss of her husband, a fighter pilot, in the Second World War. She never remarried and spent the duration of her life taking care of her mother and sister. Both passed away before her. When Wilson felt sad she said she often turned to sport and those individuals she knew through sport in order to raise her spirits and distract her from the losses she had experienced.

She had a handful of close friends, many of whom she once had coached or taught alongside in the city of Vancouver. These women were also connected to the sporting community in Vancouver and many spoke of Wilson's example as a mentor and community leader. Together these friends supported one another and helped to advance opportunities for women in sport as physical educators, coaches and administrators with various sports organizations in Canada. Wilson's sports network and the circle of friends she maintained through sport remained like family, visiting her often until she died in 2001.

The celebration of sporting feats and interesting lives serves to ignite and inspire future generations of sporting women to continue pressing for opportunities in sport. Furthermore, when celebrating women in sport, it often becomes apparent that accomplishments include extended service and mentoring. Ruth Wilson remains a member of several sport halls of fame and the story of her involvements will continue to be heralded by new generations of sporting women who have the opportunities to compete and influence others.

TAKING A STAND AGAINST DOPING
Beckie Scott Finally Gets the Gold
Jean Forrest

Through a lifetime of sports involvement as an athlete, coach and administrator, I have met many people who have inspired me in some way. For me, Beckie Scott is one person who stands out from the many athletes I was fortunate to get to know through my involvement with the Canadian Olympic Committee from 2000-2010. She is one of those rare people who through hard work, determination and a very strong code of ethics has not only established herself as a world class athlete but is also making a contribution to sport so that it will be better for those who follow her. I think she is a wonderful role model, and looking back on her 11-year career on the Canadian cross-country ski team you can see how the 2002 Olympic games were pivotal in setting the stage for her future involvement in international sport.

As Beckie Scott raced to the finish line in the five-kilometre pursuit at the Salt Lake City Olympics in 2002, I am sure she had no idea how her third-place finish would impact her life in the upcoming years. Yes, she had won a bronze medal at the Olympics and become the first North American woman in her sport to do so, but she and her coaches felt they had been robbed of the gold medal as they suspected that the two skiers who had beaten her were using performance-enhancing drugs. Most people would have moved on after the games, disappointed in the knowledge that they were unfairly beaten, but not motivated or willing to do what it would take to ensure that the people responsible for this type of cheating at the highest level of sport are held accountable. This is where Beckie Scott is different than most, and the story of her courage as she stood up for her principles and her commitment to make things right is an inspiring one.

As it turned out, the toughest battle for the medal was not on the ski slopes that day, but rather in various courtrooms from Switzerland to Russia as Scott fought to ensure that athletes who had cheated through doping would lose their medals. At the heart of the issue was whether or not the Olympic Charter would allow the International Olympic Committee to strip athletes of medals they had won in Salt Lake prior to failing a drug test. In fact the two Russian skiers, Olga Danilova and Larissa Lazutina, who had beaten Beckie that day, had later tested positive for doping prior to another race. However, it wasn't until it was learned that Lazutina had tested positive for blood doping at World Cup races prior to the Games, making her ineligible for subsequent competitions, that the IOC stripped her of her medals and upgraded Scott to the silver medal. This was presented to her in Calgary in October 2003, almost 20 months after the games. Although Scott and her supporters were happy, they knew the battle was not over, as it moved from the IOC to the Court of Arbitration for Sport.

In her fight she was supported by the Canadian Olympic Committee (COC), whose President, Michael Chambers, was also fighting to have figure skaters Jamie Sale and David Pelletier upgraded from a silver to a gold medal. The COC joined Beckie to ensure that the Olympic Charter's stipulation that athletes caught cheating at a Games should have all their medals removed be respected. It was up to the Court of Arbitration for Sport (CAS) to make a ruling. Of significant importance were the new rules brought in by the World Anti-Doping Agency stating that any athlete who fails a drug test forfeits any and all medals won in that competition. On December 18, 2003, Beckie Scott officially became a gold medal winner when the Court of Arbitration ordered the International Olympic Committee to award the medal to Beckie as a result of doping infractions by Olga Danilova. It also ruled that the IOC pay the arbitration costs that amounted to over $38,000 and over $8,000 to Scott to pay her legal fees. Many people considered this ruling to be a landmark decision in Olympic sport. Beckie became the only athlete to be awarded all three medals in a single event and also the only athlete to return two medals from the same race.

In June 2004, more than two years after the Salt Lake City games, the Canadian Olympic Committee flew Beckie and her family to Vancouver for a special press conference to present her with the gold medal she so rightfully deserved. I had been working on contract for the COC for several years at that point as their West Coast event planner, mostly on golf tournaments and large dinners to raise funds for Olympic athletes on the road to the Vancouver 2010 Winter games. Working on the press conference was a nice change, and one of my tasks was to look after the gold medal before it was presented to Beckie. I remember looking at it and thinking about what this medal in particular signified: it represented not just the athletic training Beckie had put into winning it, but also the moral, ethical and legal struggle she had engaged in. I was even more impressed when she spoke at the event, and it was evident that this battle she had fought was as much for the athletes who would follow her as it was for her. Over 500 people shared that exciting moment with her, including her parents, husband Justin Wadsworth and teammate Sara Renner, who would win a silver medal with the team sprint event at the 2006 Torino Games.

Not surprisingly, Beckie was recognized for her ethics, and in 2005 she became a member of the World Anti-Doping Agency's (WADA) athlete committee. While WADA had been active for several years, this committee was created to represent the views and rights of the athletes and help WADA face the challenges associated with developing strategies to not only detect but also deter and prevent doping in sport. Beckie was a key leader in developing the early policies and procedures for this group and has just recently been moved onto the 12-member Executive committee that is WADA's ultimate policy-making body consisting of representatives from both the Olympic movement and government. So, her work in this important area will continue for a number of years.

On February 23, 2006, Beckie was elected to the International Olympic Committee's Athletes' Commission for an eight-year term. She was competing in what would be her last Olympics as a competitor, and a few months later she announced her retirement from competitive cross-country skiing. During her 11 years on the Canadian Cross-Country ski team, she won Olympic Gold in 2002, Olympic Silver in 2006 and 17 World Cup Medals, making her the most prolific international Nordic skier Canada has ever produced.

As a member of the IOC Athletes' Commission, Beckie is a part of a consultative body that is the link between the athletes and the IOC. This commission is involved in many different activities, including the fight against doping, woman and sport issues and the IOC athletes' career program. She is also sitting on the coordination commission for the 2014 Sochi Winter Games and was active on the commission for the 1st Youth Olympic Games that were held in Innsbruck in January 2012. Her work in Canada has also been impressive as she was part of the 2010 Olympics organizing committee and has been on the Board of Directors for the Canadian Centre for Ethics in Sport and the COC Athletes Council. She has travelled with UNICEF to West Africa and has been an active ambassador for the charitable organization Right to Play. She has been honored with many awards, including being made a member of Canada's Sports Hall of Fame. During all of this she has managed to start a family and has never lost the wonderful down-to-earth personality that I'm sure many others admire. I think it can be safely said that Beckie Scott is an exceptional Canadian, and those of us with an interest in international sport will continue to watch her and feel confident that she will achieve even greater things.

RESISTING ANDROCENTRIC SPORT SYSTEMS
Turning Women Athletes into Leaders
Penny Werthner

In the early 1980s a unique program called the Women in Sport Internship Program was created to provide structured learning opportunities for young women athletes who were retiring from sport and yet were interested in remaining involved in sport. The federal government department, Sport Canada, initiated the project and it ran for a few brief years. This article is about that program, what it looked like, why it was for women only, how and why it worked, and why it perhaps should be revived.

The internship program was an idea initiated by a group of women concerned about the lack of women in leadership positions in sport in Canada. It had a very specific purpose—to develop a group of young women athletes with obvious sport experience and create an environment that would allow them to develop the skills necessary to become effective leaders within the Canadian sport system. The fact that it was funded by the federal government, albeit for a short period of time, gave the issue—lack of women in leadership positions—legitimacy. I would argue that it is still an issue for sport in Canada.

The program was designed for experiential learning. There was a director who managed all the internships and ensured that each young woman was partnered with a national sport organization for a period of six months to one year and matched with a competent mentor within the assigned organization. There was an initial meeting where the program director saw the mentor and the intern to set up a job description for the duration of the internship and to ensure that the mentor understood that the internship's prime purpose was to be a learning experience for the intern. There were numerous conversations and meetings to discuss where the intern's interests lay in order to match those interests with the possible projects that the sport organization wanted completed. It was very much a collaborative process. The intern was paid an honorarium and the sport organization obtained some projects carried out for little cost. In addition to the actual work experience, seminars on a variety of effective leadership skills were designed by the program director and facilitated by experts. The seminar topics ranged from budget management, program evaluation, policy development and board governance, to how to give effective presentations, and strong communication and conflict management skills.

This program was for women only. To understand why, we need only look at the statistics for women in leadership positions in sport which were, and continue to be, incredibly low. While women's athletic participation in sport has increased at all levels over the last 20 years, the number of women leading sport has not. With a few notable exceptions, many of our leaders in sport, such as chief executive officers, coaches and international officials, continue to be male. We know that sport in Canada, and perhaps worldwide, continues to be androcentric; that is, it is dominated by a masculine perspective. One could argue that the sporting world has many norms and conventions that are derived from traditionally male characteristics and experiences. So, as many have argued previously, we need to understand women's lives as quite different from men's and know that women often will cycle in and out and back into work within sport. Thus, this program was designed to educate the young women both on what the sport system looked like, how it needed to change, and the role they could play in that change, particularly as they developed their leadership skills.

While each young woman was set up in an organization and with a mentor—most of the mentors were male—there was also a series of seminars, led by women experts, where the young women came together and had a chance to discuss issues and concerns within a safe environment. Ann Hall's work on the gender structure of national sport organizations informed some of those discussions. Although the seminars were designed to impart specific leadership skills, they were also created so the young women could reflect on the issues they might face as they moved forward in their careers in an environment where they could freely discuss, ask questions, and learn. And for the young women, as we know from the work of Deborah Tannen on the differences between how women and men communicate, the seminars would be most effective, from a deep learning perspective, with only women present. Only in such an environment would all their voices be heard.

To know more about what the participants thought of this program, two of the participants were interviewed. One of the women, Anne Merklinger, a national level swimmer, has gone on to lead a number of national sport organizations and is, at the time of writing, the chief executive officer of Own the Podium, the organization responsible for high performance sport in Canada. The second, Anne Jardin, an Olympic bronze medalist in swimming, went on to become a teacher, but served on Swimming Canada's board for a number of years.

Anne Merklinger came to the program after completing an undergraduate degree at an American university where she had held an athletic scholarship. When asked how she would describe her experiences in the program, Anne began by saying, "I was really behind in terms of work experience because I had focused all my attention on being an athlete. This program gave me the start I needed. It got me to first. I would not be where I am today without this program." She continued, "I now recognize the value of that internship."

Anne's internship was with the sport of synchronized swimming and she worked directly with the executive director, Rick Johnson. "Rick set me up with some very specific projects to work on, such as developing a national team handbook. The projects exposed me to a number of different parts of administration. The internship gave me exposure to a new sport, and I got to watch a CEO in action everyday." For Anne, the program provided a different perspective of sport and much needed skills to move from being an intern into a series of term and full-time work in the administration of national level sport. Anne became the executive director of CanoeKayak Canada and held that position for many years, creating a transparent and very successful summer sport at the Olympic level. In 2012 she became the head of Own the Podium. By any standards, Anne has certainly established herself as a leader in the Canadian sport system.

Anne Jardin was an Olympic swimmer, earning two Olympic bronze medals at the 1976 Olympics. She was also one of the approximately 100 Canadian athletes who had to face losing a second Olympic opportunity due to the 1980 Olympic boycott. When she came into the program she had just completed an undergraduate degree in the United States. "I was just a kid, I had no idea." She said she was a bit lost wondering what she might do with a degree, but no work experience. "I flew into Ottawa for an interview for the program, but while I knew little, I knew I wanted to give back to sport." Anne was matched with her own sport of swimming and mentored by the technical director at the time, Jim Shaw. She worked closely with Jim on a variety of projects and she said, "I learned a lot, but I also brought something to the organization. I knew the sport and I brought an athlete perspective. They listened because I had some experience in the sport." She went on to say, "This program was a stepping stone for me. It enabled me to make an excellent transition from being a high performance athlete to the work world." She said her mentor Jim taught her so many aspects of running a sport organization, such as budgeting and how the funding system worked but in particular, "he allowed me to initiate some things—I saw things that needed to be done, and I did them—and he allowed me to do so. I also learned from him to look at the long term and to always try to keep things in perspective."

Anne was subsequently hired by Swimming Canada as a technical coordinator, which speaks to her contributions as an intern, and she remained in that position for five years. Upon leaving that position, she went back to university, earned her teacher's certificate and became a physical activity expert in the Ottawa school system where she remains to this day. She said that the knowledge and experiences she gained in the internship helped shape who she is and how she now teaches. "I see myself as helping students succeed."

Altogether, this program ran for only three years. When Sport Canada evaluated the program, it concluded that the program did not, in the short time frame during which it was running, increase the number of women in leadership positions in sport. All of the women participants did get jobs upon the completion of their individual internships, but not all those jobs were in sport. As a result, Sport Canada decided to not continue the program. It can be argued that often program evaluations do not consider the nature of change or how long it often takes to see real change. If the desired outcomes are not immediate, a program is often discontinued. However, experts in change management would say that changes usually take place over a long time frame and that any evaluation should factor this into consideration. Indeed, a number of the women who were part of this program did serve for many years as volunteers on boards of national sport organizations; several became internationally-recognized officials in their sport; many became leaders in the sport and fitness field, running successful businesses that were outside the direct nature of national level sport; and, some did indeed become leaders in sport at a national level. The two women interviewed for this article illustrate two different paths to leadership in sport.

In order to understand why this program was so successful in influencing how new leaders and scholars promoted, studied and understood women's relationship to sport, we must examine the program design from two distinct aspects—the women-only seminars and the concept of mentoring. As noted above, the women-only seminars were key in creating a safe and productive learning environment for the young women. They were facilitated by women who were experts in the various areas of leadership development. Most importantly, these facilitators understood the issue of gender differences in leadership roles, and incorporated that sensibility into each seminar. They understood that at every level there are problems that women face because they are women. They knew that gender issues do not occur only when women rise to the leadership level of, for example, a chief executive officer, but rather manifest at all levels. They were clear about the androcentric and homophobic nature of sport. And they understood the double bind that women face when they aspire to lead—often when women stand up and speak out they are harshly criticized. The discussion and reflective conversations that took place within the seminars enabled the young women to learn and grow into confident, aspiring leaders.

The other key characteristic of this program was the perspective it took to the mentoring process. Mentoring is designed to be an on-going relationship between two individuals that involves learning, dialogue, guiding and challenges. Mentoring can be formally or informally structured. The literature would suggest that informal mentoring is more effective, primarily because it implies that the mentee actively engages in choosing a mentor. However, formal mentoring can be equally effective as long as the relationship is carefully created. In the case of this program, the mentors were thoughtfully chosen by the program director based on a few key characteristics: they were knowledgeable leaders within their organization; they had a focus on engage-ment with the intern where the emphasis was on learning; and, they possessed a willingness to discuss, listen well and answer questions. We also know that mentorship is a reciprocal process and all the young women were chosen because they were excellent candidates. While they were young and inexperienced, they were all eager to learn, and to take responsibility for both their day-to-day work and their overall learning. Furthermore, all possessed a level of confidence to ask questions and articulate their needs. The role of the program director was to interview the potential women interns and the mentors and create successful partnerships. While there certainly were issues that needed to be resolved, over the course of the three years that the program ran, all the mentorships were effective.

In conclusion, this program was very purposefully designed to develop a group of young women athletes with obvious sport experience and create an environment that would allow them to develop the skills necessary to become effective leaders within the Canadian sport system. It is worth considering reviving this program that had a significant level of success. Given that the sport system still has a dearth of women in leadership roles, and that we have many successful women athletes with extensive sport experience, I can think of no better way to improve the Canadian sport system than by re-investing in the current generation of young women athletes who, with a structured learning environment and effective mentorship process, would bring a wonderful new, and much needed, level of expertise to the leadership of sport in Canada.

ET SI JE DEVENAIS ENTRAÎNEURE?
Guylaine Demers

Si vous jouez un rôle dans le monde du sport, vous avez sûrement remarqué que les femmes sont peu nombreuses à occuper un poste d'entraîneur. En effet, les chiffres dont nous disposons démontrent la sous-représentation des femmes à ces postes. Au Québec, nous comptons un total de 22 675 entraîneurs au sein des différentes fédérations sportives. De ce nombre, il y a un faible 14% de femmes. Du côté canadien, la plus récente étude réalisée par l'Association canadienne des entraîneurs (ACE) en 2009 révèle que seulement 26% de tous les entraîneurs universitaires, collégiaux, d'équipes nationales et provinciales et des Jeux du Canada sont des femmes. Aux Olympiques de Londres en 2012, la délégation canadienne comptait un faible 19% d'entraîneures. Pas de doute, les femmes ne sont pas nombreuses à faire le saut comme entraîneure.

Au cours des dernières années, il y a eu un intérêt constant porté au rôle d'entraîneur et sur les raisons qui incitent une personne à choisir cette carrière. L'intérêt particulier porté aux entraîneures féminines est en lien direct avec la hausse du nombre de jeunes filles qui pratiquent un sport. En effet, au cours des dernières années, le taux de participation des filles a augmenté en flèche à tous les niveaux du sport, depuis les programmes de sport communautaire jusqu'aux compétitions internationales. L'augmentation de la participation des filles dans les sports a provoqué une augmentation de la demande d'entraîneurs. Cependant, on constate que le nombre de femmes occupant un poste d'entraîneure n'a pas du tout augmenté au même rythme que la hausse fulgurante du nombre des athlètes féminines canadiennes. Étant donné la sous-représentation persistante des entraîneures, il y a lieu de se questionner pour comprendre et expliquer le recrutement d'entraîneures, leur rétention dans le système sportif et leur abandon.

On a constaté qu'avant de faire le saut en entraînement, plusieurs femmes hésitent et appréhendent un certain nombre de difficultés. Il est toujours étonnant de constater que la majorité des femmes sentent qu'elles n'ont pas les compétences nécessaires pour devenir des entraîneures et manquent de confiance en elles, et ce, même si elles cumulent de l'expérience à titre d'athlètes et qu'elles ont évolué à un très haut niveau de compétition. Dans l'ensemble, les femmes pensent qu'elles ont encore beaucoup de choses à apprendre sur la profession d'entraîneure. Elles disent se sentir capables d'occuper un poste d'assistante, mais pas d'entraîneure en chef. Elles doutent énormément de leurs compétences et cela est particulièrement évident avec les femmes qui visent des sports mixtes. En effet, les femmes sont très conscientes qu'en tant qu'entraîneure d'un sport mixte, elles auront à se battre pour prouver qu'elles possèdent les compétences nécessaires pour accomplir adéquatement leur travail. Les femmes qui visent l'entraînement de ces sports anticipent qu'elles se feront peu respecter par les garçons. Sur ce point, voici l'anecdote d'une entraîneure de badminton qui a exprimé sa frustration en ces mots : « par rapport aux gars, il fallait toujours que je leur prouve que je pouvais jouer au badminton … Pour eux, une fille n'est pas capable de faire la job … J'allais jouer contre eux juste pour leur fermer la gueule! »

Une autre difficulté anticipée par les femmes concerne la fondation d'une famille. Elles constatent qu'il est très difficile de concilier la vie professionnelle de l'entraîneure avec la vie de famille, surtout dans l'optique d'avoir des enfants. Le rythme de travail des entraîneurs qu'elles connaissent les laisse perplexes quant à la possibilité de concilier les deux vies. De plus, les femmes sont tout à fait conscientes du fait que la plupart des postes d'entraîneures qui existent sont des emplois à temps partiel. Non seulement y a-t-il peu de postes à temps plein, mais, lorsqu'il y en a, la rémunération des entraîneures qui occupent ces postes est peu élevée. Elles craignent donc devoir cumuler deux emplois si elles désirent faire de l'entraînement leur profession puisque, dans la majorité des cas, le seul salaire d'entraîneur est insuffisant pour vivre. Les femmes estiment aussi qu'elles n'ont pas les disponibilités nécessaires pour devenir entraîneures. Elles ont comme référence l'horaire de travail de leurs entraîneurs actuels qui passent souvent six ou sept jours par semaine à travailler. Sur cette base, elles ont exprimé le désir de faire autre chose dans la vie que du coaching ; elles ont d'autres intérêts. Par contre, pour celles qui hésitent à devenir entraîneures, une organisation de l'horaire de travail qui leur permettrait d'avoir une vie personnelle et familiale adéquate contribuerait grandement à leur faire faire le saut et à choisir cette carrière.

Au-delà de ces craintes, un certain nombre de femmes

choisissent tout de même de relever le défi de l'entraînement d'athlètes. Mais pour plusieurs d'entre elles, cette expérience sera de courte durée. Ainsi, la majorité abandonne la profession après moins de quatre ans en poste, comparativement à 11 ans pour les hommes, ce qui laisse supposer que les premières années d'expérience jouent un rôle important dans la poursuite ou l'abandon d'une carrière à titre d'entraîneure. On peut donc se demander à quoi ressemble le quotidien de celles qui font le saut en entraînement. Pour répondre à cette question, j'ai mis sur pied un projet avec un groupe de 12 entraîneures débutantes. Il ressort de cela que les entraîneures sont très centrées sur l'aspect humain de l'entraînement et plus particulièrement sur le côté affectif des athlètes. Également, j'ai remarqué qu'elles s'approprient spontanément les problèmes vécus et qu'elles donnent le crédit aux athlètes concernant les succès. Par exemple, lorsqu'une athlète ne réussissait pas à exécuter un geste technique, la réaction spontanée de l'entraîneure était de dire : « Je ne réussis pas à lui faire comprendre ce qu'elle doit faire, je dois essayer d'autres façons ». Elle ne disait pas : « Mon athlète ne réussit pas à exécuter correctement le geste ». Elle s'appropriait l'échec de l'athlète et ne l'imputait pas à cette dernière.

Un autre constat concerne leur estime d'elles-mêmes qui passe par le succès de leurs athlètes. Cette citation est très éloquente à ce sujet : « Le fait de voir l'évolution de mes filles me permet de me dire qu'au fond, je sers à quelque chose ». Finalement, l'ensemble du projet m'a permis de constater que leur confiance en elles n'est pas si grande que cela. Pour faciliter leur rétention dans le système sportif, les entraîneures ont identifié trois solutions: 1) travailler avec une mentore, 2) commencer à titre d'assistante entraîneure et 3) entraîner des athlètes de niveaux inférieurs; commencer à la base et progresser par la suite vers des niveaux plus élevés.

Bien qu'un bon nombre de femmes quittent la profession après seulement trois ou quatre ans, un autre pourcentage choisit de rester. La connaissance des aspects positifs et négatifs de l'expérience de ces femmes nous permettra de mieux soutenir toutes celles qui choisissent cette voie afin qu'elles demeurent en poste plus longtemps.

Les aspects positifs que les entraîneures expérimentées associent à leur travail concernent en majeure partie le côté humain. En effet, les entraîneures apprécient particulièrement le fait de voir des gens grandir à travers le sport. Elles insistent souvent sur l'importance qu'elles accordent au développement de la personne, ce qui se caractérise, entre autres choses, par l'importance accordée à la réussite scolaire de leurs athlètes. De plus, elles trouvent enrichissant de pouvoir travailler avec plusieurs personnes différentes qui leur apportent beaucoup sur les plans personnel et professionnel. Le milieu sportif représente en quelque sorte une famille où il est possible de socialiser avec des personnes partageant les mêmes valeurs que soi.

Le premier aspect négatif de leur travail concerne leur statut de femme qui entraîne des femmes. Les entraîneures constatent que le sport féminin n'obtient pas la reconnaissance qu'il devrait. Ainsi, les gestionnaires en poste consacrent plus de temps et d'énergie au sport masculin; on compare constamment le sport féminin au sport masculin, ce qui contribue au maintien d'une compétition continuelle entre ces deux entités. On rabâche sans arrêt l'argument que le sport féminin se vend moins bien que le sport masculin. Pour elles, il semble qu'il est difficile de réconcilier ces deux mondes : d'un côté, il y a les entraîneures féminines qui sont pro-éducation et de l'autre, les entraîneurs masculins qui sont pro-performance.

Les entraîneures constatent également que, dans plusieurs clubs sportifs, les femmes se voient confier les groupes d'athlètes les plus jeunes, qui participent aux compétitions à des niveaux inférieurs. Non seulement cette situation est-elle très fréquente, mais elle est perçue comme normale. D'ailleurs, les femmes qui envisagent de devenir entraîneures disent spontanément vouloir entraîner à des niveaux inférieurs.

Un autre des irritants importants pour les entraîneures concerne le peu de reconnaissance accordée à la profession. Les entraîneures perçoivent que le manque de reconnaissance est véhiculé autant par leurs propres gestionnaires que par le public en général. La précarité d'emploi et les salaires peu élevés que l'on retrouve dans le domaine de l'entraînement sportif sont des constats liés à ce manque de reconnaissance.

À partir de l'expérience d'entraîneures féminines et des résultats de différentes études, je propose trois catégories de solutions pour favoriser la présence et le maintien de plus de femmes à des postes d'entraîneure.

En termes de formation : il semble qu'il soit nécessaire d'inclure dans la formation des futures entraîneures une section qui traite spécifiquement de la réalité des femmes en entraînement afin de mieux les préparer au travail de terrain. Associé à ce thème, on retrouve la nécessité de les former sur les styles de leadership afin qu'elles trouvent leur propre style et qu'elles apprennent qu'il n'y a pas qu'une seule façon d'être un bon leader. L'autre thème important et qu'on ne retrouve pas dans les programmes existants est une formation sur la gestion de la discipline. Cela n'est pas surprenant en soi puisque les débutantes se voient souvent confier les groupes d'athlètes plus jeunes. Cela s'avère d'autant plus exact pour des sports à spécialisation hâtive, comme la gymnastique, car les athlètes qui sont initiées à ces sports sont particulièrement jeunes. Finalement, les besoins de connaître différentes stratégies d'enseignement et d'avoir accès à une banque d'exercices variés semblent une partie incontournable de la formation des nouvelles entraîneures.

En termes de soutien : tous les entraîneurs vous diront qu'ils ont appris leur métier en le faisant. L'expérience de terrain n'a pas de prix. Plusieurs entraîneurs vous confirmeront qu'ils ont développé leurs compétences par essais et erreurs. Et c'est là que le rôle du mentor prend tout son sens et devient si utile. Les entraîneures qui ont pu bénéficier du support d'une mentore ont toutes indiqué que cette aide est extrêmement utile et nécessaire. Ce qui semble différent concerne les objets de mentorat. Les entraîneures expérimentées ont davantage besoin de soutien pour faire face aux barrières liées à leur situation de femme, alors que les novices semblent avoir davantage besoin de soutien technique comme des stratégies d'enseignement ou des exemples d'exercices à utiliser.

Le développement d'un réseau non formel (networking) est une stratégie qui a fait ses preuves avec les hommes et que les femmes auraient avantage à développer. Les différentes activités regroupant des entraîneures qui partagent les mêmes intérêts fournissent des occasions en or pour initier un premier contact et développer un réseau de communication sur une plus longue période. Les femmes qui développent des réseaux solides peuvent se soutenir et s'entraider dans les moments difficiles et partager des solutions aux problèmes qu'elles vivent, qui sont bien souvent les mêmes. Les femmes ne passent pas autant de temps que les hommes à développer des réseaux non formels; le réseautage est une habileté importante pour les entraîneures dans l'apprentissage de leur métier. C'est un investissement de temps important et qui rapporte. En mars 2011, l'Association canadienne pour l'avancement des femmes, du sport et de l'activité physique (ACAFS) lançait le réseau Femmes et leadership (www.reseaufemmesetleadership.ca). Cela constitue la première initiative canadienne pour favoriser le réseautage entre les femmes en position de leadership dans le domaine du sport et de l'activité physique au Canada (réseau bilingue).

En termes de recrutement : une autre stratégie pour développer la prochaine génération d'entraîneures est l'identification d'athlètes de haut niveau avec le potentiel d'entraîner des athlètes. Devenir entraîneure n'est pas donné à toutes les athlètes, mais il y en a qui ont tout ce qu'il faut pour devenir d'excellentes entraîneures. Les caractéristiques que ces athlètes possèdent comprennent l'intelligence tactique et stratégique, une attitude positive et enthousiaste, la passion de leur sport, un haut niveau d'énergie et de grandes habiletés de communication. Les athlètes de haut niveau qui deviennent des entraîneures de haut niveau ont un avantage distinct sur les entraîneures qui n'ont pas été athlètes: elles savent comment les athlètes pensent et se sentent pendant les compétitions, parce qu'elles sont passées par là elles aussi. Cependant, nous devons être prudents et ne pas pousser trop rapidement une athlète à devenir entraîneure.

En dépit des problèmes qui sont associés à la profession d'entraîneure, toutes celles qui sont en poste avouent que cela demeure un travail très stimulant qui permet de constamment découvrir de nouvelles choses, de transmettre son savoir, de faire progresser les athlètes qui sont sous leur responsabilité et de se dépasser. Le système sportif a besoin de plus de femmes à des postes d'entraîneur et cela est particulièrement vrai pour les filles; elles ont besoin de modèles féminins. Ne sous-estimez pas l'impact que les femmes peuvent avoir auprès des athlètes, en particulier auprès d'athlètes féminines qui se reconnaissent en elles. Les habiletés de leadership des entraîneures amèneront peut-être certaines athlètes à choisir cette voie à leur tour lorsqu'elles termineront leur carrière d'athlète. N'hésitez pas à créer des réseaux de soutien, aidez les entraîneures. Il est temps de changer le monde du sport !

BUILDING FEMINIST COACHING KNOWLEDGE
The National Coaching School for Women
Yvonne Becker and Patsy Pyke

We were the lucky ones! We were the relatively inexperienced collegiate coaches who had the opportunity to become participants in the National Coaching School for Women (NCSW) during the late 1980s and early 1990s. While there is little doubt that our experiences at the NCSW improved our technical coaching knowledge and strategic abilities, the greater effect of the school was an unexpected surprise. In this article, aside from providing a glimpse into the history and vision of the school, we want to articulate how the feminist, women-centered organization of the NCSW provided us with the courage to coach in a way that empowered our student athletes and gave greater meaning to their (and our) experience of sport. We will also argue that the current, serious under-representation of women in head coaching positions in all sport levels and organizations across Canada could be rectified with the re-establishment of a women's coaching development experience.

As new collegiate coaches in 1986, seeking a professional development opportunity was an important but worrisome prospect. Learning all the x's and o's amongst experienced, mostly male, basketball coaches was an intimidating reality. In the summer of 1987, the brochure that arrived for the first National Coaching School for Women to be held at the University of Alberta provided what seemed like a safe and unique environment in which to learn about women coaching women. In addition, we would be learning from women, since the programs were designed by Kathy Shields, head coach of the University of Victoria women's basketball team, and Betty Baxter, former head coach of Canada's national women's volleyball team. Their week-long programs would include theoretical, technical and practical components: all aspects of coaching education that we needed. Upon receiving the information and schedule for the week, we noted with interest that the school staff included other well-qualified university coaches as well as university professors in the areas of biomechanics and sociology. Suddenly, there was a breadth to this learning experience that went beyond the usual offensive and defensive team strategies and included discussions about women coaching women, communication skills and the social constraints surrounding women in sport. The foresight of the school organizers was apparent when decades later, in Gretchen Kerr and Dru Marshall's article "Shifting the Culture," the authors called for this breadth and cultural shift through a sport environment "that emphasizes and rewards combinations of competition and partnership, emotional toughness and sensitivity, teamwork and individual expression, and performance and personal excellence."

Once that week ended, we knew we had experienced something special, something that made us feel that coaching was more than what we thought; this was more than what we had experienced in our times as athletes. We needed further exposure to these bright and daring instructors.

For the next seven years, the school continued to inspire. From Dalhousie University to McMaster University, to the University of Victoria and back and forth across the country, we were shown outstanding hospitality and treated to more important sessions about basketball, volleyball and, new as a pilot sport in 1990, soccer (led by Sylvie Béliveau from Canada's national team program). But integral to this process was the continued inclusion of sessions such as body image, self-concept, power, ethics, empowerment, sexuality and language. These discussions enticed us into a vision of coaching that saw it as a process of enabling that encouraged trust and unity. As the visionary for the school, Betty Baxter stated in various sessions that if sport is not positive and healthy then it is "ridiculous." For her, coaching involved empowering student athletes and eliminating hierarchies that make people feel unimportant.

As we "caught" this feminist vision of coaching, we, as participants, spent many hours outside of class times engaged in discussions that were filled with revelations about new ways we would talk with our players, new freedoms we would give them to be part of the planning for the team, new ways we would be open to the student athletes' thoughts and ideas. This process of eliminating subordination and developing shared leadership was so exciting. Because our past experience was only with coaching methods that were autocratic, narrowly technical and controlling, we often left sessions bursting with energy and plans, anticipating how we would change the way we did things. As Mariah Burton Nelson describes it in her book *Are We Winning Yet?: How Women Are Changing Sports and Sports Are Changing Women*, we were engaging in power-to coaching rather than power-over coaching.

Crucial to the delivery of the school's programs were the many partnerships that were established through the eight-year history. As an example, the first edition was endorsed by CAAWS, Basketball Canada, the Technical Committee of the Canadian Volleyball Association, the Department of Athletics of the University of Alberta, and Fitness and Amateur Sport: Women's Program. Over the next seven years, other national and provincial organizations became involved, notably: the Canadian Interuniversity Athletic Union (CIAU, now known as Canadian Interuniversity Sport (CIS)), the Canadian Colleges Athletic Association (CCAA) and Sport Canada. Brenning and McDonald stated in their 1995 article that "the National Coaching School for Women has been a very successful and innovative example of how a partnership made up of key organizations can collectively create, develop, and deliver a program that meets the needs of women." The symmetry of this statement with the vision of the school should not go unnoticed.

By the numbers, eight schools graduated 300 coaches armed with Level II and III Theory and Technical credentials from the National Coaching Certification Program (NCCP). Not included in the numbers was the transformation of the participants' coaching methodologies that altered their experiences and those of their student athletes through the vision of the NCSW. We can add to these results the proliferation of feminist coaching knowledge by all of the school's participants. After attending these coaching courses ourselves, we went off and taught our newfound knowledge to others, and not just in Canada, but internationally as well. The effects of the NCSW curriculum have multiplied many times over.

In August of 1995, the funding for the school was not renewed and it has never been re-established. Is it needed? Perhaps an overview of the coaching statistics in Canada will provide the answer.

The under-representation of women in head coaching positions in Canada is easily noted by glancing at the sidelines on courts, fields and ice surfaces all over the country. But to clarify this phenomenon, data collection can be helpful. In a 2011 unpublished study by the Canadian Collegiate Athletic Conference (CCAA), it was noted that within over 700 coaching positions (head and assistant) in the women's and men's sports of cross-country running, golf, soccer, volleyball, basketball and badminton, 11 percent of all teams were coached by women in a head coach position. When considering only women's teams, 19 percent had women as head coaches and 33 percent had women as assistant coaches. In a study of the broader context of Canadian Interuniversity Sport (CIS), the Canada Summer Games (CSG), the CCAA and national and provincial levels of competition in eight sports, Gretchen Kerr and Dru Marshall found that of 809 head coaches of women's team sports, only 35 percent were women. Again, the assistant coach numbers were higher with 54 percent of women's teams having women as assistant coaches. It appears that women cannot get past the ceiling at the assistant coach rank.

More coaching data was presented in a study entitled the "Status of Coaches in Canada" by Ian Reade in 2009. This study was monitored and reviewed by the Coaching Association of Canada's (CAC's) Project Steering Committee comprised of representatives from Sport Canada, Own the Podium, Coaches of Canada and the CAC. Of 819 high performance coaching respondents (from National Sport Organizations, colleges, universities and sports clubs) in 56 sports, 26 percent were female. With these revealing numbers, it is clear that there are barriers to women becoming involved in head coaching positions in Canada.

Research has articulated the difficulties for women in reaching coaching positions. Guylaine Demers lists several barriers in her article entitled "To coach or not?", explaining, "male control of sport, lack of role models for girls and women, success enjoyed by old boys' networks, the lack of time due to family responsibilities, stereotypes about women as coaches, employers' reluctance to run the risk of hiring a female coach ..." The myth of female frailty also plays a role in the perceived unsuitability of women as coaches. As Nancy Theberge pointed out in 1993, and later Amanda West, Eileen Green, Celia Brackenridge and Diana Woodward in 2001, because men have an assumed physical superiority, this translates to superior coaching ability. It also somehow seems to follow that men have the adaptability to coach both men's and women's teams while women are only capable of coaching women's teams.

With few women in coaching positions, they frequently receive heightened attention and scrutiny. Nancy Theberge has found that women respond to this increased pressure in two ways. They attempt to fit into the dominant culture (become "one of the boys") and they work hard to demonstrate technical ability and competence. Both of these efforts result in making women invisible as coaches or eliminating coaching practices that would be different from the male standard.

The proliferation of a particular coaching standard or practice can be traced to Canada's efforts to increase our athletes' success in high performance sport in international competitions. David Whitson and Donald Macintosh marked the beginning of what they described as the sport sciences discourse or "scientization" of sporting performance in Canada in their article "The Scientization of Physical Education." The language of sport performance and technology established a culture of professional bureaucracy in sport. To place coaching in this discursive field aligned it with what Nancy Theberge describes as the "traditional conceptions of men as rational and instrumental." She continues that women, on the other hand, are stereotypically viewed as "affiliative and expressive," which allows them to be approachable and communicative, but not considered to hold technical coaching skills. In her studies on the characteristics of effective coaches from 1995, Penny Werthner has found that male coaches may have great technical skills, but disregard their female athletes' need for greater communication in training sessions. On the other hand, women coaches are "often willing to seek out experts for help, are skilled at listening and reading their athletes, and are skilled at reflecting on their actions." It is an understatement to say that the gift from the NCSW and its instructors was the presentation and emphasis of both the technical and affiliative aspects of coaching.

In Gretchen Kerr and Dru Marshall's remarkable article, they challenge the current sport model and make a call for a "cultural shift in sport." This transformation is seen as necessary, or "gender equity for women in coaching will never be achieved." The authors note that if the seemingly impermeable boundaries would change, then sport could be opened up to women's leadership. They ask us to consider the successes of women in sport over the past few Olympics and Paralympics, and note some of the following: in the 2006 Turin Winter Olympics, 67 percent of Canada's medals were won by women; in the 2010 Vancouver Winter Olympics, 54 percent of Canada's medals were won by women; in the 2012 London Summer Olympics, 50 percent of Canada's medals were won by women. As well, increased participation by girls and women in sports such as soccer and ice hockey has been consistent each year for the past decade in Canada. However, this influx of women has threatened men's historical advantage in the control of sport, actually making it more difficult for women to become leaders and coaches. Indeed, in an article written by Nancy Theberge in 1993, she explains that women now pose "a threat to the advantages men have historically gained from their near exclusive access to and control of the world of sport." In response, men's physical superiority, a "natural" difference, establishes them at the top of the coaching hierarchy.

The cultural change necessary to transform sport and coaching encouraged by Gretchen Kerr and Dru Marshall will require activist strategies undertaken by those in the second wave of the women's movement. Engaging groups of women to critically examine practices and policies and planning alternative paths for different results is exactly what Betty Baxter envisioned for the NCSW. We were asked to see sport differently, as a place where growth of the whole person and the achievement of group goals was the objective. We were asked to see leadership differently, as an opportunity to enable the creativity and accomplishments of all members of the group and to empower those with whom we were engaged.

Were we able to recreate the NCSW, could we instill the change impetus in centres across the country and incubate the shift that is required? The US Women's Basketball Coaches Association (WBCA) must think it is possible. According to the document "Leading Lessons," each year the WBCA schedules two leadership programs that feature "collaborative and interactive educational sessions" that are designed to "go beyond the typical suggestions offered at most seminars." The events are entitled *The Centre for Coaching Excellence*, an apt and unmarked name for an important event.

Jennifer Brenning and Kathy McDonald felt that the NCSW had a bright future. In fact, in their article called "The National Coaching School for Women," they stated that the school would continue to seek "a learning model that encourages women to develop essential understandings, knowledge bases, and skills necessary to not only survive but possibly renew the sport culture."

We are the beneficiaries of the school and its visionaries; more women deserve this opportunity; sport deserves this opportunity.

HOMOPHOBIA, HYPOCRISY AND POWER ABUSE
Staying in Charge of Your Body, Goals and Achievements
Betty Baxter

I have always loved sport, loved it not for the competition, the leagues, the score or the bleachers full of parents and friends but for how it made me feel—that sense that my brain and my body were powerful, in sync somehow, and that I could do anything. From memories as early as preschool, I can recall that I felt strong physically and that I could do it, whatever it was.

But even in the early days sport was for me about betrayal: a jealous friend when I could throw the ball the farthest, or the resentful teens who felt I was suddenly too good for them when I made an all-star team.

But this story is not about early betrayals or childhood friendships. It is about my highest achievements and much bigger betrayals. This story is about power and its abuse, the pretense of progress; at its core, this story is about homophobia and hypocrisy in the sport system.

After graduating from high school in Brooks, Alberta, in 1970, I turned all my attention to playing volleyball with the goal of making Canada's national team. At the last moment after a summer of training camps, I decided not to attend the University of Calgary and instead registered at the University of British Columbia (UBC), believing that it would offer better coaching and opportunities. Working under the national coach and the Vancouver Calonas, the best club team in the country, helped me achieve national status. I very nearly made the Canadian team in July 1971 for the Pan American Games in Colombia later that year. I was one of the final two athletes cut prior to departure.

In the fall of that year I chose to play for the UBC varsity team. I was one of the star players who helped the team win the Canadian Intercollegiate Championships in 1972/73 and 1973/74, becoming British Columbia's intercollegiate athlete of the year in 1974. The experience at UBC helped me grow as a leader, and competing with the national team during the summers of 1972 and 1973 prepared me well for full-time training, touring, and competing and the World Championships in 1974. We placed 11th there, unprecedented for Canada.

Our team embarked on an intensive program for the 1976 Olympic Games in Montreal, and I was a key player in that program, becoming captain of the Canadian Women's Volleyball team prior to the Games. Although the team placed eighth of eight, we were competitive on the international scene for the first time in the country's history.

All national team athletes had a huge letdown in mid-summer 1976 when funding and support were completely cut off within days of the Games' closing ceremonies. In my case, to make enough money to return to Vancouver, I worked in isolation for six weeks out in the field for a gas development company in southern Alberta. After work, I would run along the highway to my truck to do step-ups to keep at bay the atrophic pain from my shrinking leg muscles.

The following spring I returned to the national team to train and compete and eventually headed to graduate school at the University of Alberta in fall 1977. There I played with a men's team and trained to stay in shape for international competition while coaching the U of A Pandas. I completed my course work for a master of arts in Sport Psychology that year and defended my thesis the following spring to complete the degree. I was still tremendously committed to sport and wanted to return to international competition, thinking ahead to a long career as an athlete.

The summer of 1978 had the national team rebuilding and competing in the World Championships in the (then) Soviet Union. Canada placed in the 12-15 bracket in the final round of the 24-team competition, and I was named to the tournament all-star team in Riga, Latvia. As we were heading home on the flight across the Atlantic, the head coach abruptly and without warning cut me and three other veteran players from the team. Despite the fact that I was captain of the team and we had had a strong tournament, he said that the team needed younger players to rebuild. I was 26-years-old. Although this dismissal was bewildering, it became less so when the coach resigned immediately after our return to Canada. A very good coach from Korea, he was a kind but strong authority. By cutting the senior players before he quit, he was taking responsibility for major change. We had options to apply to work with a new coach, but none of us chose to. The national program was in disarray for a year or so following our coach's exit.

That fall, I was accepted as an apprentice coach by the Coaching Association of Canada and moved to Ottawa to do apprenticeship training under the technical director of the Canadian Volleyball Association and to coach the University of Ottawa women's team. Through hard work in the 1978/79 season, the U of O team won the silver medal in the Canadian Intercollegiate Athletic Union finals. I was named Canadian Interuniveristy Athletic Union (now Canadian Interuniversity Sport (CIS)) coach of the year due to the team's rapid rise in standing, sharing the honour with the more experienced coach of the gold medal team.

I won the position of head coach of the Canadian women's volleyball team in the fall of 1979. I was 27-years-old, the first Canadian to be named as full-time national coach. I worked out of the National Sport Centre in Ottawa, where the administrative offices of many sports were housed. There, I had good professional relationships with my colleagues at the Canadian Volleyball Association and with many other sports professionals. Several of us began working on founding CAAWS to address the many areas where women were undervalued and under-represented in sport leadership. We strongly believed in a feminist perspective and felt all of sport would benefit by becoming more welcoming to women. More than three decades later, CAAWS is a multi-faceted organization still working to foster positive experiences for girls and women.

The Canadian women's team trained and toured in Canada for the summer of 1980, working at youth camps and building a profile for the program across the country. Training camps were held during both Easter and Christmas break. The young team was scheduled to participate in international competition in 1981 at the World Student Games in Romania, with extended competition in Czechoslovakia afterward.

Things were going well. I had completed my degree and my

apprenticeship as well as specialized training in Europe for two weeks that spring. I was happy and my career was thriving. I was committed to teaching young athletes to feel powerful, body and mind in sync, as I had experienced myself at the best of times. I felt ready to lead the team abroad. Then, in preparation for the tour, I began to experience the subtle, unpredictable atmosphere of discrimination.

Until this point in my athletic and coaching career, I had never disclosed my sexual orientation to my coach or association. I had come out as a lesbian to a few close friends while at UBC in 1972. I had friends who played with me on various teams who knew about my sexual orientation, and was in a relationship with a teammate at one point, but my social life was very closeted. In those days, it wasn't safe to be out. There was very little legal protection, and fear of disclosure was not unwarranted. I knew women who had been evicted, rejected by their families or had lost jobs when they were "outed" as lesbian.

While coaching the national team in the summer of 1981, I became aware for the first time that I was the subject of rumours and oblique allegations. In June or July, while the team was preparing for the European trip, the executive director of the CVA came to a training session and asked to speak to me. Although occasionally present in the stands at events, this was the first time he had come to a training session. He asked me why I was taking a particular player to Europe with the team. I answered that it was because she had made the team. He replied, "Don't you think that's like taking a fox among the chickens?" The player in question was very intense and hard working. Other players admired her as a result. She was quietly lesbian. But in the minds of many in those times, the very word "lesbian" meant immoral, deviant or perverse. I said he was making a huge assumption about the athlete and about me if he thought anything but performance influenced my team selection. He left the session without further comment.

The team's participation at the Student Games and the Czechoslovakian competition were valuable experiences, and the team returned to Canada ready to continue its program. When I returned to the CVA office after the summer's travel, another technical staff member asked to speak to me privately. He said some of his friends were gay and he had no problem with it, but I was in some trouble and he wanted to give me a heads-up. Although he didn't state any specific concerns, only implied there was some general dissatisfaction, I began to worry and searched for a sympathetic lawyer.

By the November board meeting of the organization, I was hearing rumours about my "lack of competency" for the job of national coach. One of the coaching staff justified the concerns saying, "How can parents be expected to send their young athletes to a program if they hear that the coach is gay?" While he promoted the program, he made it clear that he was not going to support me.

Just before I was to deliver my annual report, one of the women on the board came out of the meeting to speak to me in the hall and said, "You're in trouble. They're asking how the team can compete if they are in bed together." I was insulted and replied that the team was disciplined and dedicated and there was no inappropriate activity. When she admitted, "I'm not known for my courage," I understood that I would get no help from the few women on the board.

The hostile atmosphere was palpable as I made my report. I remember only one question from the session. A board member asked what the "social atmosphere" was like on the team. I replied that it was good, the athletes were committed to their goals and understood the dedication required; I had in fact had no behavioural problems on the team at all. I suspected that this question was somehow code for other concerns, but no question about sexual orientation or my personal conduct was asked.

Following the board meeting, CVA initiated an investigation of the Canadian women's team program. I had already been in contact with one of Canada's foremost feminist lawyers and learned that at that time in Canada only the province of Quebec had any legal protection based on sexual orientation. Her advice was that at best I might be able to negotiate severance pay, should I be forced from my job.

Around this time, I met in a hotel room with the executive director, technical director and president of the CVA. I believe they were informing me of the investigation. At one point the technical director, who had been my master coach for my apprenticeship, stood up and pounded the wall with his fist, glaring at me. He said, "You never would have gotten the job had I known you were gay." My reply was, "I assumed you knew. I'm the same person that I was for the 10 years I was in the national team program as a player."

Since the December training camp was already scheduled and athletes were playing with their club teams for the season, I had very little contact with my players in this period. My assistant coach, concerned the athletes would get no say in the decisions being made about the program, contacted the athletes and told them about the investigation. She urged them to write letters to the organization to make their views known. Several must have followed through. By the Christmas training camp, the CVA determined that the investigation had been sabotaged because the assistant coach and athletes were lobbying on my behalf. They interviewed each athlete at the camp asking whether she would continue in the program if there were a change of head coach. That evening, several athletes came to me in tears saying they were so sorry. They were sure I would lose my job. No other questions had been asked.

On January 17, 1982, I was on the last day of a weekend retreat in Ottawa with several sportswomen from across Canada. We were writing the first constitution of CAAWS. In a moment of extreme irony, I had to leave that meeting for an hour to go across town to the Canadian Volleyball Association offices to meet with the executive. In that hour I was terminated without cause from my position as national coach and given three months' salary in lieu of notice. The executive provided no report from the investigation, made no allegations, and included no performance evaluation. It was a short meeting!

I went back to the CAAWS committee. The head of Sport Canada and the consultant responsible for funding for CVA were there with 18 or 20 other powerful women in Canadian sport. These colleagues were outraged. There was much "we'll-see-about-that" type of comment. In fact there was nothing they or anyone could do.

In every role I had ever taken on in volleyball, I had always worked intensely to be the best I could be. As an athlete, as an apprentice, and as a young coach, I had been praised for my talent, potential, hard work and success. Now, I felt cut off at the knees and rudderless. Men dominated the CVA, and the women involved with the association were either unable or unwilling to say anything in my defense.

I was hired on contract by the head of Sport Canada for three months to consult with national sport governing bodies in preparation for a white paper on sport for the federal cabinet. I completed this contract in a kind of shell shock.

Although Sport Canada valued my work, by May 5, 1982, I decided to leave Ottawa and head back to Vancouver where I had friends and support. As I travelled across Canada, I stopped everywhere I had close relatives and came out to them. The most poignant of these conversations took place in Brooks at the table with my parents. As I was carefully telling my mother how my close relationships had been with women (awkwardly not using the words "gay" or "lesbian"), she reached across the table, took my hand, and said, "I've thought for a long time that you're lesbian." My relief was huge. My life as an out, public and political activist started at that moment with my mother's act of unequivocal love and support.

I did not set foot in a gymnasium of any kind for three years. I worked on several projects, both research and advocacy, for CAAWS and was employed as a technical writer and instructional designer by local post-secondary institutions. To build a life away from sport, I also volunteered with West Coast Women and Words and enjoyed the support and friendship of many of Canada's feminist writers while we worked together to host the 1983 Women and Words Pan Canadian conference in Vancouver.

My recovery from sport was progressing, but I remained invested in CAAWS and its objectives and believed that I could still make a difference. When the athletic director from UBC, my former coach, called in the spring of 1984 and urged me to apply for the coaching position of the UBC women's volleyball team, I happily applied. In the time period between my application and the interviews for the position, I was invited to appear on a Canadian Broadcasting Corporation (CBC) panel to discuss women and sport. The 1984 Olympic Games were proceeding without the Eastern bloc of countries and there was much interest in the "politics" of sport. The first question put to me on the panel was "Have you ever experienced discrimination as a woman in sport?"

I replied that I had been fired from the national coach position for Canada because I was lesbian. True to my commitment to always be out and proud, I came out on prime time national television. The CBC had some trouble with my statement, and supposedly in fear of being sued by the CVA for slander, they had my words dubbed over by the host. UBC Athletics must have had some trouble with it as well, for even though I had been asked to apply and was one of the most qualified coaches in the country at that time, I never was asked for an interview.

A few months later, I filed a discrimination complaint with BC Human Rights. The Council had just been revamped by the provincial government, and my complaint was denied. I had not been discriminated against as a woman since UBC had in fact hired a woman, and sexual orientation was not included in the BC Human Rights Code. Hurt and angry, I accepted that there was no place for me in sport.

Then in 1985, Kim Harris, whom I had known in graduate school, contacted me and asked if I would help with a practice for the UBC women's team. A gay man, he was the assistant coach to their second new coach in two years. After much discussion, I agreed.

I had happily played in War Memorial Gymnasium at UBC for much of my own collegiate career and had enjoyed a great deal of success, but now I found myself terrified to enter the gym. I went there alone the night before the practice and although the gym was mostly empty, my heart was pounding. When I walked onto the volleyball court, I felt like I was facing a firing squad. But, cold sweat and all, I got through it.

Kim was very supportive and after a couple of sessions helping UBC, I was asked to coach a local women's team. I agreed. This led to several good years as a volunteer community coach. Kim agreed to stay with me at any tournament out of province where we encountered CVA personnel. He wore buttons that said "out and proud," "faggot," or "homo" all over his sweat suit. Although he was playing with a men's team, he spent a great deal of time just sitting with me at women's games with his large, proud homosexual presence. I never went to a pre-tournament coaching meeting without him. Over those years, folks got used to us.

The year after the success of the 1983 Women and Words conference, the host organization in Vancouver started an annual summer writing school for women. It provided a quiet retreat-like environment with daily support and mentoring so women could get their long-planned manuscripts into publishable form.

After I had been a volunteer and member of Women and Words for several years and was back into sport as a community coach, an idea began to germinate. The pull of helping women coaches in Canada the same way we were helping women writers was irresistible. I talked to my good friend Betsy Warland, who was key to the design of the Women and Words program, and decided that the model could work for women in sport. A women-only environment would help women ask more questions and gain experience to take with them into integrated coaching and competition.

With the help of CAAWS, the CIAU (CIS) and various Canadian universities willing to supply facilities, we formed a committee and launched the National Coaching School for Women (NCSW) in 1987, based loosely on the Women and Words model.

The University of Alberta hosted the first offering. A curriculum of coaching theory topics gave women coaches a start on their coaching theory certification. We offered technical and practical sessions in basketball and volleyball. Faculty at the host university provided the theory courses, I was the head coach for volleyball, and Colleen Dufresne, head coach at the University of Manitoba and former basketball Olympian, ran the basketball section.

The school was a success and we continued for several years. It was hosted at McMaster in Hamilton, University of Manitoba in Winnipeg, Dalhousie in Halifax, and University of Victoria. Soccer was added as a third sport in Victoria in 1990. Several of the theory instructors came to every school in support of the program. In some cases, the technical coaches also taught leadership, planning or ethics sessions. The instructors were all women considered expert in their field, and fees were reasonable with some funding supplied through Sport Canada and the CIAU (CIS). In those years, approximately 300 women coaches were trained at the school.

The committee negotiated with the Coaching Association of Canada to have the courses recognized and had some success in having credit accepted by the National Coaching Certification Program.

For each offering of the NCSW, I taught a section on leadership and included several discussions on power and power abuse as well as appropriate conduct between coaches and athletes. In particular I was adamant that athletes and coaches should never be in personal relationships. If one were to start, either the coach or the athlete must leave the team. Much animated discussion occurred in these classes as interpersonal relationships between coaches and athletes are not uncommon in sport.

At the first school in Edmonton in 1987, we had a surprise visitor from Norway. An activist from women and sport organizations in Oslo was on vacation in Canada, and colleagues in Ottawa had encouraged her to drop in at the school to observe Canada's fledgling coaching school for women. She liked what she saw and invited me to attend a conference in Norway the following year. I travelled to Norway a couple of times to speak on women and leadership in sport and took on a contract coaching the KFUM volleyball club in Oslo for the 1989/1990 season. KFUM competed in several European countries, putting me back into the international world of volleyball, and I was once again recognized as a top-level coach. Living in another country had its challenges, but I thrived working with strong young athletes and seeing them develop power and confidence in their minds and bodies.

On my return to Canada, I continued as head coach for the NCSW volleyball participants for course offerings at the schools in Dalhousie and Victoria. I was re-energized and confident that somehow sport could be reformed to accept women as powerful and positive influences.

Then, at the University of Victoria, a final betrayal precipitated my leaving the sport scene permanently. The 1991 school
held in Victoria had been a success, just like the others before
it. The experiment of adding a third sport had worked, and
the committee and presenters felt good about the school. The
participant coaches left, and the instructors wrapped up with
a debrief in preparation for reporting to our partners and
planning for the following year. At the end of this session, I was
packing my car when one of the theory instructors stopped me
in the parking lot to chat. This professor had been coming to the
school to teach a section on sport science for three or four years.
We were casually chatting about the school when she asked if she
could ask me a question.

- "Sure," I said.
- "Why did you really get fired anyway?"
- "There was a rumour campaign but in fact I was fired for no
cause, with no accusations and no questions."
- "Oh," she replied, "we all thought you had had a relationship
with an athlete that had been discovered."

I was speechless!! Then I asked her (I don't think I was
shouting but I was screaming in my head),

- "How could you sit in the leadership and ethics class for
years, listening to me outline how coaches must be conscious of
their power over athletes and never have personal relationships
with them, if you believed that?"

She replied something to the effect of, "Well, it happens!"
This instructor was well respected, but I was aware, through
the closeted world of lesbian culture, that she had relationships
with her female graduate students. I had never challenged her
but had been guarded with her because I felt she was arrogant
about her authority. It had never occurred to me that because I
had never personally challenged anyone on their inappropriate
relationships, they might think that I too had relationships with
athletes.

The secrets of lesbian relationships seemed to permit other
deeper secrets of power abuse. I felt as if, once again, the floor
had fallen out from under me.

I had thought I could do anything. I thought I could change the world of sport. I was zealous about wanting to teach women they could change it too! They could coach in a new way, an athlete-centred way that would empower athletes to believe they could do anything. I was naïve.

Although I was proud and determined to be out as a lesbian, as an out lesbian still teaching and coaching, I was bucking the system. In my career, I had counseled many athletes through many personal troubles, but never crossed the line to even being their friend. Colleagues had criticized me for being too distant and not letting the athletes know me. I was so conscious of my authority and role in their lives that I was always, only, their coach.

Learning that some thought I was like them (for the theory professor was not the only woman, whether coach or professor, to let power guide her relationships) was too much for me. I could see their thinking. If everyone used power over athletes for personal gain or gratification, why not me, who had been inspired to start the school? This realization made me crazy. I had believed I had helped to create a safe space for women to learn coaching and now I was realizing that the acceptance of power abuse and the hypocrisy in sport was so endemic that it had permeated even that space, that culture. It was not safe for anyone.

The secrecy of lesbianism had collided, and in effect colluded, with the secrecy of abuse in the coaching realm. Although fearful of being out, many lesbians wanted to support me in changing the sport system. I knew of the relationships of other lesbians, but I had wanted to respect the privacy of the women who supported me, believing each would come out when she was ready and felt powerful enough. So I, and perhaps others, had been silent about abuses through sexual games and power, whether of colleagues or graduate students or athletes.

I struggled to understand. If being lesbian meant your relationships were inappropriate and must be secret, could it be that because of the socio-cultural messages we were receiving, lesbians might not be able to differentiate between inappropriate as a socially defined construct (and therefore fallible and changeable) and inappropriate as a fundamental moral principle?

Understanding came slowly. At the time, I could only think that if these presenters at the NCSW were my only allies, I could no longer be here. If this was an indication of the values of the feminists in sport who were trying to change the system, there was no hope! I could no longer believe any ethical leadership in sport was possible.

After that incident in the parking lot, I completed my duties for the Victoria school with the final report. From that point on, I had no further involvement with the sport system in any role.

The National Coaching School for Women continued for a couple of years. A very positive article was published in the *Canadian Women Studies Journal* in the mid-nineties. The article credited me as the "driving visionary" for the school and was hopeful it would have a long future, but in fact the funding was discontinued the next year. Women could obtain coaching certification only through the mainstream, male-dominated CAC program. This was a tragedy. The school was a positive tool for change in sport, but the issue of power over athletes has never been resolved. In addition, the more specific discussion about sex and relationships as tools of power, whether heterosexual or homosexual, has also never been settled. Any positive change for women cannot be permanent without a feminist analysis of these issues and a new culture in sport as a result.

I do not believe that the sport world has changed in any meaningful way, either at the CVA, or for that matter any sport organization. On contemplating my lesbianism in 1981/82, the organization could only see me as toxic to the program. Canadian life has changed greatly for lesbian, gay, bisexual, and transgendered people since then. We have legal protection in every province. TV personalities, politicians and thousands of citizens have come out to their families and communities. And yet in the world of sport, I do not see even token evidence of acceptance of lesbians or gays let alone strong program support. Sport appears to continue to reward compliance and conformity, occasionally talent and hard work, but certainly not diversity of sexual orientation or gender.

CAAWS was founded on feminist principles to improve access, visibility and promotion for women in sport. I have been very distant from the organization's activities for many years and have observed the sport system simply as a citizen, albeit an informed one. I know that CAAWS has developed resources to fight homophobia in sport (www.caaws.ca/homophobia/e/index. cfm) but despite those new resources, I don't see that much has changed. Yes, there appear to be more women coaching at high levels. Are they coaching from a feminist perspective? Do they have any analysis of the power that sport bestows on men and rarely acknowledges in women?

Certainly young girls are under as much pressure as ever to present themselves as sexualized to the male consumer. Female athletes are still very careful to have those bits of jewelry or stylized hair and costumes to show their femininity and tone down their strength. Or if strong, as evident in women's pro football, they must be sexualized via lingerie or nakedness. Only recently have I encountered young women doing physical training with pride and a cheekiness that may indicate real confidence. I suspect this behaviour happens in spite of the sport system and not because of any organizational efforts. In general, what I detect is a pretense of progress for women at a systemic level, while the abuses of power by coaches and sport leaders continue.

From time to time over the decades, the media have asked for my comments as an out lesbian who was involved in sport. Even as recently as the 2010 Vancouver Olympics, in response to requests to speak to the media about gay athletes, I was moved to ask once more, "Is there no one else still in the sport system who will talk from a lesbian perspective?" I haven't been engaged in this world for 20 years, but those who will speak and those who will challenge a system that enables homophobia and hypocrisy in pursuit of power and authority over others are very rare indeed.

My story is not rare, although perhaps more high profile than many. Women and girls still leave sport regularly because they are undervalued and cannot be who they are. Those who stay compromise and conform, and some still manage to succeed at what I hope is not too high a personal price. I still love the physicality of sport and remain fit and active. I have many young girls in my life whom I teach and observe as they learn to use both mind and body to do whatever they want. Those who move on to more organized sport always receive my caution to protect themselves. I want to instill in them that they and only they are in charge of their bodies, their goals and their achievements.

GOING ABROAD
The 1992 International Professional Development Tour
Rose Mercier

The findings of the 1992 International Professional Development Program (IPDP) are documented in "The Way Ahead for Canadian Women and Sport," the post-trip report beautifully authored by Sheila Robertson. I am not sure how many copies of the report still exist. I have one that I keep among my women and sport reference documents. The report is more than a reference. It is a marker of a unique and amazing two weeks. I had not read the report in a few years. It was immensely helpful in shaping this article. My memories of the trip endure even 20 years later.

The women who travelled together for 16 days through three countries affectionately referred to their collective adventure as a "magical mystery tour" and spoke about it in such reverent tones that others wondered just what went on in the just over two weeks they were away. The purpose of the program was compelling; the agenda for the voyage was varied and interesting. Those two factors alone might have made for an excellent study tour. But, as with any successful group activity, it was the women who made it magical. One could anticipate that bonds might form among some participants over an intense period of travelling and living together, but the group experienced the type of connectedness associated with a high performing team. Everyone just "clicked;" there was mixing and matching in the sub-groups that did different activities; no one rubbed others the wrong way; leadership flowed and shifted; humour was abundant and serious, passionate conversations were an ongoing staple of the group.

The International Professional Development Program had been part of the Canadian Sport and Fitness Administration Centre since 1972. There had been 14 previous study trips. Six, sometimes seven, professional administrators from national sport organizations or multi-sport organizations would visit one country and meet with government and non-government administrators. At the end of a trip, the group produced a report describing the country's sport structure and its component organizations and presented their findings to their colleagues whose organizations were resident in the Canadian Sport and Fitness Administration Centre. The reports were deposited in the Sport Information Resource Centre as a continuing legacy.

The program had endured over 20 years thanks to the generous sponsorship of Air Canada that provided the international air travel passes. However, the 1992 version of the IPDP was unique. For one thing, for the first time, there were 11 participants, almost double the usual number. In addition, the participants were not just Ottawa professional administrators, but came from across Canada and did not only represent national sport and recreation organizations but others as well: for instance, a report writer was included in the program. Unlike other programs, this IDPD was jointly organized by the Canadian Sport and Fitness Administration Centre, the Sport Canada Women's Program and the International and Major Games Directorate of Fitness and Amateur Sport. And finally, the most important difference was that the focus of this study tour was not a country example; instead, the IPDP was charged with examining how gender equity in sport was being addressed in three countries seen at the time as the front runners in their approach. Based on their observations, the participants were required to produce "a blueprint for action" and to become individually engaged in bringing about change.

This atmosphere of change was made possible through a confluence of timing and like-minded people being together in the right place. There were also many specific factors contributing to this moment of change. For one, the federal government was just about to release "Sport: The Way Ahead," a report that was produced by the Minister's Task Force on Federal Sport Policy. In it, the Task Force was clear that "the pace of involving and advancing girls and women across the sport continuum, and in all levels of sport organizations, must be significantly accelerated ..." Furthermore, the Canadian Sport and Fitness Administration Centre had just founded the Tait McKenzie Institute as a way of developing and advancing leadership in sport. Although I was a program officer in the International Relations and Major Games Directorate during the IDPD, after the tour, I became the first (and only) director of the Institute, and in that role, was a strong advocate of gender equity. Other strong, vocal advocates for gender equity in sport pushed the agenda forward: Wilf Wedmann, the then-president of the Canadian Sport and Fitness Administration Centre, and John Scott, the then-director of the International Relations and Major Games Directorate, were both vocal on this issue. Marion Lay, the director of the Sport Canada Women's Program, was critical in bringing about the collaboration of the three organizations.

During the IDPD tour a pattern was quickly established in each of the three countries visited: participants met with key leaders—mostly women—from universities, government, non-government organizations, sports federations, women and sport groups and municipal organizations, and visited or learned about flagship programs, with the goal of enhancing opportunities for girls and women. Connections in the three countries had been greatly facilitated by John Scott, who had previously worked with the British Sport Council and been a member of the European Sports Conference Women's Committee. The contacts in Great Britain, Norway and Sweden were generous with their ideas for making the program a substantive learning experience. The program is described extensively in the report. Following are selected highlights that introduce some of the ideas that have become hallmarks of the approach to gender equity in Canada.

In London, participants visited two community-based programs that were designed to increase opportunities for participation for girls and women. Many of the underlying principles of these programs seem familiar to us now: meet women where they are; involve those who will be involved in the program in its design; remove barriers to participation – provide transportation and childcare, make the environment welcoming to women. One idea that impressed the group was the emphasis placed on evaluation at the very beginning of program design and the rigour with which evaluation was carried out.

A central theme we found in Norway was the emphasis on having many women leaders and ensuring they occupy senior positions. Participants were introduced to the system of quotas that was an integral element in Norwegian governance and was being successfully adopted by sport. Participants also learned about the three-day leadership development program Can Will Dare, which was designed to motivate and empower women to become leaders. This idea resonated with Canadian women who had placed less emphasis on developing individual leaders and had been concentrating on trying to bring about systemic and structural changes through policy development and implementation. Leadership development programs for women became a priority upon return to Canada.

Participants had a first-person account from women who were organizing to ensure that the 1994 Winter Olympics would attend to women's interests. As indicated in the Report, the Women's Forum was established because it wasn't confident that "women's interests and needs ... would automatically be part of the planning and decision-making of the Olympic Games ... it is almost always an old boys' game."

In Sweden, participants had the opportunity to meet with Gerd Engman, former principal secretary of the Ministry of Public Administration, and were deeply impressed by her ideas. She had been commissioned by the Swedish government to write about equality for women. She is quoted in the report on her insistence that women be part of decision-making and governance: "... women make up half the population ... women bring human and financial resources to sport ... the different life experiences of women are vital and relevant to making solid decisions." The concentration on leadership in Norway was equally evident in Sweden. The Swedish Sports Confederation had adopted Can Will Dare. It also offered leadership courses to coaches that concentrated on teaching participants as well as critiquing the socialization of men and women in society. It aimed to break down stereotypes and encouraged respect for the power dynamic between athletes and coaches. Participants learned about the Swedish Sports Confederation's comprehensive plan for achieving equality in sport, which had been developed in 1989 with ambitious goals for the six-year time frame of the plan. Three years into the plan in 1992, the Confederation realized it would not be possible to achieve its goals and settled on reaching the goal of having all nominating committees consist of an equal number of women and men.

In Stockholm, participants had been invited to participate in Tjejtrampet (Girls' Tread), the 48 km women's only bicycle ride; the organizers even arranged for bicycles for the Canadians. It was a unique and amazing experience—almost 10,000 women riding a challenging course led out by an elite field of women cyclists. All of the volunteers along the route were men. Participating in the event was in one way a symbol of the hopes that participants had for the level of involvement of Canadian women and girls.

Participants translated their experiences into a blueprint for action complete with a vision for gender equity in Canadian sport. The plan identified seven major recommendations. Among these was the focus on creating a national women and sport activity plan that was fair and just for both women and men, with the aim of making Canada a world leader in gender equity in sport. Another priority was creating more access for women and girls to participate in physical activity and leadership. Finally, the blueprint for action recommended that the government share responsibility with accountability to Canadian society, paired with a financial commitment to quality programs.

When I review the recommendations articulated by the participants, I believe there has been progress since 1992. The need for gender equity in all facets of sport and physical activity has become a much stronger imperative in Canadian sport, brought about in some measure by momentum created through that IPDP. Still, I am not blind to the continuing need for courageous advocacy and strong action. There continue to be barriers to sufficient program opportunities for women and girls of lesser economic means, those newly arrived in Canada or living in Aboriginal communities. There are still too few women coaching. Internationally, gender equity still has a big agenda. One could feel discouraged. However, I remain optimistic about the possibilities.

While we can assess the degree to which the shifts articulated in the Blueprint for Action have occurred, I will leave the participants to speak in their own words about how the IPDP impacted the women who were part of the 1992 IPDP. Perhaps the passion that is still evident 20 years later is a clue to the achievement of the second goal of the program—to have participants become individually engaged in bringing about change. Then, as now, as in the future, individual leaders are essential to inspiring, enabling and sustaining change.

In 1992, Phyllis Berck was recreation planning and communication director, City of Toronto, responsible for the City's Gender Equity Program in recreation, and national chair of the Women's Legal Education Action Fund (LEAF). She explains:

"I have a lot of good memories–the group itself was loads of fun, rooming with Sheila and having all sorts of discussions with her and everyone else is a good memory, but I would say the biggest one for me is that women's cycling event we went to in Stockholm. I wish I still had my t-shirt, so I could get the name right.

I remember the 10,000 or so women and bicycles as far as the eye could see. The volunteers and support team were all men. It was a first-class event with loads of Porta-potties and a morning newspaper in each one. I think the distance was a marathon (42.2 km) but the point of the day was to get out and ride your bike on the lovely Stockholm bike routes and just celebrate being female, being active, and being alive. I loved it; it made me cry. I never thought I would see a quality women-only event be that successful."

Influence of the IPDP:

"Well, I'd say that I could see a brighter future was possible, that all countries (including Norway and Sweden) had their struggles. But the bike ride was evidence that new ways were possible. The group itself was the next generation of leadership and I found it very encouraging to be with our group. It made for a good network and indeed, as I look back on 20 years (has it really been so long?) the IPDP women have gone on to do many interesting and important things in the world of women and sport, so I think as a leadership development project, it was very successful."

Jennifer Brenning was the Canadian Interuniversity Athletic Union (now Canadian Interuniversity Sport) director of national programs at the time, and recounts:

"One of my strongest memories is this big bicycle event in Sweden; there were thousands of women in bike helmets (helmets were not mandatory in Ontario at that time). It was so inspirational to see that many women active and involved in this bicycle event. What impressed me the most about Sweden was how advanced they were in encouraging both genders and people of all ages to be active. We attended this session in which we were presented with a model that showed how young girls are impacted by nature and nurture as they grow to adulthood. It was very eye-opening how the environment can impact how women view themselves and their involvement in sport. I was very impressed by how healthy and active the Swedes and Norwegians are.

Since that time, I have been very conscious of mentoring young people. When I am asked by a student, female or male, to meet to discuss my career path or how I got where I am today, I always take the time to meet with them. I have worked with a lot of young people and enjoy assisting them in pursuing their careers."

Peggy Gallant was a professor in the Department of Physical Education at St. Francis Xavier University, as well as a Master Course Conductor, levels 1, 2 and 3 of the National Coaching Certification Program. She remembers:

"My strongest memory is of our first night, meeting all of the women who were going to be on the tour, and I remember thinking 'a whole group of women just like me,' looking for equity in women's sport, just like me, and from all across Canada. I felt, for the first time, that what I was looking for wasn't an isolated ideal; from now on I would have other women to support my requests for equity in our sport programs at St. Francis Xavier. It was like a shot of amphetamine! The other strong memory is that after speaking with Sandra Kirby and Marion Lay about how we could increase the dialogue around women in sport, I decided that I would try to develop a Gender in Sport course on my university campus and go through the process of having it approved by my department, the committee on studies and senate. After that battle was won, I became involved with introducing Women's Studies to our campus and the gender in sport course became cross-listed as it still is today. I think I became a stronger advocate for women and found a stronger voice. I still have wonderful memories of the tour where I laughed so much. I also remember what a great leader you were Rose and how patient you were. I have lots of fond memories but have to say it was the only time in my life I was able to spend two weeks with such a powerful group of women all concerned about the same things."

Vicki Gilbert was a sport consultant for the Alberta Recreation and Parks as well as provincial coaching representative for NCCP. She recalls:

"My strongest memory is when we went on the 48 km women's only bike ride (not 4.8 km as one of our group members was anticipating) through the streets and countryside of Stockholm. It was such an overwhelming, empowering experience riding alongside women of all ages, sizes, and backgrounds, just happy to be there celebrating the joy of the movement with friends, family, and other females. What also struck us Canadians was the outpouring of attention, love, respect and pride that the males of the country demonstrated for their loved ones during the event. It was a total celebration of Women!

I made a career change about eight years ago and am now a teacher working with students with special needs. While I no longer work in sport, I think the IPDP has influenced me in my current job role and my outlook on life in general. What has permeated my psyche is an underlying philosophy that we need to do everything we can to create a society where everyone feels the freedom and support to strive to reach their potential and to experience life joyfully. We have to be prepared to advocate against injustices and inequities that exist ... with respect to gender, ethnic background, sexual orientation, and physical abilities/disabilities."

Sandra Kirby was associate professor of sociology at the University of Winnipeg, and a member of the CAAWS board of directors. She remembers:

"When I was selected to the Tour, I was excited at the opportunity to travel with such fine women to England, Norway and Sweden. It was a remarkable experience with me, the researcher, writing notes on virtually all experiences we shared. The legacy for me is multi-faceted. The IPDP tour helped me find my voice. I have gone on to share important research and advocacy work with women and some men whom I met on that tour – particularly Margaret Talbot, Kari Fasting and latterly, Celia Brackenridge. It was only one year later that many of us met in Melbourne (1993) for the founding meeting of the WomenSport International. I think that in our combined efforts to advance women and sport, my own work in gender equity, gender verification, sexual harassment and abuse, child sexual exploitation and on value-driven sport is built on the pathway created by the bonds of the IPDP tour."

Marion Lay at the time was manager of the Women's Program Sport Canada. She explains:

"I think one of the greatest impacts for me was that we were treated as visiting VIPs and in each country both men and women treated the issue of women in sport as very important for their sport system for both women and men. I realized that many of the issues facing women in sport in Canada were the same types of issues/discrimination that women faced in the most progressive countries of the world. My favorite story was all of us following Rose down the street to Mama Rose's Restaurant—we were all singing and dancing—she was not only our leader on the trip but one of our most successful women and sport leaders and advocates in Canada.

The statistic that changed the approach to my work is that there needs to be a minimum of 30 percent women on boards as athletes, coaches, administrators or volunteers to have their voice heard. Since then that has been the measure I have used to ensure there is positive, real, sustainable change for women."

Rose Mercier was a policy analyst with International Relations and Major Games Directorate, and six months later became director at the Tait McKenzie Institute. She recalls:

"My strongest memory is about the emphasis by all three countries on developing and advancing individual leaders as being critical to gender equity. This was in contrast to the Canadian emphasis on systemic change through policies and organizational strategies. An idea that has stayed with me is one that I first heard in Sweden about the importance of the proportion of the minority in a group and its impact on decision-making. This was introduced in Sweden by Gerd Engman who had been commissioned by the Swedish government to write (as I recall) about equality in government. She said when a group has 10 percent women, they remain tokens; at 20 percent women become visible in the group; at 30 percent women's voices are heard; and at 40 percent women's perspective impacts and shapes decisions. I also remember learning about the Norwegian program Can Will Dare that had been adopted in Sweden and Great Britain. It was a program for women that enabled women to develop self-knowledge, self-reliance, self-confidence and self-esteem. I remember our collective realization that we needed to replicate this program. When we came back to Canada, I was in the fortunate position, as director of the Tait McKenzie Institute, to be able to make that happen. The Institute contracted Dorothy Strachan to develop what became a two-day Women and Leadership program. CAAWS eventually assumed responsibility for the program; it has since evolved to become a series of leadership skills workshops that is offered to many, many women across the country. I consider this one of the wonderful legacies of the 1992 IPDP. I have continued to believe in the importance of women discovering their capacity to lead in a different way than men.

On a personal level, I remember riding in Tjejtrampet, a women-only bicycle ride. Riding in a sea of almost 10,000 women along the trails in and around Stockholm was an unbelievable high. I also remember joining in the celebration of Norway's National Day (we felt at home in the sea of red and white) and being struck by the display of shared parenting—men and women equally engaged in tending their families. We later learned of the Norwegian mantra, 'some two have to look after the children.' We had an advance view of the Lillehammer Olympic installations and I got to experience London musical theatre for the first time."

Toby Rabinovitz was national program director, Skills Program for Management Volunteers. She writes:

"For me the whole trip was a new experience, given my background was in volunteer leadership development within the sport and recreation community. To be honest, I had not really focused on or thought much of the issues affecting gender equity within sport and recreation. Everything was a new experience and I took it all in. Meeting people from England, Sweden and Norway really challenged my thoughts and perception about what we were doing—or rather not doing—in Canada to promote women in leadership roles. I was challenged on so many fronts, and in the early part of the trip wondered why I was fortunate enough to be on the tour. Then half way through the trip on a train ride between Sweden and Norway it all came together. I remember distinctly the conversation with Marion Lay, Rose Mercier and others about how the Skills Program could contribute to the advancement of women in sport leadership by developing a series of training resources and workshops for boards. By the end of the train ride I was 'converted' to the possibilities and we had mapped out a plan for the Skills Program to develop a specific module that focused on board development and positioning women to take more of a leadership role as board member. The impact of the program on what I have done since is hard to identify. Ultimately the Skills Program did develop a module on diversity and inclusion for boards, with a specific focus on designing leadership pathways that support women in senior leadership roles. Unfortunately the Skills Program funding and administration was restructured as the module was completed, and there were no resources in place to implement the resource and I left the program in 1995.

As for what I learned, I did not realize how complicated the Canadian Sport System was until we had to present it to our hosts—I believe it was in Sweden. What really showed was how complicated and difficult it was to make any substantial change in Canada. With the Sport for All model in England (and Norway, I believe) the ability to influence change throughout the system is much easier."

Sheila Robertson was director of Editorial Services, ISI Media Services and a member of CAAWS board of directors. She remembers:

"How can time have passed so quickly—20 years since the IPDP Tour, which I can say without exaggeration, was a life changer!

I was a late addition to the delegation. Weeks before departure, Marion Lay had asked if I would write the report upon their return. I, of course, agreed. My interest was deep, not least because I was a member of the CAAWS board of directors. I remember thinking, rather wistfully, that I would love to go along. Closer to departure, she and I were discussing the project when a light bulb went off. 'I think', she said, 'you might write a better report if you were part of the delegation.' I agreed!

There were so many memorable, teachable moments that it is difficult to single out just one. Inevitably, though, my memory takes me back to Norway, a country I had visited previously and enjoyed enormously. I remember each and every session, but what stands out is the informal get-togethers, in particular dinner and discussion at the home of Goro Skou, the women's program manager of the Norwegian Sports Confederation, that included Kari Fasting, then and now one of the great thinkers on women's issues in sport, and Marit Wiig, vice-president of the Norwegian Olympic

Committee and the Norwegian Sport Federation. These were women who were strong, passionate, articulate, and who were in positions of power as were Swedish women leaders we met on our next stop—Stockholm. The conversation was thoughtful, spirited, wide-ranging—and so very inspirational.

Here were women who inspired me to do everything I could to be a positive influence on Canadian girls and women in sport. I hope, 20 years later and with a body of writing to refer to, in particular through *The Canadian Journal for Women in Coaching* and the book, *Taking the Lead: Strategies and Solutions from Women Coaches*, that I have made some contribution, spurred on in large part by the enormous learnings provided by the Tour.

As I look over the plan of action that evolved from the Tour, I am heartened to note that we have made gains in these 20 years. I note, too, that much remains to be done. Complacency is never acceptable. For me personally, the Tour is a constant reminder of the importance of striving for a world that respects, welcomes, supports, and applauds girls and women in sport."

Other participants included Danielle Laidlaw, who at the time was executive director, Bicycling British Columbia and vice-president recreation and transportation, Canadian Cycling Association; and Marg McGregor, who was executive director Water Ski Canada and later became CAAWS executive director.

YOU CAN'T BE WHAT YOU CAN'T SEE
Sheilagh Croxon

The Women in Coaching (WiC) program of the Coaching Association of Canada (CAC) is a national campaign, launched in 1987, to increase the number of coaching opportunities for women at all levels of the sport continuum.

In discussing WiC, it is important to consider the culture within sport and society at large. In 2008 the renowned ethicist John Dalla Costa commented regarding women in coaching that WiC was "attempting to change something that society has not yet figured out," and we have found that to be true. Nevertheless, we persevere.

WiC has identified a number of ongoing barriers to women in coaching, ranging from experiences of isolation and an unattainable work/life balance to a lack of experienced women to choose from. Overall, the male culture that dominates professional sports continues to cement society's image of coaching as a male domain; and with few women coaches at the national level, few other women will aspire to join the professional ranks. In short: "You can't be what you can't see."

A 2011 research study from the University of Toronto on gender equity in university sport stated, "there are disturbingly few women in leadership positions in Canadian university sport, with women occupying only 19% of the head coach positions and only 17% of the athletic director positions." In response, the authors recommended that Canadian Interuniversity Sport (CIS) and its four regional counterparts revamp their gender equity policies, create an immediate 50 percent target towards proportional female participation and develop a plan for improving leadership opportunities for women in coaching and senior administration.

Barriers to gender equity in university sport were identified, including the difficulty in attracting women to apply for coaching positions, few policies to nurture women in the coaching profession and a noticeable dissipation of efforts to have women coach women's teams. However, these barriers are not insurmountable: in addition to implementing and reinforcing gender equality policies, professional development opportunities should be provided to women coaches, while helping varsity athletes develop their own coaching skills. There should also be better integration between provincial and national sport organizations in order to recruit women from performance sport into coaching, while placing students with mentor coaches. Finally, the work/life balance issue should also be addressed; one way to do so is to use departmental funds to provide for childcare during training sessions and games.

WiC has already made a significant, positive impact on breaking down these barriers for women coaches. Impact reports confirm that the programs have contributed to retention of women coaches in the Canadian sport system. For example, 86 percent of National Team Apprenticeship Program (NTAP) coaches and 70 percent of Canada Games Apprenticeship Program (CGAP) coaches are still coaching. Among excellent examples of organizations modeling WiC to fit their own contextual realities are the Canadian Colleges Athletic Association (CCAA) and its female coach apprenticeship program, the Commonwealth Games Canada (CGC) apprenticeship program, the Aboriginal Coach apprenticeship program, women-only conferences and/ or professional development opportunities at the provincial and national levels and grants and scholarships that are offered at various levels of sport. Furthermore, WiC programs emphasize establishing a network of support, connecting women coaches with mentor coaches and working to open doors that will help advance women coaches on their career pathways.

The NTAP, which began formally in 2001, is a three-year partnership between the CAC and National Sport Organizations (NSOs) and is offered to six coaches for a three-year cycle. Each apprentice goes through a rigorous selection process, is assigned a mentor coach and attends two to three professional development seminars, the National Coach Workshop and Petro-Canada Sport Leadership sportif. The apprentice is included in senior national team activities and receives full accreditation at major international competitions and major multi-sport games where possible. The NTAP has had an impact on 40 coaches, 86 percent of whom are still involved in coaching.

It is important to keep in mind that, like athlete development, coaching development is a long-term process. Many of the women coaches have gone on to work in sport leadership and/or administration, or are still coaching. In 2007 the NTAP shifted to targeting fewer women over a longer period of time and with more financial support. This decision was made based on the knowledge that because developing coaches takes a long period of time, greater financial support needed to be provided if the coaches were to get the necessary experience to compete for top jobs. As a result of this shift, the NTAP has been more successful in getting the women to the national team level.

The CGAP is an 18-month partnership between the CAC, the Canada Games Council, and the provinces and territories. Funding is provided to two coaches per province and territory for every Canada Games cycle. WiC puts on two professional development seminars that the apprentice and her mentor coach attend. According to the terms of the program, the apprentice is included in team training for the Canada Games and receives full accreditation at the Games. This program plays a valuable role by providing coaches with the experience of working with a mentor coach at a high level, exposing them to a multi-sport situation. The CGAP has spots for 24 coaches, with two coming from each province and territory. The program has had an impact on 80 coaches, of whom 70 percent are still involved in coaching.

The National Coaching Institute (NCI) Advanced Coaching Diploma is the pinnacle of a coach's education in the National Coaching Certification Program. NCI coaches are recognized as being among the most qualified coaches and leaders of athletes and sport programs provincially, nationally and internationally. Each year, approximately 15 NCI scholarships are awarded along with approximately eight professional development grants and five NSO project grants. Of the NCI graduates, 71 percent are coaching.

Each year, 20 to 30 women are selected to attend WiC's National Coach Workshop. The workshop consistently earns a 95 percent or higher satisfaction rating from participants. This program has been significant in developing a support network for women in national team positions, providing them with enhanced professional development opportunities. The workshop has also contributed to sustaining women in these positions. The workshop is designed to facilitate a stronger network of women coaches and leaders, address the professional development and support needs specific to women coaches involved in the high-performance stream, create support mechanisms focused on sustaining women in these national team positions, discuss connections and create a support group. Year after year, women coaches come together at the workshop to experience professional development that is unique to their needs and challenges and to explore strategies and solutions on how to sustain themselves in the profession of coaching. One important outcome has been the formation of chapters of women who continue to meet following the workshop to provide ongoing mentorship and peer-to-peer support.

Another initiative of WiC is the *Canadian Journal for Women in Coaching*, with a readership of over 2,300 and a global reach. It flourishes as a unique publication on issues, strategies and solutions related to women in coaching and serves as a valuable resource for researchers, women coaches and sport organizations. The *Journal* has built a respected reputation as an informative, factual, topical and reliable publication. To celebrate the *Journal*'s 10th anniversary, the CAC, in partnership with the University of Alberta Press and with a financial contribution from CAAWS, published *Taking the Lead: Strategies and Solutions from Female Coaches*. The press prepared two electronic editions of *Taking the Lead* and the Japanese organization for women in sport translated the book into Japanese.

Until 2012, there was also a WiC luncheon, held annually at Petro-Canada Sport Leadership sportif, which featured outstanding speakers from different but complementary walks of life. This event contributed to the overall quality of the conference and has been instrumental in recognizing and celebrating women coaches and raising awareness within the sport system about the current troubling lack of women coaches.

Since 2005, the We are Coaches campaign has introduced hundreds of women to the NCCP. The objective is to increase the number of coaching and leadership opportunities for women at all levels of sport. Specifically, We are Coaches recruits, trains and retains women coaches and leaders in community sports by providing encouragement, best practice models, case studies, templates and financial support.

KEY FACTS

- In 2011, Own the Podium (OTP) reported that 146 men (86 percent) were national team coaches; 25 (14 percent) were women.

- National Coaching Certification Program (NCCP) Certified Level 1: 195,446 men and 94,401 (32.5 percent) women*

- NCCP Certified Level 2: 71,750 men and 27,315 (27.5 percent) women

- NCCP Certified Level 3: 21,148 men and 6,966 (24.7 percent) women

- NCCP Certified Level 4: 486 men and 153 (24.0 percent) women

- NCCP Certified level 5: 69 men and 9 (11.5 percent) women

 *2010 statistics

FEMMES, ÊTES-VOUS PRÊTES? PARTEZ!
Guylaine Bernier

C'est un plaisir et un honneur d'avoir été choisie pour exprimer, à travers mon expérience sportive d'une quarantaine d'années, l'évolution de la place qu'ont tenue les femmes à l'aviron, et comment elles ont pu contribuer au développement de ce sport.

Étant le 4ᵉ enfant d'une famille modeste qui en comptait onze, sans antécédents sportifs comme pour la plupart des grandes familles de l'époque, je n'avais jamais imaginé qu'un jour, je participerais comme athlète aux Jeux olympiques (JO) et que je serais intronisée au Temple de la renommée du Panthéon des sports du Québec! C'est par la natation que j'ai découvert un goût pour le sport. Comme pour beaucoup de familles, c'est par la télédiffusion des Jeux olympiques de Mexico en 1968 que les JO furent « introduits » dans notre vie.

J'ai ensuite découvert l'aviron, un sport méconnu au Québec, suite à l'invitation d'une collègue instructeur en natation. Elle avait été recrutée pour former une équipe du Québec en vue des Jeux olympiques de 1976. À l'époque, il n'y avait qu'un seul club d'aviron au Québec. La venue de l'équipe féminine d'aviron du

Québec transforma quelque peu l'ambiance du club, car il y a avait, à cette époque, une très faible participation des femmes. Je dois dire que pour l'aviron au Québec, probablement grâce à l'incroyable redémarrage de son développement en vue des jeux, l'équipe des filles bénéficiait presque du même traitement que celle des garçons, au niveau des conditions d'entraînement et de compétition. Nous devions découvrir plus tard que ce n'était pas le cas dans les autres provinces.

Comme les Jeux olympiques de 1976 se tenaient à Montréal, la province de Québec avait mis sur pied quelques années auparavant le programme « Mission Québec 76 » qui visait à avoir 30 % de la délégation canadienne formée d'athlètes du Québec. Le support financier et technique disponible était donc crucial pour notre développement comme jeune équipe.

Notre premier choc culturel est survenu lorsque l'équipe nationale a été réunie au printemps 1976 pour un camp d'entraînement à Welland, en Ontario. Nous avions appris à ramer en français et nos entraînements avaient toujours été en français. L'incorporation dans notre bateau (un quatre de couple avec barreuse) de deux rameuses anglophones a donné lieu à quelques surprises sur le plan des communications, situations heureusement pas trop critiques au niveau des résultats de course. La barreuse, qui était aussi francophone, faisait un travail extraordinaire, mais sa difficulté en anglais créait quelques fois la confusion dans les actions qu'elle nous demandait de faire, comme par exemple la manœuvre suivante « right with your left » soit « droite avec votre gauche » voulant plutôt dire « back with your left », soit « dénager avec la (rame) gauche ».

Le processus de sélection olympique n'a pas été facile à plusieurs égards. Particulièrement lorsque des membres de l'équipe devaient quitter alors que moi, je poursuivais. La participation aux Jeux olympiques de 1976 a été extraordinaire; quelle expérience comme athlète, quelle expérience de vie! L'entrée dans le stade olympique, dans sa ville, dans sa province, dans son pays, demeure un moment intense, chargé d'émotions qui, même après 36 ans, me donne encore la chair de poule.

Pour l'aviron, les Jeux olympiques de 1976 ont vraiment été un moment charnière pour son développement parce que c'était la première fois que l'aviron féminin était au programme des jeux. Nous étions donc la première génération d'athlètes féminines olympiques en aviron, et c'est ce qui explique que plusieurs d'entre nous sont devenues à bien des égards des pionnières dans le développement de l'aviron.

La participation des femmes en aviron aux Jeux olympiques de 1976 a vraiment contribué à sa promotion autant au niveau national qu'international. La mise en place d'une Commission des femmes à la Fédération Internationale des Sociétés d'Aviron (FISA) est une des retombées importantes. Au Canada, l'inclusion des femmes en aviron aux Jeux olympiques a permis de revoir les pratiques établies dans les clubs à travers le Canada, alors qu'on y privilégiait principalement les hommes (équipement, temps d'entraînement, douches, etc.).

D'ailleurs, un petit groupe composé principalement d'Olympiennes de 1976, dont je faisais partie, s'est réuni pour identifier les problèmes et les lacunes ainsi que des pistes d'amélioration. Pour ce faire, nous avons demandé à la Canadian Amateur Rowing Association (nom de l'association nationale à l'époque, devenue Rowing Canada Aviron) de créer le « Women *Ad Hoc* Committee » pour aider à l'amélioration des conditions pour le développement de l'aviron féminin.

Je nous vois encore entrer dans cette salle de conférence, pleine de fumée épaisse des cigares, toutes jeunes et décidées que nous étions face aux membres du Conseil d'administration, principalement des hommes d'un certain âge pour ne pas dire d'un âge certain, qui avaient malgré tout accepté de nous entendre. Ils se demandaient bien ce qu'on voulait, car à leurs yeux, l'association fonctionnait très bien. Utilisant notre vécu, nous leur avons présenté les situations d'iniquité et d'exclusions concernant les conditions d'entraînement (équipement, entraînement, installations, accès aux vestiaires, douches, etc.), afin de les convaincre de la nécessité d'un comité pour l'avancement des femmes au sein de l'association. Ce comité veillerait à l'intégration de l'aviron féminin et à fournir aux femmes des conditions équitables.

La création du Comité *ad hoc* fut un premier gain dans la reconnaissance de l'importance de l'intégration de l'aviron féminin au Canada. Ce changement d'orientation a contribué à la venue d'un plus grand nombre de filles et de femmes et à leur intégration dans les programmes d'activité (y compris au niveau de l'équipe nationale). Dans certains clubs, ceci ne s'est pas fait sans heurts. Plusieurs d'entre eux mirent plusieurs années à y parvenir. Quoi qu'il en soit, le changement était inévitable et nécessaire.

Le Comité *ad hoc* qui faisait rapport au Conseil d'administration de l'association nationale a mis fin à ses travaux plusieurs années plus tard, une fois que l'aviron féminin a été suffisamment intégré et que les clubs faisaient preuve d'équité et d'ouverture.

Un autre élément qui a aidé au développement de l'aviron féminin fut l'extraordinaire succès de l'équipe féminine aux Jeux de Barcelone en 1992 avec, entre autres, celui de Silken Laumann malgré une grave blessure infligée lors d'un brutal accident sur l'eau quelques mois à peine avant les jeux. Ceci fit qu'à la fin des années 90, la participation des femmes pour l'ensemble des clubs d'aviron au Canada fut supérieure à celle des hommes.

Ma participation à ce comité *ad hoc* s'inscrivait dans une démarche plus globale. En effet, pour l'aviron au Québec, si les années précédant les Jeux olympiques de 1976 furent exceptionnelles pour le développement du sport, les lendemains de cette grande fête furent malheureusement plutôt dramatiques. La faillite de la fédération provinciale d'aviron mettait un frein au développement de l'aviron, avec la perte de beaucoup de bateaux achetés pour les Jeux dont le Québec devait hériter. La perte d'encadrement technique et surtout la perte du support financier pour plusieurs années subséquentes comptent parmi les conséquences les plus dramatiques.

L'équipe du Québec disparut; à peine quelques personnes décidèrent de poursuivre et je n'avais plus personne pour m'entraîner ni d'entraîneur. Comme je travaillais à temps plein depuis déjà plusieurs années et que j'adorais ma carrière professionnelle, je ne pouvais pas quitter le Québec pour aller m'entraîner ailleurs au Canada, bien qu'invitée avec l'équipe nationale.

Malgré tout, il m'apparaissait important de redonner à la communauté sportive puisque sans les bénévoles engagés dans le développement de mon sport, je n'aurais pu découvrir l'aviron et me rendre aux Jeux olympiques. Et je crois que c'est cette valeur qui m'a incitée à faire tout ce que je pouvais comme bénévole pour aider au développement de mon sport et de l'aviron féminin, et il y avait beaucoup à faire.

J'ai donc poursuivi comme entraîneur à mon club – comme il y avait peu d'entraîneurs, le fait d'être une femme n'a pas été un problème. J'ai dû acheter mon propre moteur pour l'embarcation d'entraîneur, mais c'était le prix à payer pour une plus grande flexibilité. L'année suivante, ce qui fut le plus étrange, mais stimulant, fut d'entraîner une rameuse (Sandra Kirby) qui avait été ma partenaire de bateau aux Jeux olympiques, venue de Victoria à Montréal pour poursuivre ses études.

Toutes les deux, de par notre implication et notre enthousiasme, nous avons influencé plusieurs jeunes filles (et garçons aussi …) à s'engager à la pratique de notre sport. Les conditions étaient plus difficiles, faute de moyens financiers à cause de la faillite, mais le recrutement de nouveaux athlètes et leur progression comme athlètes se poursuivaient et les succès s'accumulaient.

Il y avait peu de régates au Québec et l'arbitrage se faisait surtout par des juges arbitres de l'Ontario jusqu'à ce qu'un membre de mon club demande à l'association nationale de former quelques personnes. C'est sur son invitation que j'ai donc décidé de devenir juge arbitre national. Je n'aurais jamais pu imaginer que cette décision me conduirait un jour à nouveau sur la scène internationale et me ramènerait aux Jeux olympiques.

Il n'y avait pas beaucoup de femmes juges arbitres au Canada, et au Québec, j'étais la seule. L'arbitrage, faut le dire, était plutôt réservé aux hommes, peut-être aussi parce que l'aviron féminin par le passé n'était pas très populaire. Dans ce contexte, comme femme, il fallait faire ses preuves et là aussi, il ne fallait surtout pas commettre d'erreurs ! Il a fallu plusieurs années avant qu'une femme occupe la position de juge arbitre en chef à une régate nationale. Comme le Championnat du Canada s'est tenu au bassin olympique à Montréal en 1987 et les années subséquentes, j'ai donc été favorisée à cet effet.

Pour contribuer davantage au développement de l'arbitrage, la certification au niveau international était un atout. Ayant été acceptée par l'association nationale comme un des trois candidats à l'examen, j'ai dû me préparer seule pour l'examen car je le faisais en français et il n'y avait aucune femme certifiée à ce niveau au Canada à qui je pouvais me référer.

L'examen prévu à Indianapolis durant les Jeux PanAméricains en 1987 a été davantage difficile pour moi, car les représentants de la Fédération Internationale des Sociétés d'Aviron (FISA) avaient oublié qu'il y avait une candidate francophone parmi les candidats du Canada et des États-Unis. Cela fut une belle surprise tant pour eux que pour moi (le français était pourtant la langue première de la FISA à l'époque!). J'ai dû passer l'examen écrit en anglais, même si j'avais tout étudié en français et que mon anglais était passable. Malgré ma grande appréhension avant de connaître les résultats, je fus soulagée lorsque j'appris que j'étais acceptée à l'examen pratique, qui fut, lui aussi, réussi.

En devenant juge arbitre internationale au Canada, mon objectif était déjà de faire en sorte qu'il y ait d'autres femmes qui le deviennent. Pour devenir juge arbitre international, il faut d'abord être juge arbitre national et avoir au moins trois ans d'expérience. Il fallait en faire la promotion et surtout inciter sur une base individuelle d'ex-rameuses, par exemple, à devenir juge arbitre. Il me fallait aussi servir d'exemple, car si j'avais été capable de le faire, elles aussi le pourraient.

Sur le plan du développement du sport, l'arbitrage était (et est toujours) un peu le parent pauvre du sport de l'aviron, comme dans d'autres sports d'ailleurs — il y avait beaucoup à faire et j'estimais que mon expérience de rameuse olympique pourrait y contribuer de façon positive. Je me sentais prête pour m'impliquer davantage dans le recrutement et la formation de juges arbitres tant au Québec qu'au niveau national, en me joignant au comité national des juges arbitres.

Ma nomination par la FISA en 1994, comme membre de la Commission d'arbitrage fut pour moi un grand honneur et une très belle reconnaissance qui a aussi grandement changé la suite de mon cheminement en aviron.

Au niveau national, ma nomination a suscité quelques remous auprès de certains juges arbitres internationaux canadiens, car ils me considéraient jeune, avec peu d'expérience, de surcroît une femme et en plus francophone du Québec ! C'était une assignation convoitée et c'était la première fois qu'il y avait une personne du Canada à cette importante commission. Il aura fallu quelques années pour que chacun réalise que cette assignation n'était pas de tout repos et ma crédibilité ne fit plus de doute.

Au niveau de la FISA, depuis son existence de près de 100 ans, j'étais la première femme au sein de cette commission et mes collègues ont dû s'ajuster à la présence d'une femme, ce qui n'était pas en soi évident.

Les débuts n'ont pas toujours été faciles : n'ayant pas de mentor, il fallait tout de même se débrouiller. Rapidement, j'ai réalisé tout ce que cette assignation voulait dire en responsabilités. C'est le plus haut niveau d'arbitrage, les responsabilités pour les régates sont considérables et à cela s'ajoutent la formation, la certification, la révision de la réglementation, etc. Avec le recul, je n'étais pas vraiment préparée pour tout cela. Heureusement, mon expérience de rameuse olympique et mon expérience professionnelle m'ont beaucoup aidée. Heureusement aussi pour les grands événements, tels les championnats du monde, les Coupes du monde, les régates des Jeux olympiques, etc., il y avait plusieurs membres de notre commission ainsi que d'autres personnes de la FISA et l'entraide était vraiment fantastique.

Par ailleurs, pour les événements continentaux pour lesquels j'étais désignée, la plupart du temps j'étais la seule représentante de la FISA avec tout ce que cela implique comme situations à gérer. J'ajouterais aussi qu'agir à ce niveau n'est pas toujours facile, sachant que dans certains pays, être une femme dans une position de leadership ou d'autorité ne fait pas vraiment partie de la culture. Il faut donc tenir compte de cette réalité pour assumer son leadership et ses responsabilités.

Par ailleurs, et c'est le beau côté de la médaille, par ma présence et mon travail, je pense avoir réussi à démontrer aux femmes de ces pays qu'il est possible de le faire. C'est donc un encouragement pour qu'elles s'investissent dans cette voie et aussi renforcer leur confiance en elles. L'estime de soi est souvent ce qui fait toute la différence, d'où l'importance d'encourager et de supporter les femmes. Chaque occasion qui se présentait était une opportunité unique de pouvoir faire une différence.

Pour moi, l'expérience acquise au niveau international devait contribuer à enrichir la qualité de la formation et les conseils dans mes interventions au Canada et à participer encore davantage à l'identification de candidates potentielles pour l'arbitrage tant au niveau national qu'international.

En comparant les statistiques sur le pourcentage de femmes certifiées juges arbitres FISA (international) qui indiquent une participation de moins de 4 % au début des années 1990 passant à près de 23 % en 2012, je ne peux que me réjouir du chemin parcouru. Pour le Canada, ce n'est qu'en 2006, soit 19 ans après ma nomination, que nous avons eu une 2e juge arbitre FISA. Depuis, deux autres femmes se sont ajoutées en 2010.

En guise de conclusion, ce que je retiens de tout cela, c'est qu'il faut s'impliquer si l'on veut que les choses changent; que cela prend souvent une dose d'audace, de courage et de confiance en soi pour s'aventurer. Mais cela en vaut la peine.

J'ai aussi réalisé qu'à travers mes activités, je devenais souvent un modèle pour les autres femmes et que cela pouvait les stimuler dans leur cheminement personnel. J'étais fière de ce que j'accomplissais (et que je continue d'accomplir) et je souhaitais que d'autres puissent le faire aussi, d'où l'importance de les aider et les encourager à poursuivre leur voie. Être un modèle ça veut aussi dire être une référence et pour cela il faut faire du mieux qu'on peut. J'ai toujours eu en tête la devise de ma mère : « Ce qui mérite d'être fait, mérite d'être bien fait ». Et cela m'a toujours servi.

L'aviron féminin au Canada s'est bien développé. Nous pouvons être fières de nos athlètes qui brillent sur la scène internationale, mais il reste encore beaucoup à faire. J'ai acquis une expérience riche et extraordinaire comme membre de la Commission d'arbitrage de la FISA que j'ai quittée après une quinzaine d'années, et j'en garde de merveilleux souvenirs ainsi que le plaisir d'avoir rencontré des gens formidables.

Acquérir de l'expérience est une chose, mais ce qui est important c'est de pouvoir la transmettre à d'autres, et c'est ce à quoi je continue de travailler.

I SIMPLY STOOD AND SPOKE FOR WOMEN
Real Change Hurts
Wendy Bedingfield

I was a graduate student in Indiana when the state votes on the Equal Rights Amendment were taking place. I was so astonished when the amendment failed! However, my thinking went no further, as I had yet to even consider the idea that change can be orchestrated by humans, that it doesn't always come from Moses bringing tablets down a mountain. I am not an historian, indeed, my thoughts are almost entirely of the future. I am completely out of my element in this attempt to sort out how I became a change agent for women in sport. It makes me uncomfortable, but I am familiar with this uncomfortable state. It is, I believe, the normal state for women who work to make change.

In 1976 I arrived as a young faculty member at the University of Alberta to find a vibrant, welcoming academic unit with, most importantly, a significant number of strong, able, well-respected women. We formed friendships first, action groups later. Ann Hall introduced me to the Alberta Status of Women Action Group, and my education began. I have very clear memories of the stories women told about becoming destitute following divorce and of the subsequent campaign for revised matrimonial property legislation. I learned about the "power of the story" and the demand for flawless data in advocacy work. Perhaps just as important, I discovered during these years the single talent that I could bring to the task at hand—a high-speed brain-to-tongue connection.

My memories include chairing a meeting of several hundred women trying to determine whether or not the organization should adopt a pro-choice position. I remember presenting a brief on matrimonial property to a Royal Commission. I remember the collective outrage and subsequent actions necessary to maintain the inclusion of women in our Athletics Department's administration. My role in these events was small, although it often appeared large. The knowledge, the ideas, the strategies came from very talented groups. I simply stood and spoke.

The group is the most essential element to making change. Learning how to build and maintain that group was another essential lesson I was lucky enough to learn. What fun it was to spend hours listening to smart women share their knowledge and ideas. I changed my mind every day in this very safe place we had created for ourselves. And when I did venture forth to advocate a position, I knew I had the group to pick up the pieces and plan the next step.

I was fortunate to be selected as one of six Albertans to attend the very first National Coaching Certification Program's Master Course Conductor workshop. (I perhaps should point out that this appointment had not a thing to do with any knowledge or ability of mine, but was instead an outcome of our Alberta group's advocacy for women's inclusion in sport.) I was still nursing my daughter, and the Coaching Association of Canada agreed to provide accommodation for her and her caretaker while I attended the workshop, an accommodation I understand to be far less than universal in Canadian sport 33 years later! In any case, it was at this event that I began to understand the art of facilitation. Many years later, I have read, studied and practiced facilitation skills and know that these skills are key to working for change in organizations.

A second important learning opportunity to come my way by chance came via Canadian Interuniversity Sport, formerly the Canadian Interuniversity Athletic Union. I was a member of this organization's Women's Committee. Most sport organizations had a women's committee in those days. It was an accommodation of the demand to include women in sport. The Sport Canada Women's Program provided help for these committees by teaching us how to plan. It was a powerful experience. We sat together, developed a realistic picture of our position, and set out goals and actions to move ahead. Suddenly, change seemed possible. Five years later, we were able to add women's soccer to the list of university championships, but not before another valuable lesson was learned: the importance of positioning advocates within and without the system.

By the mid-1980s, women working in sport were still anomalies. Abby Hoffman was director of Sport Canada, and university sport had had its first woman president. The importance of positioning advocates both within and without the organization or system became clear. One can choose from which vantage to operate, but the chance of success is greatly enhanced when advocates from both positions cooperate and coordinate.

Real and successful change is driven by a strong vision. It was thrilling to experience the engagement of Canadians in the women's soccer competition at the 2012 Olympics, and I have tried to remember whether any of us envisioned such a scene 30 years ago. Was this the vision that drove our planning? I am sure that having a vision is key to pushing for change, and I do remember the incident that led me to develop envisioning as a hobby. Bob Steadward was a member of Alberta's faculty when I arrived. I recall him describing the future of Paralympic Sport to me. In the late 1970s what he envisioned was astonishing! But in 2012 we have attained what he had dreamed of, and now the next vision is ready for us to pursue. And so, I envision the soccer field in the 2016 Olympics. It is populated with terrific women athletes, women trainers and managers and with women coaches!

Perhaps connected to the idea of vision is the ability to denote the "givens" that we accept in running our organizations. It is a given that we elect our leaders, that we religiously follow Robert's Rules of Order, that women's events serve as preliminary to the main contest, and so on. In the early 1990s, I worked on a university sport committee attempting to sort out various governance questions. Our committee of five—three men and two women—worked hard over a two-year period. In the end, after many hours of discussion, data collection, lobbying, socializing, pushing and pulling, the organization figured out a way to ensure that both its general assembly of over 100 and its board were gender balanced. It was hard slogging for all of us, hard to let go of time-honored, entrenched ways of governing and working, and hard to invent and develop the courage to try new ideas. I learned so much of value from this group.

An academic in my real life, I learned the value of academe from Cathy Macdonald, a member of the university sport committee. Cathy brought us mountains of literature on models for change and social action. She helped us envision a very different organization from any that we had known. Somehow we came to understand the magnitude of our task and argued, cried and tried until we got there. I learned to look for help, knowledge, advice, ideas and support from both inside and outside the sport world. The agony of working to a solution in our own group made us a cohesive unit, and we learned that we needed to enable the larger collective to work through the issues just as we had. We saw the necessity of providing a supportive, safe, respectful place to challenge each other. We came to understand that real change takes time, incredible patience, effort, skill and energy.

This process for change also hurts, not all the time, but certainly for a significant portion of it. I remember not only the excitement of our discussions but also the agony, as women pondered the political ramifications of calling ourselves feminists in the sports world, of addressing sexual orientation as a sport issue, of insisting that girls and women be on every agenda. I remember longing for a few minutes to relax as "one of the guys" as I stood to speak, yet again, about gender equity. That safe place to return to, that group of advocates, has to be there. Making change is simply not an individual sport nor is it for the faint of heart.

Leadership, to me, is very different from managing, administering or instructing. To lead is to take people someplace new, to make change, to create. It requires some idea of what that place looks like, not necessarily in terms of its final appearance, but certainly in terms of the values and principles on which it will be built. And then there is the getting there. Having a group is the first essential. We can neither build a vision nor work for change alone. Learning the skills that keep groups together and committed, identifying, using and valuing the special skills of each member enable us to build community. Learning to facilitate large discussions, to lead planning exercises and to write briefs and position papers are all things that matter.

I think there is indeed a body of knowledge and a skill set acquired by this kind of leader, although I do not want to advocate for the haphazard, trial and error, learn-on-your-feet education of my generation of women. Today, we have CAAWS, a group instrumental in my development, and the many resources they offer; theirs is a better way.

In the end, leadership fits well with sport performance. It takes time to learn the skills. It requires many hours of practice. And then, it requires performance before a critical audience. Sometimes it all goes wrong. The winner is the one who learns from the errors, works some more, and is brave enough to enter the public arena again.

BRINGING FEMINISM TO SPORT
A Continuing Challenge
Guylaine Demers, Lorraine Greaves, Sandra Kirby, Marion Lay

Making change for women in sport in Canada between 1960 and 2010 was a challenging and rewarding ride. Struggle, heartbreak, joy and disappointment were part of the journeys not only for the athletes but also for the coaches, program and policy developers, politicians and academics. The changes required activism, organization, strategy and most of all, passion. They necessitated an application and integration of feminism into sport, as activists across Canada shifted patriarchal and tradition-bound systems in sport organizations, coaching programs, governments, schools and the media.

And these women and men made a big difference, as this book shows. Much has changed in the past 50 years for women in sport in Canada. Transformation began in the 1960s when equality for women began to be demanded, signaling a shift away from a culture where women had to seek "permission" to play. The challenge then became a fight for access to resources, often publically funded, in the 1970s. By the 1980s, equity in sport was the goal, a much more subtle and meaningful challenge for sport activists and female athletes alike. The 1990s saw the emergence of a very visible leadership in the women and sport arena, setting the stage for incredible changes in policy, programming and resource allocation for girls and women, and the shifting of power in key sport organizations. In addition to these achievements, was the introduction of a slew of great role models for a whole new generation of girls looking for opportunities in sport, coaching and leadership.

But the last decade, post-millennium, has been a time of continued challenges for some time-honoured feminist ideals in sport. There have been marginal increases in women coaches for the national teams, but their representation is still small. There have been increased numbers of events for women in the Olympics and Commonwealth Games, but there are still many hurdles to cross to make the picture truly equitable. And at the university level, the proportion of women coaches has actually declined in Canada.

Perhaps public and political leaders think everything necessary has been accomplished for women and girls in sport, as the emergence of girls' and women's hockey takes root in the Canadian consciousness, and as legal battles are won to provide room, funding or acknowledgement of girls' rights to play. Or, perhaps the women and sport movement simply needs revitalization, as younger women and girls emerge onto the playing fields, perhaps not realizing that only two or three decades ago those fields were not open to them.

Whatever the reason, we have recently experienced some reversals of the feminist ideals. For example, the insertion of sexist and sexualized imagery and practice into women's sports has consistently plagued the field, even at the Olympic level. For example, beach volleyball features women in scanty outfits and has become a huge sexualized attraction for audiences and media, and nude fundraising calendars have been sold featuring women's rugby players. At the same time, vigorous legal fights have had to be mounted to get women's ski jumping admitted into the Olympic lineup.

In 2013, the women and sport movement is still crucially important, but also critically in need of continued activism and advocacy, especially from younger women and younger athletes. This is the intergenerational challenge of the women's movement, played out among sport activists and aspirants.

By 2010, some would say that the momentum to improve women and sport had slowed or stalled. Has pressing for change for women in sport become "old news," victim to the general resistance to the term "feminism"? Whatever the reason, there had been subtle, sometimes unnoticed, backtracking on key issues. For example, past gains on equitable representation of women and men on National Sport Organizations boards were eroded or stalled in some sports, while others held their own.

Similarly, the proportion of women coaches was stalled or reversed. While these patterns were different by sport, very few sports experienced a rise in the number of women coaches. More recently, at the time of publication in 2013, cuts in government funding to women and sport organizations at both federal and provincial levels have struck serious blows to forward movement.

Key questions and issues remain: who will be next to hold the feminism and sport torch? Young women of today have had access to almost any sport they wanted, so the need for activism and advocacy may seem less urgent. Feminism is not necessarily part of the young female athlete identity, and indeed may be seen as passé, despite the fact that there is more support for fighting for rights and more visible responses to discrimination than 50 years ago. But change for the better is simply not a given. Vigilance is required to ensure we don't slide backwards.

Feminist activism in sport remains important, perhaps even more important now than ever. However, it requires strategic approaches addressing some more nuanced and complex challenges. There are strong pressures not to offend funders, for feminists to be "closeted," and for more diversity issues not to be addressed head on. Advocacy is not encouraged at this time in Canada for federally funded organizations such as CAAWS. So the resistance and reaction continue. While there are more "professional sport options" for women such as soccer there are also the Lingerie Leagues, including contracts for occasional "accidental nudity" and the bikini roller derby, and of course, beach volleyball. Even the best women athletes in these situations may find that professional options require them to be sexualized and exploited.

What else can be done? There are no direct consequences for continuing to discriminate against women in sport in Canada. There are no measurable targets, goals or quotas against which to measure either progress or backward movement. Our federal policies regarding women in sport have no compliance criteria, demonstrating a general lack of commitment to change. For the most part, we do not set measureable standards or targets, goals or quotas in the same way as some Scandinavian countries do. Nor do we have any legislation such as *Title IX* in the USA, prohibiting sex discrimination in federally funded educational programs, which has had a positive impact on women's school and college athletics. In order to make sustainable and measurable progress for women in Canada, accountability measures such as these must be considered. Is the time for encouragement and gentle pressure to adopt better practices simply over?

At the international level there are still significant discriminatory practices facing women. Ongoing sexual abuse and harassment of girls and women in sport and complex discussions about transgendered athletes directly and indirectly determine who gets to play, the fundamental fight that the women and sport movement was formed to address. While all new Olympic sports must now have equal events for both women and men, existing ones continue to discriminate against women. For example, in Olympic rowing, there are eight events for men that allow for a total of 28 men to compete. The women's program, by comparison, includes only six Olympic events allowing 20 women to compete. These sorts of rules create a double standard, where equality is supported only in some Olympic sports. Clearly, the arguments for equality that have been made for decades are still relevant, and feminism itself remains keenly important to women and sport.

As Marg McGregor, one of our authors, wrote: "By the 2030s, if I have any granddaughters, I hope that they will be able to take part in any sport on an equal and open basis with their male friends, spend their energies on getting prepared to play and not on trying to be allowed to play, be lauded for their performances and not for their looks, not feel afraid that they will be harassed and not feel ashamed of who they are."

Let's all hope for such times.

NOTES ON AUTHORS /
NOTICES BIOGRAPHIQUES
DES AUTEURES

BETTY BAXTER is an Olympic athlete, international coach, adult educator and organizational development consultant. She has been candidate for Member of Parliament, equity officer and instructor for civic leadership. An outspoken advocate for equality on gender and sexual orientation, she is a school trustee passionate about ethical leadership in public life.

YVONNE BECKER, an Associate Professor in the Department of Social Sciences at the Augustana Campus, University of Alberta in Camrose, Alberta, teaches in the areas of gender in sport and physical activity, research methods in physical education, and health and wellness.

WENDY BEDINGFIELD grew up in Newfoundland and graduated from Memorial University. She completed her PhD at Indiana University in 1978. She was a faculty member at the University of Alberta until 1988 and spent the remainder of her career at Acadia University. Her work in sport began in the 1970s and continues.

SYLVIE BÉLIVEAU a entraîné l'équipe canadienne féminine senior de soccer qui se rendait pour la première fois à la Coupe du Monde de Football Féminin de 1995. Instructrice pour la FIFA, elle a fait partie de groupes d'étude technique lors de Coupes du Monde de football féminin senior et des Jeux olympiques d'Athènes et de Londres. Pendant 8 ans, elle a agi en tant que présidente du Conseil d'administration d'Égale Action, une association québécoise œuvrant pour la participation des femmes dans le sport. Elle a été introduite au Temple de la renommée du soccer canadien.

PHYLLIS BERCK has been involved in sport her whole life, as a competitor, as a recreation participant and as an activist in gender equity. She has been recognized by various organizations and received the Queen's 50th Jubilee Medal for her efforts. She is a provincially ranked marathon and half marathon runner.

GUYLAINE BERNIER est une athlète en aviron médaillée et a participé aux Jeux olympiques de 1976. Membre de la commission d'arbitrage de la Fédération Internationale des Sociétés d'Aviron de 1994 à 2010 elle en était à ce titre à ses 5ieme Jeux olympiques et paralympiques à Beijing en 2008 et en 2010 aux Jeux olympiques de la Jeunesse. Guylaine dirige maintenant sa propre entreprise de consultation en gestion.

The Honourable **IONA CAMPAGNOLO** (P. C., O. C., O. B. C.) was elected as one of nine women Members of Parliament in 1974. Prime Minister Pierre Trudeau named her as Canada's first Minister of Fitness and Amateur Sport in 1976, where she served for three years. Presently retired, following service as British Columbia's first woman Lieutenant Governor 2001-2007, Ms. Campagnolo lives on Vancouver Island.

CINDY CRAPPER is Coordinator, Sport for Life for the City of Vancouver and liaison with the Women in Sport Committee. She has worked extensively with vulnerable populations in recreation and is currently aligning

Sport Strategy with the Canadian Sport for Life model. Cindy is a Windsor Essex County Hall of Fame inductee and was the first woman to pass the firefighters' test in Vancouver.

KERI CRESS resides in Winnipeg with her silver labrador retriever, Beatrix. She holds a Kinesiology degree from the University of Manitoba and works in sales. Keri continues to play hockey in the ASHL and is a member of the Winnipeg Roller Derby League All Star team as "Violent Femme."

CHARMAINE CROOKS, C.M, is a five-time Olympian, Olympic silver medalist, a member of the Canadian Olympic Committee and a former International Olympic Committee member. She served on the founding Boards of the World Anti Doping Agency, Athletes CAN, Right to Play and the 2010 Olympic and Paralympic Winter Games. Charmaine is a recipient of the Order of Canada.

SHEILAGH CROXON is a three-time Olympic Coach in synchronized swimming. She assisted the Canadian team to a silver medal finish in 1996 and led them to a bronze medal finish in 2000. She was the leader of WiC from 2004-2012. She is now head coach of the synchronized swimming program at the Granite Club in Toronto.

NIKKI DRYDEN is an Olympic swimmer and human rights attorney. She writes, speaks and advises on issues at the nexus of sport and human rights, including athletes' rights and gender discrimination. Nikki is on the Editorial Board of LawInSport, supports Olympic campaigns for Human Rights Watch, and assists WomenSport International.

GUYLAINE DUMONT a été une athlète de niveau international pendant plus de 20 ans, autant professionnel en Europe et au Japon que dans le sport amateur. Elle prodigue maintenant ses conseils auprès d'athlètes, d'entraîneurs et de parents de sportifs à titre de thérapeute en relation d'aide spécialisée dans le sport. Un des points saillants qui s'ajoutent à sa persévérance, et sa résilience, c'est son cheminement intérieur qui lui a permis de réaliser son rêve olympique à 36 ans alors maman d'une fillette de 3 ans.

HILARY FINDLAY is a professor in the Department of Sport Management at Brock University and a partner with the Sport Law & Strategy Group. The focus of her research is on legal issues affecting sport, particularly those impacting the regulation of sport organizations both domestically and internationally.

JEAN FORREST has lived in Vancouver since 1979, when she played on the Canadian Field Hockey team while attending UBC. Since then, she has had a career in sports and recreation management, working and volunteering for organizations including the YMCA, Sport BC, Canadian Olympic Committee, Field Hockey Canada and the BC Sports Hall of Fame. She is married with three children.

JANICE FORSYTH is an Assistant Professor in the School of Kinesiology, Faculty of Health Sciences at the University of Western Ontario. Her primary research area is in Canadian sport history, with a specific interest in contemporary Aboriginal sport practices. She is a member of the Fisher River Cree First Nation, Manitoba.

MARGARET "PEGGY" GALLANT is a professor in the Department of Human Kinetics at Saint Francis Xavier University, where her research focus is on sport leadership. While a varsity athlete at St. FXU, she competed in basketball and field hockey and was a member of the dance team. Today she is an avid recreational runner and dancer.

AUDREY R. GILES is Associate Professor in the School of Human Kinetics, University of Ottawa. Her interdisciplinary anthropological research focuses on the discursive production of tradition, health, community, gender equity and safety, within a sport and recreation context, usually in the Canadian Arctic and sub-Arctic. She is especially interested in qualitative research, particularly emergent methodologies.

FIONA JOY GREEN, PhD, has been an avid swimmer, runner and cyclist throughout the last five decades and hopes to continue being active for as many days as come her way. She teaches Women's and Gender Studies at the University of Winnipeg and is author of *Practicing Feminist Mothering* (Arbieter Ring).

SUE GRIFFIN is a self-proclaimed Passion Pusher and Canadian leader in Strategic Fundraising Alliances. She is President and CEO of the BC Sports Hall of Fame. A passionate educator, she teaches at Vancouver's British Columbia Institute of Technology. In her spare time, Sue can be found on the squash courts and volunteering as Chair for ProMOTION Plus.

M. ANN HALL is an author and retired professor who taught for over 30 years at the University of Alberta. She has published extensively on gender and sport, and her most recent book is the award-winning *The Grads Are Playing Tonight!: The Story of the Edmonton Commercial Graduates Basketball Club*.

JENNIFER HUGHES is a freelance writer, with numerous articles published in magazines such as *Style at Home, Canadian House & Home, Canadian Gardening, Today's Parent* and *Canadian Family*. A former Torontonian, she has found balance living in a small town outside of Ottawa with her husband and three children.

PATTI HUNTER is the General Manager of KidSport Victoria, a co-founder of ProMOTION Plus Victoria and one of the founding members of ProMOTION Plus BC. She is past-Director of Health and Wellness for the Vancouver YWCA and of the 2010 Legacies Now province-wide Physical Activity and Healthy Living Initiative.

SUE HYLLAND is President and CEO of the Canada Games Council. Previously, she was the Executive Director of the Canadian Association for the Advancement of Women and Sport and Physical Activity and spent nearly 18 years with the Canadian Olympic Committee. She lives in Ottawa with her husband and three children, and is an active participant, coach and volunteer in local sports.

CHRISTIANE JOB is a PhD Candidate in the Faculty of Kinesiology, University of Calgary. Her research focuses on the intersection between sociology of sport, feminist theory and sport history. Currently, she is focusing on narratives of older women athletes with the aim of informing new policies and best practices for maintaining, promoting and inspiring older athletes.

LORI JOHNSTONE is strongly committed to creating and promoting values-based sport, increased participation, improved wellbeing and the achievement of excellence. A former national champion in racquetball and a member of Canada's National Racquetball Team for seven years, Lori's contributions to sport as a leader, advocate and change agent have been widely recognized.

JUDY KENT has been President of Kent Consulting Inc. since 1984. She has authored several books and publications, made keynote presentations on all continents and facilitated world summits. She is Past President of Commonwealth Games Canada and the Canadian Lifesaving Society. Currently, she is Lead Facilitator for Generations for Peace, Amman, Jordan working to bring conflict transformation to communities in war-torn countries.

BRUCE KIDD is a Professor in the Faculty of Kinesiology and Physical Education and Warden of Hart House at the University of Toronto. In the early 1960s, he was Canada's best distance runner, winning a Commonwealth championship and competing in the Olympic Games.

ÉLAINE LAUZON has played volleyball internationally and as a member of the national team. She was a representative on the COC athletes' committee and was sport administrator for Volleyball Canada, Manitoba Special Olympics and Volleyball Québec. After having her first child, she became the first Director General of Égale Action, where she spearheads change to ensure girls and women are encouraged and given equal opportunity to participate in sport and physical activity at all levels in Québec.

MICHELLE LEE was born in Ottawa, Ontario and has been an athlete and lover of sports her whole life. Her passion is to teach and promote female athletes. This is her first book contribution, which she hopes will help further female participation in sports.

NANCY LEE is a life-long supporter of all things sports. She sits on the boards of CAAWS, the Canadian Commonwealth Games, Right to Play Canadian Advisory Board, Toronto Emerging Athlete Fund and the U of T Varsity Alumni Board. She is Chief Operating Officer for the Olympic Broadcasting Services Vancouver and past Executive Director of CBC Sports.

PAMELA LEWIS is a founding member of the Canadian Association for the Advancement of Women and Sport and was on the Board of Directors during its formative years. She is on the Board of the Bearpark Foundation, which supports the legacy and vision of the late Bob Bearpark by providing equitable coaching education in British Columbia for women and men. Pamela is a Certified Executive Coach, and currently lives in Victoria, British Columbia.

VANESSA LODGE-GAGNÉ completed her M.A. at the University of Ottawa. Her thesis focused on the sporting experiences of Aboriginal athletes who won a Tom Longboat Award from the Maritimes region of Canada. She is currently the Acting Senior Manager for the Aboriginal Sport & Wellness Council of Ontario.

KARIN LOFSTROM is Executive Director at CAAWS in Ottawa. She has been an active participant, volunteer, leader, mentor and advocate for girls and women in sport and physical activity, both in Canada and internationally. Karin's commitment to achieving gender equity in the Canadian sport system is shared through her collaborative approach.

MARG MCGREGOR has worked in leadership positions with the Canadian Olympic Committee, Canadian Interuniversity Sport, and CAAWS. Marg graduated from McGill with a Masters of Management. She is a recipient of Canada's Top 40 Under 40 Award and was the chef de mission to the 2006 Paralympic Games and the 2002 Commonwealth Games. She volunteered at the 2010 and 2012 Olympics.

ROSE MERCIER is a Kingston-based consultant in leadership development and organization development with a life-long involvement in sport. A founding mother of CAAWS, Rose's contribution to gender equity in sport was acknowledged by the National Herstorical Award and the Queen's Jubilee Medal. She continues to be involved with the CAC Women in Coaching programs and the *Women in Coaching Journal*.

SYDNEY MILLAR is National Program Director at CAAWS. She has travelled across Canada delivering workshops and presentations on how to create positive programs and inclusive environments to engage more girls and young women in sport and physical activity. Sydney has a Bachelor of Kinesiology from McMaster University and a Master of Arts in Human Kinetics from the University of British Columbia.

DIANE PALMASON has been involved in sport as an athlete, coach and administrator since the 1950s. Her participation in the founding of CAAWS led to volunteer and professional roles in Canadian sports organizations, including Manager of Sport Canada's Women's Program in the late 1980s.

SYLVIE PARENT est professeure adjointe au Département d'éducation physique de l'Université Laval. Ses intérêts de recherche portent sur la protection des jeunes athlètes contre diverses formes de violence. Mme Parent travaille actuellement au développement d'un cadre d'intervention québécois en matière de protection des jeunes évoluant dans le milieu sportif.

AMY PASTERNAK is from Winnipeg and grew up playing boys' hockey, men's field lacrosse at a provincial level, and playing and refereeing men's box lacrosse. Amy has a Bachelor of Science in Biochemistry. She now works at the Children's Hospital in Winnipeg as a Diagnostic Medical Sonographer and continues to play and coach various sports including female hockey.

JESSE PASTERNAK was born and raised in Winnipeg. She played boys' hockey for 11 years, men's box lacrosse for 14 years and men's field lacrosse for 4 years, including playing on the Manitoba

Men's Provincial Field Lacrosse Team for 2 years. Jesse now lives in Edmonton, Alberta where she works as a neonatal intensive care nurse and plays in a ball hockey league.

DANIELLE PEERS is a Paralympic Bronze Medalist, World Champion and World MVP in wheelchair basketball. She is currently a PhD candidate and Vanier and Trudeau Scholar at the University of Alberta, where she studies the relationship between disability sport and human rights in Canada. Danielle is also a filmmaker, public speaker, coach and activist in her community.

PATSY PYKE graduated from Saint Francis Xavier University and started her coaching career at Mount Saint Vincent University in Halifax as head coach of women's basketball and soccer. She attended the National Coaching School for Women five times. Patsy is Program Coordinator and Professor in Recreation and Leisure Services at Algonquin College in Ottawa.

SHEILA ROBERTSON is the editor of the *Canadian Journal for Women and Coaching*. In 2010 she was named a Top 20 Most Influential Women in Sport and was honored with the 2011 CAAWS Marion Lay Herstorical Breakthrough Award. She also received a Canadian Sport Award for Communications.

LAURA ROBINSON is a former member of the national cycling team, has covered six Olympics as a journalist and has written the same number of books. Today she is an award-winning writer and filmmaker. She still loves to ride her bike, and disappear for long periods of time on cross-country skis.

TRICIA SMITH C.M. O.B.C. BA LLB LLD (Honorary) is a Partner at Barnescraig & Associates, a Sports Arbitrator with the SDRCC, VP of the Canadian Olympic Committee, and Member of the Executive Committee of the

International Rowing Federation and the International Council of Arbitration for Sport. She is an Olympic, Commonwealth and World Championship medalist.

JANNA TAYLOR is an instructor in UBC's School of Kinesiology, teaching courses in the sociology of sport and leisure. A past director of parks and recreation in Port Coquitlam, she received the Vancouver YWCA's Women of Distinction Sports and Recreation award in 1993. She has been involved in women's issues for decades, serving on numerous boards and committees.

SARAH TEETZEL is an Assistant Professor in the Faculty of Kinesiology and Recreation Management at the University of Manitoba. She is a research affiliate of the Health, Leisure and Human Performance Research Institute and the Centre for Professional and Applied Ethics. Her research investigates applied ethical issues in sport pertaining to doping, eligibility and gender.

HEATHER THOMPSON, originally from Ottawa, lives in North Vancouver with her family and enjoys the outdoor recreation it has to offer. She works at an independent school in Vancouver and enjoys working with very young children to discover their abilities in Physical Education class through dance, gymnastics and games.

PENNY WERTHNER is the Dean of the Faculty of Kinesiology, University of Calgary. A former Olympic athlete in the sport of athletics, her research is focused on women and sport issues, coach learning and coach education, and performance psychology using bioneuro feedback with Olympic athletes and coaches to optimize performance.

ERIKA VINES grew up in Ottawa, attained PHE/Sociology and B.Ed degrees from Queen's University, is

a wife, mother, and sports enthusiast. She has held world and national sailing titles, worked as Racing Co-ordinator for Canada's national sailing authority, is a sailing coach, CORK board member, and actively supports Kingston Yacht Club's youth sailing program.

HEATHER WALKER-WADDELL played for the winning BC Girls' Basketball team in 1953. The following year, she competed in Track and Field at the British Empire Games. She has played basketball for Canada in two Pan American Games, in 1955 in Mexico and in Chicago in 1959. She also played for the University of British Columbia Basketball Team in 1959.

HAYLEY WICKENHEISER is a five-time Olympian and is most well-known for her leadership of the Canada National Women's Hockey team to three Olympic gold medals, though she has also represented Canada as a member of the national softball team that competed in Sydney in 2000. On the ice she breaks not just records, but also stereotypes. Off the ice, she is a respected business woman and philanthropist.

Photo Credits

Thank you to
Jessica Kozak
for her diligent
and careful photo
research.

Every effort has
been made to trace
the original source
of photographs in
this book. Where
the attempt has
been unsuccessful,
we would be pleased
to hear from
copyright holders so
that we can rectify
any omission in
subsequent editions.

PART ONE
PAGES 6 & 7:
Library and Archives
Canada / 1990-112 NPC

PAGE 62 (top):
Library and Archives
Canada / NIC-5767

PAGE 62:
Library and Archives
Canada / PA-074583 /
Edwin C. Guillet
Collection

PAGE 63:
Library and Archives
Canada / PA-043029 /
William James Topley

PAGES 64 & 65:
Laboratoire de recherche
sur la culture corporelle
des Québécois (LARECQ),
Université Laval

PAGE 66:
Courtesy of QMI Agency

PAGE 67:
Laboratoire de recherche
sur la culture corporelle
des Québécois (LARECQ),
Université Laval

PAGE 68:
Laboratoire de recherche
sur la culture corporelle
des Québécois (LARECQ),
Université Laval

PAGE 69 (top):
Courtesy of Marion Lay

PAGE 69:
Library and Archives
Canada / PA-174392 /
Duncan Cameron

PAGE 70 (top):
Courtesy of Ann Hall

PAGE 70:
Courtesy of Bruce Kidd

PAGE 71:
Courtesy of John
Cameron

PART TWO
PAGES 72 & 73:
Winnipeg Free Press /
Phil Hossack

PART THREE
PAGES 114 & 115:
Canadian Association
for the Advancement of
Women and Sport /
Courtesy of Karin
Lofstrom

PAGE 190 (top):
Courtesy of Sandra Kirby

PAGE 190:
CBC Still Photo
Collection

PAGE 191:
Courtesy of JoJo Carrier

PAGE 192 (top):
Courtesy of John Vines

PAGE 192:
Courtesy of Lucille Lessard

PAGE 193:
Courtesy of Johanne
Falardeau

PAGE 194 (top):
Courtesy of Heather
Thompson

PAGE 194:
Courtesy of Keri Cress /
Stew McCulloch

PAGE 195 (left):
BC Sports Hall of Fame
& Museum / 6115.1

PAGE 195 (right):
Courtesy of Amy and
Jesse Pasternak

PAGE 196:
Courtesy of Dave Holland

PAGE 197 (top):
Courtesy of Jennifer
Walinga

PAGE 197:
Canadian Press / COC /
Mike Ridewood

PART FOUR
PAGE 198:
Courtesy of Guylaine
Demers

PAGE 277:
Canada Soccer

PAGE 278:
Canada's Sports Hall
of Fame

PAGE 279 (top):
Canadian Press / Cromby
McNeil

PAGE 279:
Courtesy of Sandra Kirby

PAGE 280:
Courtesy of Guy Menard

PAGE 281 (top):
Courtesy of Beckie Scott

PAGE 281 (far right):
Courtesy of Hilary
Findlay

PAGE 281:
BC Sports Hall of Fame

PART FIVE
PAGE 282:
Canadian Press / Frank
Gunn